GIVE ME YESTERDAY

GIVE ME YESTERDAY

AMERICAN HISTORY IN SONG, 1890-1920

BY LESTER S. LEVY

Calligraphy by Henry W. Hoffman

UNIVERSITY OF OKLAHOMA PRESS · NORMAN

By Lester S. Levy
Grace Notes in American History: Popular Sheet Music from 1820 to 1900 (Norman, 1967)
Flashes of Merriment: A Century of Humorous Songs in America, 1805-1905 (Norman, 1971)
"Give Me Yesterday": American History in Piano Music, 1890-1920 (Norman, 1975)

Library of Congress Cataloging in Publication Data
Levy, Lester S
  Give me yesterday.
  Bibliography: p.
  1. Music, Popular (Songs, etc.)—United States—History and criticism.
2. Songs, American—History and criticism.   I. Title.
ML3561.P6L5   784'.0973   74-18119
ISBN 0-8061-1241-7

To Eleanor—Again

PREFACE

THIS BOOK could not have been completed without assistance, both in the field of research and in that of literary criticism. For help "beyond the call of duty," I am deeply indebted to the personnel of the Reference Department of the Enoch Pratt Free Library, Baltimore. They spared no efforts, regardless of the consumption of time, in a thorough research on numerous subjects germane to the stories behind the songs.

Special thanks are extended to those publishers who graciously permitted me to make use of the melodic lines and/or words of the lyrics of a number of songs for which they held copyright privileges. I have tried diligently to confirm the copyright status of each song used in the book. If any errors or oversights have occurred, they have been inadvertent.

Acknowledgments are made to the following publishers: Belwin Mills Publishing Corp., Irving Berlin Music Corporation, Broadway Music Corp., Leo Feist, Inc., T. B. Harms Company, Edgar Leslie, Edward B. Marks Music Corporation, Edwin H. Morris & Co., Inc., Will Rossiter, Shapiro Bernstein & Co., Inc., Shawnee Press, Inc., Jerry Vogel Music Co., Inc., Warner Brothers Music.

I want also to acknowledge with deep thanks the work of Evelyn Wagner, who once again has dug through a myriad of books and periodicals to come up with hard-to-find data which has formed an essential part of the book.

Thanks, too, to Henry H. Hoffman, first-chair flutist of the Salt Lake City Orchestra, for his calligraphic expertise, which is displayed on all the music reproduced.

For the ultimate development of the stories, and the style in which they are presented, I have turned, as twice before, to my "severest critic." As may be suspected, she is my life partner, and it is to her that I dedicate, with affection, *"Give Me Yesterday"*: *American History in Piano Music*.

Lester S. Levy

Pikesville, Maryland
July 31, 1974

CONTENTS

Preface   *page* vii
Introduction   1
1. Show Biz   5
2. Getting Around   49
3. The Big Fellows   97
4. The Ladies, God Bless 'Em   139
5. Growing Pains   169
6. The Muscle Men   197
7. The Tragic Era   223
8. Relax Is All   251
9. Progress! Progress?   301
10. From Different Angles   347
Bibliography   393
Index   405

ILLUSTRATIONS

Color

"Asleep at the Switch"	*following page* 130
"Sousa's Band Is on Parade To-Day"	146
"San Antonio"	306
"Hold Fast!"	322

Black and White

"Mary Pickford, the Darling of Them All"	*page* 10
"Poor Pauline"	19
"Castles in Europe"	25
"I'm After Madame Tetrazzini's Job"	31
"My Cousin Caruso"	38
"The Gaby Glide"	44
"On the Old Fall River Line"	50
"Won't You Come Up and Spoon in Coey's Balloon 'Chicago'"	59
"Give Me a Spin in Your Mitchell, Bill"	71
"Hold Fast!"	75
"Asleep at the Switch"	88
"The Ironmaster"	100
"Mister Dooley"	103
"Sousa's Band Is on Parade To-day"	108
"Standard Oil"	117
"Get on the Raft with Taft"	123
"We Take Our Hats Off to You, Mr. Wilson!"	131
"Oh! You Suffragettes"	142
"Salvation Nell"	152

"The Gibson Bathing Girl"   158
"September Morn (I'd Like to Meet Her)"   164
"My Pretty Little Kickapoo"   172
"San Antonio"   186
"Arizona Prospector"   188
"The Victors"   200
"Jim-a-da-Jeff"   212
"Dorando"   218
"The Hall-Mills Case"   228
"Why Don't They Set Him Free?"   234
"The Iroquois on Fire"   238
"Just as the Ship Went Down"   244
"With Mary Ann on a Merry-Go-Round"   252
"As We Go Down the Pike"   264
"I'm the Guy"   272
"Look Out for Jimmy Valentine"   279
"At the 'Funny Page' Ball"   291
"Bessie and Her Little Brown Bear"   296
"Meet Me on the Boardwalk, Dearie"   302
"She Couldn't Keep Away from the Ten Cent Store"   311
"Hello Central, Give Me Heaven"   320
"The Flatiron March and Two-Step"   327
"The Song of the N.C.R."   329
"In Panama"   342
"March of the 1/8 Brigade"   348
"Our Soldiers Again Are Marching"   353
"Stick to the Union, Jack"   365
"Tammany, a Pale Face Pow-Wow"   373
"Dr. Munyon"   378
"When America Is Captured by the Japs"   385

GIVE ME YESTERDAY

INTRODUCTION

IN THE DAYS when vaudeville flourished, sixty and more years ago, nearly every show included one solo act by a full-chested tenor (Irish, whisky, or just double-chinned). After going through his vocal paces, and being recalled for the standard encore by the applause of the audience, he would pull at the heartstrings of the ladies—and many of the gentlemen too—with a rendition of everybody's favorite ballad, "Turn Back the Universe and Give Me Yesterday."

Ernest R. Ball's tearjerker of 1906 has not had the staying qualities of the much-loved masterpieces of a Stephen Foster, for instance; but its sentiments remain valid. Who among us would not welcome the gift of a magic wand which, when hopefully extended, would transport us, young once more, to the happy years of growing-up-hood?

To restructure those yesterdays we have help from the inside—from the writings of the people who were there when things happened. And as so often was the case, the things that happened were set to music. When history of one sort or another was being made, great deeds and small foibles both came to the fore as subject matter for song writers.

In an earlier book, *Grace Notes in American History*, I mentioned some of the musical sagas of old—Moses recounting in song the passage of the Israelites through the Red Sea and blind Homer singing of the prowess of Ulysses. Later minstrels were to chant of the glorious episodes of their monarchs. Eventually, here at home, songs to commemorate all sorts of occasions made their appearance. When a statesman was nominated for the presidency, when a disaster at sea occurred, when gold was found in California, when women's fashions altered sharply, when a new canal was opened, when the continent was first spanned coast to coast by rail, when

I

people commenced riding bicycles—all such occurrences, comprising the developing history and the mores of the country, were described in song.

Nor could the American sense of humor be denied by our musicians. From the early 1800's, lyricists and melody men merged their talents toward the production of comedy in song. So entertaining were many of these pieces that I was impelled to do a second book, *Flashes of Merriment*, in which many comic songs of the nineteenth century were brought back to life.

So now there emerges the third volume of the trilogy. Through the first decades of the twentieth century, when the piano remained the instrument for general family and stage use, there were plenty of happenings for people to sing about. The early 1900's are rich in songs about characters who made current news in the papers—about sports and sportsmen, theatrical entertainers, financiers, and murderers.

These are some of the heroes and nonheroes of this book, the folks of the new century who are presented to us in musical form. We learn, too, about innovations in the life of the people—the telephone, the Boardwalk in Atlantic City, the automobile, the funny papers, the art shocker in a community of staid churchmen.

The book is grouped into ten sections, and each of the several dozen songs falls, more or less naturally, into one of these slots. First comes "Show Biz," with songs written about some of the most attractive entertainers of the early 1900's—folks like Caruso and Pearl White and Mary Pickford. Next in line is "Getting Around," which is illustrated by songs describing various methods of locomotion in vogue during the period. This is followed by "The Big Fellows," a pair of presidents plus others who made their own marks, including Mr. Dooley, the era's greatest political satirist. "The Ladies, God Bless 'Em" includes disparate segments of femininity, running from Salvation Army lassies to Gibson Girls. "Growing Pains" introduces songs written about some of the new territories and about Texas, a state which seems to grow larger year by year.

The adoration of the athlete is pointed up in "The Muscle Men," where the college football teams and the track stars are revered along with the great prize fighters. Disasters and murders used to make fine fodder for the song writers' appetites, and "The Tragic Era" includes a taste of both subjects. But it was just as much fun to write about fun, and so the next section is called "Relax Is All." Here we can find music about the St. Louis World's Fair, the gentleman burglar, and the greatest cartoonist of the early 1900's, Rube Goldberg. Following this subject comes "Progress!" and, caustically,

"Progress?" The verdict is left for the reader to decide, as he mouths the words of songs about the cash register, the "Five and Dime," and the Panama Canal.

And finally, there are a few bits and pieces too good to be omitted, and grouped together under "From Different Angles." Here will be found material about Tammany and Wall Street and the geriatric cases who held together the Grand Army of the Republic, and incredulously, about the possibility of a newly awakened Japan overrunning the United States.

Of such is the book put together. It is contrived for entertainment, for reminiscence, and for reviving catchy melodies, six decades and more behind us. Our country's history is well worth preserving. Songs help keep green the fading laurels that our heritage has earned.

I
SHOW
BIZ

Mary Pickford

She was a beautiful little girl with golden ringlets, a captivating smile, and innocent blue eyes. Alistair Cooke, the world-famous newspaper correspondent, once said that she was "the girl every young man wanted to have for his sister." She was the screen's Pollyanna, the girl who knew that everything would come out all right in the end. But she didn't stand around and wait for things to happen; she *made* them happen. Behind that sweet smile and those big wide eyes was a razor-sharp mind, whose analysis of figures would do credit to any IBM computer. From the age of five, Mary Pickford knew exactly what she was after—fame and money. And she pursued her objectives as ruthlessly as a hungry cat stalking a mouse.

Mary was born Gladys Smith in 1893 in Toronto, Canada. Her father died when she was four years old and her mother struggled to ward off the threat of poverty which threatened her, little Gladys, smaller Lottie, and baby Jack. She felt obliged to rent the master bedroom in her house, and it was soon occupied by the stage manager of a stock company. The gentleman needed two small children for tiny roles in his current production, *The Silver King*, and with much persuasion he prevailed on Mrs. Smith to allow her daughters to take the parts. Gladys' first professionally spoken words, before a paying audience, were "Don't speak to her, girls; her father killed a man!" The young stage moralizer was to carry her code of righteousness over the decades that lay ahead of her.

Before Gladys was nine the Smith family was playing in one-night stands in New York state for the aggregate sum of twenty dollars a week in *For a Human Life* (originally *The Little Red Schoolhouse*). From *Human Life* the family was drafted en masse into *The Fatal Wedding*, a play in which Gladys was given her first starring role. Bright handbills of magenta and orange were circulated along the streets proclaiming "*The Fatal Wedding* with Baby Gladys Smith is a Wonder."

After a few years of steady road work, Gladys determined (determination was her middle name) to make the New York scene, and to beard in his den the mightiest lion of them all, the great showman, David Belasco. A combination of wheedling and belligerent tactics gained her an approach to the maestro, who, like everyone else who encountered her, succumbed to her charms. He gave her a part in the new play he was preparing to produce, but he did not approve of the stage name of Gladys Smith, and suggested that his new young performer call herself Mary Pickford. So then and there, as it were, a star was born.

For three years Mary was a fixture as Betty Warren in Belasco's *Warrens of Virginia*. By the end of that period she had reached her full height of five feet and trained her eyes on the up-and-coming movie industry, still in the pre-Hollywood era, which meant that most of the infant studios were in New York. Encouraged by her ambitious mother, Mary took a trolley to the Bioscope Studios on East Fourteenth Street, and confident as ever, was taken on—for two days and ten dollars—by David W. Griffith of the Biograph Company. Griffith "made her up" personally for her first picture, and she came on as an extra in a film called *What Drink Did*. Her appearance in her initial try ended on the cutting floor, but the next day she got a part as a ten-year-old girl in *Her First Biscuits*, and immediately afterward was rehired for a bigger role in *The Violin Maker of Cremona*. Mr. Griffith was so well satisfied with her performance that he put her on a weekly salary of forty dollars, and Mary was off and winging.

The following winter the Biograph Company was filming in California, where Mary was impressed by a young scriptwriter named Mack Sennett. Sennett had formed an opinion that if Mary's name could be given as the author of his stories, they would receive more serious consideration from producers. But righteous little Mary was not in a frame of mind to permit the Pickford name to be connected with a ridiculous film in which policemen made clowns of themselves, and she thereby passed up the golden opportunity of soaring to instant fame as the originator of the Keystone Cops.

No doubt she frowned also at Mr. Sennett's absorption with glamorous bathing beauties, whose charms, enhanced by Sennett's idea of scanty swim suits, decorated so many of his comedies. The leggy girls were the subjects of a 1919 song written by Ray Perkins, with the title "Help! Help! Mr. Sennett. I'm Drowning in a Sea of Love." The chorus goes, in part:

> Help, Help, Mr. Sennett, Help!
> I'm drowning in a sea of love;
> Just because those bathing girls of yours,
> Have got me always thinking of 'em. Gee, I
>   love 'em!
> Each peach, strolling on the beach,
> Won me when she winked and smiled;
> If you need a life-guard just call upon me,
> For I'd like to offer my services free;
> Help! Help! Mister Sennett help! Your bathing
>   beauties are driving me wild.[1]

In those days, the names of movie actors and actresses were of little interest to audiences. Those with more important roles were billed in theater lobbies with descriptive appendages. Mary, for example, came to be known as "Blondielocks," "Goldilocks," or "The Girl with the Curls." Eventually she was called "The Biograph Girl," and this title remained her pseudonym for longer than any of the others.

In 1905 in Oshkosh, Wisconsin, Carl Laemmle, the manager of a clothing store was greatly dissatisfied with his lot. He decided to leave Oshkosh and tackle a brand new venture, the opening of a nickelodeon movie theater on Milwaukee Avenue in Chicago. Within a few years he was making movies in a New York studio, calling his small outfit the Independent Motion Picture Company, soon abbreviated to "Imp" pictures. When in 1911 Laemmle, with acumen and colossal nerve, lured Mary away from Biograph with an offer of $175 a week, he nicknamed her "Little Mary," and advertised "Little Mary Is an Imp Now!"

But little Mary was not destined to be an Imp long. Back she went to Biograph, which began to circulate her name on posters and handbills. Even this was not enough for the eager young beaver. When she learned that David Belasco was preparing a new play, *A Good Little Devil*, for the New York stage, she deserted Griffith, her old director at Biograph, sought out Mr. Belasco and was assigned a fat part in his show at the healthy salary of $200 weekly.

For a short while she was happy on Broadway; but the career of a film actress had been carried into her blood stream, and the infection could not

---

[1] "Help, Help, Mr. Sennett." Words and Music by Ray Perkins. Copyright 1919 by Mills Music Inc. Copyright © renewed 1947. Used by permission.

be overcome. Naturally the money involved was important, so when Daniel Frohman and Adolph Zukor, a former furrier's apprentice from Hungary, who together had just started a film company which they called Famous Players, offered Mary a fourteen-week contract at $500 a week, she snapped at it. Ever since the early days of her childhood, Mary had set this figure as a goal to be attained by her twentieth birthday; she reached it shortly after she turned nineteen. Up and up her value climbed; after *Tess of the Storm Country*, in which Mary gave her greatest performance to date, and probably saved Famous Players from threatened bankruptcy, she could have named her own figure.

Meanwhile, her marriage to Owen Moore, a screen actor, had gone on the rocks, and Mary, while her fame grew, had periods of severe despondency during one of which, she confided in her autobiography, she even considered taking her life. And still she was always smart enough to be able to retain the affection of her fans. As a girl in her early twenties, she was the most famous woman in America. When in 1917 a woman's magazine, *Ladies World*, conducted a popularity contest, Mary Pickford received some 1,147,000 votes, a half million more than her closest competitor. The owner of Grauman's Hollywood Theater gave her the title by which she was best known, "America's Sweetheart." Yet, when she was told one day that she had drawn a larger throng than the president of the United States, she expressed the thought that a white elephant taking a morning stroll would have drawn a bigger and more curious crowd than either of them.

At twenty-two she was getting a thousand dollars a week; at twenty-five she was making a million dollars a year. Part of the enormous increase was occasioned by her professional envy of the huge salary of Charlie Chaplin, the other enormous drawing card in the film industry. Mary, fully aware of her earning power for her employers, had no scruples about putting the "bite" on them for every available penny, and for a deal which would give her a place alongside Chaplin on the salary scale.

Songs about Chaplin testified to his great popularity. One, written in 1915 by William A. Downs and Roy Barton, described his famous rib-tickling shuffle thus:

Put your two heels close up tight,
Swing your cane, fix your hat just right.
Shuff, shuff, shuff, shuff, shuffle with ease
Pointing your toes out at ninety degrees.
Next you raise your right foot so,
Round, round, round on the left you go,
Oh, joy. 'at a boy
That's the funny Charlie Chaplin walk.[2]

And yet the two were good friends; they worked together to sell Liberty Bonds and to whip up patriotism for World War I, in which, incidentally, Mary sent two ambulances to France and adopted six hundred members of the Second Battalion of the First California Field Artillery, who became known as Mary Pickford's fighting six hundred, and who carried—every one of them—a gold locket with a miniature of Mary.

Long before then she had been receiving five hundred letters a day from her devoted admirers; at her peak of popularity they came in at a rate of more than ten thousand a week.

Her new contract stipulated that her pictures should feature no other player; when she traveled to or from California she was guaranteed parlor car transportation for her mother and herself, and for any services outside New York a motor car was to be at her disposal. All of her pictures—but no one else's—were to be made in the "Mary Pickford Studios," and if she made pictures in California during the winter, she was to have a stage to herself. What a tyrant—but what a delectable tyrant! And what a good investment for her producers!

In 1914, after she had captivated the public in her appearance in the screen version of *A Good Little Devil*, a team of three song writers, Dave Radford, Daisy Sullivan, and Richard A. Whiting, brought out a song entitled simply, "Mary Pickford, the Darling of Them All." The writers' admiration was unbounded.

When the day is dreary and is filled with care,
Mary's smile can make the sunshine ev'rywhere,
This world is full of girlies, but I'll give you
    all the rest,
Just leave me pretty Mary, little Mary is the best.

[2] "That Charlie Chaplin Walk." Words by William A. Downs, Music by Roy Barton © Copyright MCMXV, Harold Rossiter Music Co. U.S. Copyright Renewed MCMXLIII. Copyright assigned to Shawnee Press, Inc., Delaware Water Gap, Pa. 18327. International Copyright Secured. All Rights Reserved. Used by Permission.

MARY PICKFORD
THE DARLING OF THEM ALL

WORDS & MUSIC
BY
DAVE RADFORD
DAISY SULLIVAN
RICHARD A. WHITING

JEROME H. REMICK & CO.
NEW YORK   DETROIT

Mary Pickford

There's a lit-tle fai-ry who has won my heart,— She's so cap-ti-vat-ing with her dain-ty art,— I've on-ly seen her pic-ture, but I love her just the same,—And here's my lit-tle se-cret Ma-ry Pick-ford is her name.—

Chorus

She's the dar-ling of the mov-ies,— For she's "such a lit-tle queen,"— And she stepped right down in-to my heart— From a mov-ing pic-ture screen—— Fai-ry Ma-ry dain-ty as a dres-den doll— Such a "good lit-tle dev-il" Could make Sa-tan on the lev-el, Ma-ry Pick-ford you're the dar-ling of them all.——

2. When the day is dreary and is filled with care,
Mary's smile can make the sunshine ev'rywhere,
This world is full of girlies, but I'll give you all the rest,
Just leave me pretty Mary, little Mary is the best.
CHORUS

CHORUS: She's the darling of the movies,
    For she's such a little queen;
    And she stepped right down into my heart
    From a moving picture screen.
    Fairy Mary dainty as a Dresden doll
    Such a 'good little devil' could make Satan on
        the level,
    Mary Pickford you're the darling of them all.[3]

Around St. Valentine's Day, 1920, a ranch house outside the town of Genoa, Nevada, was occupied by Gladys Mary Smith Moore. Nearby was the town of Minden, where, in the courthouse G. M. S. Moore soon filed suit for divorce from Owen Moore, claiming desertion. Moore, who happened to be in Minden, shortly thereafter was served the papers in the divorce proceedings and promptly disappeared. The divorce was granted on March 2, after which Mary announced to the newspapers that she intended to make her permanent home in Nevada and would remain near Minden for a long time.

A little more than three weeks later, Douglas Fairbanks gave a small party at his home in Beverly Hills. The guest of honor was Mary Pickford. Other guests included the Reverend J. Whitcomb Brougher, pastor of Temple Baptist Church, and a deputy clerk, R. S. Sparks. At the party Sparks issued a license for Mary Pickford, 26, to wed Douglas Fairbanks, 36. The following day the couple was married by Brougher.

On April 16, the attorney general of Nevada filed suit to set aside Mary's divorce decree, charging collusion, fraud, and unlawful testimony. The story made newspaper headlines all over the country, and threatened disaster for Nevada's highly profitable divorce industry. Two years later, after the news and editorial columns of the press had had long and titillating reports from all involved, the Supreme Court of Nevada sustained the Pickford divorce, and Mary's good name, which had hung in the balance to the horror of millions, was cleared once and for all.

When Mary reached the age of thirty-five, she decided that the time had come to cut off her curls. Her waist-long hair had never before been trimmed, and the operation was a traumatic experience, both for Miss Pickford and for Fairbanks, who burst into tears when he saw what she had done. But Mary, as always, was motivated by the advantages that might

---

[3] "Mary Pickford, the Darling of Them All." Words and Music by Dave Redford, Daisy Sullivan, Richard Whiting. © 1914 Remick Music Corp. Copyright Renewed. All Rights Reserved. Used by Permission WARNER BROS. MUSIC.

accrue from her action. Soon she was at work on her first talking picture, *Coquette*, giving a superior performance which won her the Academy Award. This was followed by *The Taming of the Shrew*, the only picture in which Mary and Douglas appeared together. By that time the gap between them had replaced the old love match, but not until six years later did Mary bring suit for divorce.

In 1937 her third marriage took place, this one to Charles B. ("Buddy") Rogers, a popular actor in his own right, and a man who, on the screen, exemplified the pure and beautiful—masculinely, of course—much like Mary did in her earlier pictures. A bit later two adopted children rounded out her family life, and for her old public she became a living memory.

Today's sophisticated moviegoer would probably be horribly bored if another little "Girl with the Curls" was projected on their screens. But in the early years of the twentieth century, before we had outgrown the simple joys of the simple life, Mary Pickford symbolized the concept of ideal young innocence, the quality of young girlhood prized above all others.

"Poor Pauline"

Pearl White, a girl who lived dangerously throughout her career as a heroine of the silent movies, was born March 4, 1889, in the town of Greenridge, Missouri (population 300). Like all of her sisters, she was named after a precious jewel. She was the ninth—and the last—child of a mother, who after losing five of the nine, died giving birth to Pearl.

Pearl's first recollection was of a weekly bath in a wooden tub with two of her siblings. She describes herself as an ugly brat with a head too big for her husky body. Her father had a bit of an income, but little ambition. His house was untidy and remained so until he remarried, when Pearl was six. Pearl's stepmother was a beautiful woman and a stern ruler. She took charge of the household at once, cleaned up her home, and remodeled it to suit her wishes.

At seven Pearl had the opportunity to see her first "Uncle Tom" show, when a traveling company put on the famous "Uncle Tom's Cabin" in Greenridge. It happened that the show's Little Eva took sick that evening, and with the help of an older sister, Pearl persuaded her father to let her substitute for the ill child. She got through the part without mishap and was invited to repeat her performance the second night of the show. This time, as Eva was ascending to heaven after her death scene, she spied her father in the audience. This so unnerved her that she lost her balance and plunged to the floor, howling with fright and pain.

Now misfortune commenced to strike the family. Pearl's stepmother's baby died. The family decided to move to Springfield, Missouri, where they rented an attractive house, and where Mr. White took a fling at local real estate and soon lost his savings. Pearl continued her schooling, but for two hours every day before trudging to the schoolhouse, she sawed the wood that the family required for heating and cooking. During her Christmas holidays she worked as a cash girl in a store. Summers, she picked berries for the farmers. After a full day's work she would bring home an aching back and sixty to eighty cents.

Pearl was sturdily built, and she enjoyed exercise. She had a trapeze in the woodshed and spent considerable time performing on it. A capable artist, she felt that the circus was the best career for her. When she had just passed her thirteenth birthday she met a circus performer named Mrs. DeVere, who was so impressed with Pearl that she found her a job on the bars, during her school vacation. It was a great start—eight dollars and board per week. She lived in the circus cars with the rest of the troupe and was convinced that she was on her way to a fabulous career. But it was not to be. One night, while doing a giant swing on the bars, her wrist gave way; she fell, fractured her collar bone, and terminated her circus career abruptly.

There followed two more years of schooling with a job in the summer, this time in a printing office, where she worked from 8:00 to 6:00 for four dollars a week. But at fifteen, when she had enough of school, she was employed by a Dr. Diemer, a patent-medicine manufacturer with a side line; he owned a stock company and a theatre. In some of the rooms connected with the theater he packed his "Anti-Grippine" pills into boxes and executed the mail orders that came in for them. Here he also printed the theater programs, an undertaking which brought Pearl her next occupation. Hers was the responsibility of taking charge of the printed programs and distributing them. This activity gave her the chance to meet the manager and director of the stock company, which played two different shows each week, with matinees on Saturdays and Sundays. It was not long before she managed to work herself into small parts, then into better ones, while she took lessons in drama—principally Shakespearean material—from one of the female members of the company.

In her second season—she was nearing seventeen now—she was awarded some more impressive parts. But her Springfield career was nearing its close. A performance of *Monte Cristo* produced the catastrophe which ended it. Pearl's role was that of Prince Albert, who was required to fight a duel with Monte Cristo. The duelists used swords with buttons sewn on the end of them so that no damage could be done to the participants. In an unrehearsed thrust, Monte Cristo rammed the end of his sword into Prince Albert's open mouth. Pearl impulsively bit down on the sword, the button became dislodged, and a neat hunk of the roof of Pearl's mouth was sliced off. The blood streamed out; Pearl burst into tears and then in a frenzy jumped on poor Monte Cristo. In the midst of a free-for-all, the curtain was rung down and the performance wrecked. Wrecked, too, was Pearl's career in repertory.

But she couldn't abandon the stage. She transported herself to Memphis, where she teamed up with the "All Star Stock Company" at fifteen dollars a week, adopting the professional name of Mazie Hall. After a short stand in Memphis the company took to the road. In two months they were in South Carolina—and bankrupt.

Pearl had saved sixty dollars from her salary. Somehow she became convinced that an assignment as stewardess on a boat plying between New York and Cuba would be a glamorous occupation. She got the job, all right, but she became so violently seasick once she was on the water that she left the ship in Havana. Here she accepted an offer to appear in a variety hall, this time under the pseudonym of "Miss Mazie." Between the wage paid her and the coins which the theater's patrons tossed on the stage when they wanted encores, she saved two hundred dollars.

Now came another brilliant idea. She had been told that talent such as hers was appreciated in South America, so she bought a steerage ticket for Buenos Aires, where she arrived on her seventeenth birthday. For a few weeks she managed to secure odd work here and there, but her heart wasn't in it. She was terribly homesick, so she found a freighter bound for New Orleans and boarded it. From New Orleans it was a comparatively easy train ride to Memphis, then back home to Springfield.

Once more her father found employment for her, this time as an apprentice seamstress, a job which lasted for four months before she was discharged, to emerge as a nursemaid for three small children.

When she reached her eighteenth birthday she was off with another stock company. She was Mazie White now, a name which she used for about eight weeks, when she was stranded once more, this time in Emporia, Kansas. By now she decided that her own name was the best after all, and

Pearl White it was, from then on, through Kansas, then on to the big name towns—Chicago, Kansas City, New Orleans—where she saw her first moving picture.

In 1907 she married an actor named Victor Sutherland, and soon afterward seems to have disappeared from public view for about three years, finally turning up in New Jersey and, when seeking work, ferrying across to New York City. She was still a stock company actress, finding small jobs in Asbury Park, New Jersey, and South Norwalk, Connecticut.

The melodramas in which she appeared were so overdone, the shouting so loud, that after a few months she lost her voice. It was then that she conceived the idea of looking for parts in moving pictures, which of course were "silents." The first name on her list of prospects was Edison. She was unable to find the studio, however, and settled for another one, the Powers Film Co., which was producing movies in the Bronx in a converted livery stable. She made an impression on the director, Joseph A. Golden, and he gave her a job at five dollars a day. Her first picture took two days to produce. Shortly thereafter she was offered steady employment at $30.00 a week. When she first saw herself on the screen, she was so disappointed that she rushed out of the studio and did not reappear for several days. However, after deciding to come back, she continued with Powers for six months.

After that she skipped from one company to another—the Lubin Company in Philadelphia, Pathé Frères in Jersey City, and the Crystal Motion Picture Company, where she appeared in slapstick comedy and called herself the company's chief pie slinger.

By July 1913 she had amassed the enormous sum of $6,000 with which she decided to take a holiday in Europe. At the dock there was a cameraman who was eager to take her picture, which appeared in the papers with the heading "Pearl White leaves for Europe." With her face and name now in the public eye, she was on her way to real stardom.

When she returned, Pathé had started to work on serials in the Jersey City plant, and the company offered Pearl a part in a series of episodes entitled *The Perils of Pauline*, a title which was supposed to have been given to the firm by William Randolph Hearst. When Pearl read the contract submitted to her, she refused to sign it. It would have forced her to participate in many dangerous undertakings. For a while she resisted the contract's attractive terms, but then when she realized that she had been a minor success as an acrobat and trapeze artist, she decided to sign and to submit to Pauline's many trials. The least difficult of them was to learn to play tennis!

However, she was faced with episodes which were much more heart-stopping. She was to fly in a plane which crashed to the ground. She was to drive an automobile through water, fire, and sand. She was to jump overboard from a yacht just before it blew up. She was to stand in a captive balloon when the villain cut the rope, sending her soaring skyward; then she would have to drop an anchor which was to catch in a tree, descend 250 feet on the rope, reach a cliff on a mountain, and be pelted by rocks. All these exciting activities she did with much practice before the actual film.

She practiced jumping off moving trains and automobiles several times before each picture was shot and she worked out in a gymnasium before every scheduled struggle or fight. She never used a double to perform her stunts for her. Each serial was patterned along the same lines, based on action and suspense. The end of each episode left her in an apparently inescapable situation with no way out, until the following week's episode revealed her method of escape. One critic opined that the basic overtones of the dangers involved were height, depth, fire, water, speed, weight, and edged tools.

One stunt got her into a really serious situation. In May, 1914, the episode of the week was to show her climbing into a balloon and to have it ascend skyward, leaving her stranded in it until the following week. The balloon was supposed to have been under control from the ground, but it was set loose by mistake, and in a short time was four thousand feet above the Palisades, drifting down the Hudson, then across Manhattan and Brooklyn. Fortunately for Pearl she was not alone in the balloon. Its owner had hidden in a pile of canvas on board, and when the balloon was on its merry way, he came out to attempt to lower it. He had brought his lunch with him too, and while the balloon was drifting over Central Park, Columbus Circle, the Plaza Hotel, and St. Patrick's Cathedral, he and Pearl had their sandwiches and beer. Pearl was terrified when a terrible storm came up as they were near the Statue of Liberty, but they got through safely and eventually landed in open country along Long Island Sound.

A career like Pearl's could not escape the sort of publicity furnished by the popular song writers of the day. In the midst of the weeks of suspense during the serializing of *The Perils of Pauline*, a new song made its appearance. Called "Poor Pauline," it achieved instant acceptance. The music by Raymond Walker, was bouncy, the lyrics, by Charles McCarron, simple but engaging.

2. Handsome Harry's always near, he will save her never fear.
   Just in time he will appear, when Pauline's in peril.
   On a roof she fights for life, villian (*sic*) sticks her with a knife,
   "Marry me or be my wife!" what will Pauline do?
   But soon balloon with anchor swings around,
   Pauline is seen and rescued up side down.

   The chorus:
   > Poor Pauline, I pity poor Pauline,
   > One night she's drifting out to sea,
   > Then they tie her to a tree,
   > I wonder what the end will be,
   > This suspense is awful.
   > Bing! Bang! Biff! They throw her off a cliff,
   > They dynamite her in a submarine,
   > In the lion's den she stands with fright,
   > Lion goes to take a bite,
   > Zip goes the film—Good-night!
   > Poor Pauline.[4]

In April, 1916, in New York, she hung from the roof of a building on Seventh Avenue, and at a height of several hundred feet burned her initials in large letters on the wall, a stunt which made front-page headlines. Immediately after the United States had entered World War I, she was lashed to a steel cable being used in the construction of the twenty story Bush Terminal Building and hauled to the top, throwing down American flags and recruiting circulars during her upward journey. When she was lowered to the ground she shouted, "I have done my part; now you do yours," and walked to a recruiting booth followed by thirty young men who signed up forthwith.

She became immensely wealthy. Her income after the war was supposed to have reached a figure of $10,000 a week, which she spent lavishly. Among her acquisitions were a Park Avenue apartment, a large summer house on Long Island, a French maid, $25,000 worth of jewels, a $14,000 Rolls Royce, and a sporty Stutz which she drove herself.

Six years and one husband later, she had a nervous breakdown and was ordered to the mountains by French doctors. She had by this time been converted to Catholicism and announced that she would retire to a convent in the French Alps. Apparently she never quite made it.

[4] "Poor Pauline." Words: Charles McCarron, Music Raymond Walker © 1914 All rights for the USA and Canada controlled by Broadway Music Corp., c/o Walter Hofer, 221 West 57th Street, New York, New York. Used by Permission. All Rights Reserved.

POOR PAULINE

MISS PEARL WHITE
STAR OF THE FAMOUS SERIAL
PHOTOPLAY
"THE PERILS OF PAULINE"

WORDS BY
CHAS. McCARRON
MUSIC BY
RAYMOND WALKER

BROADWAY MUSIC CORPORATION
WILL VON TILZER PRESIDENT
145 WEST 45ᵗʰ ST. NEW YORK

Poor Pauline

I'm as wor-ried as can be   all the mov-ie shows I see   Have that aw-ful mys-ter-y,

"Paul-ine and her per-ils." On a rope they dan-gle her, then they choke and stran-gle her, With an

axe they man-gle her al-ways some-thing new,— To make   you shake—they give her Par-is

green,— Of course her horse—will neigh, "Nay Nay Paul-ine."   Poor Paul-ine, I pit-y

poor Paul-ine,— One night she's drift-ing out to sea, Then they tie her to a tree, I won-der

what the end will be,   this sus-pense is aw-ful.   Bing! Bang! Biff! they throw her off a

cliff—They dyn-a-mite her in a sub-ma-rine,— In the li-ons den she stands with

fright, Li-on goes to take a bite Zip goes the film   Good-night   Poor Paul-ine.

CHORUS: Poor Pauline, I pity poor Pauline,
   One night she's drifting out to sea,
   Then they tie her to a tree,
   I wonder what the end will be,
   This suspense is awful.
   Bing! Bang! Biff! They throw her off a
    cliff,

They dynamite her in a submarine,
Then the villain takes her on his knee,
Wonder what we're goin' to see—
Zip goes the film—Oh Gee!
Poor Pauline.

In the 1920's she acquired for herself in Biarritz the Hotel de Paris which had once been a chalet of the Empress Eugenia. She kept the Empress' bedroom for her own apartment, but turned the drawing room into a gambling casino, which remained open until her health made her give it up. In her late years she was a familiar figure in the gambling spots and night clubs of the Riviera. She became rather fat when she was in her forties and was always dressed in expensive French clothes and wore diamond studded anklets. When she died, her jewelry was sold for $75,000.

Her funeral service, performed by a Catholic priest, was attended by a dozen people. Poor Pauline!

The Castles

She came from New Rochelle, New York; he came from Norwich, England; together, they formed the greatest "society dance" pair that ever trod a ballroom floor.

Irene Foote met Vernon Castle (Blyth was his family name, Castle his stage name) at a swimming party in New Rochelle, when she was seventeen and he was twenty-three. It was not, by any means, love at first sight. He had come to the United States four years before with his sister and brother-in-law, both actors, and Vernon had landed a small part shortly after his arrival in a show called *The Orchid*, produced by Lew Fields. Since Irene was stage-struck her first thought, after being introduced to Vernon, was that he might help her find a professional part. Physically he did not appeal to her; his lanky frame was not built for girls to swoon over—five feet, eleven inches tall and tipping the scale at hardly more than one hundred eighteen pounds. But he was a means to an end, and she nagged him to arrange an audience for her with Lew Fields until finally he succumbed.

Irene, a tall, willowy blonde who was always impeccably dressed, was a very nervous dancer as she tried to impress the great Mr. Fields in a huge dark theater. She began with a pseudo-Spanish number which she called "Benita Caprice," and which seems to have combined the use of castanets, a tambourine, and a pair of hard heels for the stamp act, adding a sort of cancan to spice it up. Fields and Castle conferred in the lobby after Irene's performance, and, sure enough, Fields came up with an offer in a third or fourth road company of a show called *The Midnight Sons*, playing the Colorado circuit! But Irene's parents, Mr. and Mrs. Foote, put their respective feet down on the proposition, so their daughter could not accept it.

Nevertheless, a second opportunity came a few months later in Brooklyn, New York. Irene Foote made her professional debut on the stage in a small part in *The Summer Widowers*, playing for two weeks before the show's demise. Irene, who had about three lines to speak, attracted little attention; on the other hand, a much younger girl, with a mass of curls, played a whole scene and stole the show. The youngster, who had a violent crush on Vernon, was introduced to Irene. Her name was Helen Hayes.

After *Widowers* Irene was offered a part in a new play, *The Henpecked*. It was 1910, and on Christmas Day Castle asked her to marry him. His roles now were of sufficient importance to be worth a salary of seventy-five dollars a week. The wedding took place in May, and the young couple had a short honeymoon in England, after which each accepted a part in *The Henpecked* —Vernon a large one, Irene's was insignificant.

After the New York run, the show took to the road. In Kansas City Vernon was approached by the American agent of a French producer of revues, who wanted him to come to Paris to appear in a new show called *Enfin en Revue*. Vernon wangled a part for Irene, and the two were off to fulfill their new contract. They entranced the French audiences at the Olympia Theater with a quaint dance act about a tin soldier and a paper doll, a number which marked the beginning of their success as dancing partners. As a finale, they put on their own version of a new ragtime dance which was just coming into its own in America, the "Grizzly Bear," a lively number which consistently brought down the house.

But the backstage odors of some of the Paris stages were overwhelming, and the Castles were overwhelmed. They soon left the Olympia and secured an engagement at the Café de Paris, thanks to a French agent who had seen their act. In the small cabaret atmosphere of the Café de Paris they were an instant smash hit. For nearly six months they appeared at the Café nightly, interspersing their shows with private engagements and command performances. At last the Castles were "big time."

Back in New York, they accepted an engagement with the Café de l'Opéra at Broadway and Forty-second streets. At each of the small tables in the restaurant a neat card announced that Mr. and Mrs. Castle would appear at twelve o'clock. Shortly before that hour, they would slip to their table, and at midnight the floor would be cleared, a spotlight from the balcony would pick them out, and they would glide off to the music of Europe's Society Orchestra.

These days marked the zenith of the ragtime era, and the Castles demonstrated their own version of each new dance craze. Gone was the waltz; the one-step was the standard dance; but those couples who felt like bouncing or jumping or hopping could express themselves in the Grizzly Bear, the Turkey Trot, the Camel Walk, the Bunny Hop, and the Lame Duck. For such exhibitions, the Castles were the leading instructors.

In some dance halls, participants had to abide by a strict moral code. It was against the law to hold your partner too tightly. When patrons on the floor drew within six inches of each other, bouncers would tap them on the shoulder and ask them to widen the gap. In fact, an inventor tried to market a belt of metal, with a nine-inch bar protruding, to keep the dancers at the proper distance. Fortunately this was a complete failure.

Vernon and Irene's most popular innovation was the Castle Walk. It was a simple little number, but it brought the Castles much notoriety, and much money too. Their book on modern dancing describes the steps as follows: "First of all, walk as in the one-step. Now, raise yourself up slightly on your toes at each step with the legs a trifle stiff and breeze along happily and easily, and you know all there is to know about the Castle Walk. To turn a corner you do not turn your partner round, but keep walking her backward in the same direction, leaning over slightly—just enough to make a graceful turn and keep the balance well—a little like a bicycle rounding a corner . . . and then straighten up and start off down the room again. It sounds silly and is silly. That is the explanation of its popularity!"

At this time the Castle School of the Dance was turning people away, and the Castles were induced to expand their teaching activities and open Castle House, where Vernon taught a minimum of six hours a day. At first the people who sought instruction at Castle House paid two dollars an hour on weekdays, except on Fridays, when the charge was increased to three dollars. But Vernon soon learned that for his avid followers the sky was the limit, and his rate eventually went up from a dollar a minute to one hundred dollars an hour.

Once more the stage beckoned to them. Charles Dillingham was producing Irving Berlin's first musical comedy, *Watch Your Step*, and the Castles were wanted for leading roles. Such an opportunity could not be turned down, so in 1914, three years after their last previous appearance behind the footlights, there they were again, delighting audiences with their versions of the tango, the polka, and the fox trot. The number with which they brought down the house was "The Syncopated Walk," one of Berlin's smartest songs, with a melody that almost begged people to dance to its catchy beat.

Their restaurant, "Sans Souci," located under the sidewalk at 42nd Street and Broadway, was filled with supper guests, who danced Castle steps on a linoleum floor. "Castles in the Air," "Castles by the Sea," were other dance and supper places where Vernon and Irene made more or less regular appearances.

A four-week whirlwind tour, covering thirty-five cities, drew enormous crowds. Billboards proclaimed "The Castles are coming—Hooray! Hooray!" as the company, with its superb band, led by the popular Jim Europe, delighted their thousands of admirers. Most of the time they played two cities a day—a matinee in Rochester and an evening performance in Buffalo. Their exhibition dances comprised not only the accepted society dances of the day, like the tango, the maxixe, and the one-step, but included other more exotic and intricate numbers, such as the lulu fada, the furlane, and the pavanne. Each exhibition ended with a contest among the spectators and the award of a cup to the winner.

In December, 1915, Vernon bade good-by to his wife and his profession to prepare for enlistment in the British Royal Flying Corps. He took his aviation course at Newport News, Virginia, and earned his pilot's wings there. Then, before departing for England, he and Irene gave two farewell shows before record audiences on two successive Sunday nights at the gigantic Hippodrome in New York. The theater was jammed; three hundred people were forced to sit on the stage. The Castles performed four dance numbers to the music of Sousa's band. It was a particularly difficult period for Irene, who was still in the cast of *Watch Your Step*, now playing in the middle west. She would catch a special train from Pittsburgh or Cincinnati after her Saturday night show, get to New York for the Hippodrome appearance, and leave directly after the performance so that she could be back on the *Watch Your Step* stage on Monday night.

The following May, shortly before Vernon was dispatched to France with his squadron, Irene sailed to England to spend six days with him. The day after she landed, the pair appeared at a benefit performance at the Drury Lane Theatre before Queen Alexandra. They were nervous before they started, but their spirits had been bolstered by the discovery that Jim Europe's band was in England and available to them. Once again they captivated a packed house, and Alexandra applauded with the rest.

Many instrumental pieces were written for them, but those to which they most enjoyed dancing were composed by Jim Europe himself. "The Castle Walk" was probably the best known; "Castles in Europe" came close behind

in popularity. The title page of each showed the attractive couple doing one of their most popular steps. Each piece was written in fox trot or one-step time—simple, but catchy, and most of all, danceable.

Castle, after a series of memorable actions over the lines in Europe, was sent back to the United States to train pilots for the Royal Canadian Air Corps. At Fort Worth, Texas, his plane crashed on a training flight, and Castle was killed.

A few days after the fatal accident, the *Christian Science Monitor* editorialized the contribution of the Castles: "The Castles showed and taught people of two continents how modern dances ought to be danced. They eliminated vulgarity and replaced it with refinement. They restored poetry to motion. Multitudes of people who had no time to waste upon ordinary dancing, as participants or spectators, took kindly, and even enthusiastically, to their dancing exhibitions and instructions. Little by little the Castles changed the atmosphere of the dance hall. Little by little, too, they made it possible for discriminating people to witness with some degree of pleasure stage and screen dancing. Unconsciously, perhaps, because with all their popularity and success they remained as modest as they were unaffected, the two achieved a notable social reform. Dancing was running down to the depths when they first came upon the scene, and before the war separated them they had reversed the current. The Castles furnished an illustration of the good that may be accomplished in any calling if the effort is rightly and skillfully directed."

Teamwork—teamwork! A winning team can be a thing of beauty. And certainly in their field, the handsome Castles were the winningest team of all.

Oscar Hammerstein

THE TIME: December 3, 1906
THE PLACE: West 34th Street, New York City
THE MAN: Oscar Hammerstein
THE OCCASION: The opening of the Manhattan Opera House
THE POPULAR VERDICT: A smashing triumph

Oscar Hammerstein, the entrepreneur, the speculator, opera's superbuff, had pulled it off. He had challenged the great Metropolitan Opera Company, and he had emerged from the duel healthy and anxious to continue the fray. For four glorious seasons his exciting performances were studded with some of the brightest stars in the operatic firmament, while the competition between the rival companies became more and more bitter, and, as a corollary, more and more disastrous. The inevitable happened. In the spring of 1910, the wealthier Metropolitan absorbed Mr. Hammerstein's operatic interests, and the Manhattan Opera Company was no more. But during its short, and much of the time merry, life, it was a dynamic, news-provoking organization, the sort of company that Oscar Hammerstein delighted to operate.

Hammerstein's early life had been that of a Horatio Alger hero set to music. Leaving his native Berlin in 1863 at the age of fifteen, after a quarrel with his exacting father, he used his meager savings to buy passage to America on a cattle boat. In New York he went to work making cigars at a salary of two dollars a week. In his spare time he studied English and attended the theater. His ambition was unbounded, and as he became more proficient at his occupation his income increased, so that after less than a dozen years he was able to devote time and capital to other interests. The most absorbing of these were the musical theater and the accumulation of real estate. Combining the two, he built his first theater, the Harlem Opera House, on 125th Street, in 1889, following which he erected several more. His specific love was the opera; within two months of its opening the Harlem Opera House was staging performances in English of *The Bohemian Girl, Carmen, Der Freischütz* and others. Some of Hammerstein's vocal performers were of high rank, others questionable. One soprano who had a star billing in *The Bohemian Girl* was singled out by critics. The *New York Times*, discussing her rendition of the beautiful aria, *I Dreamt I Dwelt in Marble Halls*, observed that the singer dwelt in halls "half a tone lower than those occupied by the orchestra."

Before long Hammerstein's name was becoming legendary—if such may be said about a man still in his early forties. One legend—a true one—occurred in 1893. Oscar was lunching with a few theatrical friends, and a discussion arose as to how long it would take to write an operetta. All except Hammerstein concurred in the opinion that a minimum of two months would be required. Hammerstein insisted that he himself could turn out the words and music for such a production in forty-eight hours, provided one of the other diners, Gustave Kerker, would orchestrate the score. His friends regarded the statement as ridiculous, whereupon Oscar offered to bet $100 to bolster his rash pronouncement. The wager was accepted, and Oscar Hammerstein locked himself in a room on the top floor of the Gilsay House, to emerge forty-eight hours later with a light opera in three scenes called *The Kohinoor*. The show, orchestrated by Kerker, was produced in the fall of that year at Koster and Bial's Music Hall on Broadway and ran for six weeks. Hammerstein, flushed with the apparent success of his brain child, transferred the production to his Harlem Opera House. Apparently the theater-goers on Broadway were of a different breed than those on 125th Street. The Harlem production closed with disastrous results after a one-week trial.

Hammerstein could not resist trying his hand, from time to time, at composing. In 1896 he wrote and produced a new light opera, *Santa Maria*, a monumental financial disaster. Later, when the show went on tour, its advance publicity indicated that it had played for one hundred nights in New York, a statement which appears to have been considerably exaggerated. Oscar's lyrics for the big waltz song, "Santa Maria, My Joy, My Pride," could not be termed highly original:

> Oh, ravishing this is,
> No words describe such bliss
> No mortal ever loved as I,
> And, angel, oh so beautiful,
> And so enchanting angel white,
> Entrancing child of light,
> My eyes, I lift on bended knee,
> My thanks above to thee!
> Maria mine!

Hammerstein's fortunes rose and sank like the waves in mid-ocean. He made money quickly and lost it just as quickly. Whenever he made it, he would build another theater; in all, he erected thirteen—in New York, Philadelphia, and London—always on other people's money, to the full extent of his borrowing capacity. And when his luck ran out, he had no sympathy for his hapless creditors.

In 1898, upon the closing of his enormous Olympia Theater, the president of the New York Life Insurance Company, which held a mortgage on the property, wrote Hammerstein asking that a representative of the company be permitted to take charge of the theater's financial transactions. Oscar replied immediately: "I am in receipt of your letter, which is now before me, and in a few minutes it will be behind me. Respectfully yours, Oscar Hammerstein."

A year later another theater, the Victoria, was under construction. A contractor had not been paid and served notice on Oscar that until $2,000 was forthcoming, no roof would be put on the building. That afternoon Oscar was riding on a trolley car attempting to think of a solution. A girl sitting beside him said, "I was in the chorus of *Santa Maria*. You were very good to me." When Oscar explained how times had changed, and what a predicament he was in, the girl led him by the hand to her bank, drew $2,000 from her account, and gave it to him. Later Hammerstein used to say, "It shows that if opportunity does not come knocking at your door, you may be sitting beside her in a streetcar."

Hammerstein's greatest triumph was in the opening of his own Manhattan Opera House in 1906. The Metropolitan had been in operation since 1882 and had been in virtually complete control of grand opera in New York. Some think that Hammerstein's prime reason for building an opera house was his intense dislike of Heinrich Conried, the director of the Metropolitan. At any rate, Hammerstein, while putting up his own opera house, tried by every means to lure some of Conried's stars to head the large casts he was assembling for his performances. Unsuccessful in his efforts, he set about the task of inducing the great singers of Europe to come to America. A visit to the continent enabled him to secure contracts with some of the greatest artists, Nellie Melba, Luisa Tetrazzini, Mary Garden. At home, he completely dominated every phase of the construction of his theater. He was owner, architect, builder. His optimism was dynamic, his spirits high, his courage matchless. He had no fear of the financial dragons who controlled the destinies of the Metropolitan; he was St. George in a frock coat instead of a suit of armor, a high silk hat instead of a helmet, a cigar (he smoked twenty-five a day) instead of a gleaming sword. And, indeed, he fought the good fight.

That hat, incidentally, was a kind of trade-mark. The angle at which Hammerstein wore his ever-present top hat was usually indicative of the man's mood. When the financial and orchestral skies were clear, the hat was tipped jauntily over one eye. When trouble stalked the stage, Oscar wore his hat squarely down on his head, as if to weather any approaching storm. If the storm passed, and it was possible to relax again, the hat went to the back of his head, and anybody could ask him for any favor. To think of Hammerstein without his hat was—well—unthinkable. It was rumored that he wore it while sleeping—if he ever slept. Hammerstein's high silk hat was part of the man himself, like Will Rogers' lasso, like the Hathaway shirt man's eyepatch, like General Grant's cigar.

The whole country was interested in the Manhattan's opening night. It fulfilled every promise; the three-thousand-seat theater was sold out; the standees in the rear were packed almost to the point of suffocation. At the conclusion of the performance of *I Puritani*, Hammerstein, along with the featured artists, was brought out for bow after bow. One paper reported that with the fall of the final curtain Oscar cried out, "I did it!" And he did it again and again, scoring one triumph after another.

Hammerstein's major coup was undoubtedly the acquisition of Luisa Tetrazzini. The superb coloratura soprano, after enjoying several years of great popularity in South America, had had a phenomenal success at Covent Garden in London and was being eagerly sought by impresarios around the world. Hammerstein determined to bring her to America at any cost—the cost was high but she was worth it. Four days before her debut at the Manhattan Opera Company, Hammerstein had received mail orders alone amounting to $25,000 for a house with a dollar capacity of $11,500.

On January 15, 1908, Tetrazzini was introduced to her first New York audience in *La Traviata*. The audience went berserk. Her phenomenal voice, aided by her acting ability—remarkable in a woman built like a super-Brunhilde—generated a delirium on the vast assemblage which the newspapers found difficult to put into words. The people cheered, they screamed, they cried; Tetrazzini, overwhelmed by the reception, was in a flood of tears herself. The next morning she was front-page news in the New York newspapers. The brightest of Hammerstein's stars was in the ascendant.

From that moment on, no coloratura soprano ever challenged her position; she remained at the top of the operatic ladder until her retirement many years later. She was Hammerstein's Liebestraume, his "Love Dream," and "love," to Oscar, was synonymous with "money." Whenever a Tetrazzini performance was announced, the house was sold out within an hour. It was reported at the close of the season that Hammerstein had made $250,000; if such was the case, much of his profit can have been attributed to Madame Tetrazzini.

She gained weight over the summer, as was readily visible when she appeared as Lucia in the fall of 1909, with John McCormack, the twenty-five-year old Irish tenor, at the Manhattan's second performance of the season. But after she had blown a few kisses to the audience and settled down to the serious business of singing, her bulk was forgotten and the silvery cascade of pure notes was all that mattered.

Tetrazzini's massive frame seemed impervious to physical ailments; she never missed her "turn at bat." All the more strange that during her second year with Hammerstein a veteran composer like Gus Edwards should write a song, "I'm After Madame Tetrazzini's Job," indicating that she was ill, even though the lyrics were in a humorous vein.

I'm After Madame Tetrazzini's Job.

Please tell me have— you seen dear Mis-ter Op-'ra-steen I got a see-a heem queck—— Here in de pa-per wrote, there is one lit-tle note Says Tet-raz-zin-i she's seek— Poor Mis-ter Op-'ra-steen he must-a feel— so mean Tears from de eyes— on his face— Soon he'll no lon-ger mourn, 'Cause Tet-raz-zi-ni's gone I come to take— her place.—

Refrain

I can sing— just like Tet raz-zin,— If you will just give— me one chance— I sing Ver-di, just like a Bir-die I put them all-in a trance, So won't you please, Mis-ter Ham-mer-stein, let me sing Puc-ceen for the mob, Then I'll sing for you till next sum-mer,— for I'm af-ter Ma-dame Tet-raz-zin-i's job.——

2. I'll sing-a Traviat first thing right off the bat
   Wait till my Carmen I spring.
   I bet-a feefty cents, he thinks I am immense
   After Aida I sing
   I do Somnambula grrr-eater than any star
   Almost a make you to weep
   Queek he will make de choice,
   Say that my granda voice
   Put Tetrazzini to sleep.

   CHORUS

   They ran, in part:

> Please tell me have you seen dear Mr. Op'rasteen
> I got a see-a heim queek
> Here in de paper wrote, there is one little note
> Says Tetrazzini she's seek.

Then, burlesquing arias from popular operas, the chorus goes:

> I can sing just like Tetrazzin,
>
> . . . .
>
> So won't you please, Mr. Hammerstein,
> Let me sing Pucceen for the mob!
> Then I'll sing for you till next summer
> For I'm after Madame Tetrazzini's job[5]

Gus Edwards, who published the song in addition to writing the words and music, had many hits to his credit after the turn of the century. Probably the greatest of all was "School Days," a nostalgic waltz; its sheet music sales were in the millions.

The title page of "I'm after Madame Tetrazzini's Job" shows a rapt diva lilting her best for Mr. Hammerstein, who sits stolidly in an arm chair, his high silk hat squarely on top of his head (was there another storm to weather?), his eyes closed, a long cigar between his lips, pondering a decision on the lady's operatic ability. But he knew that she could never take Luisa Tetrazzini's place in the hearts of her devout admirers. Nobody would ever do that.

Nothing good lasts forever. Temperamental Oscar quarreled heatedly with two of the people who were most important to his continued success, Cleofonte Campanini, the Manhattan's principal conductor, and Mrs. Clarence Mackay, one of its most affluent and influential patrons. Campanini

---

[5] "I'm After Madame Tetrazzini's Job." Words and Music: Gus Edwards © 1909 by Mills Music Inc. © Renewed 1937 by Mills Music Inc. Used by Permission.

returned to Italy at the end of the 1909 season; Mrs. Mackay then gave up her box, and so did many of her well-to-do friends.

The opening of the new season lacked the glitter of those that had preceded it, and the heretofore fulsome newspaper reviews no longer appeared on the front page. Even though Tetrazzini and John McCormack still "packed them in," deficits mounted, for both the Manhattan and Metropolitan Opera Houses were trying to outdo each other and were indulging in competitive extravagances. But it was the Metropolitan, with the assistance of its wealthy clientele, that had the staying power. And in the end Hammerstein surrendered. At the age of sixty-three, and for a consideration of one and a quarter million dollars, he agreed not to produce grand opera in New York, Chicago, Philadelphia, or Boston for a ten-year period.

Luisa Tetrazzini gave her last New York performance for Hammerstein on March 26, 1910, in *Lucia di Lammermoor*. With the closing of the curtains at the conclusion of the final act, Hammerstein's reign at the Manhattan Opera House ended, though he did manage to bring Tetrazzini and his other stars to Boston for nine more performances before disbanding them.

Ten years later Oscar was in no condition to revive his master opus. He had died in August, 1919. Of the great individualist there remained only a memory of a ghostly figure with a Van Dyke beard, in a high hat, smoking a long cigar.

Enrico Caruso

He was only forty-eight when he died. So active had he been, so much had been crammed into his professional career, that it was hard to believe his life span was so short. The world grieved when word came from Naples on August 2, 1921, that the incomparable Enrico Caruso had passed away, the golden voice of opera stilled. Crowds of Italian-Americans gathered around the bulletin boards of the New York newspapers and wept when the announcement appeared. He was mourned by operagoers from London to Chicago to Mexico City to Buenos Aires, and by the men and women associated with him at the Metropolitan—Geraldine Farrar, Amelita Galli-Curci, John McCormack, Antonio Scotti. The *New York Times* editorialized, "There was no second. There is, there will be, no likely successor."

Madame Marcella Sembrich, one of the Metropolitan's leading sopranos, who sang opposite him for many years, recalled, "Well do I remember his debut. I had never met him before, but once I heard him sing, I knew him for the great artist that he was. . . . There were times when he was suffering from a cold, when he would say to me: 'Unless this cold improves we had best not try the high notes tonight. But if I should feel equal to them, I will give you the signal, a pressure of the hand will let you know that I am feeling fit.' And then at the critical moment would come that pressure of his hand and then his voice rising and soaring away over the audience in those thrilling measures."

Even tin-pan alley acknowledged his stature. Soon after his death, George A. Little and Jack Stanley wrote a schmalzy lament, in waltz time, entitled "They Wanted a Song Bird in Heaven, So God Took Caruso Away." The lyrics went like this:

> Just like a beautiful rose that has flown,
> When into the heart of the world it has grown
> Gone is a flower that we learned to love,
> To bloom for the Master and Maker above!

> Chorus: They needed a song-bird in Heaven
> To sing when the angels would play
> So God told the angels where one
>   could be found,
> They came and they took him one day.
> He's gone to that sweet land of sunshine
> Forever and ever to stay
> They needed a song-bird in Heaven,
> So God took Caruso away.[6]

Caruso was thirty years old when he first sang at New York's Metropolitan Opera House. The Metropolitan was ten years younger; the great opera house had been erected in 1883 and was dubbed by one veteran manager "the new yellow brewery on Broadway." In 1892 it had been badly damaged by fire, but it was restored in time for the next season's opening with the addition of a Diamond Horseshoe which surrounded the boxes filled on opera nights with the members of New York's most opulent families.

These families, and the rest of the huge group of operagoers, were cool to Caruso his first season. They had been enamored by his predecessor, the lyric tenor Jean de Reszke, and there was no immediate indication that they were ready to accept the dictum of "off with the old love, on with the new."

---

[6] "They Wanted a Song Bird in Heaven, So God Took Caruso Away." © 1921 by Mills Music Inc. © Renewed 1949 by Mills Music Inc. Used by Permission.

It took a full year before the audiences and the critics realized that the Metropolitan's manager, Heinrich Conried, had discovered a golden nugget worth a fortune to his company.

That second season Caruso was a work horse. Not only did he appear thirty times in New York, but he was sent all over the country from Boston to San Francisco for twenty more performances. At the close of the American season, he was off to Europe for a few months, and caught Paris in a highly receptive mood. One hundred twenty-two thousand Parisians attended one of his outdoor performances.

After the 1905–1906 season in New York the artists were off on another cross-country tour, reaching San Francisco the middle of April. In the early morning hours of April 17, after a superlative performance of *Carmen*, Caruso and his fellow singers were awakened by vast rumblings which to some portrayed the advent of the end of the world—the earth shuddered mightily; buildings toppled; glass shattered. The artists fled their hotels in various stages of dress and undress. Caruso apparently was bewildered and thereafter was the subject of assorted legendary experiences. One reporter had him scantily clad, sitting on a valise in the middle of the street, and begging for a pair of pants. Another had him wandering around the lobby of the St. Francis Hotel in pajamas and a fur coat, and muttering, " 'Ell of a place! I never come back here." A third had him fighting with a Chinaman who had tried to steal a small trunk which Caruso was guarding on Market Street. Still another had him sleeping under a tree all the next night, afraid to trust himself under a roof. Eventually he, along with the other artists, came safely back to a world where the ground was solidly anchored.

In the fall, a week before the Metropolitan was to open its season, Caruso made newspaper headlines of a nonmusical nature. He had always enjoyed walking in Central Park and looking at the animals which were caged there. One afternoon, while he was meandering through the monkey house, he was accused by an angry woman of annoying her. Annoying? Pinching? Just what was it? At any rate, the woman insisted that a policeman arrest Caruso, which was promptly done. At the stationhouse he was able to contact the management of the Metropolitan, who put up bail for his release. For days the papers recounted and speculated on the incident, weaving all sorts of insinuations.

Caruso was deathly afraid that the threatened blot on his character would cause operagoers to turn against him, and when he was preparing for his opening-night role as Rodolfo in *La Bohème*, he was highly agitated.

Fortunately, his audience was not concerned about any monkey business on the part of its favorite tenor. He received an enormous spontaneous ovation, so heartfelt that between the scenes, he broke down and sobbed, "New York is still my friend."

A few days later he was in the Yorkville police court to answer the charges that had been made against him. Fortunately, he had nothing to fear; no woman appeared to accuse him, but the court fined him ten dollars anyway before they let him go.

In the fall of 1908 he received his most severe emotional blow. His mistress from his more youthful days, Ada Giachetti, who had borne him two sons but who had later become estranged from him, visited him in New York. Caruso had hoped there might be a reconciliation, but instead the couple quarreled hopelessly, and Miss Giachetti then returned to Europe with a substantial amount of cash which Caruso had proffered as a settlement for all their differences.

The tension of these unpleasant encounters had a deleterious effect on the great man. Time after time he was obliged to cancel scheduled appearances; on twenty-one nights that winter Caruso failed to "go on" as advertised. When he sailed for Italy in the spring of 1909 he was perturbed; he felt sure he had a serious throat ailment which would destroy his ability to sing again. So widespread were the reports that he was losing his voice that a team of popular song writers, Billy Dunham and Al Piantadosi, wrote a gruesome little number called "Good-bye Mister Caruso." The chorus goes like this:

> Oh poor Mister Carus
> His great-a big-a voice he's-a lose
> No more he sing in Opera grand,
> He's gone-a back to Italy to peddle banan
> He was one big-a chump
> Smoke-a cigarette and make-a fool with the monk,
> Good-bye I cry good-bye Mister Carus.

Apparently the public had a long memory, for this was three years after the monkey-house incident.

In Milan a specialist removed an obstruction from one of Caruso's vocal cords. This was a flare-up of an old trouble for which Caruso had undergone similar treatment before his fame had mounted. Fame is costly. His first throat operation had cost him ten dollars; the second was six thousand. But the golden voice was restored, and when the lights dimmed at the

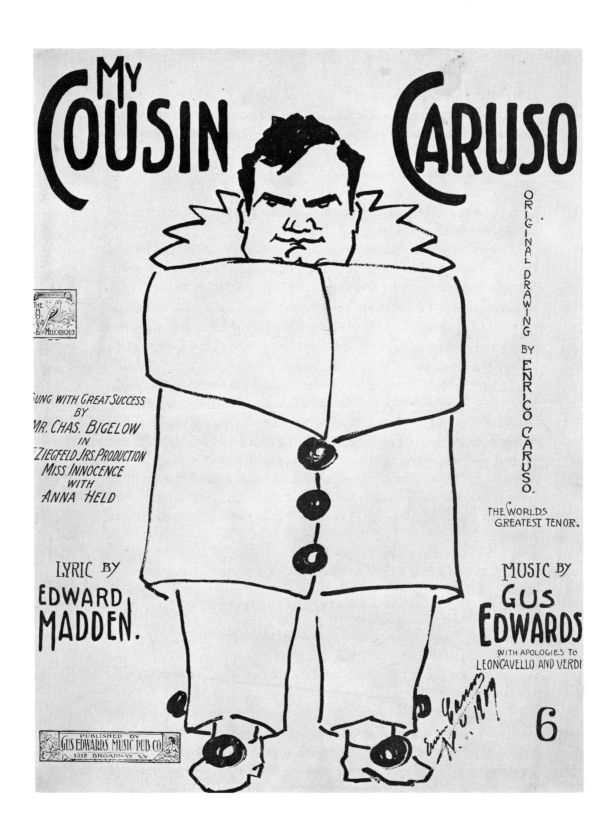

"My Cousin Caruso"

Poor man, Mis-ter Ham-mer-steen, He's-a turn-a green, Feel-a ver-a mean; Talka craz

Tro' da fun-na hat, Down at the Op'-ra house Man-hat.— He's-a lose won-der-ful Ca-rús,

Sing-a lak' de deuce, Sing-a da P's and Q's Hisa mudd' she's my fad-der's brud, Data

mak' him my cou-sin Ca-rus.— My— Cou-sin Ca-rus - o Say, kid, when he cut loose,

Dat Op'-ra House justa shaka like-a dis - a like dat He mak' dem all cry "Bra - vo Grat - si,"

When he sing Pag-li-ac - ci His voice so sad - a— Drive de la-dies all mad - a,

Oh! what's de use,——— He's my Cou-sin Ca-rús.—

2. One night something is de mat',
Op'ra fall-a flat,
Good-bye "Traviat,"
Can't find Carus Da great-a man,
Up at the Metropolitan,
Ten million people get-a sore,
Jump up with a roar,
Pusha de building o'er
They yell Carus no want-a come,
Grand Op'ra it goes on de bum.

CHORUS: My Cousin Caruso Say, kid, when he cut
loose,
Dat Op'ra House justa shaka like-a dis-a
like dat
He mak' de Ladies tear out de rat-a,
When he sing Traviata
His voice so dream-a
Lak'-a peaches and cream-a
Oh! what's de use,
He's my Cousin Carus

Metropolitan for Caruso's first night of the new season, the magnificent voice rang out as gloriously as ever.

A few months before the malicious innuendoes of "Good-Bye Mister Caruso" had appeared on the sheet-music stands, a song with an entirely different point of view had made its appearance and attained instant popularity. Gus Edwards, one of the most popular song writers of the day, wrote a melody for "My Cousin Caruso," to which Ed Madden wrote the lyrics. In the chorus Edwards had cunningly woven a theme from Pagliacci.

> My Cousin Caruso Say, kid, when he cut loose,
> Dat Op'ra House justa shaka like-a dis-a like dat
> He mak' dem all cry "Bravo Gratsi,"
> When he sing Pagliacci
> His voice so sad-a, Drive de ladies all mad-a
> Oh! What's de use, He's my Cousin Carus.[7]

The title page was designed by Caruso himself, who thereupon displayed to the public a second, and quite impressive talent; he was revealed as a skilled cartoonist. Self-taught, he had developed the art of caricature to a degree matched by but few of the cartoonists of the day. So entertaining were his sketches of close acquaintances that eventually, to the delight of his admirers, a number of them were reproduced in book form.

Caruso's cartoons were many and highly prized. Most, naturally, were of musical personalities, but best of all he enjoyed drawing caricatures of himself. He never tried to flatter; some of his portrayals of the artists, usually in costume, would have been considered cruel had anyone else sketched them. But Caruso had a broad sense of humor; he pulled no punches when he sketched his friends. There was nothing intentionally mean or biting about his work; it was so good-natured that his subjects were always flattered rather than hurt.

One of his great friends was Geraldine Farrar, the handsome American soprano who frequently sang opposite him. He drew numerous caricatures of her. At times she objected, half in earnest, but she could never be annoyed with him for long. When told by a friend of one sketch of the two of them singing a duet, she inquired, "Did it show me with a mouthful of big teeth—tombstones?" When told that that was the general impression, she replied, "I knew it! He always drew me like that! And each time I objected

---

[7] "My Cousin Caruso," by Gus Edwards & Edward Madden Copyright 1909 by Mills Music, Inc. Copyright © renewed 1936 by Mills Music, Inc. Used by Permission.

he would say, 'but I have never seen you, Geraldina, with your mouth shut!' "

He became a rich man. At a salary of $2,500 a concert he was earning over $100,000 a year from his operatic performances. At least a million dollars came to him from his recordings, which included about two hundred songs, arias, and hymns. During a twenty-year period he made records for the Victor Talking Machine Company—later R. C. A. Victor—and for European record companies.

And yet he was not greedy for money. In 1914 he was offered $4,000 for each performance; he refused the increase, indicating his satisfaction with the lesser amount he had been receiving. But for a concert in another country—that was quite different. For an outdoor concert in the great bull ring in Mexico City, with the rain pouring down on a delirious audience of 25,000, he received $15,000; for a short season in Havana he was paid $10,000 per concert; in Buenos Aires he got $7,000 an evening. But, at least, each of his hearers was treated to a unique experience; Caruso's voice never went off the gold standard.

Nothing is forever. On Christmas Eve, 1920, he sang the part of Eleazar in *La Juive*. The following day he collapsed in his bathtub with a severe attack of pleurisy, and the great man's days of glory were over. For weeks he struggled back from a frightening case of bronchial pneumonia; then, in the early summer, when it was felt that his strength had been sufficiently restored, he sailed with his young wife, Dorothy Benjamin Caruso (whom he had married in August, 1918), his baby, and his household staff, for Italy. But he no longer had the staying power; his health had been too severely impaired, and in another two months it was all over.

For fifty years music lovers have longed for another Enrico Caruso. Has the mold been broken? Can there be another such golden voice? Can such sounds burst again from a human throat? Anyone interested is asked to wait for the next installment of this unresolved hope. Please be patient; it may be ten years, or twenty, or thirty, or never.

Gaby Deslys

The little girl from Marseilles was quite sure of herself. It did not matter that her mother was a washerwoman. Nor did it matter that her parents had placed her in the Convent of St. Marie. Little Madeline Caire had only one interest—the stage. She was convinced that she was born for it. So at sixteen, as the twentieth century dawned, she took the first step necessary to fulfill her ambition; she ran off from the convent and made her way to Paris, where she obtained an engagement in a variety theater at an equivalent of ten dollars a week.

She was a dancer with an acrobatic style. She was a singer with a better-than-average voice. But these attributes would not have been sufficient to propel her to the heights, had it not been for her sparkling personality, which, augmented by a striking face and figure, found favor with her audience, and moreover, with some important admirers.

Like many stage people, she was dissatisfied with her name, so she selected another. "Gabrielle" appealed to her, "Gabrielle of the lilies." "Gabrielle" slid into "Gaby," and "Gaby Deslys" was the sobriquet under which she became the toast of Europe and eventually the darling of America.

Gaby was shrewd. She had a keen sense of the value of publicity, and an iron will which drove her forward. Her forward march included the conquest of the affections of King Emanuel of Portugal. This alliance gained her an enormous amount of the sort of notoriety upon which she was building her career. Materialistically it brought her a great fortune in jewels, for Emanuel was lavish in showering gifts upon his enamorata. Gaby was a pearl gatherer, and the king draped her in a king-size pearl necklace which was the base for what later became one of the world's costliest pearl collections. Other extravagant gifts so depleted the royal treasury, that the Portuguese revolution which took place after the *affaire* resulted in large part from the nation's indignation at the profligacy of their monarch.

The gorgeous Gaby flitted from flower to flower. Reports had it that she was the mistress of King Alfonso of Spain. The young men of Paris, London, and Berlin lost their heads over her. They wrote her for assignations, or sometimes just to tell her how attractive they found her. For example, one letter from England read: "I saw you at the Palace on Saturday night last and I felt I must . . . tell you what I think of you. If I were older I should have fallen in love with you and then I should have made you marry me, but as I am only seventeen and poor, I cannot very well do that." Another man wrote: "I was glad when the curtain went down, for you played upon my feelings so. My heart went up and down with your every movement."

Gaby's movements were quite definitely provocative; her décolleté costumes had the men squirming in their seats, and her dance maneuvers included the high kicks so enjoyed by the patrons of the baldhead row. An English organization, calling itself the Purity Brigade, announced: "The publicity given to the performance of Miss Gaby Deslys aroused the attention of the Purity Campaigners." One of the Purity gentlemen, preparing to give evidence against several of Miss Deslys' turns, stated: "I have no hesitation in saying that the turns I refer to are not fit to be seen by women, girls, youths, and children."

One rapt theatergoer, when reminded that his wife was prettier than Gaby, and had prettier ankles and arms and a more beautiful figure, said, "It is queer. I never look to see what bloomers my wife has on . . . but there is something about Gaby, you know, isn't there?"

Lee and Jake Shubert, a theatrical team whose productions numbered into the hundreds, were convinced that Gaby Deslys would captivate an American audience and they made the necessary overtures. Gaby had refused other offers to go to New York. She admitted it was just a question of money. She told Alan Dale, a writer for *Theatre Arts* magazine, "I have had so many offers to go to New York but I refuse to go. New York will not pay me enough." And further: "In New York I must rehearse for twenty days, and they refuse—they dare to refuse—to pay me for rehearsals. I protest. It is unheard of. It is an insult. To rehearse for twenty days for nothing—*Oh, la-la-la! Que c'est drôle!*" In other words, ridiculous!

She described to Dale a sketch she was planning for an appearance in London: "It is very, very frank . . . . It has been submitted to the authorities and they will allow it . . . . Of course, evil to him who evil thinks. I play it very delicately, very daintily, and it is most artistic. But it is what you call just a bit shady. I do not think New York would like it."

But Gaby did go to New York, courtesy of the Shuberts. At her 1911 debut at the Winter Garden, the "sexy French chanteuse"—as she was advertised— ran into difficulties. Not with her salary, which was $4,000 a week, but with the presentation of her material. Her heavy accent made the lyrics of her songs nearly unintelligible, and her voice failed to thrill the audience, who indicated a decided preference for her costars, two young fellows in black-face named Al Jolson and Frank Tinney.

Lee and Jake, nothing daunted, tried again. Once more they featured her with Jolson, this time in a production entitled *Vera Violetta*. By now Gaby's pronunciation of English had improved markedly, and she captivated the crowd. Another young person, as yet unrecognized, was in the cast, a young female with an hourglass figure; her name was Mae West. But in 1911 the men didn't come up to the Winter Garden to see Mae; they came up to see Gaby.

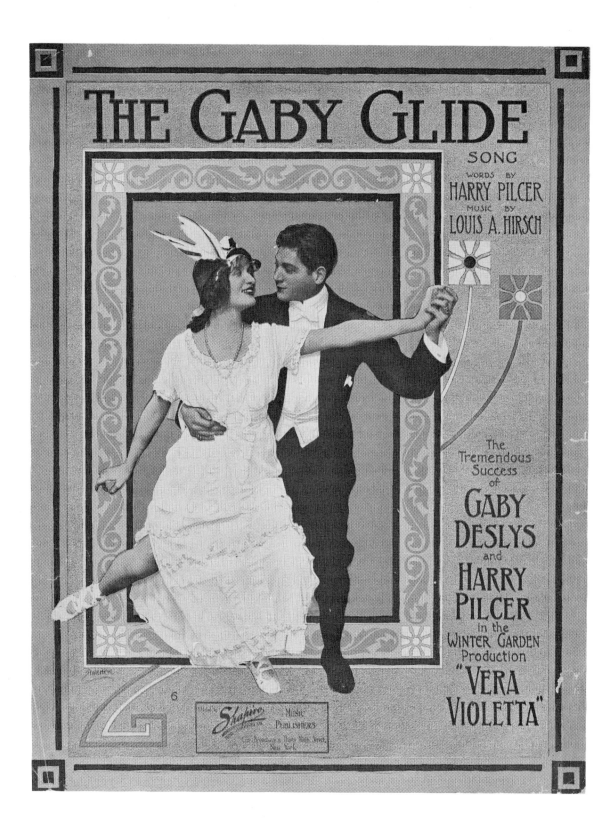

One musical number was the sensation of *Vera Violetta*. It was built around a song called "The Gaby Glide," for which the words were written by Harry Pilcer and the music by the veteran Louis A. Hirsch. Pilcer was, at that time, one of the best-known "society" dancers in America, a handsome, well-built young man, and Gaby's dancing partner in the show.

The title page of "The Gaby Glide" carries a photograph of Deslys and Pilcer executing a step in their dance number, and beaming at each other while so doing. The song has a catchy syncopated beat; it was a best seller in 1911, though it did not attain the popularity of another syncopated song written in the same year by a young fellow named Berlin. Irving Berlin's modest little work was "Alexander's Ragtime Band."

Pilcer's lyrics were exciting and even suggestive:

2. We are going crazy 'bout this new dance bewitching
   We can't stop our feet at all, they feel such an
        itching,
   You are in the air, floating here and there,
   Not a single care comes a-stealing.
   Talk about your other rags, why they aren't in it
   You feel all the joys of life in one single minute,
   For you travel so, with a lot of go,
   Can you stop? I guess "No"
   It's a big joyful dip, it's a heavenly trip.[8]

CHORUS: Oh! oh! That Gaby, Gaby Glide;
        It's just a real Parisian slide
        Prance along as though you were upon the boulevard
        Dance it here and dance it there and keep on dancing
             hard ...

After Gaby's success in *Vera Violetta* she had a kinder spot in her heart for the American stage. After further successes in the capitals of Europe she was back in the United States in 1914 in *The Belle of Bard Street*, where her best-received song was "Who Paid the Rent for Mrs. Rip Van Winkle When Rip Van Winkle Was Away?" However, before her success in a New York theater she had been subjected to a bit of rowdyism at the usual New Haven tryout, where she was pelted with missiles by obstreperous Yale students. Bananas and cigarette boxes were thrown at her, and she was nearly felled by a bag of peanuts which hit her in the forehead. The gallant police closed in and arrested three of the principal troublemakers, one of them the son of a United States senator from Minnesota.

[8] "Gaby Glide." Harry Pilcer & Louis A. Hirsch Copyright 1911 by Shapiro, Bernstein & Co. Inc. 666 Fifth Avenue, New York, N.Y. 10019 Copyright renewed and Assigned. USED BY PERMISSION.

The Gaby Glide

Ev-'ry-bo-dy's rav-ing 'bout the real French-y Two Step, Ev-'ry-bo-dy wants to

do this smart fan-cy new step, It's a fun-ny bear, Par-is on a tear, Well, I do

de-clare it is class-y. Gab-y brought the dance and it's got us all a go-ing,

Since she came no oth-er twirl has had an-y show-ing, It's a mu-sic treat,

for your danc-ing feet, It is flash-y but neat— Just a twist and a

Chorus

bend,— that you hope will not end.— Oh! Oh! that Gab-y, Gab-y

Glide;— It's just a real Par-is-ian slide,— Prance a-long as though

you were up-on the boul-e-vard;— Dance it here and dance it there and keep on danc-ing

hard.— Start in to the side, do the Par-is ride, Swing up near— then wide.—

Va - len -tine   gets   out.

Oh! Oh! that Gab-y, Gab-y Glide,—— Don't lag or let your feel -ings

hide,—— Do the side step, trip and then go back the oth-er way,— Do the for-ward

dip, and see how you be-gin to sway,— Oh! Oh! that Gab-y, Gab - y Glide.——

side - tracked the west - bound freight —— And the mid -night ex- press

All in safe- ty flew by, While—Tom was a- sleep at the switch.——

holes in sweit- zer cheese. ——

2. We are going crazy 'bout this new dance bewitching,
   We can't stop our feet at all they feel such an itching,
   You are in the air, floating here and there,
   Not a single care comes a stealing.
   CHORUS

In 1915 one critic commented: "Gaby Deslys is an instance of a triumph of unscrupulous advertisement; that she has gone to the front owing to her unfaltering resolution that the public should see a good deal of her. She is more than a clever dancer with a talent for décolleté."

Her last appearance in this country was in 1916, and when she sailed for London in April, a reigning musical star, Nora Bayes, gave her a big farewell party which started at midnight, and at which every facet of theatrical life was represented. A charwoman danced with Sam Bernard, the producer. A stage manager swapped stories with a leading actress. The property man, the electricians, the ticket takers all were there to say good-by to Gaby; the guests even included a trained dog named Jasper. Of course Harry Pilcer, her old dancing partner, was there. Rumor had it that at one time he had been engaged to her, a report vehemently denied by Gaby.

From 1916 on she was weakened by bouts of illness. Several throat operations proved unsuccessful, particularly since she always insisted that the surgeons take pains not to scar her neck. A throat infection in 1920 proved fatal. The entire French theatrical world attended her funeral at Notre Dame, which was so crowded that many could not gain admittance.

Except for her famous jewels, which were bequeathed to her family, and a set of diamond cuff links, left to Harry Pilcer, her fortune of millions of francs went eventually to the poor people of Marseilles.

About this time another song came on the market. It was called "The Little Good-For-Nothing's Good for Something, After All." The writer *couldn't* have been thinking of Gaby, could he?

2
GETTING AROUND

"The Old Fall River Line"

Harry Von Tilzer, a man who used to boast that he had written the tunes for a thousand songs, must have been a sentimental fellow. Most of his lyricists supplied him with the sort of boy and girl material that represented the bread-and-butter fare in the elaborate menu of popular music served to sheet-music buyers.

Probably there was never a melody committed to paper by Von Tilzer that couldn't be whistled by anyone (provided he had half an ear) after he had heard it played a couple of times. Certainly "On the Old Fall River Line" falls into this category.

In 1913, when the song was written, the Fall River Line was a favorite attraction of honeymoon couples, both genuine and simulated. Far less expensive for New England newlyweds than a trip to Niagara Falls, the overnight run to New York in a four-hundred-foot-long steamer seemed almost made to order for brides and grooms. In fact, the line catered to them; one of their earlier steamers built in the 1860's advertised nine bridal rooms.

The Fall River Line came into being in 1847, as the Bay State Steamboat Company. It formed a link, along with the Fall River Railroad Company, in the increasingly important transportation service between Boston and New York. Daily the "cars from Boston" met the *Bay State*, one of the first two ships of the new line, drawing up to the Fall River wharf and disgorging their passengers from the toylike coaches.

The *Bay State* was the luxury vessel of her day. A 1,500-ton monster, she was 315 feet long, the largest steamer to traverse the inland waters of America. She had a 1,500-horsepower engine. A writer of the period said about her, she "is a noble specimen of steamboat architecture." He might

have added that her table was renowned. In the forward cabin, passengers sat at long candle-lit tables, where they could partake of a delicious supper for fifty cents. Of course, they had to suffer some small discomforts on the trip; for instance, on cold winter mornings they would have to break up the ice in their water pitchers in order to proceed with their ablutions.

In those early days there was great competition between the ships of rival lines, and races were the order of the day—or, in reality, of the night. On the *Bay State's* first run to Fall River in May, 1847, she was challenged by the *Oregon*, the queen of the Stonington Line. The two vessels plowed through the night toward their first destination, Newport, which the *Bay State* reached ahead of her opponent, nine hours and fifteen minutes after leaving New York, a glamorous showing for those days.

But the beaten *Oregon* could have proud memories of a later glory. A month after she had met her match in the *Bay State*, her owner, "Live-Oak" George Law, a former day laborer, had challenged another Stonington boat to a race up the Hudson River from the Battery in New York, with a $1,000 wager plus a sizable hunk of prestige to reward the winner. The cocky competitor was the *C. Vanderbilt*, named for her owner.

The two boats started on a June morning before a crowd of cheering spectators and churned their way neck and neck—or rather paddle and paddle—for thirty miles up the river. At Ossining a slight collision damaged the *Oregon's* wheelhouse, but she did not slow down. The opposing boat, however, became mired in confusion, with Vanderbilt relaying so many orders to his pilot, and with so many bells sounding in the engine room, that the bewildered engineer stopped his engine dead, thereby spotting the *Oregon* a substantial lead.

This advantage was seriously threatened when Law's boat ran out of coal. Desperately he sent his crew off to scavenge any available wood they could lay their hands on. Chairs and loose benches were turned into fuel; and after they were gone, the berths, doors, and wainscoting made the supreme sacrifice. The *Vanderbilt* was bearing down, but the gap was too wide to be closed, and the *Oregon* limped over the finish line a battered winner.

Some years later the financiers of Wall Street discovered that the Fall River Line was a big money-maker, and they moved to acquire ownership. The man who gained eventual control was Jim Fisk, the shrewd capitalist and railroad magnate who at one time or another seemed to have a finger in everything which required millions of dollars to operate. Fisk took over the line in 1869, when its mainstays were two 3,000-ton behemoths, the *Bristol* and the *Providence*. Each could transport 800 passengers in a luxurious style to which few of them could have been accustomed. They promenaded on thick carpets to the chant of 250 caged canaries, every bird named personally by Fisk. (He probably had had ample practice christening Pullman cars). He was a childish, often softhearted, giant, bestowing personal favors on people who appealed to his fancy or his vanity, giving an occasional free trip to a stranger, or a pension to an old-time employee. Fisk met a violent death in 1872, and the line changed its name to the Old Colony Steamboat Company, to pass under the control of the Old Colony Railroad.

Now came the *Pilgrim*, far more luxurious than the *Bay State*, a 390-foot-long giant, with a gross tonnage of almost 3,500. The *Pilgrim* was launched in 1882. She had sleeping accommodations for 1,200 passengers, and was lighted with 1,000 incandescent electric lights (seven years before the White House used them). The Fall River Line was now *the* way to travel between New York and New England. Among the names on the passenger lists were presidents Grant, Arthur, Harrison, Cleveland, Teddy Roosevelt and F. D. R., and various Astors, Rockefellers, Belmonts, and Vanderbilts.

In 1908 there appeared a newer and bigger "Queen of the Sound." She was christened the *Commonwealth*. Four hundred fifty-six feet in length, she so impressed those who traveled on her that writers were hard put for words to properly picture this gorgeous creation. She was an "apartment house boat." "No less than seven architectural styles were incorporated. The garden cafe on the main deck was a glimpse of a Parisian sidewalk afloat." She was "an effulgence of glory—a fairyland that moved and had being." This was the ship that inspired Von Tilzer and his lyricists, William Jerome and Andrew B. Sterling, to write the catchy "On the Old Fall River Line."

The theme was the age-old one, Von Tilzer's standby—boy meets girl. Boy got girl, too; but he seemed to have cause to regret it later, when he sang:

> On the old Fall River Line, on the old
>   Fall River Line
> I fell for Susie's line of talk and Susie
>   fell for mine.
> Then we fell in with a parson, and he tied
>   us tight as twine,
> But I wish "oh Lord" I fell overboard on
>   the old Fall River Line.[1]

---

[1] "On the Old Fall River Line." Music Harry Von Tilzer, Words William Jerome, Andrew B. Sterling. Copyright © 1913 Harry Von Tilzer Music Publishing Co., Copyright Renewed. Reprinted by Permission of the Publisher, Harry Von Tilzer Music Publishing Co. A division of T. B. Harms and Company.

On The Old Fall River Line.

Talk a-bout your spoon-ing and moon-ing, Take a trip to Bos-ton its fine

Sail-ing up the bay, boys, "Hur-ray" Boys I was on the up-per deck when I met mine,

I said "Sue—in your sail-or suit— You look cer-tain-ly cute."——— On the

old Fall Riv-er Line— On the old Fall Riv-er Line— I fell for Sus-ie's line of

talk And Su-sie fell for mine— Then we fell in with a par-son, And he tied us

tight as twine— But I wish "oh Lord" I fell ov-er-board On the old Fall Riv-er

Line:—

2. When the boat is landing they're standing
   Spooners by the dozen, and more
   While the captains calling and bawling
   "Is there anybody wants to go ashore,
   Ev'rybody just answers then, turn the boat round again.

   CHORUS

53

Most popular songs of the preradio days had their place in the musical sun for a few months, and then were pushed aside to make way for successors. This was not the case with the "Old Fall River Line." It maintained its place in the hearts and on the lips of the singing public year after year.

World War I arrived, and in the barracks of the training camps in New England the old favorite became a new favorite. In the YMCA huts, and around the barrack pianos, the men continued to sing it lustily. Long after the war came to an end, the song retained a large degree of popularity and continued to attract a following well into the 1930's.

But then, with the depression clamping down on so many American landmarks, the Fall River Line approached the point of oblivion. Controlled at this time by the New Haven Railroad, which was struggling to remain solvent, the ninety-year-old line was dealt a mortal blow when a struggle between the American Federation of Labor and the new CIO involved her crew. The men struck on July 12, 1937, and six days later the Fall River Line announced the suspension of service.

Von Tilzer was dead by this time. A handful of his songs lived on, but not "The Old Fall River Line." It was dead too.

"Won't You Come up and Spoon in Coey's Balloon 'Chicago'"

Coey's balloon, as tall as a junior skyscraper, was of early twentieth-century vintage, and a great favorite with the lighter-than-air-ophiles. But it was far, far from serving as an American pioneer. The first recorded balloon ascension in this country was made by a thirteen year old named Edward Warren, who, on June 24, 1784, volunteered to occupy the basket of a thirty foot high balloon in a field near Baltimore, and who rose in it to a height sufficient to warrant cheers from the "gazing multitude below," as the *Maryland Journal and Baltimore Advertiser* of the following day described the onlookers.

This daring feat was much too early to excite any composers to honor it with a musical tribute, and in fact it was not until more than fifty years later that we run across the first sheet music published in the United States with ballooning as its subject matter. Entitled compactly, "The Balloon Polka," and composed by Anton Wallerstein (a European, born in Dresden in 1813) it appeared about 1850 with a beautiful title page, picturing a balloon floating over a placid body of water with paddle wheelers and sailing ships to add to the decor. Many of Wallerstein's popular dance compositions—there were some three hundred of them—were published and widely circulated in the United States. "The Balloon Polka" was merchandised by a New York music publisher along with several other Wallerstein polkas, so the picture of the balloon occupied only the top portion of the title page, the rest of which carried scenes to illustrate other dances, "The Brunette Polka" and "The Adriatic Polka," mentioned on the composite cover.

Four years later, a Baltimore musician, James E. Magruder, composed a polka in honor of a veteran aeronaut, George Elliott. Elliott, who undertook his first flight in 1834 and remained a practicing balloonist for fifty years, had cast loose from a large amphitheater near the Baltimore railroad station one fine May evening in 1854. The event had been extensively advertised in advance, with the result that three thousand persons bought tickets to the amphitheater, where, prior to the ascension, they had been treated to a concert by an orchestra under the direction of a Professor Bear.

After rising a thousand feet, Elliott had soared in a northeasterly direction before coming down in an agricultural area some eight miles distant. The impressive take-off having been witnessed by such a large crowd of cheering people, Magruder felt disposed to write a light musical composition in conjunction with the feat, and "The Aerial Polka" quickly appeared, with a stunning title page showing the likeness of "Professor" Elliott superimposed on a swaying balloon and with a sprightly melody that would set any foot tapping.

In 1868 an Englishman named Leybourne wrote the words and music of "Up in a Balloon," a song which became so popular that it quickly spanned the Atlantic, where pianists and singers by the many thousands played and sang:

> Up in a balloon, up in a balloon,
> All among the little stars sailing
> round the moon.

The first aeronaut to whom a song writer paid homage with words as well as music, was Frederick Marriott. Marriott, born in England in 1805, had formed a partnership with two fellow countrymen to promote their "Aerial Steam Transit Company." Unfortunately the steam escaped, the company went on the rocks, and in 1848 Marriott embarked for California to seek his fortune in the gold fields a year before the forty-niners started flocking in. His fortune ultimately was amassed in a different sort of gold field; he became a banker of note. Later he founded and edited the *San Francisco News Letter*.

His interest in aeronautics had not diminished, and in 1869 he invented a flying ship which he called the *Avitor*. This was essentially a cigar-shaped balloon thirty-seven feet long, controlled by a rudder and elevator and powered by a steam engine operating two propellors and supplying loco-motion. In his *News Letter* he described the successful operation of his model, but he failed to secure a government appropriation to develop it commercially. He continued his efforts to enlist federal aid, but it was never forthcoming, and Marriott's death in 1884 spelled *finis* to all dreams for the future development of the flying cigar.

But his memory lived on. In 1897 a San Franciscan named S. H. Marsh wrote "The Song of the Aeroplane" or "The Flying Machine," dedicating it to "the memory of the late F. Marriott." The title page portrays a crude likeness of the *Avitor* with the big cigar in full flight over the peaceful countryside. The song's words go like this:

> Now high, now low away I go
> A twist of wrist will lift me,
> The steerer's hand has full command
> In any way to shift me.
> Forward or back or tack and tack,
> There's nothing that can stop me.
> A touch I fly towards the sky
> A touch will gently drop me.
> Foul wind or fair, what need I care,
> I've automatic motion
> I want no land on which to stand
> I scorn to plough the ocean.

Sounds pretty cocky, doesn't it, six years before Orville and Wilbur Wright wrote history at Kitty Hawk.

The Wrights did not inspire any musical hosannas, but some who followed them did. One was a Frenchman, Louis Bleriot, a man who was to set many enviable records. The French were aviation bugs in this pioneering period of the twentieth century's first decade, and Bleriot was at the head of his class. A successful manufacturer with plenty of capital at his command, Bleriot, who enjoyed nothing more than experimenting with his theories, was the first man to place an engine in the nose of an airplane. He was also the first, and probably the only, man who is reported to have crashed fifty times without ever suffering a serious injury.

Among Bleriot's greatest triumphs was the first conquest of the English Channel by air. In the spring of 1909 the London *Daily Mail* offered a prize of one thousand pounds to the first man who could take a plane across the Channel. To navigate the twenty-mile stretch over water was not as simple as it appeared, even though land flights of three times the distance had previously been made. Visibility might be near zero; there were no guiding landmarks, no instruments, no altimeter if one ran into fog, no gauge of speed. On July 25 at four o'clock in the morning Bleriot took his monoplane into the air near Calais, circled the coast, and then set off for Dover. In less than forty minutes he had crossed the Channel and put his plane down behind Dover Castle. Thereupon Dover exploded in the greatest demonstration that little city had ever experienced. The streets were packed with people, flags waved, and guns were fired. And why not? It had been demonstrated conclusively that England was only a few minutes away from the continent. Soon there was available the "Bleriot Valse," by Travnyik Bela, with descriptive phrases indicating the stages of Bleriot's accomplishment: first his "meditation in his garage," then "among the clouds," and finally the "arrival in England" to a swelling crescendo of sound. On the title page the little plane is seen approaching the English coast, above which appear the words "Rule Britannia."

But the day of the balloonists, and music to mark their accomplishments, was not yet a thing of the past. And here is where Charles Andrew Coey makes his dramatic entrance. Charles Coey was a born promoter. A transportation buff, his interests carried him from bicycles to automobiles to balloons and back to automobiles again. Coey came to Chicago from New York State in 1898, with a few dollars in his pocket and an idea for a new contraption for bicycles. After four years of marketing this gadget, he seized on the early popularity of the automobile and in 1902 opened the first public garage in Chicago. Soon he went into the auto livery business and then took on the franchise of the Thomas Flyer car, the product of a pioneer automobile manufacturer.

In 1906 he arranged with the R. R. Thomas Motor Car Company to deliver the first taxicabs to Chicago. Coey promoted the inauguration of his taxi company by engaging the famous Floradora sextette to tour the city's boulevards in Coey taxis, with batteries of newspaper photographers to record the event on camera. The taxi business proved an immediate success; soon Coey was operating a hundred cabs, each of which grossed an average five dollars an hour. It was not long before Coey became a wealthy man. Shortly thereafter he was racing Thomas Flyers, winning one twenty-four-hour race, during which he traveled almost eight hundred and fifty miles.

But now a new idea entered Coey's mind; he began to think about balloons. He was a man of impulse; he ordered the world's largest free-sailing balloon, naming it *Chicago*. The balloon, when fully inflated, was reported to stand ten stories high.

His most spectacular ascension was made in 1908. Rising in Chicago, the balloon traveled northeast across the Great Lakes to West Monkton, Ontario, a distance of approximately four hundred miles, establishing a free balloon record which stood until 1932. The inhabitants of the little town where Coey ended his flight were so overwhelmed at sharing the spotlight with the noted Chicagoan that they named their public park for him.

Coey's taxi business no longer engrossed his attention and he sold out to a Chicagoan named John Hertz, who later was to establish the Hertz Drive-It-Yourself company. He even dropped the coveted franchise for the Thomas Flyer.

Within months after his first flight the 38-year-old bachelor had taken a bride from Kansas. And where did they go on their honeymoon? On a balloon trip, of course—with attendant publicity. Nothing else would have been fitting for the man who by this time had attained not only the presidency of the Aeronautique Club of Chicago, but also of the prestigious Federation of American Aero Clubs.

Such a man deserved a song, and he got it. In 1908 two Chicago song writers, Victor H. Smalley and Bernie Adler, came through with a number bearing the mouth-filling title of "Won't You Come Up and Spoon in Coey's Balloon 'Chicago.'" The title page not only depicts the great balloon soaring high over the treetops but in the foreground is Colonel Coey himself, completely equipped for flight, with baggy Norfolk-jacketed suit, buckled shoes over what appear to be leather puttees, carrying an oversized valise which may have contained either sandwiches or equipment, and to top it all a straw sailor hat perched firmly on the aeronaut's head.

The song's hero is tired of automobiling, so he puts this proposition to his girl:

I've seen Colonel Coey, He's filled me with joy,
He's loaned me his gas-bag "Chicago,"
With you by my side to Venus I'll ride
With nothing but kisses for cargo.

CHORUS: Won't you come up and spoon in the Colonel's balloon
Up in the clouds so blue.
A fly to the sky, just you dear and I
In a basket that's just built for two.
It's high diddle diddle, the cat and the fiddle,
We'll see the cow jump o'er the moon.
We'll cast off at seven and ride up to heaven
So come up and spoon, up in Coey's balloon.

Come Up and Spoon in Coey's Balloon "Chicago."

Said young John-ie Steel Miss Mar-gie I feel So tir-ed of au-to-mo-bi-ling

I gaze at the skies With a soul full of sighs In cloud-land I want to be

steal-ing — I've seen Colon-el Coey, He's filled me with joy, He's loaned me his

gas-bag "Chi-ca-go"— With you by my side To Ven-us I'll ride With no-thing but

Chorus

kiss-es for car-go. Won't you come up and spoon In the Colon-el's bal-loon Up in the

clouds so blue— A fly to the sky Just you dear and I In a bas-ket that's just built for

two —— It's high did-dle did-dle The cat and the fid-dle We'll see the cow jump o'er the

moon —— We'll cast off at sev-en and ride up to heav-en So come up and spoon

Up in Coey's bal-loon.

2. The gay milky way They travel by day
The wise old sun smiling and blinking
The moon came at night, But they asked for
   more light
So he set the wee stars all a winking.

Will you marry me? I love you said he,
And constancy swore by the stars
She answered, ask Pa, For consent he said
   "Pshaw!
Why see I've all ready got Mars."

Coey eventually experienced financial misfortune. In 1912 he introduced an automobile, the "Coey Junior," which, priced at $425, was to compete with the product of Henry Ford. It was no contest, and Coey and his machine fell on hard times, from which he later extricated himself by marketing a mineral water and establishing a health resort. Unfortunately neither the water nor the resort inspired any music composers.

The year after Coey's various balloon antics, a spate of airplane songs burst on the American scene. In 1909 airplanes were being developed by individual experimenters in almost every part of the world, with the Americans leading the pack. The song writers kept step with them. There was "How I Caught My Girl," about the fellow whose girl friend was always out with a rival in a big automobile until, as he relates it:

> In despair I bought an aeroplane
> And here's how I caught the girl.

He promised her:

> We will take a sail in my aeroplane
> Up where the shooting stars play
> We will chase the big bear
> Back to his lair
> And glide on the milky way.

Then came a second romantic gentleman, who sang about "Beautiful Jane in My Aeroplane."

> Beautiful Jane in my Aeroplane
> Up like a bubble of dry champagne.
> Don't seem to care when up in the air,
> Never has storm on the Brain
> Drawing ozone in her wireless 'phone,
> Raises her system a semi-tone,
> O what a great sprawl, if she ever should fall,
> Out of my Aeroplane.

And then there was the prolific composer, Albert Von Tilzer, who, with Junie McCree, wrote "Take Me up with You Dearie." The title page shows a modish pair hanging out of a cockpit, the girl costumed as if she were going on an automobile ride, the man in a modish business suit with a stiff collar and a derby hat. Their objective is the first wedding in the sky, as the lady sings:

> Take me up, up, up with you dearie,
> Away up to the sky,
> Sail around the moon for a quiet spoon,
> Just the parson, you and I.

Let us float, float, float through the clouds
And just have a lot of fun.
We'll go up, up, up as two
And then come down as one.

The French aeronauts, whose flying skill almost blanketed the field for a few years, were suddenly faced with a brilliant American contender, Glenn H. Curtiss. Like several other pioneers of air travel, Curtiss had first won attention by exploits on the ground. He had started in upper New York State as a bicyclist who, after defeating the local champion, began to build his own bicycles. Soon he was manufacturing motorcycles, and racing them too, setting one speed record after the other.

Then in 1907, Curtiss met Dr. Alexander Graham Bell, inventor of the telephone, who ordered from him an engine to be installed in an experimental tetrahedral kite. This diverted Curtiss' attention from ground locomotion to aviation, and within months he had built his first plane, which he christened the *June Bug*. On July 4, 1908, the little *Bug* astounded the public, as well as Curtiss, by breaking all distance records for heavier-than-air craft; it traveled 5090 feet before touching the ground.

Record-setting was Curtiss' avocation, and he capped the climax in 1910. The *New York World* had offered a $10,000 prize to the first flyer to cover the 150-mile distance down the Hudson River between Albany and New York in twenty-four hours. Curtiss was the first entrant. On June 1 he set out from Albany in his new plane, the *Albany Flyer*, and after landing in Poughkeepsie to refuel, resumed his flight, maintaining an average speed of fifty-two miles an hour. Curtiss followed the Hudson as far as the Statue of Liberty, which he circled before setting his plane down on the parade ground at Governor's Island.

This feat was noted by a composer named Julius K. Johnson, who quickly wrote a march and two step entitled "King of the Air," dedicated to "Mr. Glenn H. Curtiss, the famous aviator." The title page is illustrated with a photograph of Curtiss at the steering wheel of his biplane, superimposed over a sketch of Manhattan along the riverbank. Curtiss wears a sport costume with dark jacket, light trousers; heavy goggles are affixed to his cap. The description of the picture reads "Mr. Glenn H. Curtiss and His Celebrated Prize Winner 'The Hudson Flyer'."

For years thereafter Curtiss' principal efforts were in the field of naval aviation, and one of his famous Navy-Curtiss flying boats was the first to span the Atlantic Ocean by air in 1919.

In later years new heroes of the air were greeted with songs in their honor. Charles Lindbergh's spectacular flight in 1927 brought out scores of songs, from "Hello Lindy" endorsed by the mayor of St. Louis, to "Captain Lindy, He Flew for the Red, White and Blue." The whole country was wild with pride and the encomiums of the song writers were overwhelming. "Hello Lindy" by Dave Silverman and Larry Conley was dedicated to "America's Flying Hero" and went, in part:

> Who's that ev'rybody wants to meet?
> Who's that fellow did that daring feat?
> Gee, I'd like to meet him,
> I'd be proud to greet him
>
> . . . .
>
> Flying o'er the dark and stormy sea,
> In his airship he made history,
> "Flying Fool" they named him,
> Now the world's acclaimed him.

Vincent L. Micary, the writer of "Captain Lindy," put it this way:

> Lindy, the flying Hero,
> Oh boy, how he did go,
> No time to eat, no time to sleep,
> Only to watch that he did not fall
> Into the ocean below . . . .
> Lindy just kept on flying
> Fading right out of sight,
> He made the trip, in his airship,
> Sailing into the night.
> Thirty-three hours to make the flight.

> CHORUS: Captain Lindy, our hero tried and true,
> He flew for the Red, White and Blue
> The wind and the ocean, he steered clear,
> With the Spirit of Saint Louis. He had no fear,
> Just like an eagle, away up in the sky
> Watching the great big world roll by.

When Clarence Chamberlin and Charles Levine followed Lindbergh with a flight from Roosevelt Field, New York, across the Atlantic on June 4, 1927, they insured themselves against starvation by including in their equipment ten chicken sandwiches on toasted rye bread, two bottles of chicken soup, a bottle of coffee, and half a dozen oranges. Their destination was Berlin; before take-off they received a cablegram from that city telling them that all Germany was awaiting their arrival and that they should be

63

prepared for a royal welcome. They nearly made it to their destination; after almost two days in the air they came down 4,100 miles from New York and 110 miles from Berlin.

Following their feat even non-English-speaking song writers saluted them. To capture the patronage of New York's large Yiddish-speaking population, a writer named Gus Goldstein composed and wrote Yiddish words for a song the title of which, translated, was "Levine, Levine, the Jew with His Machine." The title page is illustrated by a photograph of Levine superimposed on a sketch of Chamberlin's Bellanca monoplane, the *Columbia*. For the Yiddish-speaking public, who were proud of their Jewish "hero," not only is Chamberlin's picture missing from the cover; his name does not even appear in the song.

The other member of the "big three" among the airmen of that period was Richard E. Byrd. He too had spanned the Atlantic in 1927, and in the course of his illustrious career had two important "firsts" to his credit; he had been the first man to fly over the North and South Poles. Following a second, and extensive, exploratory trip to the South Pole, which netted the United States much valuable information and Byrd a slew of citations, he was the subject of a 1935 song, "Byrd, You're the 'Bird' of Them All," by Howard Johnson, who saluted him thus:

> Byrd, Oh! what a "bird" you are,
> Byrd, Your wings have led you far,
> Over the North and the South Pole you flew
> If there were East and West Poles you'd conquer
>   them too.
> Hail to all your gallant crew.
> Thru snow and ice they rallied at your call
> Good-bye to ice floes tossing
> You're thru with wintry crossing
> Byrd, you're the "bird" of them all.[2]

For a span of nearly a hundred years our gallant airmen have been honored in the field of popular music. Has the custom staled? No such musical ovations greeted the first astronauts or the moon-men. And looking ahead it appears unlikely that a manned trip to Mars or Jupiter will inspire tomorrow's Von Tilzers to record such feats in song. Such must be the sacrifice our present-day, or future, heroes will pay for breathlessly scientific accomplishments. A bit of a pity, though, isn't it?

---

[2] "Byrd, You're The Bird of Them All." Howard Johnson. Copyright 1935 by Shapiro, Bernstein & Co. Inc. 666 Fifth Avenue, New York, N.Y. 10019. Copyright Renewed and Assigned USED BY PERMISSION.

"Give Me a Spin in Your Mitchell, Bill"

A MITCHELL? What's a Mitchell? Some sort of animated roulette wheel? A new dance? A record album? You're cold—very cold. A Mitchell, friends, was one of the twenty-two hundred makes of automobiles that have been introduced to the public since that exciting day in 1893 when J. Frank Duryea first steered a single-cylinder horseless carriage along the rough streets of Springfield, Massachusetts.

And, looked at from the vantage point of the 1970's, the Mitchell was an unusually popular car. Its company lasted for twenty years, from 1903 to 1923, and that's more than can be said for the great bulk of names that were created by automobile companies to capture the imagination of the American public for over three quarters of a century.

Names? They were a dime a dozen. Here is a sampling of new cars introduced to the public, with the year of their advent: 1900—Friedman; 1902—Long Distance; 1903—Okey; 1907—Bugmobile; 1908—Browniecar; 1910—Available; 1914—Sphinx; 1917—Ben Hur; 1919—Luedinghaus-Espenscheid; 1922—Harrigan; 1923—Static.

Possibly one reason automobiles like these failed to appeal to the public was because it was so difficult to conceive of a song about them. Can you envision a song writer getting away with "In My Merry Bugmobile," or "My Merry Friedman," or "My Merry Luedinghaus-Espenscheid"? But let us not disturb the very dead. Some cars whose names "made" song titles will be introduced a bit later.

Possibly because the conception of an automobile was such an innovation to composers of popular music, some of the early writers added to the novelty by depicting the owner of this new mode of transportation as a black man. One of the very first pieces of automobile music, composed by Frank P. Banta, is entitled "Kareless Koon, an Ethiopian Two Step." This 1899 instrumental piece has a title page which portrays a well-to-do black couple riding in a taxicab of the period, ostensibly an electric carriage run by storage batteries and electric motors. The gentleman in the cab, which is chauffeured by a white man, is tossing handfuls of coins to youngsters on the street, thereby demonstrating his affluence.

The following year the famous song writing team of J. W. and Rosamond Johnson composed "My Creole Belle." Here, too, the handsome woman on the cover is operating another electric vehicle, with a groom behind, as was customary with smart horse-drawn carriages. Say the Johnsons:

> Upon your heart she puts a spell,
> This fascinating Creole Belle.

Seventy years ago there were no antidefamation regulations protecting foreign-born Americans, or blacks or Indians, for that matter. Italian, Irishman, Jew, and German were lambasted mercilessly if the song writer was so inclined. Nor was the Negro spared, though in his case the lampooning was directed for the most part at an exaggeration of his dialect. Witness "Just Come Aroun' Wid an Automobile," written in 1902 by R. Melville Baker and Josephine Sherwood, and with a cartoonlike cover depicting a black couple cruising in a smart automobile of the period, with the words "The Black Ghost" printed on the hood. Following their car is a gentleman in horse and buggy, to whom the lady driver makes these cutting remarks:

> I don't ride in no hitch like dat;
> Ole style buggy hitched to a rat,
> You come aroun' wid an automobile
> 'lectric pow'r wid a blown up wheel,
> I'se outgrown a horse or a bike,
> Dey can't strike de gait I like.
> If wid me you want to speel
> Jes' come aroun' wid an automo-automobile.

But not all the early music relied on dark-complected subjects. Dave Reed, Jr., one of the more prolific talents of the day, based his popular 1902 song on the cry of the period "Git a Horse!" His offering goes:

> Automobile coming down the street,
> Git a horse, git a horse;
> You will hear this all along the beat,
> Git a horse, git a horse.
> When you're just about to turn a corner,
> A rock or something hits you in the ear,
> You say your pray'rs and think you are a goner,
> But soon the saying falls upon your ear.
> CHORUS: Git a horse, git a horse;
> It's enough to make your angel brother cross.
> All the young ones in the land in your path
>   are sure to stand,
> Then they dodge away and yell with awful force,
> "Git a horse, git a horse."
> You're mad enough to kill the kids of course
> But a hint to you I'll drop. If you want to
>   make them stop,
> Git a horse, git a horse.

The name of the famous racing driver, Barney Oldfield, became practically immortalized when the Oldsmobile came on the scene near the beginning of the century. And who among us can't whistle or hum the melody of Gus Edwards' and Vincent Bryan's still great "In My Merry Oldsmobile," which was one of the bright features of 1905's song crop.

But there was an even earlier automaker which made musical use of its name, the Studebaker Brothers Manufacturing Company of South Bend, Indiana. In 1899, Studebaker induced—that would probably be the right word—one L. Marda to write "The Studebaker Grand March," a rousing number in six-eighths time, sounding a bit like a little brother of one of John Philip Sousa's impressive heavyweights. The front cover contains two vignettes, one of the first Studebaker shop—actually a barn—in 1850, the other the original Studebaker home near Gettysburg, Pennsylvania. But the *back* cover—that tells one how far the company has come. The great plant depicted, the "Studebaker Vehicle Works," covers 98 acres and has an annual capacity of 75,000 vehicles—vehicles, not automobiles. The types of vehicles are listed, and automobiles are mentioned, but only as one of over one hundred different items, which include, among their scores of horse-drawn and hand-propelled apparatus, police ambulances, bobsleds, cabriolets, dump cars, doctors' buggies, furniture vans, lawn sprinklers, omnibuses, undertaker's wagons, victorias, and wagonettes. Nevertheless the automobile made the team, for Studebaker had been experimenting with motor vehicles since 1897.

Probably the first music to include the word "automobile" in its title was "The Automobile Spin," a gavotte written in 1899 by Grace Walls Linn. Published in Indianapolis, the cover depicts two young ladies traveling sedately in their "electric" along a country lane. The car carries the name of H. T. Hearsey Vehicle Co., a bicycle manufacturer and a distributor for the smart little two-passenger model manufactured by the Waverley Electrical Company of Indianapolis. The Waverley was one of the few automobiles exhibited in 1898 at an electric show in Madison Square Garden, New York; in the country's first exclusive automobile show, given in the "Garden" two years later, the Waverley was again on hand.

The record of its actual sales remains shrouded in mystery. It is known, at least, that the Hearsey Vehicle Company bought a Waverley for the use of its executives, though hardly for their secretaries or girl friends, which leaves the identity of the young females on the "Automobile Spin's" title page a mystery. And, sad to relate, the Waverley's existence was not much longer for this world.

Like the Waverley, all but two of the early automobiles about which music was written have departed from the field of transportation. One of these two is, of course, the Oldsmobile, and the other is, of course, the Ford. There were many songs written about Ford cars, such as, for example, "Henry's Made a Lady Out of Lizzie," and "Mr. Ford's Little Jitney Bus." The first Ford musical selection was promoted by the company itself, which published, in 1908, "The Ford March and Two-Step," by Harry H. Zickel. The cover shows a handsome girl, nattily attired, at the steering wheel of a Ford runabout, while an equally handsome collie serves as her escort. The back cover goes in for promotion, as did Studebaker nine years before. With a slogan, "The Ford: A Car for Business and Pleasure at the Right Price," four models are depicted. The first is a runabout standing on a snowy street; a man carrying a satchel has just alighted, and the inscription reads, "The busy doctor finds it always ready." Just below it is a derby-hatted man driving a two-seated model; a trunk is strapped behind. The caption: "It takes the salesman anywhere." Next is a big car, chauffeur driven, with adults riding front and back, and the words "For touring, dependable and economical." The last sketch has father and mother on the front seat, with Junior in a propped-up seat in the rear, holding on to his sailor hat for dear life. The descriptive matter reads: "A source of pleasure for the whole family." A list of Ford branches follows, along with the statement, "Agencies in a thousand towns and cities."

Well could Ford blow his horn in 1908; that was the year when he brought out his Model T, which was the closest thing to a staple the industry ever had, and which showed its heels to all would-be competitors for twenty years.

But the competitors were music conscious too, and although most of them fell by the wayside eventually, they tried piping their little songs and hoping the automobile-buying public would dance to their tunes. Even though their names may be legend, or more probably forgotten, today their music has its peculiar appeal, particularly to curiosity seekers.

First came the Rainier, which made its appearance in 1905 and hung on for half a dozen years. In 1907 the company arranged a tie-up with a brewery in Seattle to publish a song, "There's Something Else Goes With It," with a lithographed title page depicting two good-looking girls in a Rainier automobile. The "something else," of course, was Rainier beer, the product of the Seattle Brewing and Malting Company.

A verse, in part:

> It may be in an auto that you take a lively spin . . .
> But when the trip is over then for something
> else you call . . . .

CHORUS: There's something else goes with it that you
    like to think about;
There's something in its spirit that you
    cannot do without.
Yes, something else goes with it . . . .
What? Rainier, Rainier, Rainier.

The well-built Jackson car went on the market in 1902 and hung on for twenty-one years. A widely distributed song, "From Earth to Mar [Mars, that is] in a Jackson Car," was written in 1908 by C. D. Paxton and Carl Carlton. The wide distribution was arranged by the Jackson Automobile Company and its dealers. The title page shows a photograph of Jackson's Model E, shooting through space in the direction of various extraterrestrial bodies, as the man in the moon exclaims, "No Hill Too Steep, No Sand Too Deep." The back cover pictures a series of popular models, with a dozen trophies won by the Jackson, and a detailed list of their successes in three years of competition.

The song:

Last night as I lay sleeping an angel
    appeared unto me,
With great white wings a-sweeping and
    thus spoke unto me,
Away up yonder in the great milky way
    among comets and the stars,
They're using automobiles today and
    the best are the Jackson cars.

CHORUS: From earth to Mar, from star to star
It's always the same in sunshine or rain,
No hill too steep, no sand too deep
For the good old Jackson car.

The Mitchell introduced its song in 1909. It had no need to blow its own horn in an advertising campaign; the words and melody were catchy enough to appeal to a legitimate publisher, the Music House of Laemmle, a name to become famous after a few years when Carl Laemmle stepped up the ladder to head Universal Pictures, the great producer of screen extravaganzas. The Mitchell song was the product of C. P. McDonald and J. W. Gilson. It had a merry swing:

Billy Maloney loved Maggie Mahoney
A squeezable, pleasable pearl;
Maggie was sighable, quite glorifiable,
And a most eyeable girl.
Nightly she'd meet him and brightly she'd
    greet him

> And smile in her cute little way;
> He'd say, "shall we go, dear, and take in
>   a show, dear,"
> And she'd answer, "no dear," and say:
>
> CHORUS: Give me a spin in your Mitchell, Bill,
>   My goodness gracious! I can't keep still;
>   Buzz me along on the boulevard,
>   Let 'er go, Willie boy, good and hard,
>   Throw it wide open, I'll hold on tight,
>   I don't care a fudge if my hair's a fright;
>   There's nothing that gives me such keen
>   delight
>   As a spin in your Mitchell, Bill.

Then in 1910 came the "Cole 30 Flyer," with words and music by J. Lee Bowers. The Cole had gone into manufacture the previous year, and it stayed around until 1925. A handsome job it was, too, judging by the high-styled runabout on the song's cover, with a begoggled driver and bedustered young lady smartly ensconced in it.

The song tells of a proposal to his girl by the young gentleman who owns a nondescript car. She spells out the conditions and stipulates in her acceptance:

> You will win me, Bill, heart and soul,
> If you buy a Cole;
> Down through the woods and down thro' the dale,
> Ride smoothly and swiftly as on a bird's tail;
> You ask me to be true—
> I'll tell you what to do;
> Just sell that old wheel, buy an automobile,
> Get wise and buy a Cole.

In 1913 the automobile that people sang about was the Mercer. Essentially a sports car, it was a great favorite on the tracks. It bowed to the public in 1909, and the name continued popular until 1925, when it passed out of the picture. "In My Mercer Racing Car" was written in 1913 by Axel Christensen and John S. Meck. The title page is illustrated with a sketch of a young couple in a low-slung runabout, ostensibly speeding along a tree-shaded road at night with headlights glaring. The pair is eloping, as the song points out. The first verse says:

> Hasten, hasten, dear; now the coast is clear ....
> Hug me while I steer!
> With my Mercer car that gink Lochinvar
> Has got not a thing on me!

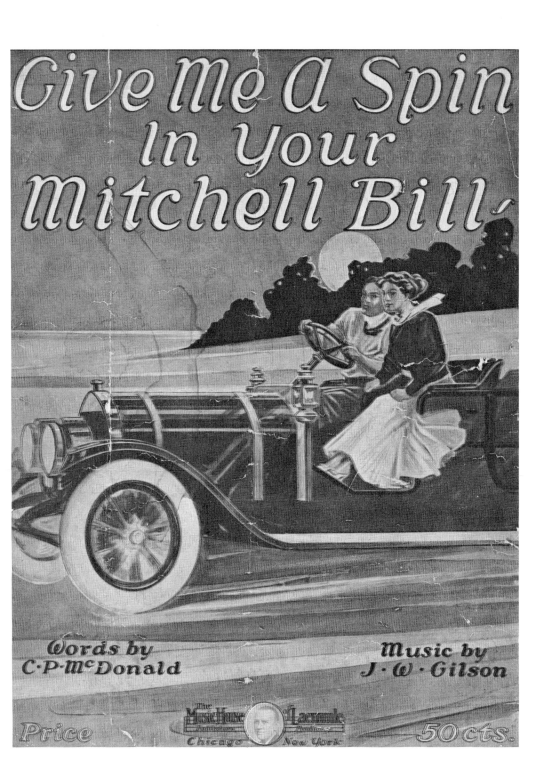

Give Me A Spin In Your Mitchell, Bill

Bil-ly Ma-lon-ey loved Mag-gie Ma-hon-ey, A squeez-a-ble, pleas-a-ble pearl;

—— Mag-gie was sigh-a-ble, quite glo-ri-fi-a-ble, And a most eye-a-ble girl.——

Night-ly she'd meet him and bright-ly she'd greet him And smile in her cute lit-tle way——

He'd say, "Shall we go, dear, and take in the show, dear?" And she'd an-swer, "No dear," and

Chorus

say:—— Give me a spin in your Mitch-ell Bill,—— My good-ness gra-cious I

can't keep still;—— Buzz me a-long on the boul-e-vard,—— Let 'er go Wil-lie boy, good and

hard,—— Throw it wide o-pen, I'll hold on tight,—— I don't care a fudge if my hair's a fright;

There's no-thing that gives me such keen de-light As a spin in your Mitch-ell Bill.——

2. Gee this is jolly, look out for the trolley,
   There, Willie, oo golly, that's near;
   Mercy, don't blow up Bill, you'd better slow
     up Bill,
   That copper's watching us dear.
   Chugging and churring, in moonlight and
     whirring

Along at a merry old clip;
"Ain't it delightful? although the speed's
  frightful,
Don't mind me, Bill, just let 'er rip."

CHORUS

And the second verse:

> What you didn't pack? Well, we can't go back
> Papa's on the track.
> Hear the "Old Man" shout. He's a game old scout
> But he's losing out.
> Though it's awful bad we will beat your dad
> Gee, I'll bet he's mad
> Here we are, Hooraw, and your foxy old paw
> Will soon be my father-in-law.

CHORUS: In my racing car like a shooting star,
> Thru the silent night we'll fly.
> With the throttle wide, like the wind,
>> we'll ride
> And watch the country flashing by!
> Courage! Lady fair! We will soon be there,
> For it matters not how far.
> Ere the rising sun you and I'll be one,
> Thanks to my Mercer racing car.

Two years later it was the Packard that came in for musical treatment, and with the Packard, back came the Ford. Harold R. Atteridge and Harry Carroll put together that most fanciful of all automobile songs, "The Love Story of the Packard and the Ford." Their fairy tale follows:

> By a lonesome little curb in a lonesome little town
> On a lonesome little Ford a lonesome Packard looked
>> down
> And the great big car heaved a great big sigh
> For the little Ford so modest and shy,
> "You shouldn't travel 'round alone, you should
>> have a chaperon"
> Said the Packard, in a language all its own,
> "In my garage, you know, if you will only go,
> I've a cozy, cozy cunning little home."

CHORUS: "Honk! honk!" said the great big Packard,
> "Aaa! Aaa!" said the little car,
> Said the Packard: "Won't you come and cuddle closer?"
> But the Ford said: "I can't go far."
> "But you see how much I need you,
> And I love you there's no doubt,
> Come and marry and we'll have a little Buick,
> You can't afford to run about!"

In the lonesome little town now the Ford cannot be found,
For the Packard towed it far away with hardly a sound,
And they're married so they say. Twenty little Buicks gay
Round their little turning table are found,
And now they liven up the scene, when they're drinking
    gasoline,
Big and little Buicks gather 'round, and then
They start to toot and shout, and then they holler out:
"Daddy Packard, won't you sing to Ma again?"[3]
CHORUS

Other wonders of yesteryear attracted composers, the Overland, about which Professor E. B. Beal wrote "The Overland Success Grand March" about 1915, and the Peerless, which was born in 1900, but which had to wait seventeen years before that great song writer and comedian, Joe E. Howard, wrote a musical toast to it:

The Peerless, the Peerless, Made in the U.S.A.
Of all the cars from coast to coast, it stands the
    best today.
The Peerless, the Peerless, come on if you can spell,
It's P double E R L E double S, the Peerless let us yell.

Then there was the automobile named for the great flying ace of World War I, Captain Eddie Rickenbacker. For five years, from 1922 to 1927, the company struggled to achieve success. Leo Wood's 1923 song "In My Rickenbacker Car" stresses his preference for his car rather than a girl:

Much better and better she's getting each day,
No one will part us, on that you can bet,
I know when I'm old she'll be running yet.

CHORUS: ... She's not a bit expensive like most sweethearts are;
    Always there when I need her all I do is feed her,
    It's my Rickenbacker car.

It seems strange that of all the motor cars sung about so bravely in years gone by, most have lacked the intestinal fortitude to justify their song makers' undying faith in them. Save for automobile museums, the waters of history have closed over the remains of the gallant Peerless, the sturdy Mitchell, the romantic Cole, the flying Mercer, and hundreds more of makes which the song writers by-passed. Rest quietly, old four-wheeled friends. Today's superhighways belong to your superdescendants.

---

[3] "The Packard and the Ford." Harold R. Atteridge & Harry Carroll. Copyright 1915 by Shapiro, Bernstein & Co. Inc. 666 Fifth Avenue, New York, N.Y. 10019 Copyright Renewed and Assigned. USED BY PERMISSION.

The Only Trolley Car Song

HOLD FAST!

HOLD FAST TROLLEY COMPANY

WORDS BY
WILLIAM JEROME

MUSIC BY
JEAN SCHWARTZ

PUBLISHED BY
SHAPIRO, BERNSTEIN & VON TILZER
NEW YORK 45 WEST 28TH ST   CHICAGO 55 DEARBORN ST

FIELDS & WARD

Starmer.

Hold Fast!

I got a-board a trol-ley car to take a ride up town,— There was no place to sit down,— on my face I wore a frown;— 'Twas dur-ing busi-ness hou-rs ev'-ry seat was oc-cu-pied,— It seemed as if no-bo-dy had a home, I won-der why we ev-er care to roam;— A la-dy fair would get a-board at al-most ev'-ry street,—And with a smile so sweet,— she'd try to get a seat;—A-bout two hun-dred thous-and peo-ple walk'd up-on my feet,—The words I said I would-n't dare re-peat, Oh!— the words I said I would-n't dare re-peat;—— Oh! me! Oh! my!—I thot I'd die!— Ev'-ry time I heard the old Con-duc-tor cry!—

Chorus

"Hold! Fast! don't you lose your nerve! Grab your la-dy by the arm we're going 'round the curve! Keep your wits a-bout you and you'll nev-er get a jar, If you lis-ten to the man who runs a trol-ley-ol-ley car!" show girls, good-ness grac-ious, Will be driv-en out by geish-as, When A-mer-i-ca is cap-tured by the Japs.——

you Suff-ra gettes!——

2. The car was over crowded folks were hanging on the straps,
Girls had bundles in their laps, came from Macy's store perhaps;
There wasn't room for breathing and you couldn't turn your head,
For fear you'd bunk it into some one's face,
And this is what we call the "human race,"
They slamm'd us in and they jammed us in and piled us up in stacks,
The Irish, Dutch and Blacks, stuck elbows in our backs;
You couldn't carve your way out with a carving knife or axe,
Remember I am telling honest facts,
Yes, remember I am telling honest facts;
Transfer! Dear Sir! Please ring the bell!
Keep still don't you hear the old Conductor yell!
CHORUS

The Trolley Car

> The car was overcrowded, folks were hanging on
>   the straps,—
> Girls had bundles in their laps,—came from
>   Macy's store perhaps;
> There wasn't room for breathing and you couldn't
>   turn your head,
> For fear you'd bunk it into some one's face,
> And this is what we call the "human race;"
> They slamm'd us in and they jammed us in and
>   piled us up in stacks,
> The Irish, Dutch and Blacks, stuck elbows in
>   our backs.

That was in 1901.

> Take a car, take a car,
> Wherever you go take a car,
> It beats all your hansoms and automobiles,
> If you're out for pleasure that travels on
>   wheels.

And that was in 1905.

> To the tune of the grinding wheels
> All hands start doing funny reels.
> Here, there, someone would swear,
> The conductor gets excited and rings up the
>   right amount of fare.
> Now you glide on the trolley ride, how you slide,
> And when the car goes round a curve you begin
>   to swerve,
> Grab for a strap, fall in some woman's lap,
> Clang, clang, watch your step.
> Ding ding, That's the trolley car swing![4]

"The Trolley Car Swing" was the work of a leading words-and-music team, Joe Young and Bert Grant, around the time of the first World War. It was a big hit in 1912.

An integral part of urban life for more than a thirty-year period, the trolley car, as we view it in perspective, was only a link in the chain of urban transportation accomplishments that has run from public hacks to fleet express buses and even fleeter undersurface railways. But what a powerful link it was! Reaching its full growth at the turn of the century, it became a

---

[4] "The Trolley Car Swing." Joe Young Bert Grant. © 1912 Remick Music Corp. Copyright Renewed All Rights Reserved Used by Permission of WARNER BROS. MUSIC.

hub around which the wheels of the city's industry, its daily business, its educational facilities revolved. The speed with which it was able to negotiate distances, the comfort—for those days—of transport, brought city dwellers within easy access of any local point of destination. The trolley was one of the great conveniences of its time.

Its early progenitor was the omnibus, a public hack plying a specific route along city streets, the driver perched high above the closed interior so that he might spot any likely passenger who hailed him. For a few pennies the horse-drawn vehicle would deposit the "fare" at his destination. Omnibuses proved popular, for cities had grown too large for convenient walking.

But they had their defects, too. They were slow, and the riding was rough. The passenger had to pay his fare by working his way up the aisle and thrusting the money at the driver through a small trap door in the roof. This proved awkward, particularly when the coins proffered were of a value which required change to be returned, and which in turn resulted in minor delays. As a solution, small boys were hired to stand in the back of the bus and collect fares. These youngsters were of course the ancestors of the trolley car conductor.

It was not many years after the omnibus was operating in the big cities of the east before it was challenged by an appalling enemy—the horsecar. This required the laying of iron rails on the city streets, but the result was a vast improvement in carrying capacity and the comfort of the passenger. From the 1830's on, when the best-known horsecar line began its run in New York City over a mile of track in the uptown area, reaching all the way north to 14th Street the days of the public hack were numbered. The first car built for the new line was a glorified, thirty-passenger stagecoach on rails. Its designer, a young wagon builder named John Stephenson, secured a patent for its construction, signed by President Andrew Jackson. This so excited him, the prospect of the "animal railway" so captured his imagination, that he threw all his resources into the building of new cars and went flat broke during the depression of 1837. Nothing daunted, he secured permission from his creditors to continue in business, and within another six years he had paid off all his debts and was on his way to becoming the most famous car builder in the world. When he died, full of years, in 1893, his factory was producing twenty-five cars every week.

Meanwhile horsecars had become a necessity in every large city. By the fifties they had not only extended over Manhattan and Brooklyn, but they were appearing in Boston, Chicago, Philadelphia, Pittsburgh, Cincinnati, and elsewhere. Then they spread into smaller towns, with routes which usually ran from the depot or steamboat wharf along the main street, past the principal hotel, and out to a terminus at a beach, camp meeting ground, or cemetery. Strangely, cemeteries were always regarded as traffic builders.

Until the period of the Civil War, drivers of horsecars occupied a high perch, similar to that utilized on the omnibus. But then new designs were introduced, and the driver was moved to a front platform, a position accepted later by motormen on trolley cars.

Many stories were told about the purchase of horses for the streetcars. New York's bustling Third Avenue line had 1,700 horses. It preferred gray ones, advancing the theory that gray horses were not as distressed by hot weather as were steeds of other colors. In Boston, where the Metropolitan Railroad utilized 700 cars, it required 3,600 animals to "horse" them. Most roads set a limit on the number of years of service a horse could endure; some disposed of the animals automatically after three or four years. There were always tales of a few exceptional beasts with supernatural powers. One was a gelding named "Old Crooked Tail," working for the North Chicago City Railway. He was the star performer of the line, pulling cars on it for twenty-two years, seven days a week, and racking up a total mileage of 102,540. Almost half way to the moon!

Before the trolley car came into its own, various other contraptions had their little fling. There was the steam-drawn streetcar, and there were cars propelled by compressed air, hot water, naphtha, and ammonia gas. A common type of steamcar operation utilized a separate steam "dummy," so named because its construction was intended to give passengers the idea that it was an ordinary car. But it had a boiler and a small steam engine, and it generated enough power to carry several other cars in tow.

The "dummy" often proved more popular than the cars behind it. In 1885 a composer named Frederick G. Carnes and a lyricist named Sam Booth wrote "Riding On the Dummy." The title page portrays a "dummy" with a car in tow, ascending a steep grade in San Francisco. Twice as many passengers occupy the "dummy's" seats as those in the car in the rear. The song goes:

> Of all the ways of travelling, By coach or
> carry all,
> By steamer stage or railway car, The dummy
> beats them all,
>
> . . . .

> One bright and sunny afternoon, From off the
>   crowded street,
> A lady stepp'd upon the car, But could not
>   find a seat;
> Oh! take my seat, a gallant said, Oh! thank
>   you sir, said she,
> A sudden jerk, and down she sat, Right on a
>   deacon's knee.

By far the most successful pretrolley urban vehicle was the cable car. It was developed by Andrew Hallidie, a California manufacturer of wire rope, after he had witnessed a horrifying horsecar accident on one of the steep San Francisco hills. To the street-side observer, all that could be seen of the mysterious mechanism was a metal-rimmed slot between the two car tracks. The cable car itself was operated by a man standing in the middle of the car, working long levers extending through the floor and controlling the car's speed and mobility. Hallidie's first half-mile line, skirting Clay Street's sewer systems and gas and water mains, cost nearly one hundred thousand dollars to construct, and the company skirted bankruptcy before the successful demonstration of the invention in 1873 made the cable car famous. A rival San Francisco line, opened in 1878, is still operating.

Once the trolley car had proven its worth, its competition in the field of urban transportation was, to all intents, wiped out. The electric cars had struggled for supremacy for years; in fact, back in 1847 a Professor Moses Farmer had demonstrated a two-passenger electric car. But neither this little pioneer, nor others that followed it from the 1850's on, were able to unravel all the snarls that impeded the wide use of electric transportation. Even Thomas A. Edison, who built a small dynamo-driven car in 1880, could not develop his creation into a practical vehicle.

But the era of the trolley would soon be at hand, and three men in three different locations were hard at work to make the new day dawn. One was English-born Leo Daft, who developed a two-ton electric locomotive, which he called the "ampere," and which drew current from a third rail. In November, 1883, on a trial run near Saratoga, New York, using the tracks of a narrow-gauge scenic line, he hooked a passenger car onto the little engine, and propelled his "train," carrying sixty passengers, at a steady eight miles an hour. However, Mr. Daft became too enthusiastic. On a downhill grade he "let her rip," and she hit fifteen miles an hour, a speed too great to maintain safely. A sharp curve threw the train off balance and she left the rails and plunged over on her side. Fortunately, none of those aboard was hurt.

Daft picked himself up, and staring disconsolately at the wreck of his dreams, muttered over and over, "We *were* going too fast."

But Daft did not give up easily. Soon he was promoting "electrical rides" behind small locomotives in Boston and on Coney Island. One of the demonstrations at Coney was observed with great interest by the general manager of a horsecar system in Baltimore, who invited Daft to develop his ideas in that city. The result was a partial success—a three-mile electric line operating on a regular schedule. New problems caused an early demise of Daft's Baltimore project, but he continued to promote his inventions in New York, New Jersey, and Connecticut, where he replaced the objectionable third rail with grooved-wheel "trollers" (from which the word "trolley" was derived), which rode on two overhead electric wires.

By 1900 superior designs had replaced Daft's innovations, but a series of legends about the Daft cars made the rounds for a long time. One had to do with complaints about the trolley company's service in a Connecticut city. On instructions of the mayor, a city official was sent to investigate the ability of the cars to stop on brief notice. The gentleman stepped into the street in front of the car, held up his hand and ordered it to halt. The car pulled up short all right, but the troller coasted on until it was jerked to a stop by its wires, whereupon it fell off and hit the official in the head, hospitalizing him for six weeks. That did it; Daft cars were immediately and permanently barred from the city.

The second trolley-minded inventor was Charles J. Van Depoele, a Belgian, who ran away from his family in his teens and came to America. His operations were centered in Chicago. He had no use for electrified rails but instead utilized an overhead wire with a trolley wheel pressed up against it. From Chicago Van Depoele was able to attract streetcar lines in Indiana, Wisconsin, and elsewhere; but like Daft, he had his problems.

The running rails were used as the return half of the electrical circuit. Most of the rail joints were so loose that the current would find a better underground route to the powerhouse. Mostly, this was by way of buried gas and water pipes, and soon these began to corrode electrolytically. The result was a slew of pipe burstings which shattered the already shaky reputation of the electric cars. Then the telephones, which were using the ground as part of their circuits, became intermittently useless, transmitting only a steady buzz when a transit car was in operation.

The "third man"—who had no connection with the titular hero of a great movie produced decades later—was Frank Julian Sprague. He it was who ironed out the most glaring defects which had plagued other innovations and nursed the budding street railway system into full flower. A mathematical wizard from Connecticut, Sprague had attended the United States Naval Academy in Annapolis, and after his graduation had managed to get a leave of absence to study new technical developments which were being displayed at the Crystal Palace Exhibition in London. There the idea of electric transportation became fixed in his mind, and he conceived a self-adjusting, upward-pressure contact to a trolley. Not knowing that Van Depoele was also trolley conscious, he waited too long before applying for patents and then found Van Depoele had a prior claim. Eventually a method of mutual use was agreed upon.

After retiring from the navy, Sprague went to Menlo Park to work for Thomas A. Edison, but he could not accommodate himself to Edison's distrust of the academic-trained scientist and left him after a year. He started on his own in 1884, forming the Sprague Electric Railway and Motor Company, with next to no capital but a plenitude of brains. Sprague's motors won instant favor; even Edison endorsed them. In the spring of 1887 at the age of twenty-nine he accepted the assignment of equipping the city of Richmond, Virginia, with a complete electrified street railway system. His contract called for completion in ninety days, a foolhardy undertaking for the young man, and, as it turned out, an impossible one. For months the Richmond syndicate stood poised on the brink of bankruptcy; then, just as it was ready to take the plunge, Sprague commenced regular service, and, despite one misfortune after another, kept the cars running.

Financially Sprague had fared badly on the deal, but as news of the success of the service spread, his name became famous. The first city to bid for his services was Boston; before 1890 more than two hundred streetcar systems throughout the United States were either operating or under construction, more than 90 per cent based on Sprague's patents.

By 1900 more than two billion dollars had been invested in traction companies, which operated on fifteen thousand miles of track and utilized more than thirty thousand trolleys. Most large transit companies used two types of cars, the enclosed model which carried passengers from the cool days of autumn until late in spring, and the open cars, which appeared on the tracks early in June and caught whatever summer breezes were available as they cruised leisurely along their routes. The open-car trolleys acquired great popularity among the masses, who often rode them on warm evenings just to cool off. Clubs or lodges or groups of factory workers would organize a trolley party and charter an open car for a night ride to the beach or Electric Park. The summer cars were equipped with canvas side curtains, which the conductor could lower at the start of a rain squall. In such instances the boys and young men, who so often preferred attaching themselves to the running boards rather than sitting on the uncomfortable wooden slats inside, would be forced to take shelter in one of the rows of seats, usually standing, uncomfortably crowded, in front of the men and women who foresightedly had occupied the available spaces.

The companies disliked the open cars. Not only did they require a large additional investment for stock which could be utilized for only a few summer months, but the rate of accidents on the open cars far outran those on the others. One prime reason was that passengers were tempted to board or dismount from the open cars before they had come to a dead halt; and while most men and boys became adept at this feat, from time to time a less deft gentleman would fail to time his action and fall on his face or suffer even more serious or painful injury. Posting signs reading "Wait till the car stops" had little effect on the daring young men on the flying trams, nor was there any hesitation on the part of the injured to file damage suits against the company. And while it was noted that most men left a moving car facing the direction in which it was traveling—the proper position for a descent, by the way—most women faced the rear as they stepped down, which frequently threw them off balance, if the trolley had not completely stopped, and occasionally resulted in a form of backward somersault both unladylike and embarrassing.

In addition to the winter and summer models, there were many special styles of trolley cars for special purposes. There were, of course, snowplows and sweepers. There were sprinkler trolleys and postal trolleys and quick-lunch cars for company employees. In many cities trolleys served as hearses. A special hearse car named "Dolores," operating in Baltimore, was frequently booked up to her capacity of two or three funerals a day. The Dolores had a special casket compartment with a wide glass door which permitted the casket to be seen from the street, with a rail against which the floral tributes could be banked, with black leather chairs in the casket compartment for the principal mourners and additional seats in the rear for mourners of less immediate family relationship. Complete charges for all these niceties, with a motorman and conductor thrown in, ran from twenty to twenty-six dollars.

There was no hearse on hand, however, for the trolley's ultimate demise. When the nineteen twenties ended many of the streetcar lines were in deplorable shape, both as to finances and physical condition. One company after another converted its equipment to buses, or ceased existence altogether. The thirties and forties saw the end of the line, as far as all but a few die-hard groups were concerned; and today about the only trolleys to be seen are on view in museums.

A few trolley buffs still exist. One, a resident of the state of Washington, wrote a doleful ballad, some years ago, which ended thus:

> But oh! may there never come the day,
> Be it ever yet so far,
> When a child will go to his dad and say,
> As a youngster might, in his curious way,
> What was a trolley car?

The Railroad Men

If we were to rephrase a Mother Goose rhyme and substitute for the first line, "Sing a Song of Railroads," the song that would occur to 99.44 per cent of those people who could recall any such music would be the one that starts, "I've been working on the railroad."

Okay—so *who's* been working on the railroad? All sorts of fellows: engineers, signalmen, conductors, porters, switchmen. And in the old days, when railroads were the lifeline of the giant industries that bracketed the United States, men of these vital occupations were recognized and glorified by the song writers of the country, as shall soon be demonstrated.

Before introducing some of these songs, though, notice might be taken of the importance of the individual railroads in the field of popular music. For every road worthy of a timetable, no matter how insignificant, was sooner or later honored by a march or polka or quickstep.

Even before the first American steam engine shuffled along the first track at a speed of some eight miles an hour, the anticipatory mind and skill of a Baltimore composer, Arthur Clifton, had produced the first march in railroad history, "The Carrollton March," which was copyrighted on July 1, 1828, and was "performed at the ceremony of commencing the Baltimore & Ohio Railroad on the Fourth of July 1828." The piece was dedicated to "the Hon. Charles Carroll of Carrollton," a gentleman something over ninety years of age, who was the last surviving signer of the immortal Declaration created more than fifty years earlier. When Carroll pushed his shovel into the ground to turn the first earth, he declared, "I consider this among the most important acts of my life, second only to my signing the Declaration of Independence."

So impressed were Baltimoreans with the advent of this amazing method of transportation that a second composer, Charles Meineke, capitalizing on their excitement, was impelled to follow Clifton's lead at once. Just two days after the "Carrollton March" had been copyrighted, Meineke registered his own "Railroad March for the Fourth of July," dedicating it to "The Directors of the Baltimore and Ohio Railroad."

From then on it seemed as if every new railroad had its musical sponsor. Only a fraction of the compositions can be mentioned here. They did homage to the smaller roads as well as the giants. The "Syracuse Rail Road Quick Step" was written by I. P. Wind in 1840; the "New Orleans and Great Western Railroad Polka" by Theodore La Hache (a musician of real importance) in 1854; the "Kansas Pacific Railway Grand March" in 1872. On behalf of the big fellows, Van der Weyde wrote the "Erie Railroad Polka" in 1851; James N. Beck wrote the "Fast Line Gallop" in honor of the Pennsylvania Railroad in 1853; Albert H. Fernald composed the "Union Pacific Galop" in 1870; and William C. Rehm wrote a "Southern Railway March" in 1895. Throughout a sixty-year period a plethora of compositions poured forth in recognition of the Burlington, the Rock Island, the Lehigh, the New York, New Haven and Hartford, the Northwestern, the Wabash, the Louisville and Nashville, and numerous other lines of all shapes and sizes.

On rare occasions, a road might find itself the subject of musical criticism. Such a situation arose in the late 1850's, when the Philadelphia and Reading Railroad, which owned large anthracite coal holdings, permitted a controlling interest in its stock to be acquired by British capitalists. The president of the Reading, Robert D. Cullen, seems to have been under the domination of the English cabal, headed by Robert McCalmont. The thought of British money controlling an important American institution like the great Reading Railroad was anathema to some patriots. A song resulted; whether it was inspired by minority American stockholders is not known, nor is the name of the author. The title is "The Reading Railroad and Its President," and it is written to the tune of "Yankee Doodle." Here are some of the verses:

'Tis said a corporate body ne'er
Was with a soul invested.
The Reading Railroad Company
This logic has suggested.

The only principle he has
Is what he holds invested;
So for the corporate interest, he
Felt deeply interested.

That if the body had no soul
Yet held a heart undaunted
An Englishman unnaturalized
Was not the head it wanted.

No matter if the course pursued
Brought ruin and disaster;
McCalmont spoke and Cullen must
Obey his foreign masters.

So when the Great Dictators spoke,
Then Cullen cried, hosanna!
Not with much skill, because he lacked
The "blandishment of manner."

Or let the great McCalmonts send,
And take away their poodle.
We want no foreign curs to bite
Those who sing Yankee Doodle.

The pounds of cure are not as good
As ounces of prevention.
Let Cullen then go hang himself,
And bless us by *suspension*.

The lives of a train's passengers and crew were at times at the mercy of men who never rode with them, the signalmen and switchmen. Toward the end of the last century there was developed a system of interlocking switches and signals, whereby a switch had to be in the proper position before the signal indicated that an engineer could bring his train forward.

Apparently some of the song writers had not kept up with the innovations of the railroad, as was the case of one Charles Shackford, whose touching ballad, "Asleep at the Switch," brought tears to many eyes when it appeared in 1897. Wrote Shackford:

CHORUS: Asleep at the switch
The president read,
And my wife and child
Were on board he said
But as he read on
His stern face relaxed,
This road shall reward,
Such heroic acts,
He sat at his desk
And fill'd out a check,
And sent it with all dispatch
'Twas for Tom's daughter Nell
For her brave deed that night,
While he slept his last sleep at the switch.

The midnight express will be late here tonight,
So sidetrack the Westbound freight
Those were the orders that Tom had received,
As he passed through the roundhouse gate
Tom was the switchman, with heart true as steel,
And duty was first in his breast,
But the thought of his boy who was dying at home
Crazed Tom and he fell at his post
The shrill whistle blew on the freight for the west.
The rumble was heard of the midnight express.

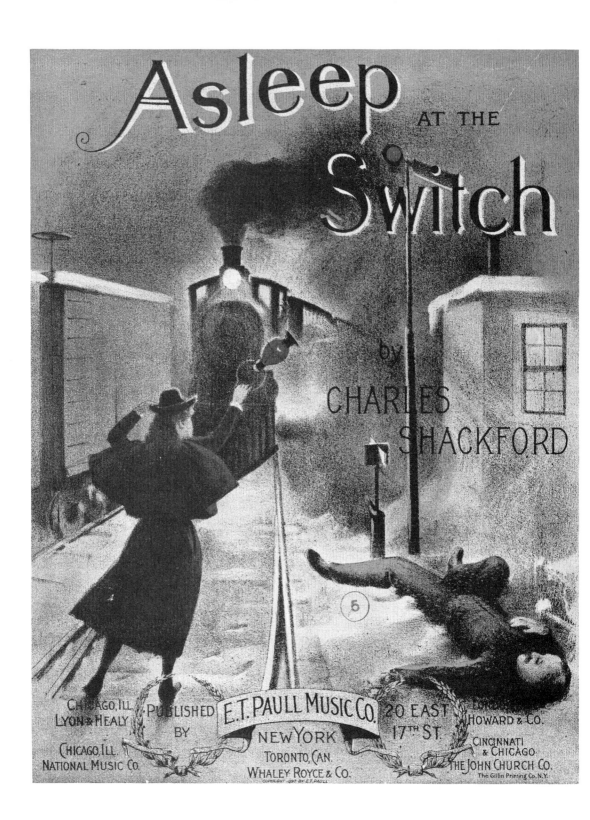

Asleep at the Switch

The mid-night ex-press will be late here to-night,— So side-track the West-bound freight

— Those were the or-ders that Tom had re-ceived,— As he passed through the round house

gate —— Tom was the switch-man, with heart true as steel;— And du-ty was first in

his breast —— But the thought of his boy who was dy-ing at home crazed Tom and he

fell at his post —— The shrill whis-tle blew on the freight for the west—— The

Refrain

rum-ble was heard of the mid-night ex-press A-sleep at the switch—— And

no warn-ing light,—— To sig-nal those trains—— That rushed through the night— When

down to the switch—— Ran Tom's daugh-ter Nell— The cri-sis had past—— His

boy would get well, — She caught up the light —— And waved it on high— And

2. The freight slowly back'd on the main track again,
The men called to Tom good-night
Only the sob of a girl made reply,
And they saw by the engines light
Tom lying flat at his post where he fell,
And there with her head on his breast,

Was his brave daughter Nell who had saved all their lives
And those on the midnight express.
Each man on the freight for the west bared his head
For Toms heart had stopped at his post he lay dead.

CHORUS: Asleep at the switch and no warning light,
   To signal those trains that rushed through the night
   When down to the switch ran Tom's daughter, Nell,
   The crisis had passed his boy would get well.
   She caught up the light and waved it on high,
   And sidetracked the westbound freight.
   And the midnight express all in safety flew by,
   While Tom was asleep at the switch."

But we must not fault Tom—no, no! The second verse reveals the sad truth.

   The freight slowly back'd on the main track again,
   The men called to Tom goodnight.
   Only the sob of a girl made reply,
   And they saw by the engine's light
   Tom lying flat at his post where he fell,
   And there with her head on his breast
   Was his brave daughter Nell who had saved all their lives
   And those on the midnight express.
   Each man on the freight for the west bared his head
   For Tom's heart had stopped at his post; he lay dead.

CHORUS: (and the pay-off):
   Asleep at the switch, the president read,
   And my wife and child were on board he said,
   But as he read on his stern face relaxed,
   This road shall reward such heroic acts,
   He sat at his desk and fill'd out a check,
   And sent it with all despatch,
   'Twas for Tom's daughter Nell, for her brave deed
       that night,
   While he slept his last sleep at the switch.

Signalmen, like switchmen, have their crises, as is illustrated by Will H. Friday, Jr., in his 1896 story of the "Signal Man." Our hero tells why he developed such an aversion to his job:

   You see that box just over there? 'Tis where we
       switch fast trains,
   From side tracks to the center rails; it takes
       good nerve and brains.
   For if you're too late at the switch, a second,
       naught can check
   A terrible collision, which means awful death
       and wreck!

Well, it happened that one Christmas day the signalman's wife left him and their boy to go off on a little toot—by train, of course. The boy accompanied his father to the signal box; but after a while he wandered off. Now hold on to your hats:

> The day grew late; my boy had thought he'd heard
> his mother's train;
> I left the box to listen, sir, then looked for
> him in vain.
> My God! on came the "limited". My son, I cried
> is lost,
> For I must turn the fast express no matter what
> the cost.
> And then my eyes glanced down the track; I saw
> with bated breath,
> My boy there on the center rails, right in the jaws
> of death!
> Oh what can save! the local stops; the express
> onward flies
> I did my duty, Heaven knows, my boy's the sacrifice!

CHORUS: (finally)
> Another eye had seen him there, a heart that
> could not swerve,
> With courage all undaunted and a hand with
> steady nerve,
> His mother, swift as eagle's flight, to clasp
> her boy drew nigh
> She'd left the train and saved him, just as the
> express dashed by.

The duties of a passenger-train conductor were not usually as vital to the safety of his charges as those of other railroad men. One requisite is that of good breeding, whether innate or acquired. A conductor, says one source book, must be a "polished gentleman." He must be a student of human nature, equipped to deal with the myriad personalities that add up to a trainload of passengers. He must prepare to be conciliatory, but cannot waver from the railroad's regulations. He may have to soothe a truculent man "under the influence," convince a woman that her ten-year-old daughter cannot ride without a half-fare ticket, assist non-English-speaking foreigners, and comfort timid women who are traveling for the first time. In addition he requires the qualifications of an expert bank teller handling money, making change, and keeping accounts.

In 1881 there appeared "The Railroad Conductors," a song with words by Frank Dumont and music by W. S. Mullaly, an experienced writing team. The words:

The car conductor is a king, when on his railroad train,
He swings his lantern to and fro to start and stop
    again;
He wakes the sleepers one and all, and tickets they
    must show,
Or put the price into his hands or off the car they
    go....

CHORUS: The locomotive whistle blows, the wheels go
    round and round,
All aboard or you'll get left, just hear that
    awful sound,
It means the boiler's full of steam, it's got
    a mighty pow'r,
We'll soon be speeding at the rate of sixty
    miles an hour.

The conductor, indicate the song writers, does not experience a rough life on the cars. The second verse:

In palace cars we take our ease, and read the
    daily news,
If friends should offer fine cigars, I'm sure
    we'd not refuse;
And ladies, too, will sweetly smile when we
    collect the fare,
We "pass" them free and never think the company
    will care;
"Dead heads" never bother us, or try to "beat"
    their way
We signal to the brakeman if they don't quickly
    pay;
"Punch the tickets, —keep the cash," this motto
    bear in mind,
By doing this we'll soon become the owners of the
    line.

In that same year James Collins wrote the "Song of the Rail," which pays additional tribute to the conductor, who is apparently a well-satisfied servant of his railroad.

I am a gay conductor on a Western railway car,
I travel night, also by day, so many miles afar.
The ladies smile so sweet on me, and call me duck
    and dear,
For which the comp'ny pays me just twelve hundred
    dollars a year.

I never beat my company, and I'm always most polite,
I'm kind to nervous women when they get into a fright,
That is, when they are pretty, and young and fresh
    and fair,
For I'm a gay conductor on the Western Railway Car.

In most of the ballads written about railroad men, the hero was the engineer. Throughout the last quarter of the nineteenth century and into the twentieth, songs about gallant engineers could always be found in the music department of retail stores around the country. "The Faithful Engineer," "My Dad's the Engineer," "The Message of the Dying Engineer (or Just Tell Wife)," "An Engineer's Love," and "Casey Jones" were some of the titles. Casey was by far the most popular of these thrilling tales. Written in 1909, it developed into a folk legend, and the devil-may-care Casey was soon an object of adulation among all railroad buffs.

Most of these songs managed to inject a babe into the picture. There is no doubt that in real life engineers made an effort to save men and women also, and even cows and pigs. But a song writer could not whip up much sentiment for an engineer—or our above-mentioned friend, the signalman— if he merely rescued a man or a cow. On the other hand, helpless children were godsends to the lyricist who aimed at a real tear jerker. "Saved from Death" is a perfect example. Written a hundred years ago with words by George W. Hersee, and music by J. W. Bischoff, it plunges into its subject boldly, with an introduction:

A child sat on a railway track, heedless of coming harm,
It cared not for the clashing bell or whistle's loud alarm,
On sweeps the train with whirlwind rush. Ere many moments fly
The little joyous bud of life a fearful death must die.

Still on the fiery monster came. The hearts of all stood still,
And through the veins of ev'ry one there shot a sick'ning chill.
Out from her home the mother rushed. She shrieked in anguish
    wild,
"Oh, God of heaven, strike me down, but spare, o spare, my
    child."

The engineer sees the child. The whistle screams down brakes,
And as he throws the lever back no nerve or muscle shakes;
He then climbs out on his engine, quick, yet with bated breath,
To try if God will nerve his arm, to save the child from death.
And as he feels his way along, and on the pilot stands
The mother moans, "God give you strength," then falls
    upon the sands.

His eye is quick, his nerve is great, his soul knows
    no alarms,
O, God, that wheel will crush the child! No, no, 'tis
    in his arms!
Great God in heaven, we thank thee now, 'tis safe
    within his arms!

Another important component of train personnel has not been forgotten by the song writers. This adjunct of every first-rate passenger train is the pullman porter. As prominent a writer as Irving Berlin recognized the porter as songworthy; his "Pullman Porters on Parade" was published in 1913. Others before him had written on this subject. One who apparently was impressed by his personal experiences was Charles D. Crandall, who wrote "Porters on a Pullman Train" in 1890. His porter sings as follows:

We need no introduction, you can see just who we are,
Porters on a Pullman train,
Standing at the platform of the sleeping car,
Ready, quick and willing to explain.
Where you are located; we must be remunerated,
Don't forget the little friendly tip.
We think you oughtah give us a qua'tah,
For then you'll have a very pleasant trip.

Chorus: Porter, porter, give us more air,
    Porter, the window please close.
    Porter, this pillow is hard as a rock,
    Porter, come give us more clothes.
    Porter come here, porter stay there,
    All night the people complain
    We are porters, dandy porters,
    And we run on the vestibule train.

It seems that no songs about baggagemen have been written, but one of the saddest of all railroad songs has, as its location, the interior of a baggage car. This is "In the Baggage Coach Ahead," written in 1896 by the popular Gussie L. Davis. To hear this touching ballad three necessities must be available, a pianist, a vocalist, and a large dry handkerchief. Here we go:

On a dark stormy night, as the train rattled on,
All the passengers had gone to bed,
Except one young man with a babe in his arms
Who sat there with a bowed down head.
The innocent one began crying just then,
As though its poor heart would break.
One angry man said, "Make that child stop
    its noise,

For it's keeping all of us awake."
"Put it out" said another, "Don't keep it in
     here,
We've paid for our berths and want rest."
But never a word said the man with the child,
As he fondled it close to his breast.
"Where is its mother? Go take it to her,"
This a lady then softly said.
"I wish that I could" was the man's sad reply,
"But she's dead, in the coach ahead."

CHORUS: While the train rolled onward,
              A husband sat in tears,
              Thinking of the happiness,
              Of just a few short years,
              For baby's face brings pictures of
              A cherished hope that's dead,
              But baby's cries can't waken her,
              In the baggage coach ahead.

The great days of rail travel in this country lie far behind us. Today a ride on a passenger train for most of us is more of an innovation than a flight in a plane the size of a football field. But it is good to remember the time when the railroad was the only means to get around the United States, and to take cognizance of the men who ran the trains and who made them run.

3
THE
BIG
FELLOWS

Andrew Carnegie

IN MAY, 1848, a small, bright-eyed twelve-year-old boy set out from Glasgow, Scotland, in an eight-hundred-ton sailing ship. The ship's destination was New York, where she deposited the boy with his family seven weeks later. The voyage would be hardly worth mentioning—thousands of families were then leaving their homes in Great Britain for America—except for the fact that the name of the boy was Andrew Carnegie.

Three weeks after landing, the family was in Pittsburgh, where William Carnegie, Andrew's father, pursued his occupation as a weaver. But Andrew, with just five years of formal schooling, was anxious to augment the family's income, and wasted no time in finding a job. Andrew was definitely no time waster. He started as a bobbin boy in a cotton factory in Allegheny City at a salary of a dollar and twenty cents a week. At work before dawn, no surcease (except for a brief lunch period) until after dark, it was a consuming, wearying existence. However, Andrew was conscientious and industrious, and as a result he was shortly on his way up to bigger and better things. Soon he was earning two dollars a week, then, as a telegraph messenger boy, eleven dollars and a quarter a month.

Now there opened up to him a new dimension in his life. Colonel James Anderson, who possessed a library of four hundred books, announced that he would open his library to working boys, who would be permitted to borrow any book in it on a Saturday with the understanding that it be returned the following Saturday. Andrew seized the opportunity avidly, and his self-education began. A "Webster Literary Society" was formed by Carnegie and a few friends, which gave them the chance to discuss at length the ideas gleaned from Colonel Anderson's books, and which developed in Carnegie the self-possession that enabled him to address an audience so effectively and so forcefully. Decades later, when Carnegie put into operation the establishment of free libraries across the country, one of the first, erected in Allegheny, was dedicated to Colonel Anderson, "Founder of Free Libraries in Western Pennsylvania"—so reads Carnegie's inscription.

At sixteen he was on the road to economic independence. He was in succession a telegraph operator, a clerk in the office of a Pennsylvania Railroad executive, and superintendent of the railroad's Pittsburgh Division. When the Civil War broke out his old chief with the railroad was appointed assistant secretary of war and Carnegie was called to Washington as one of his important aides. The two men remained there until 1864, when they returned to Pittsburgh to help operate the Pennsylvania Railroad's heavy traffic with the government.

Carnegie, now twenty-four, was ready to make use of the skills and knowledge he had acquired during the preceding few years. He organized a rail-making company, a locomotive works, and a bridge company, all of which proved successful ventures. The Keystone Bridge Works was Carnegie's special pride; he regarded this company as the pioneer of all his iron and steel projects.

Until the 1870's, when the Bessemer process of making steel was perfected, the country's railroads had been running on iron rails, which wore out rapidly and often required replacement after about six weeks of constant usage. Carnegie's steel rails put an end to that expensive procedure; the Pennsylvania and Baltimore and Ohio railroads became enormous customers for them.

Young Carnegie's energy was prodigious; he erected one huge plant after another, each one enormously profitable. Earnings came to some forty million dollars a year.

Eventually, in his sixties, he was induced to dispose of his great business. The man who started the chain of events leading to the sale of the Carnegie Steel Company to a group of bankers headed by J. P. Morgan was Carnegie's protégé and close friend, Charles M. Schwab. Carnegie had plucked the nineteen-year-old Schwab from his menial job in Spiegelmire's general store in Braddock, Pennsylvania, twenty years before, in 1881.

Schwab had given a speech in December, 1900, before a group of the country's top business executives, painting in glowing colors the expanding future of the steel industry. Mr. Morgan was one of the invited guests, and as Schwab waxed eloquent, Morgan was entranced with the prospects he described. Personal conferences between Morgan and Carnegie followed. The result was a transaction of almost half a billion dollars of which Carnegie himself received three hundred million.

For his great wealth he had some of the most significant uses to which an individual's fortune has ever been committed. One of his first writings on the subject was entitled "The Gospel of Wealth" and appeared in 1889. His gospel, which had many aspects, fell into two main parts—the advantages of poverty and the responsibilities of surplus wealth. He contended that wealth should be held in trust for the benefit of the entire community. This places a formidable task upon the rich man, who will be held derelict in his duties if he fails to use his millions to communal advantage.

Once Carnegie was asked for his opinion as to the best endowment an ambitious youth might hope for. He replied, "The greatest of all advantages with which he can begin life is that of being poor. The man who wishes to make millions should not be born with a silver spoon in his mouth. He must feel that it is sink or swim with him!"

It is rightly said that giving is one of the most difficult of arts. Andrew Carnegie mastered this art as few other individuals have ever done. After the gift of his first public library in 1881 (it went to his birthplace, Dunfermline, Scotland) he invested in such libraries forty million dollars more. He established the Carnegie Institute in Pittsburgh, a Carnegie Hero Fund, a Carnegie Endowment for International Peace and a sum for the erection of a Palace of Peace at The Hague, trusts for Universities in Scotland, for the advancement of teaching, a relief fund for steel workers, and even a fund for simplified spelling boards. For these and many other causes his combined gifts came to more than three hundred million dollars.

His overwhelming desire was for the maintenance of peace between nations. The revenue from his endowment for international peace, set up in 1910, was to be administered (in his words) for "the abolition of international war, the foulest blot upon our civilization." Three years before, he had accepted the presidency of the Peace Society of New York. In an address before the students of the University of St. Andrews in Scotland in 1905 he had spoken of Lincoln's bitter aversion to slavery, and had said, "Let us resolve like Lincoln, and select man-slaying as our foe, as he did manselling." Small wonder that up until the beginning of World War I, Carnegie's name was almost synonymous with international peace efforts.

Even in the field of popular music were there tributes to him. In 1913

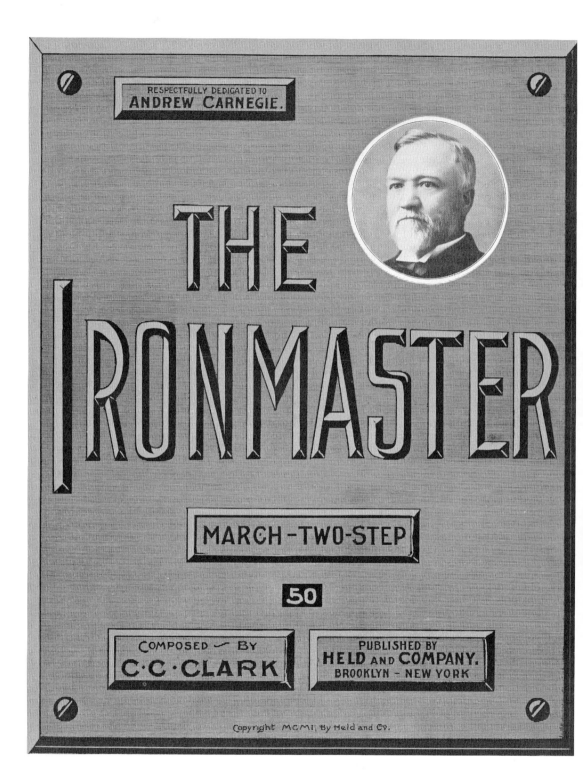

there appeared a brisk march entitled "Dawn of Peace," written by Henry Dellafield and dedicated to Andrew Carnegie. Just below the title is a quotation from the writings of Andrew Carnegie: "Music is the servant of everything good, and belongs to the great sisterhood which labors in any way and in every form to improve, educate and refine humanity."

Another march, dedicated to him, had been published a dozen years earlier. This one was "The Ironmaster," composed by C. C. Clark. Shortly after its publication Mr. Carnegie disposed of his great company and the ironmaster became the great philanthropist, a title which he never claimed for himself. One of his biographers, Barnard Alderson, calls him "a trustee for the English-speaking race." However he may be regarded, he was certainly an inspirational figure for all who have confidence in man's sense of justice for his fellow man.

Mr. Dooley

SEVENTY-FIVE YEARS AGO, in Chicago, one of the best-loved Americans of his day was making his observations known, not only around the country but around the world. The man who found himself in this enviable situation was a self-effacing, unprepossessing-looking fellow of Irish descent named Finley Peter Dunne, better known—*much* better known—as Mr. Dooley.

His home town had not yet embarked on the exhibitionism which would, in a few decades, make it the hub of so many assorted activists and activities. Unknown to Mr. Dooley's stage there lurked in the wings some of the most brutal gangsters, the slickest utility magnates, the chewyist chewing gum, and the toughest legislators in the United States. It was also furnishing the country with some of its leading educators, architects, industrialists, and musicians; and it felt entitled to boast of its greatness in one of the catchiest songs of the twenties, which began, "Chicago, Chicago, that toddlin' Town." But all this was long after Mr. Dooley had made his delightful mark.

Peter Dunne (later on he prefaced his name with his mother's maiden name) was born in 1867. At home he was considered bright, but his high school record offered no corroborating evidence. When he graduated from West Division High, he stood last in his class.

Dunne hankered to be a newspaper man. Before he was seventeen years old he started in that occupation as an office boy with the *Chicago Telegram*. Soon his little stories of day-to-day life began to appear, and other newspapers evidenced interest. He was lured away from his five-dollar-a-week job at the *Telegram* to one at eight dollars with the *Chicago News*. Dunne was a literary butterfly. By the time he was twenty-one he had flitted away from the *News* to become city editor of the *Chicago Times*, which he left after a short while to take charge of the editorial page of the *Evening Post*. His dreams now seemed to be coming true; he looked forward to becoming a great publisher and to writing editorials which would have their influence on public opinion.

Ironically, his brilliant sense of humor was the spoiler of his grandiose aspirations. The managing editor of the *Post*, impressed by Dunne's keen wit, asked him to write a series of unsigned humorous articles for the paper's new Sunday edition—at ten dollars apiece. The first of the articles, in Irish brogue, appeared on December 4, 1892. The dialogue was purported to be between James McGarry, a public-house keeper whom Dunne called "Colonel McNeery," and John J. McKenna, a politician.

One day, wrote Dunne, McGarry was in the rear of his barroom when his bartender, Mike Casey, opened the door and asked him if George Babbitt was good for a drink. "Has he had it?" inquired McGarry. "He has," said the barkeep. "He is," answered McGarry. The articles soon attracted such widespread reader attention that McGarry became concerned about the notoriety that he and his bar were receiving. So Dunne permitted "Colonel McNeery" to return to Ireland and replaced him with an Irish bachelor who was to become one of the greatest characters in American literature. His name was Martin Dooley. In 1896, Dooley's faithful listener, Mr. Hennessy, was "born" and was fated to become Dooley's stooge for the rest of his days.

Mr. Dooley had by that time become the most celebrated and entertaining philosopher to appear in the American press. He editorialized, he sermonized, he even denounced, all with a wit and charm that rendered defenseless any antagonists whose opinions clashed with his own. He could criticize any movement or individual or happening that was the current front-page news sensation; yet so gentle, so pleasant, so sparkling were his remarks that nobody took offense.

His devotees included a host of men in the highest circles of government, one of the staunchest admirers being President Theodore Roosevelt. Roosevelt (probably one of the toughest men who was ever in the White House) had strong sympathy with what was then called reform and with early strains of the civil rights movement. For example, during Roosevelt's term

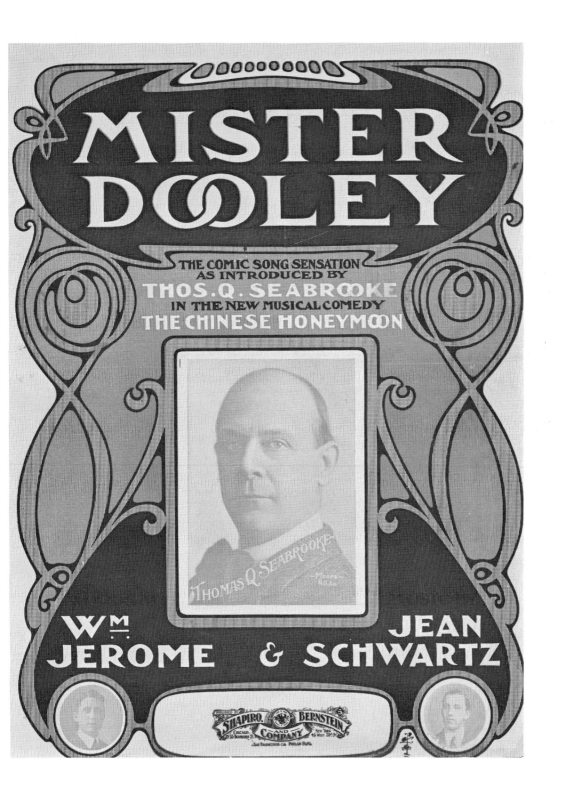

Mister Dooley

There is a man that's known to all, a man of great re-nown—A man whose name is on the

lips of ev-ery one in town— You read a-bout him ev-ery day you've heard his name no

doubt.—And if he ev-en sneez-es they will get an Ex-tra out— For Mis-ter Doo-ley

Chorus

For Mis-ter Doo-ley—— The great-est man the coun-try ev-er knew—— Quite dip-lo

ma-tic——And dem-o-cra-tic—— is Mis-ter Doo-ley oo-ley oo-ley oo.——

2. Napoleon had an army of a hundred thousand men—
   He marched them up the hill and then he marched them
       down again—
   When they were up why they were up—on that I'll
       bet a crown—
   And though Napoleon marched them up who was it called
       them down.
   'Twas Mister Dooley
   'Twas Mister Dooley
   He always knew a little parle vou
   With Boni Partee
   A la Ma Carty was Mister Dooley, ooley, ooley oo.

3. This country never can forget, forget we never will—
   The way the boys at San Juan they went charging up the hill
   Though Teddy got the credit of that awful bloody fray
   The hero who deserved it and the man who saved the day
   'Twas Mister Dooley
   'Twas Mister Dooley
   Like a locomotive up the hill he flew
   Who drove the Spaniards
   Back to the Tanyards 'twas Mister Dooley, ooley, ooley oo.

4. Now Wireless Telegraphy is cutting quite a dash
   And messages across the sea, are sent now like a flash,
   With all the great inventors it has made an awful hit,

And but few of them acknowledge that the man invented it
Was Mr. Dooley, Mr. Dooley
To Edison he taught a thing or two,
And young Marconi, eats macaroni,
Along with Mr. Dooley-ooley-ooley-oo

5. Of Washington you've heard the tale about the Cherry tree,
In fact it seems to be a part of Yankee History,
Who cut that tree his father said,
And George began to cry
Oh, father dear said little George,
I cannot tell a lie
'Twas Mr. Dooley, Mr. Dooley,
His father said now Georgie is it true,
With meditation, was it Carrie Nation,
Or Mr. Dooley-ooley-ooley-oo.

6. Who settles all the labor strikes,
Without a word or blow,
And sees the men who work receive the right amount, of dough,
Who causes them to arbitrate,
Who uses all the grease,
To keep the men of capital and labor both at peace.
It's Mr. Dooley, Mr. Dooley,
A man reporters like to interview,
Who changed the manner of Marcus Hanna,
Sure 'twas Mr. Dooley, ooley, ooley-oo

7. Of course you all remember the reception to the Prince,
And every one who met him, voted Henny was immense,
He said he had a bully time while he was over here,
But the only man he ever met could beat him drinking beer.
Was Mr. Dooley, Mr. Dooley,
He drank more than the German's they could brew,
The great adviser to Bill the Kaiser,
Is Mr. Dooley, ooley, ooley-oo

8. Columbus he came over here in 1492
When New York was a vacant lot, if History is true
'Twas down at Castle Garden he first put his foot on land,
And as he did, the first one there, to grab him by the hand
Was Mr. Dooley, Mr. Dooley,
And he took him up Columbus Avenue
With head uncovered, said we're discovered,
Did Mr. Dooley, ooley-ooley-oo

9. The great "400" haven't any leader so it seems
They want a man to show them how to eat their cakes and creams,
It once was Ward McAllister who led the merry pace,
And they claim there's only one man who can ever take his place
Its Mr. Dooley, Mr. Dooley
Who writes the jokes for Chauncy M. Depew,
It seems that Chauncey took quite a fauncy,
To the jokes of Mr. Dooley, ooley, oo-oo

10. A doctor in this city, once his business it was bad,
His name it was unknown, for not a customer he had,
But now his name is famous his success it is assured,
Just through a certain party, that this certain doctor cured,
'Twas Mr. Dooley, 'Twas Mr. Dooley,
That made the Doctor known to me and you,
For Dr. Munyon once cured a bunyon,
For Mr. Dooley-ooley-ooley-oo

in office he invited Booker T. Washington, the great negro president of Tuskegee Institute in Alabama, to be his luncheon guest at the White House. This was shortly before Roosevelt ran for reelection in 1904, and it caused a storm of excitement around the country, for the thought of a black dining with the president was an unheard-of occurrence. Mr. Dooley's comment is as pertinent today as it was then: "Well, annyhow, it's goin' to be th' roonation iv Prisidint Tiddy's chances in th' South. Thousan's iv men who wudden't have voted f'r him undher anny circumstances has declared that undher no circumstances wud they now vote f'r him."

Mr. Dooley had no compunction about criticizing anyone with whom he disagreed, even the Supreme Court. Many of his writings became famous, among them his comments about the infallibility of the Supreme Court. He said, "No matther whether th' constitution follows th' flag or not, th' Supreme Court follows th' iliction returns."

To his friend Mr. Hennessy, Mr. Dooley expressed these thoughts about the vice-presidency: "Th' prisidincy is the highest office in th' gift iv th' people. Th' vice-prisidency is th' next highest an' th' lowest. It isn't a crime exactly. Ye can't be sint to jail f'r it, but it's a kind iv a disgrace . . . .

"It is princip'lly, Hinnissy, because iv th' vice-prisidint that most of our prisidints have enjoyed such rugged health. Th' vice-prisidint guards th' prisidint, an' the prisidint, afther sizin' up the vice-prisidint, con-cludes that it wud be betther f'r th' country if he shud live yet awhile. 'D'ye know,' says th' prisidint to th' vice-prisidint, 'ivry time I see you I feel tin years younger?' "

It was not surprising that the popular song writers found him an apt subject for the piano. The "Mr. Dooley March" was published in 1901, and the enormously popular "Mister Dooley," with music by Jean Schwartz and words by William Jerome, was incorporated in 1902 into a musical comedy called "The Chinese Honeymoon." Not too many people will remember "The Chinese Honeymoon"; "Mr. Dooley" was an instant hit.

Dunne had not known that the song would be introduced in the show, but one of his close friends, William C. Whitney, was in on the secret. He took a box and invited Dunne to share it. Suddenly a popular singer advanced on the stage, turned in Dunne's direction, and as a spotlight focused on the embarrassed Dunne, the singer started as follows:

> There is a man that's known to all, a man of
>   great renown
> A man who's name is on the lips of everyone
>   in town

You read about him every day, you've heard his
      name no doubt
And if he even sneezes they will get an extra out.
CHORUS: For Mister Dooley, for Mister Dooley
      The greatest man the country ever knew
      Quite diplomatic and democratic
      Is Mister Dooley-ooley-ooley-oo.

There were ten stanzas and the audience loved every one.

America has produced many humorous writers. Some, such as Artemis
Ward and Hosea Bigelow (James Russell Lowell's creation) preceded
Dunne; John Kendrick Bangs and Will Rogers followed him. All were
great favorites with the public, but none enjoyed the enormous amount of
admiration and the tremendous following that belonged to Mr. Dooley.
This lovable little man, whose wit eliminated the old conception of the
United States about the "Shanty Irish" and helped to bring respect to that
large segment of Americans of Irish extraction, carried his own brand of
greatness wherever he went. In our current problems with minority groups,
maybe what this country could use again is a little "Dooleyism."

John Philip Sousa

He took his band to Boston. He took it to St. Louis. He took it to Atlanta,
to Spartanburg, South Carolina, to Butte, Montana, to San Francisco. He
was a sensation on the Continent. He played in Paris, in Brussels, in Liege,
in Berlin, in Hanover, in Heidelberg, in Dresden, in Munich, in Nurem-
berg, in Amsterdam. An article in an English journal proclaimed: "Sousa
is entitled to the name of 'March King,' quite as much as Strauss is to that of
'Waltz King.'"

In 1905, a pair of song writers, Add. Vance and Chas. Kohlman, produced
a song in march time entitled "Sousa's Band Is on Parade To-day." It goes:

In rain or sleet it is a treat to hear the music sweet,
Kazoo kazip, Oh let 'er rip.

. . . .

There's a problem I have solved your weary brain to thrill
Great men have worked upon it night and day
Have you noticed that a horse goes faster down than up
      a hill,
For Sousa's Band parades today.
CHORUS: When you hear Mister Sousa's band a-marching down the
      street,
      The trombones and the cornets blaze away.
      Maggie Gee Whiz and shiftless Liz upon the corner meet,
      For Sousa's Band is on parade today.

107

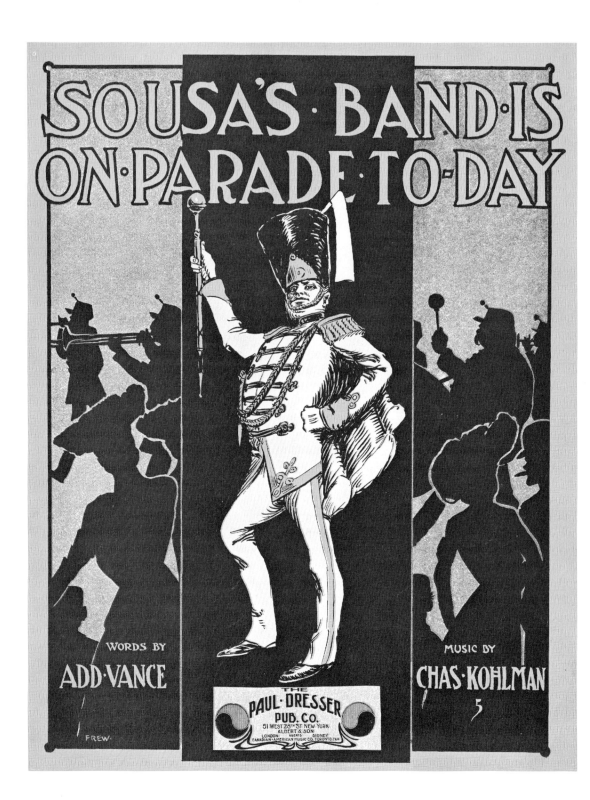

Sousa's Band is on Parade Today

A big brass band give it a hand is com-ing down the street, The pic-co-lo — — from Ko-ko-mo — — The man who beats the bass-drum and his board-bill used to be in Bar-num's show — I'll have you know — The man who plays the trom-bone used to pick the old ham-bone — And you could hear him pick it far a-way — Bring out your pick-an-ni-nys and your shov-els and your picks, for Sou-sa's Band — pa-rades to-day —

Chorus

— When you hear Mis-ter Sou-sa's band a march-ing down the street, The trom-bones and the cor-nets blaze a-way — Mag-gie Gee Whiz and shift-less Liz up-on the cor-ner meet, For Sou-sa's Band is on pa-rade to-day. —

2. In rain or sleet it is a treat to hear the music sweet, Kazoo kazip
Oh let 'er rip
There's just one way to dodge bananas with your dainty feet,
If you are flip, give them the slip
But there's a problem I have solved your weary brain to thrill
Great men have worked upon it night and day
Have you noticed that a horse goes faster down than up a hill,
For Sousa's Band parades today.
CHORUS

He was the march king, no question about it. His first great march, "The Gladiator," appeared in 1886 and spread like wildfire. It was followed in rapid order by one hit after another. But wait a minute!

John Philip Sousa was no infant prodigy like Wolfgang Amadeus Mozart, even though he got off to an early musical start. At the age of thirteen and a half, when he was all of four feet nine inches tall, he was enrolled as a member of the United States Marine Band. He was not expected to participate in the band's concerts; rather, his position was that of apprentice, putting up music stands, distributing the parts, and running errands, while he perfected the art of playing the trombone. Sousa's father, Antonio, himself a trombonist in the Marine Band, was not to have the pleasure of seeing his son become a great "horn" man. Although he reenlisted in 1872 at the age of eighteen for a five-year term as a principal musician, third class, Sousa was discontented. His real source of happiness was as a violinist, at which he was skilled, rather than as an indifferent trombonist. He was short in stature, a bit over five feet six, but even shorter in temper; and he became embittered when one day he was humiliated by the supercilious attitude of the Marine Band's new conductor. With the help of an acquaintance in the State Department, he was able to secure a release from the band, and gladly discarded the striking red, gold-trimmed, jacket and blue pants which he had worn so resplendently for nearly five years.

For a short while during his nineteenth summer he led an orchestra performing at a Washington variety stage, at the same time continuing to study the violin. Meanwhile the creative urge descended upon him. His first small effort, which he called "An Album Leaf," written for violin and piano, was dismissed as "Bread and Cheese" by his instructor, Professor Espata. But Sousa was not discouraged; rather he was inspired to continue his compositions while his violin earned for him a modest living.

At twenty-two he was writing madly. He had fallen in love with a girl named Emma Swallow, the daughter of a clergyman. Emma fancied herself a poetess, and Sousa was determined that some of her poems, set to his music, should attain popularity. As a matter of fact, he managed to get one published; "Ah Me! Ancient Ballad" was the title on the song cover. Sousa wrote the music in six-eighths time, a tempo that would later be used for some of his most stirring marches. But in this early effort he indicated the piece was to be performed andante lamentabile, an appropriate pace for the saccharine lyrics:

> A knight there was of noble name,
>   Ah me!
> A knight of wond'rous deed and fame,
>   Ah me!
> He wooed a lady, wooed and won,
> No fairer lady 'neath the sun,
> She lived and smiled for him alone,
>   Ah me!

But then, the song related, the knight lost his interest in the girl and rode off. Sousa, too, ran into difficulties in his affair with Emma. He had become engaged to her, but her mama and papa did not approve; so, like Emma's literary knight, her real one was a renegade too. He left her to seek a fairer flower elsewhere, while she found another boy friend acceptable to her parents.

Sousa's new enamorata was a little sixteen-year-old Philadelphian named Jennie Bellis. His feelings were reciprocated, and soon he was a married man. Song writing was in his blood, but it was not profitable; fiddling was. As a violinist at Philadelphia theaters he earned enough so that he could devote part of his time to compositions. He was not a classicist; he wrote with tongue in cheek for the man in the street. For example, in 1877 he sold a song, now a collector's item, called "The Free-Lunch Cadets":

> We circumnavigate the town for ev'ry free-lunch bar;
> We go from east to west and back, and travel wide and
>   far.
> We sometimes get into a bar where lunch has just run
>   out,
> And all that's left to feed upon is the smell of
>   sauerkraut. . . .

> CHORUS: Oh, sauerkraut and barley-soup, and corn-beef by the
>   slice,
> Red herrings sprinkled o'er with salt, we tell you
>   they are nice
> Limburger cheese and mushroom-pie, and hot corn by
>   the ear
> You wouldn't have, you couldn't get, a better bill
>   of fare.

He was sure that humorous songs were his bent, and the following year he continued in a humorous vein with "Smick, Smack, Smuck." Herewith the first verse and the chorus:

> I loved a maid long years ago,
> A queerer girl no one can show,
> She had a wart upon her nose,
> And eyes that looked just like a crow's,
> She had a failing, I must say,
> 'Twas to be kissing all the day,
> She'd kiss at morn, she'd kiss at noon
> She'd kiss from July up to June.
>
> CHORUS: Face to face, and nose to nose,
> Smick, smack, smuck, and away she goes;
> Lay her eye-brow on your collar,
> Hug her so that she can't holler,
> Tell her that you're always true,
> Squeeze her 'till her face turns blue,
> Keep it up for fifteen hours,
> Then begin anew.

That same year Gilbert and Sullivan produced *Pinafore* in London. It was an instant success and within months came to the United States, where it created a sensation. Sousa played in, and at times conducted, the orchestra of a company performing *Pinafore* in and around Philadelphia, moving upward, after a bit, to greater prominence by presenting the musical at the Broadway Theater (later Daly's Theater) in New York.

The company's leading actress was often carelessly off key in her vocal numbers, pitching her voice noticeably sharp, while at the same time she was not fastidious when donning her costume, so that occasionally up to two inches of petticoat would show beneath her gown. This combination of annoying traits so disturbed Sousa that one night, when he was conducting the orchestra, he felt impelled to dispatch this note to the young woman: "Dear Madam: Please raise your petticoat two inches, and lower your voice one inch. J. P. S."

Sousa was soon touring the country, fiddling in orchestras, arranging scores, and composing. When he was twenty-five years old his talents were recognized by the organization that had given him his start a dozen years before; he was offered the leadership of the Marine Band. Sousa had always wanted to lead a prestigious band, and now that ambition was gratified. The remuneration did not compensate for the prestige. After twelve years of arduous service, his salary was only about fifteen hundred dollars a year. His musicians received from thirteen to thirty-eight dollars a month, depending on their rank, plus some clothing money and the princely sum of thirteen cents a day for "rations."

But he did play at all the important government functions. Five presidents, from Hayes to Harrison, enjoyed the Marine Band's concerts at the White House. Fortunately, practicing and performing were not so time consuming as to prevent Sousa from composing. Some of his most stirring marches, among them "Semper Fidelis" and "The Washington Post March" were written during this period.

In 1892 a Chicago business syndicate offered to quadruple the salary Sousa was receiving if he would leave the Marine Corps and organize his own concert band. This was a proposition that he could not justifiably refuse, though pressure was applied to insure his remaining with the Corps. He requested his release from service with the government, and after a wait of nearly three months it was granted.

On the day Sousa's band opened its first season in September, 1892, Patrick Garfield Gilmore, the most popular band leader of the day, died suddenly. Sousa was saddened by the death of a man who had been hailed as the finest in his field up to that time and who was to be remembered ever after as the composer of one of the great songs of American military history, "When Johnny Comes Marching Home." Gilmore's bandsmen looked for new leadership, and Sousa, quick to take advantage of the situation, induced almost a score of the best musicians of Gilmore's band to join him. These men, along with Sousa's great trombonist, Arthur Pryor, formed the nucleus of a band which excited every audience that had the good fortune to hear it.

And all the while, Sousa composed—marches, songs, musical comedies (or "light operas," as they were then called). He became the most popular entertainer in the country. Every march he wrote was eagerly welcomed, and quickly set to dance tempo. Letters were addressed to him in envelopes bearing only the words "The March King, U.S.A."; they were straightway delivered. He redesigned the big Helicon tuba carried by, or rather, curled around the body of a bandsman. The blast of the instrument was too powerful to suit him, so he instructed the Wurlitzer Company to create a gentler giant of a tuba, diffusing its tone and softening its blare. The new horn was christened the Sousaphone.

His greatest marches became standard fare for every band in the country. No concert was complete without "El Capitan" or "Semper Fidelis" or "The Manhattan Beach March" or "The Stars and Stripes Forever." His prodigious output comprised over one hundred marches, over fifty songs, and many other works which included light operas, suites, fantasies, and even novels.

He was fortunate in securing first-rate collaborators for the songs of his comic operas. One number which scored an instant hit and remained popular for decades was "A Typical Tune of Zanzibar," the words for which were written by Charles Klein in Sousa's great musical "El Capitan." To a simple, but delightful melody in six-eighths time, Klein contributed a simple but delightful ballad, the first verse going:

> Under the window he softly crept,
> While father and mother and Towser slept;
> Then plunking a tune on his light guitar,
> He warbled a ballad of Zanzibar.
> From out her chamber emerged the maid,
> Begging the name of the tune he played,
> Said he as he plunked his light guitar,
> " 'Tis a typical tune of Zanzibar."

But, alas:

> Quickly she leaped from the casement high
> Into his arms and ready to fly,
> But Towser had heard the light guitar
> And the typical tune of Zanzibar.
> They buried them down by the ocean's spray,
> Where oft at night, (so neighbors say;)
> Is heard the plunk of a light guitar,
> And the typical tune of Zanzibar.

In 1906 another great lyricist, Harry G. Smith, joined Sousa in writing the book as well as the words of the songs in another hit, *The Free Lance*. Could the young people of the late 1960's have possibly found inspiration here for one of their own phenomenal successes? Because sixty years before the delightful musical *Hair* captivated New York, Sousa and Smith introduced a charming little number, "Hair" by name, as one of the featured songs in *The Free Lance*. Here are the lyrics.

> What makes a man a poet or musician?
> What makes a man succeed at any game?
> What makes a man win out in his ambition?
> I have a theory about the same,
> For instance, there's the old time hero Samson,
> Such muscles as he had are very rare,
> A lady friend attracted by a ransom,
> Caught him asleep and slyly cut his hair.

CHORUS: It was his hair, that got him there,
> You mostly always tell a great man by his hair,
> Tho' philosophers have said,
> All depends upon the head,
> Not at all, it all depends upon the hair.

You are the great piano playing wonder,
Whose noise, the av'rage thunderstorm can drown,
All other iv'ry pounders knuckle under,
When Mister What's-his-namesky comes to town.
They talk about his technique so artistic,
His genius, we know, is very rare,
The ladies think he has a magic mystic,
It isn't that at all, it is his hair.

CHORUS: It was his hair, that halo fair,
That makes the girls adore and love him ev'rywhere,
Oh his technique and his touch,
Are not really such a much,
It's that wonderful chrysanthemum of hair.

John Philip Sousa's songs, captivating though many of them were, and enhanced by the work of the best lyricists of the time, are all but forgotten today. But his marches live on. Rare is the man who fails to thrill at the swell of a great brass band breaking into "The Washington Post March" or "The Stars and Stripes Forever." They are as American as apple pie.

"Standard Oil"

IN 1907, when John D. Rockefeller was nearly seventy years old and the country's richest man, he was chastised severely by Kenesaw Mountain Landis, a judge only a little over half his age. The chastisement was in the form of a $29,240,000 fine plastered on Mr. Rockefeller's "baby," The Standard Oil Company of Indiana.

The judge found the oil company guilty of violations of an act forbidding secret railroad rates. The decision was a momentous one, and the publicity enormous. Not only were the newspapers overflowing with oil, but the drippings seeped through to other media, including that of the popular song. And this is the way they sang about Mr. Rockefeller and the whopping fine:

2. Now "Rockefeller" is no fool
For long ago he went to school
And learned to read and write and spell,
And some words looked like O-I-L.
   S-T-A-N-D-A-R-D
Another word he liked to see,
They looked so good to "Johnny D."
He added on the Come "pay" ny.
CHORUS

3. Some States appear to hold their breath,
While others aim to cause the death
Of this "Oil wagon" called a trust,
Which surely will be hard to bust,
And if it busts I think they'll find
The same old thing bob up behind.
Yes surely we are in the toil
Of ever lasting Standard Oil.
CHORUS

4. But who can tell now if you please,
   Just how much oil twill take to grease
   The track that causes things to slide
   Around the bend or to the side?
   We know there's "fingers in the pie"
   This is a truth we can't deny;
   There's others who will share the spoil
   Of what is called the Standard Oil.
   CHORUS

5. "John's" fortune is so very large
   A corner off would fill a barge.
   Could buy a city large or small,
   And own the Rail Roads one and all.
   Could stretch his twentys to the moon
   And if the earth was one balloon
   Could cover it with shining gold
   With millions more down in the hold.
   CHORUS

6. He had a very winning "smile"
   And many Rail Roads did beguile
   He said I'll give you something back
   If only Standard Oil you'll pack.
   Remember this is on the dead
   (I think thats what the old man said)
   And when they answered "You are on"
   A friendly smile came over John
   CHORUS

7. When our good President had seen
   That John D's plans were mighty mean
   This freezing little fellows out
   His "thinker" then began to doubt.
   He said its time to blow the horn
   And call the cows in from the corn
   And sure enough he started in
   To put him out, and will he win?
   CHORUS

8. The rich old man was hard to find.
   He knew they had an "ax to grind."
   And when they found him O ho! ho!
   All he would say was "I don't know."
   Now you wont censure him for that.
   It is not nice with Judge to chat.
   Nor is it wisdom if you please
   But "Thank you" for the witness fees.
   CHORUS

9. O "John" we feel so very bad,
   To think that when you was but a lad
   So many schemes got in your head.
   Why did you not play golf instead?
   We fear you did not think of us;
   You've got us in an awful muss
   We can't forgive you John for this
   For things are terribly amiss!
   CHORUS

10. Two nine two forty! O! O! O!
       ($29,240,000)
    Was something awful don't you know!
    But then you brought it on yourself
    By laying too much on the shelf
    Now come dear John and sin no more
    Bestow your shekels on the poor.
    We know you've given much away
    But "Uncle Sammy" wants his "pay."
    CHORUS

CHORUS: Two nine two forty! O! O! O! ($29,240,000)
        Was something awful don't you know!
        But then you brought it on yourself
        By laying too much on the shelf.
        Now come dear John and sin no more
        Bestow your shekels on the poor.
        We know you've given much away
        But "Uncle Sammy" wants his "pay."

This was the tenth verse of a song entitled "Standard Oil," by F. L. Hill and A. F. Scheu, with a title page depicting a figure whose head is an oilcan (resembling markedly the tin woodman in the *Wizard of Oz*), with the initials J. D. R., superimposed. To the title are added the words "Oils Well that Ends Well—a Gusher"; the song is dedicated to Judge Kenesaw Mountain Landis.

The chorus pays tribute to President Roosevelt:

> Oil, oil, oil has got us in its toil,
> But Teddy says the trusts have got to go;
> And when this man behind, gets a thing
> set in his mind,
> You can bet your bottom dollar 'twill
> be so.

It had been more than forty years since John D. Rockefeller had first invested his savings in an oil refinery. No astrologer back in 1862 would have dared to predict the unbelievable figures to which Rockefeller's fortune would mount by the turn of the twentieth century. But he had chosen an industry in which the qualities of ruthlessness, shrewdness, and derring-do could lift a man to the top, even though at times it might destroy him in the end. Oil was the gambler's blue chip, and with nerve and luck he might win a fabulous pot.

The daring speculator in oil in those early days of the 1860's was the embodiment of an imaginary character known as "Coal Oil Johnny," the symbol of sudden, flaring wealth, which might at almost any instant be succeeded by abject poverty as his balloon collapsed. "Coal Oil Johnny" inspired John Brougham to write a number which he called "Coal Oil Tommy," and which he inserted in his drama of the 1860's, *The Lottery of Life*.

Irish-born Brougham, had, in his youth, gone to England, where he became an actor, song writer, playwright, and eventually theater owner. Having less executive than acting ability, he soon lost his Lyceum Theatre and in the late 1840's decided to come to America. Here he wrote, produced and acted in a number of successful plays. His lyrics for "Coal Oil Tommy" were set to the well-known melody of "Champagne Charlie," by an English composer, Alfred Lee.

> I've come from Pennsylvania some city life to see, and
> You may bet your boots, I'll have the biggest kind
> of spree, with
> My pockets stuffed with greenbacks and a skin full
> of rye,
> Amongst the oyster cellar swells a jolly boy am I.

Upon the road I drive the very spiciest of drags
Behind a pair of thoroughbred four thousand dollar nags,
That didn't allow me never to take no one elses dust,
I'd sell them both for oatmeal if they wer'nt always
    first.
CHORUS: And Coal Oil Tommy is my name, Coal Oil Tommy is my name,
    Good for any game tonight my boys, Good for any game
      tonight my boys.
    Coal Oil Tommy is my name, Coal Oil Tommy is my name,
    Good for any game tonight my boys, Hi! Ten strike
      set 'em up again.

Except for the fact that Tommy and John D. were oilmen, they bore no resemblance to each other. Rockefeller started out in 1855 as a Cleveland bookkeeper at a salary of twenty-five dollars a month. He was frugal; his savings went into a produce commission firm, which by 1862 had brought him enough to invest four thousand dollars in a small "oil refining" business.

As the antithesis of Coal Oil Tommy, he reverenced order as much as he revered the church. He despised gambling, and he despised something else too—competition. By 1870, Rockefeller's name was synonymous with the word "oil," at least as far as Cleveland was concerned. But of course, Cleveland was only his jumping-off-point.

His business acumen was overwhelming; his ruthless methods to achieve complete control of his industry were destructive to anyone or any company who strove to bar his progress. To achieve his objective of cornering the market in the distribution of oil, he had to be able to deliver the product cheaper than his competitors could. This goal was attained in 1872 by the formation of a Pennsylvania corporation, the South Improvement Company (Rockefeller and his associates were major stockholders), to deal with the railroads in the transportation of oil.

The corporation entered into contracts with the major carriers, stipulating "that the party of the second part (the railroad company) will pay and allow to the party of the first part (South Improvement Company) . . . rebates." And herein lay much of Rockefeller's success in accumulating great wealth; here was his overriding advantage over his competitors.

Now, it was not unusual in that period for railroads to arrange for special terms to favored customers. There were various means of achieving such sought-after consideration. Bullying, gentle persuasion, gifts of stock to railroad officials, and other tactics alternated with a pooling of railroad and corporate interests. The South Improvement Company used them all.

They went even further—and here is where they overstepped the bounds of whatever propriety that contract with the railroads could have claimed. For one of its additional clauses read: ". . . and on all oil transported for others, drawbacks." In other words, Standard Oil's competitors paid the railroads full transportation rates, but a percentage of these charges was credited, not to these shippers, but to the South Improvement Company.

It was only a short time before other oilmen learned of the unfair advantages accruing to South Improvement. They descended on the Pennsylvania legislature with such a storm of protests that the charter of the company was repealed; but during the forty days of its brief existence it had undermined the spirit of a large number of independent oil refiners, who realized that they could not play Mr. Rockefeller's game. By the end of 1872, Standard Oil absorbed twenty of the twenty-six refining firms in the Cleveland area. Within the next few years the volume of Standard Oil's refinery business grew enormously; by the 1880's they controlled 90 per cent of the industry in the United States.

The word "trust" soon appeared in newspapers and in speeches by various statesmen. The oil refining operations of Standard Oil were, naturally, so classified. In 1890 and 1892 the courts of New York State and Ohio ruled that trust agreements, which tended to create monopolies, were contrary to law, and in 1892 the Standard Oil Trust was dissolved.

One state did cater to the trustlike structures—New Jersey—and Rockefeller was quick to take advantage of this situation. In 1894 he had incorporated his business under New Jersey laws; and from 1899 on, the parent company operated out of that state. In that year the charter of the Standard Oil Company of New Jersey was amended; its capital was increased more than ten times the former declared value, and its stock substituted for that of the remains of the old Standard Oil Trust and twenty of its constituents.

Other affiliates operated under their own names. The Standard Oil Company of Ohio, formed originally in 1870, remained theoretically independent, as did Standard Oil companies in Indiana, Kentucky, and elsewhere.

It was all peaches and cream until Theodore Roosevelt ascended to the presidency. He proceeded with caution at the outset, as if he could not make up his mind as to whether or not trusts and holding companies were basically injurious to the country's welfare. But once he had decided that the Sherman Antitrust Act of 1890 (which stated that every combination in restraint of trade is illegal) was being flagrantly violated, his course was set. He pursued big business relentlessly; and the bigger the business, the more determined was his pursuit of it. Standard Oil as an entity appeared doomed to destruction.

Two enactments of Congress, the Elkins Act of 1903 and the Hepburn Act of 1906, dealt with abuses of big business, one of the most flagrant of which was the matter of rebates still being given by railroads to favored shippers. Hardly had a Missouri affiliate of Standard Oil been fined more than $1,000,000 for violating the antitrust law when a new, and far more spectacular, case set the company back on its heels.

The Chicago and Alton Railroad was a prime carrier of oil for the Standard Oil Company of Indiana. Conclusive proof was introduced to indicate that the railroad, in violation of the Elkins Act, accepted from the shipper the sum of six cents per hundredweight, whereas the published and correct charge was eighteen cents. Forty-one-year-old Judge Landis, presiding at the jury trial in Chicago, was a new federal appointee, a hotheaded liberal who was irritated by Rockefeller's attempts to avoid being obliged to testify. The jury brought in a verdict of guilty against the company, whereupon Landis resorted to arithmetic. Fourteen hundred and sixty-two carloads of oil had been shipped over the Alton Railroad at the six cent per hundredweight price; Landis levied a fine of $20,000 per carload, which added up to the figure stated at the beginning of this article, $29,240,000.

On the morning that Landis announced his decision, old John D. was golfing with friends on his Forest Hills estate. A messenger came tearing across the fairway and put a note into Rockefeller's hand. It contained the bad news. Rockefeller read it, and then said calmly: "Well, shall we go on, gentlemen?" His next shot sailed one hundred and sixty yards toward the hole. When one of his foursome bolstered up courage at the next hole and asked, "How much is it?" the old man replied, "The maximum penalty, I believe. It is your honor. Will you gentlemen drive?"

The result was highly satisfying to most of the people of the country. Vincent Bryan, one of the better song writers of the day, gave much of the credit to Roosevelt. In "Theodore," a song he wrote in 1907, he says:

> I've travelled all around the world. I've
>   sailed on every sea;
> Met ev'ry king and potentate; including
>   old John D.
>
> . . . .
>
> But there's a ruler greater still; no doubt
>   you've heard his name

CHORUS: It's Theodore, the peaceful Theodore;
         Of all the rulers great or small
         He is the greatest of them all.

And farther along:

         Not long ago the railroads owned the whole
             United States,
         Their rates were high to farmers, but a
             trust could get rebates.
         Who stopped this crime of freight rebates
             among the railroad men?
         Who fixed it so the railroads carry people
             now and then?[1]
         CHORUS

As a footnote to what appeared to be a crushing blow to Standard Oil, it should be noted that the company appealed the decision. A year later, when another judge in the federal circuit court found that Landis had erred and ordered a retrial, Judge Anderson instructed the jury that "the government has failed to prove its charge." The verdict was "not guilty"; the government had to pay the costs. Roosevelt was furious, but helpless.

Landis was to achieve a new form of publicity nearly a score of years later, when he was chosen to be organized baseball's first commissioner (or czar).

And Rockefeller lived for another twenty-nine years. When he died in 1927, he was nearly ninety-nine years old. Roosevelt had been dead for eighteen years. Of the enormous fortune that old John D. had accumulated, hundreds of millions had gone into charitable enterprises. Science and medicine are his eternal debtors. And though of course he couldn't realize it, he was following the admonition of those young song writers who back in 1907 had advised him

         Now come dear John and sin no more
         Bestow your shekels on the poor.

"Get on the Raft with Taft"

HE WAS NOT THE SORT of candidate to stimulate wild enthusiasm among the electorate. He was quiet, courtly, considerate. The song writers did their best to help rouse the great mass of people who had remained enthusiastic Teddy Roosevelt fans. Among the most widely sung of the campaign songs for the big man from Ohio was one by the team of Abe Holzman and Harry

[1] "Theodore." W/M Vincent Bryan. Copyright 1907 by Shapiro, Bernstein & Co. Inc. 666 Fifth Avenue, New York, N.Y. 10019. Copyright Renewed and Assigned. USED BY PERMISSION.

D. Kerr, "Get on the Raft With Taft." To Holzman's catchy martial music, Kerr wrote:

2. The greatest man that ever ran the greatest land on earth
   Is Teddy R., whose shining star is only in it's birth.
   We'd like some more of Theodore, but Theodore has said,
   That TAFT was meant for President to follow in his stead.
   CHORUS

3. His running mate's from New York state, we'll all give him
        a hand;
   Our votes he'll get, and you can bet the second place he'll
        land.
   Jim Sherman's square and always fair, in due respect to him,
   All democrats must doff their hats to dear old "Sunny Jim."
   CHORUS

4. Of Bryan's bluff we've had enough, he'd talk you deaf and
        blind,
   The million trusts he's goin' to bust are only in his mind.
   Seems he has run since Washington first started in the game,
   If his legs were gone, he'd keep right on a running just the
        same.
   CHORUS

        The time has come, the fight is on,
        We've picked the man to run;
        For President, Ohio sent her noble, worthy son.
        The man we need, the man to lead
        Our strong and mighty craft,
        Through storm and sea, to victory,
        Is William Howard Taft.

   CHORUS: Get on the raft with Taft, boys
           Get in the winning boat,
           The man worth while, with the big glad smile,
           Will get the honest vote.
           We'll save the country sure, boys
           From Bryan, Hearst and graft;
           So all join in, we're sure to win!
           Get on the raft with Taft.[2]

---

[2] "Get on the Raft with Taft." W/Harry D. Kerr M/Abe Holzman. Copyright © 1912, Renewed 1940 LEO FEIST INC. Used by Permission.

Then, to let the hosts of Roosevelt admirers know that the song's sentiments did not imply any desertion from the acknowledged leader, Kerr's second verse proclaimed:

> The greatest man that ever ran
> The greatest land on earth
> Is Teddy R., whose shining Star
> Is only in its birth
> We'd like some more of Theodore
> But Theodore has said,
> That Taft was meant for President
> To follow in his stead.

Oh, and one more slap at the opposition:

> Of Bryan's bluff we've had enough,
> He'd talk you deaf and blind.
> The million trusts he's goin' to bust
> Are only in his mind.
> Seems he has run since Washington
> First started in the game
> If his legs were gone, he'd keep right on
> A-running just the same.

William Jennings Bryan, a fighter to the end, had already been knocked out in his first two bouts, once in 1896 and again in 1900. Here he was, up for the third time and as cocky as ever. One of his admirers, an Illinoisan named S. M. Hawk, produced a good song for his idol:

> He's an orator, a scholar too,
> A man whose every aim
> The best things for our country will assure.
> When banks are run on plans he drew
> All honor to his name
> Our money will at all times be secure

> CHORUS: Billy Bryan is the lion of the hour
> In the hearts of all the people is his power
> As the moments come and go while he travels
>   to and fro
> The clouds upon his welcome never lower.
> He will lead his hosts to battle in the fray
> And it's ten to one that he will win the day
> For our Teddy says he's out and there's no one
>   else about
> Who can hope such pop-u-lar-i-ty to stay.

Bryan's plans for operating the banks were several decades ahead of his time, as will be noted later. And as for there being no other successor to Teddy, Roosevelt himself had the last word. But first things first.

And first of all, Taft did not want the highest honor. He was a lawyer by profession, a judge before he was thirty. The law was his true love; and to him the pinnacle to which he aspired was the chief justiceship of the Supreme Court of the United States, a goal which he was eventually to achieve twenty odd years after his calls to service in other branches of the federal government.

After the electorate of Ohio had endorsed him for a full term in the Superior Court of Cincinnati, to which he had been appointed in 1886, his climb to the presidency involved no further vote getting until the big show-down on November 3, 1908. The rungs on Taft's presidential ladder began with his appointment as solicitor general in 1890, as a judge on the federal circuit court, and then, to his consternation, as a commissioner to the Philippine Islands to help bring order out of the chaos existing as an after-math of the Spanish-American War. This post, which Taft filled so ably, led in turn to that of governor general of the Philippines, and then, under Roosevelt to an important cabinet post as Secretary of War, succeeding Elihu Root.

Roosevelt held Taft in the highest esteem. The extent of this regard is exemplified in a letter he wrote to Taft in 1903 before the latest appointment. "If there were only three of you. Then I would have one of you in the Supreme Court, . . . one of you in Root's place as Secretary of War, . . . and one of you permanently Governor of the Philippines." In fact, there could well have been three of him, had he been divided physically—three thin fellows, true. For Taft in December, 1905, as Secretary of War, was close to being a monstrosity, tipping the scales at 326 pounds.

A few weeks later Taft and his wife were dinner guests of President Roosevelt in the White House. After dinner the president led them to the library, dropped into an easy chair, closed his eyes, and intoned: "I am the seventh son of a seventh daughter and I have clairvoyant powers. I see a man weighing three hundred and fifty pounds. There is something hanging over his head. I cannot make out what it is . . . . At one time it looks like the presidency, then again it looks like the chief justiceship."

"Make it the presidency," said Mrs. Taft.

"Make it the chief justiceship," this from Mr. Taft.

In 1908 he was Roosevelt's hand-picked choice for succession to the presidency. But Taft was by no means as yet assured of his party's faithful support, and defections occurred among dissident groups. One faction, in order to alienate the Jewish vote, claimed that Taft had shown traces of anti-semitism. Another attempted to estrange the Negroes by citing his action in punishing severely a black battalion for unpardonable conduct in a riot which occurred while he was Secretary of War. The military men in the party were reminded that Taft had insulted one of their idols, General Ulysses S. Grant, by remarking in a Memorial Day speech that Grant was addicted to strong drink. But there was no single strong opponent of Taft's to make a fight on the floor of the Republican National Convention when it met in Chicago, so Taft, Roosevelt's man, was nominated on the first ballot.

This action stimulated some song writers to put forth their best efforts, which, unfortunately, were not of high quality this time. The most widely sung was a work by Monroe Rosenfeld, the lyricist, and "Rosie Lloyd," the composer. Rosie Lloyd's name does not appear elsewhere in the popular music field, and could well have been a pseudonym used by Rosenfeld, who was one of the most prolific song writers of the period. His great successes include "Take Back Your Gold," "Those Wedding Bells Shall Not Ring Out," and other tearjerkers of the gay nineties. But Rosenfeld, if such "Lloyd" really was, in Taft's day was an older and soberer fellow, as witness his lyrics in "B-I-Double L-Bill":

> Thro' the land ringing grand
> Is a name known to fame, that we all love, so dear!
> And we stand, hand in hand,
> At his loyal command, his noble cause to cheer!
> So for our statesman let us all fall into line,
> He's the man that we want in Nineteen Nine!
> And we'll sail on the raft, crowded down fore and aft,
> For our good ——— Bill ——— Taft!

> CHORUS: B-I-Double L-Bill! Good, old honest Bill!
> He's the Bill to start each mill,
> And we'll have him, yes we will!
> He'll get in for the next four years,
> Let's all give him three hearty cheers!
> B-I-Double L-Bill, Taft's no counterfeit Bill![3]

The second verse is slightly more inane.

Then came another entry, this one by J. M. Hagan, and called "Step Into Line for Taft," with a by-line, "A Continuation of the Big Stick and Square Deal Policy." The words of the verse, with the elimination of Taft's name, could almost be number 87 in a Methodist hymnal:

---

[3] "B-I-Double L-Bill." © copyright E. B. MARKS MUSIC CORPORATION. Used by Permission.

Step into line for Taft, boys, hold fast the
    winning hand,
Shout, in his name advancing, 'We shall possess
    the land!'
Rally from plain and mountain, Tho' falt'ring
    hosts oppose;
Raise high the flag victorious, over the fallen
    foes.

CHORUS: Step into line, boys, Taft shall be our song;
    Stand by the leader of the conq'ring throng,
    Step into line, there's vict'ry in the air;
    We'll place our leader in the Presidential
    chair.

But Bryan elicited enthusiasm from his own followers. One of them, Geo.
W. Gale, dedicated to "The Great Commoner" his "Line Up for Bryan, the
Battle Song of Democracy." It went like this:

Like the rolling of the thunder echoes loud the
    battle song,
'Tis sung throughout the nation with a chorus
    good and strong,
We are coming from the mountain and we're coming
    from the plain,
From village, town and city you can hear the
    grand refrain.

CHORUS: Line up for Bryan, boys, that's the battle cry,
    Line up for Bryan, how the fur will fly.
    There's a hot time coming in the sweet bye and bye
    When we line up for Bryan in the morning.

A determined lady song writer from Pennsylvania, Mrs. Annie Bassett,
minced no words in her endorsement for "Our Good and Honest Taft":

There's a war-cry from Chicago that's spread unto
    the sea,
A summons to the battle for the gallant and the
    free.
Yet a battle without bloodshed and a fight all free
    of graft,
The battle of the voters for our good and honest Taft.

There was blood in our election in the time of
    shall and shan't,
When we feared to vote for Lincoln and we risked
    our lives for Grant.

Now we cast the ballot fearing nothing more than
    autumn rain,
And our peace will grow more peaceful under Taft
    whom 'tis said shall reign.

CHORUS: Thank God that we are freemen
            And can vote for whom we will
            We spread our starry banner
            Freely forth from dome and hill.
            Hurrah then for our freedom
            Let us cheer him with a will,
            The man though slated president
            Is just a plain man still.

Indeed, Taft was just a plain man, but Bryan—there was a different breed. Bryan was an individualist, a moralist who romanticized as he sermonized. And he was bursting with ideas to protect and to strengthen the economy. As a superb politician, he realized he must capture the minds of the public by presenting issues—issues that they could be persuaded were in the country's best interests. In his 1896 campaign, and again in 1900, the issue had been the free coinage of silver. In 1908 he tried new approaches. He plugged for strict governmental control of the railroads. And he sought for a means to prevent any recurrence in the immediate or distant future of the panic of 1907 when the public's confidence in the national banks had been badly shaken.

Bryan proposed a solution much like the one adopted twenty-five years later when Franklin Roosevelt assumed the presidency; he advocated the imposition of a tax on national banks and on any state institution endorsing his idea in order to set up an insurance fund to guarantee the safety of bank deposits. In 1933 FDR's proposal was welcomed with enthusiasm. But in 1908, while there appeared to be widespread endorsement for the idea, Teddy and Taft were flatly opposed to it on the ground that an enactment would require strong, solid banking establishments to support those which were weak or recklessly managed. The Republicans had alternative propositions which struck many of the public as far less attractive. Nevertheless, the issue was not sufficiently pressing to sway a majority of the electorate into Bryan's camp, and Taft was able to ride on Roosevelt's coattails, despite his opponent's colorful image as contrasted with his own paler one.

Bryan continued his strenuous efforts, and as late as September his followers entertained high hopes. Samuel Gompers, the powerful leader of organized labor, had endorsed the Democratic candidate, and he and the unions which he controlled offered formidable opposition to Taft.

They attacked his early record of supposedly antilabor actions when he served on the federal circuit court. They pointed to an instance in 1894 when he imposed a six-months prison term on a labor leader who had instigated a railway rebellion, and they pointed to several of his decisions which appeared to be against the interest of labor.

Taft had no apologies to make. At a big Chicago meeting of railway trade organizations he explained and defended his decisions; and he vowed that if the same problems were presented to him again he would take the same sort of action as before.

And the song writers kept his name before the people, as in this offering of Rudolph Aronson, "The Man of the Hour," whose title page, embellished with an almost life-size portrait of the candidate, proclaimed that the brisk march and two-step was "respectfully dedicated to the Hon. William Howard Taft."

> Our leader we hail, and from mountain and vale,
> We are rallying for Taft the nation's choice.
> With true honest might, he is firm in the Right,
> And we pledge to him a loyal heart and voice!
> The proud ship of State he will soon navigate,
> And of good old solid statesmen he's the flow'r!
> From sea unto sea, Taft our choice e'er shall be
> For Bill Taft is the man of the hour!

Roosevelt was his coach, suggesting subjects for campaign speeches, even advising him how to show off any athletic prowess for the eager press photographers. Teddy, who was a tennis buff, would warn Taft, who was a golf buff, when to invite the photographers to snap him in action. Said T. R., "On horseback, yes; tennis, no, and golf is fatal."

The big man had no difficulties on November 3, 1908. He beat Bryan by a million and a quarter votes; the electoral ballot gave him a two-to-one victory over the Democrat. Little did he surmise that in four years time he would be utterly degraded in his attempt to succeed himself, and that with the exception of Utah and Vermont, who together were good for eight electoral votes, he would be deserted by his countrymen from coast to coast. This was a shameful way to treat a future chief justice of the Supreme Court!

"We Take Our Hats Off to You, Mr. Wilson"

The title of this song will soon have little or no meaning to the great majority of Americans. This is not because the average young person will

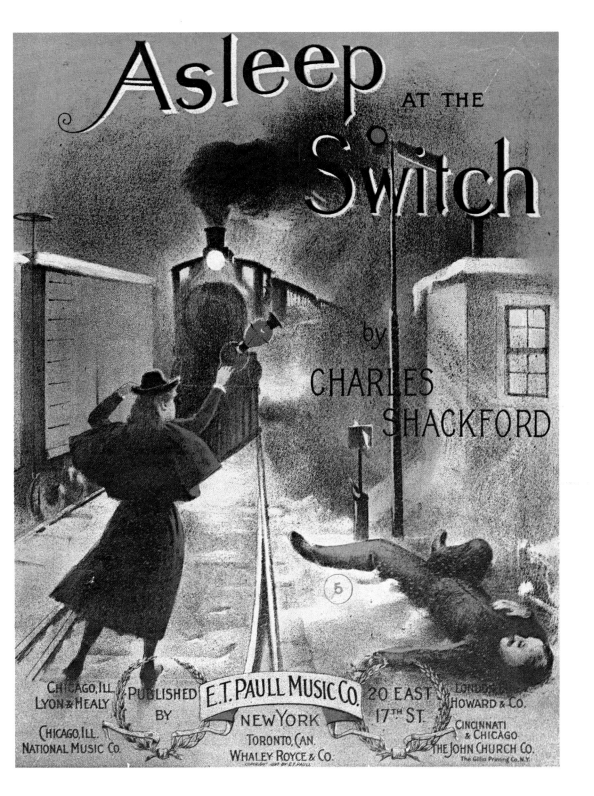

WE TAKE OUR HATS OFF TO YOU - MR. WILSON

Words and Music *By* BLANCHE MERRILL

PORTRAIT OF MR. WILSON USED BY PERMISSION

Published by LEO FEIST, Inc., New York

5

not know who Mr. Wilson was; rather, it is because most of them don't know what a hat is. And furthermore, unused to the quaint customs of past generations, those who are aware that some old fogies go around in things called hats won't understand why one should take his off, after he puts it on—except when he goes indoors. But we old fogies know that the removing of the hat in the presence of a distinguished personage is a mark of the greatest respect; and in 1914 practically every American was full of respect for his high-minded, intellectual, peace-loving president.

World War I burst upon Europe in midsummer 1914. The people of the United States were horrified. Many first- or second-generation Americans could not refrain from partisan feelings for the country of their ancestry. But the president kept a strong grip on his and his nation's emotions, and he steered his course to keep free of foreign entanglements.

Among his most fervent admirers were the song writers, who were soon translating the president's policies into musical idiom. The first to produce a real hit was a girl by the name of Blanche Merrill, who was later to furnish material to such stage stars as Fanny Brice, Nora Bayes, Eva Tanguay, and Willie Howard. A few weeks after Sarajevo Miss Merrill, not yet out of her teens, wrote the words and music of a song which catapulted into popularity almost overnight.

2. Your Uncle Sam is mighty proud,
   He's proud he picked you from the crowd,
   He's proud that you have shown the world your worth;
   You've sought peace with ev'ry nation,
   Steered us through all tribulation,
   And made our land the greatest land on earth.
   You've set up a standard for the world,
   The flag of peace you've unfurl'd.
   Chorus

    Greater than a gladiator, you're the world's
      big mediator, . . .
    We'd trust you in any kind of fuss,
    We're glad you belong to us.

Chorus: We take our hats off to you, Mister Wilson,
    Our hats are off to you,
    You're the man of the hour, you've stood
      like a tower,
    And know what to do for the red, white and
      blue.
    You're the right kind of man in the right
      kind of place,

> Like Washington and Lincoln you've set a pace;
> They know at home and abroad
> Your pen is greater than a sword,
> We take our hats off to you.[4]

The president made a powerful appeal to the nation, warning all Americans against any breach of neutrality, and ending his plea with "Shall we not resolve to put upon ourselves the restraint which will bring to our people the happiness and the great and lasting influence for peace we covet for them?"

His words so touched a Chicago song writer, W. R. Williams, that he immediately translated them into music and verse in "We Stand for Peace While Others War." Prefacing the song with a note stating "This 'Peace Poem' was inspired by President Wilson's appeal to Americans to remain neutral in thought and deed," Williams wrote:

> We stand for peace, while others war,
> Tho' war we know is sin;
> But Uncle Sam's a neutral power,
> And we must stand by him.
> We can't take sides—for all the world
> Will suffer for this wrong,
> And we'll pray that every nation
> Right their wrongs by arbitration,
> And that "Home Sweet Home" will be
>   their National Song.[5]

During the first months of the conflict, other song writers adopted a similar vein. The team of Casper Nathan and F. Henri Klickmann contributed "Uncle Sam Won't Go to War":

> Uncle Sam won't go to war,
> That's not what the U.S. got united for.
> Let all Europe fight, if they must,
> But the Yankee motto is, "In God we Trust."
> When war clouds roll by once more,
> Things will be the same as before
> Our country's always free, [tune of "My Country
>   'Tis of Thee"]
> No matter what may be,
> Uncle Sam won't go to war.[6]

---

[4] "We Take Our Hats Off to You Mr. Wilson." W/M Blanche Merrill Copyright © 1914, Renewed 1942 LEO FEIST INC. Used by Permission.

[5] "We Stand for Peace While Others War." Copyright © 1914 by Will Rossiter. Copyright renewed 1941. Used by Permission.

[6] "Uncle Sam Won't Go to War." Copyright MCMXIV, Frank K. Root & Co. U.S. Copyright Renewed MCMXLII. Copyright assigned to Shawnee Press, Inc., Delaware Water Gap, Pa. 18327. International Copyright Secured. All Rights Reserved. Used by Permission.

Into 1915 the hopes for peace still prevailed. In that year the greatest of the antiwar songs appeared. It was "I Didn't Raise My Boy to Be a Soldier." The work of two veterans of tin-pan alley, Alfred Bryan and Al Piantadosi, the smart melody was matched with passionately appealing lyrics:

I heard a mother murmur thro' her tears:

CHORUS: I didn't raise my boy to be a soldier,
I brought him up to be my pride and joy,
Who dares to place a musket on his shoulder,
To shoot some other mother's darling boy?
Let nations arbitrate their future troubles,
It's time to lay the sword and gun away,
There'd be no war today, if mothers all would say,
"I didn't raise my boy to be a soldier."[7]

But soon came horrible misgivings. The steamship *Lusitania* was sunk by a German submarine; well over a hundred Americans went down with her. As might have been expected, there was introduced at once a new song, "When the *Lusitania* Went Down," and the nation's hopes for peace began to dim. Another well-known writer, A. Seymour Brown, expressed the confidence of the people in their president's decisions, offering as his contribution "Go Right Along Mister Wilson."

Go right along Mister Wilson,
We're all for you strong;
You speak for us as a nation,
And we're for the nation right or wrong,
In war or peace it's just the same,
We'll leave that up to you.
We know that you will do the best that
can be done,
For it is one for all; and all are for
that one,
And so you go right along Mister Wilson,
And we'll all stand by you.[8]

In December, 1915, Wilson, a widower, was married to the vivacious Mrs. Edith Galt; and one team of song writers, Thomas Hoier and Jimmie Morgan, seized the occasion to promote the president's candidacy for a second term. They wrote "Four Years More in the White House":

[7] "I Didn't Raise My Boy to Be a Soldier." W/Alfred Bryan, M/Al Piantadosi Copyright © 1915, Renewed 1943 LEO FEIST INC. Used by Permission.

[8] "Go Right Along Mr. Wilson." W/M A. Seymour Brown © 1915 Jerome H. Remick & Co., Copyright Renewed. All Rights Reserved. Used by Permission WARNER BROS. MUSIC.

Come on, ev'rybody, come on ev'ryone.
I'll tell you 'bout the wedding, down in
    Washington.
Our President was married, by the altar took
    his stand,
With a true blue Yankee beauty, First lady
    in the land.

CHORUS: So here's to you, Mister Wilson!
    Here's to your lovely bride!
    When you were marching to the altar,
    The nation marched right by your side.
    You've kept us out of trouble,
    You've been faithful and true blue,
    And four more years in the White House
    Should be the nation's wedding gift to you.[9]

Despite the increasing problems of foreign blockades, of outrageous meddling in American affairs of state, and of constant threats to American shipping, most of the country still struggled to refrain from conflict. The song writers were still, for the most part, on the side of peace and staunchly behind the president's efforts to preserve it. In 1916, Al Dubin, a youngster who would become one of our most popular lyricists within a few years, joined forces with Jos. A. Burke, another talented youngster, and George B. McConnell, to acknowledge Wilson's greatness. In a song called "The Hero of the European War," Dubin wrote:

If you're English or German or French,
And your heart's 'cross the sea in a trench,
While you're sympathizing, you wonder who'll be
The hero of the biggest war in history.
When the guns are laid away, and Peace has come
    to stay,
Whose name will be famous that day?

CHORUS: Is it Hindenburg or Joffre
    Who will wear a hero's crown?
    Who will be the one, just like Washington,
    When the European war is done.
    In my mind there's just one hero,
    Woodrow Wilson's name will live forever more,
    For there's no doubt of it, he kept us out of it,
    And he's the hero of the European War.

[9] "Four Years More in the White House." W/M Thomas Hoier & Jimmy Morgan. Copyright © 1916, Renewed 1943 LEO FEIST INC. Used by Permission.

135

But the rumblings of discontent with the president's efforts to preserve neutrality grew louder, despite the appeals of leaders to refrain from violent action. A plea from another song writer, John P. Hall, to support Wilson, in "Don't forget That He's Your President," admonished:

Don't forget that Woodrow Wilson is your president,
And he fills that honored chair
Where Washington and Lincoln sat
At least let your judgment be fair.
Love ev'rything that is American
Thank the Lord for the blessings He has sent,
Stick to the old Red, White and Blue,
Stick to Mr. Wilson, too
Don't forget that he's your president.

And yet there was a tremendous amount of uneasiness around the nation, among people who were fearful that we would be drawn into the fighting. Some song writers believed we should be prepared for that eventuality. In 1916, George Graff, Jr. and Jack Glogau expressed such thoughts in "Wake Up, America!"

Have we forgotten, America, the battles our
    fathers fought?
Are we ashamed of our history in the peace
    that fighting brought?
Must we be laughed at, America, while our
    swords turn weak with rust?
Is the blood of our fathers wasted? And how
    have we treated their trust?
Is Columbia the gem of the ocean? Is Old Glory
    the pride of the Free?
Let's forget ev'ry selfish emotion, United
    forever let's be!

CHORUS: Wake up, America
    If we are called to war,
    Are we prepared to give our lives for our
        sweethearts and our wives?
    Are our mothers and our homes worth fighting
        for?
    Let us pray, God, for peace, but peace with
        honor,
    But let's get ready to answer duty's call,

> So when Old Glory stands unfurled, let it
> mean to all the world,
> America is ready, that's all.[10]

In the 1916 election the president ran on his record with the slogan, "He kept us out of war." It was one of the closest presidential races in the nation's history. Wilson appeared to have suffered defeat until the late returns from the Pacific Coast states brought in a tremendous popular vote for him, and assured him of reelection. Fresh songs in support of the president burst forth. One bore the title, "Be Good to California, Mr. President, California Has Been Good to You." Another, "Once More He Is Our President," by a writer named Billy Repaid, sang:

> We've prospered under him as ne'er before.
> Peace and contentment reach from shore to
> shore,
> Under his administration we've become a
> wealthy nation,
> There are many things that we should thank
> him for.
> We could show appreciation in one way,
> You bet we did it on election day.

> CHORUS: Let's shout "hooray" for Woodrow Wilson,
> He is the man the country needs,
> He kept us out of war, that's what we're
> thankful for,
> He's prov'd the man that's right, always
> succeeds.
> That's why we gave him a second term in
> office,
> We knew his time would be well spent,
> Tho' New York went strong for Hughes,
> Woodrow Wilson couldn't lose,
> Once more he is our President.

But the end of neutrality was plainly in sight. Just a month after Wilson's second inauguration, he stood before Congress and asked for a declaration of war. With only three congressional objectors, the president received the backing of his legislative body, and the United States became a full-fledged ally of England and France.

Immediately the popular music of the country took on martial tones. George M. Cohan led the parade with "Over There." Irving Berlin's offer-

---

[10] "Wake up America." W/George Groff, M/Jack Glogau Copyright ©1916, Renewed 1944 LEO FEIST INC. Used by Permission.

ing was "It's Your Country and My Country," and an old musical war horse, Andrew B. Sterling, teamed with Arthur Lange to produce one of his best numbers, "America, Here's My Boy." Sterling's "brave mother" speaks:

America, I raised a boy for you,
America, you'll find him staunch and true,
Place a gun upon his shoulder,
He is ready to die or do.
America, he is my only one;
My hope, my pride and joy,
But if I had another, he would march beside
    his brother:
America, here's my boy.[11]

Woodrow Wilson's dream of keeping his country free from entangling alliances had vanished. Today there are people who regard him as a visionary rather than a realist. Some contend that America would have brought World War I to an earlier and less sanguinary end if we had declared war on Germany immediately after the *Lusitania* was sunk, as Theodore Roosevelt demanded. But such observations are moot today. Wilson could not have been called a pragmatist. On the other hand he remains as one of the most idealistic of America's presidents.

[11] "America, Here's My Boy." W/Andrew B. Sterling M/Arthur Lange © Copyright 1917 by Edwin H. Morris & Company, Inc. copyright renewed and assigned to Edwin H. Morris & Company, Inc. Used by Permission.

4

THE LADIES, GOD BLESS 'EM

"Oh! You Suffragettes"

THE NINETY-FIRST CONGRESS, passing out of existence with the expiration of the year 1970, took an action in that year which indicated its confidence in American youth. With scarcely any political skirmishing it gave all American citizens from eighteen to twenty-one the right to vote in federal elections.

To those young people, and to their parents too, it would have been startling to realize—had they stopped to think about it—that for nearly three-quarters of our country's two-hundred-year-old history, their female ancestors were denied the privilege that was accorded these youngsters at the first go-around.

It is true that in a few state elections women were qualified to enter a ballot box; but no *presidential* ballot bore a feminine X mark until after the great knockdown, drag-out fight in which the antisuffragists were finally kayoed in 1920. It was a long, hard struggle, dating all the way back to the eighteen forties, when women whose names were later mentioned with reverence—Susan B. Anthony, Elizabeth Cady Stanton, Lucretia Mott, Lucy Stone—first let their country know that, in their opinion, they were not getting a fair shake.

These brave girls and their successor generations eventually achieved some of their goals; toward the end of the nineteenth century a handful of western states agreed that there was reason to their demands, and acceded to them. Not until after the freed male slaves had gotten the franchise under the Fifteenth Amendment were women allowed to vote, first in Wyoming territory, then in Colorado, Idaho, and Utah; still later in Illinois, Montana, and Nevada.

The writers of popular songs, which mirrored the country's political undulations and other foibles, paid little heed to the battle for universal suffrage. Occasionally, in the mid-1800's, a humorous ballad on the subject would emerge. For example, in 1876 there appeared a song called "Rights of Ladies," with words by Dennis McFlinn, the pseudonym of a writer named A. G. Weeks, and music by a mysterious composer known only as "Van." This was the period when Irish immigrants were considered the most ignorant of the new arrivals into the United States; so to make a real burlesque of the issue, the verses were written in an Irish dialect to point up the ridiculous theory that any stupid woman would have the opportunity to vote if suffrage went bisexual—and even to be elected to office.

> Hurrah! for the good time a comin,
> Whin ladies shall vote like the men,
> Och, wont the people be a bloomin,
> Wid fithers and crinoline thin.
> Election day thin I am thinkin
> Will be the great day of the year,
> Whin lasses and lads will be drinkin
> Together the candidates beer.
>
> An thin whin we mate in convention,
> The ladies of course will be there,
> An' maybe somebody will mintion,
> Me Biddy to sit in the chair.
> An' maybe for office select her,
> Wid four or five dollars a day
> It's meself twould vote to elect her
> An put in me pocket the pay.
> An' thin whin election approaches
> An' the lasses are marchin' the street
> Wid big bands of music and torches,
> An' Biddy asthanding the trate;
> I'll be on the sidewalk hurrahin'
> For me own darlin' Biddy McFlinn,
> Wid a chile in me arms, an drawin'
> A cab wid another one in.
>
> An' whin all the votin' is over,
> An' Biddy's elected, shure thin
> I'll live like a pig in the clover
> Wid Honorable Misses McFlinn.

After the turn of the twentieth century, new, dynamic leadership inspired the ladies to launch more vigorous efforts than ever. British-born Dr. Anna Howard Shaw, minister, author, and doctor of medicine, was the most gifted orator of the woman suffrage movement. President of the suffrage association for over ten years, her golden voice could carry through the length of the vastest halls, and her glowing phrases and gentle humor had an appeal that warmed the hearts of her audiences. Carrie Chapman Catt was born in the middle west, where she studied and taught. In 1890 she took up the cudgel for the National American Woman Suffrage Association, for which she organized and campaigned intensely.

In 1900, Susan B. Anthony, the pioneer leader of the movement, chose Mrs. Catt to follow her as president of the organization. When, four years later, Mrs. Catt surrendered the presidency, Dr. Shaw took over; and when she, in turn, stepped down in 1915, back came Mrs. Catt to see the women's battle fought to a successful conclusion on the floor of Congress, and to see the Nineteenth Amendment to the Constitution ratified by three-quarters of the states within a little over a year. The thirty-sixth and deciding state to endorse the amendment was Tennessee; the date was August 26, 1920, the greatest Ladies' Day in American history.

But for a number of years before that significant event the United States was treated to the sort of *Sturm und Drang* that only a group of militant women can summon up. The suffragettes—for that is the only printable name by which the ladies were known—were probably the most persistent peaceful hecklers this country has ever known. They picketed, they paraded, they prattled, and they posed problems to law-enforcing officers throughout the land. When should they be left alone, and when should they be arrested? When should they be challenged, and when ignored?

The woman who was most adept at mobilizing and directing the army of suffragettes was a quiet, frail young Quaker named Alice Paul. She had had a thorough indoctrination before demonstrating her skill at organizing a following. After attending Swarthmore College and the University of Pennsylvania, she went to England, where she continued her studies in history, politics, and sociology and where she submitted her doctoral thesis on the status of women. Just at this time (1912) the militant suffragists in England, led by Mrs. Emmeline Pankhurst, were demonstrating most violently, and the impressionable Miss Paul interrupted her studies to participate in their often unladylike activities and to go to prison with some of their leaders.

The phrase "Votes for Women" was adopted by the British Women's Social and Political Union in 1903, and shortly thereafter the English women had injected themselves forcefully, and often violently, into the political scene. They interrupted party meetings with impromptu speeches, intruded into the homes and offices of top-ranking statesmen, and they campaigned vigorously against candidates whom they believed to be unfriendly —Mr. Winston Churchill for one. Led by Mrs. Pankhurst and her two daughters, the women so aroused the ire of conservative male gatherings that they were manhandled, beaten, and jailed and were subjected to other indignities. Alice Paul was an early neophyte in the movement but soon became an activist and was subjected to arrest, forced feeding, and other punishments.

When she left England to return to the United States, she was convinced that the British suffragists were fighting for the women of the entire world, and she was determined to assume a militant attitude in this country to force it to acknowledge woman's rights to the franchise.

The publicity given the movement in England had so penetrated the press of this country that some of the popular song writers felt impelled to popularize it still further. In 1912 a team from New Jersey, J. J. Gallagher and B. A. Koellhoffer, took note of the English origin of the revived suffrage activity here in a song entitled "Oh! You Suffragettes."

2. They tell me America is the land free for all,
   And all that you need here is plenty of "gall."
   The spinsters o'er in London!
   They have plenty of that,
   And I think if they came here they would surely grow fat.
   I don't mind the girls showing plenty of grit,
   They may all wear our trousers as long as they fit,
   But if they are too stren'ous just make this your bet,
   They'll surely burst the trouser and then!
   Oh you Suffragettes.
   CHORUS

            I've come to America from the old mother soil,
            Where the suffragette spinsters are making
               things boil.

            . . . .
            I nearly was hazed,
            By Suffragettes in war paint who were hot on
               the scent,
            They took me for a member of the house of
               Parliament.

CHORUS: They're growing too strenuous by jingo,
These women on mischief are bent!
With brick bats they've smashed all the
windows
And raided the House of Parliament!
They're wearing men's collars and
shirt-fronts,
Less bashful are these sweet Coquettes;
They're after our votes, just as well as
our notes,
And our trousers! Oh! you Suffragettes!

The title page of the song pictures a parade of nice-looking girls, carrying a banner reading "Votes for Women." It would all appear sweet and peaceful except that in the background is a well-dressed lady heaving bricks through a plate-glass window.

Alice Paul did not approve of brick throwing, but she was a champion of every form of nonviolent action. In fact, she was entirely too energetic for the more conservative Dr. Shaw and Mrs. Catt. As chairman of the Congressional Committee of the National American Woman Suffrage Association, her report for 1913 jolted the older ladies. Whereas in the previous year the association had allocated ten dollars for work with Congress, the committee under the first year of Alice Paul's chairmanship expended twenty-seven *thousand* dollars! Shaw, Catt, and company decided that a time had come for a parting of the ways, and they so acted immediately. They took the high road and Miss Paul took the low road, forming an independent body known as the Congressional Union for Woman Suffrage.

The older women had grown fearful of Miss Paul's more aggressive methods ever since Woodrow Wilson had been inaugurated president in March, 1913. On the day before his inauguration, when he arrived at Union Station in Washington from New Jersey, he had looked around him and inquired, "Where are the people?" Back came a prompt reply, "On the Avenue watching the suffragists parade." The parade brought forth some fireworks. The women had obtained a permit to march, but the police protection proved inadequate; rowdies attacked the women, ten thousand in number, and all but broke up the peaceful demonstration. A short time later the chief of police was unostentatiously retired.

Within a few days, a deputation of suffragists, headed by Alice Paul, appeared before Wilson, soliciting his support for an equal suffrage bill. The president resorted to the time-honored run-around by promising, "This subject will receive my most careful consideration."

In 1914 there appeared a song by Lucenia W. Richards, a dedicated suffragist from Chicago—"Suffrage March," she called it simply. The title page depicts a calm-faced woman bearing a banner with the words "Universal Suffrage." On the back of the title page Miss Richards sets forth her message in stirring terms. Here is part of it:

Hail! Sisters in the cause—I salute you—Hail!...
Your opportunity is at your door. Grasp it!...
Never miss a chance to utilize what power has been
    given you. Vote the ticket which will give you
    more power....
Woman's suffrage stands today a solid shaft of marble;
    from it, your hands must help to carve a monument
    for all time.
Every hand must grasp its chisel and leave its imprint.

As for the song, about which the writer exhorts "May its martial strains awaken the best fires that burn within us," here are some of the lyrics:

We're a band of suffragists,
Fighting for the cause we love.
We are in the fight to stay to reach the goal,
'Till side by side with gentlemen,
We sheathe the sword and grasp the pen.
Cast our ballots, claim our rights from
        poll to poll
To our brave and noble sisters
Fighting far across the sea,
We extend the hand of love, as we waft a
        prayer above,
To our God who leads the right to victory.

CHORUS: Onward is the battle cry
        Of suffrage just and right
        We will trust our loyal Captain
        He will lead us in his might.
        We will ne'er retreat an inch
        Until opposition's done,
        And all the world proclaims to us
        That women's rights are won.

It was only natural that the movement was to come in for a fair share of ribbing. One song writer who felt inclined to "needle" the ambitious ladies was a woman named Grace Heller. Her 1913 song bore the title "Everybody Works but Ma (She's an Advocate of Woman's Rights)." Here are some of the lyrics:

Have you heard why mother and father can't agree;
Poor old pa must stay at home while ma goes on a spree.
She joined the woman's movement, and wears a bloomer skirt;
Now father has to cook and do the work.
Mother bought an auto, to sport around the town,
Father sweeps the house while she goes out with Mister Brown.
She brings men home to dinner, who promise her their vote;
Since ma is leader, father is the goat. (Poor father)—

CHORUS: Mother kissed the ice man, and she kissed the baker boy.
Then she kissed our landlord, now we get our house rent free,
oh joy.
Father asked her how she could, and he caught it on the jaw.
She's an advocate of woman's rights and everybody works but ma.

In 1916 in Chicago a new party—The Woman's Party—was born, with thousands of women assembling for the birth. Their power became enormous. Convinced that Wilson had no idea of granting them the franchise, many of them fought savagely for the election of Charles E. Hughes, his Republican opponent, often with huge banners reading, "Vote Against Wilson! He kept us out of suffrage!" As a result, several states which had previously adopted equal suffrage switched their votes in 1916 from Democrat to Republican, and Wilson emerged the winner only with last-minute help from the Pacific coastal states.

Without the president's endorsement, the hope for equal suffrage was futile. So the women besieged his sanctuary. In January, 1917, the first pickets appeared—women standing at the White House gates. They stood there quietly, carrying banners reading "We Shall Fight . . . For Democracy," and "Mr. President! How Long Must Women Wait for Liberty?" For three months, day after day, the pickets besieged the gates, trying in vain to secure an audience with Wilson.

When war was declared in April, the women were more determined than ever that they must have a hand in approving austerity measures which would affect the country. They were picketing the Capitol now, as well as the White House, and they were bombarding their congressmen with demands for support. Eventually, the dogged persistence of the suffragettes broke down the patience of their prey, and the chief of police ordered the women arrested for "obstructing the traffic." Required to pay fines of twenty-five dollars each or to serve three days in jail, the women unanimously chose the latter course. As the picketing continued, more and more women were arrested, and sentences were lengthened. They served their

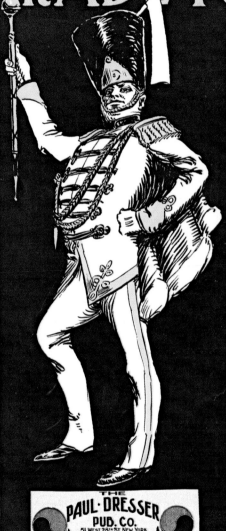

SOUSA'S · BAND · IS
ON · PARADE · TO-DAY

WORDS BY
ADD · VANCE

MUSIC BY
CHAS · KOHLMAN

5

FREW.

THE
PAUL · DRESSER
PUB. CO.
51 WEST 28TH ST NEW YORK
ALBERT & SON
LONDON · AGENTS · SIDNEY
CANADIAN-AMERICAN MUSIC CO. TORONTO CAN

terms in Occoquan Workhouse, a dismal Virginia prison which nauseated but did not intimidate the valiant ladies.

The picketers suffered an additional indignity. One August day, as they stood outside the White House gates, they were suddenly set upon by men in the armed forces of the United States. Alice Paul was knocked down three times by a sailor in uniform, and other women were struck and thrown to the pavement. The following day the women were attacked by a mob led by fifty policemen, who bruised the suffragists' hands and arms while wresting away and destroying their flags and banners. Further protests followed.

That fall there was held the 1917 Gridiron Club dinner, an annual affair given in Washington by the press club, at which various national figures who were present are lampooned. One of the songs creating the most amusement among the guests, including President Wilson, was written to the tune of "Tenting on the Old Camp Ground."

> We're camping to-night on the White House
> grounds,
> Give us a rousing cheer;
> Our golden flag we hold aloft,
> Of cops we have no fear.
> Many of the pickets are weary tonight,
> Wishing for the war to cease;
> Many are the chilblains and frost-bites too;
> It is no life of ease.
> Camping tonight, camping tonight,
> Camping on the White House grounds.

The charge never varied; "obstruction of traffic" was the only offense which could be leveled at the picketers. But to obstruct traffic now drew terms of six days to six months, with an exceptional sentence to Alice Paul, whom the judge committed to seven months in the Washington jail.

Nothing intimidated the determined women. Soon the war came to an end. A new tactic, "watchfires of freedom," was added to the steady picketing. A large urn was placed on the sidewalk in a line with the front door of the White House, lit with wood from a tree growing in Independence Square, Philadelphia. Into the fire the women threw, ceremoniously, copies of speeches and books of the president concerning "freedom," "democracy," and "liberty."

From the archives there was found an ancient statute prohibiting the building of fires in a public place between sunset and sunrise. This discovery gave the local courts an additional implement for serving jail sentences on the offenders. Hunger strikes in jail shortened some of the terms; the women continued their sidewalk demonstrations.

Meanwhile, one by one, congressmen were won over to the side of the suffragists, until, in the spring of 1919, the national suffrage amendment had clear sailing. Whether the astute generalship of Mrs. Catt or the unintimidated tactics of Miss Paul's valiant army carried the heavier weight is a moot question today. One can only recall that well-known advertising slogan of the 1950's, "Never underestimate the power of a woman."

The Salvation Army

THE GREAT WHITE BEARD below the long crooked nose had been a physical trade-mark of the patriarchal figure for so many years that many of his followers must have thought he was born with it—or at least acquired it in his youth. It was terribly impressive, as was everything else about William Booth. "The General," to his army and to thousands of admirers. A powerful predecessor to a succession of later evangelists who were to sway their own adherents in due time—Billy Sunday, Aimee Semple McPherson, Billy Graham—General Booth was more than a preacher; he was the founder of a movement which symbolized love for the poor and the unfortunate, and which was universal in its appeal to the better instincts of man.

Born in England in 1829 to poverty-stricken parents, he commenced his missionary activities before he was twenty. His independent "East London Mission" became after some years the "Christian Mission" and finally in 1877 the Salvation Army.

As Mr. Booth and his wife, who shared his evangelical fervor, preached in England and Wales, they attracted a large number of converts who joined their ever-increasing retinue like a crowd of camp followers. These people had been among the lowest of the low before the Booths gathered them in; they included drunkards, poachers, and notorious criminals, their characters altered by their contacts with the evangelists, and they were called by Booth "The Hallelujah Band."

So well known became the phrase that it soon attracted the attention of the popular song writers, who were always attuned to a new incident or a new movement, which aroused the interest of large numbers of people. As a result, "The Hallelujah Band," a lively ditty, made its appearance in sheet-music form about 1870. Originating in England, it soon crossed the Atlantic and was published in Philadelphia. The names of English parks and towns were eliminated, and American names substituted, as indicated here:

I was an artful dodger once but now you'll understand
I'm a most exalted member of the Hallelujah Band,
Our doings are notorious and here I may remark,
We've lately held a picnic in the grounds of Fairmont
    Park.
It was a glorious morning and we made a jolly start,
Like angels going to Dixey in a cover'd Carrier's cart,
So brotherly and sisterly of friends about a score,
And such a lot of loving lambs you never saw before.

CHORUS: Then you may go to Cape May Burlington or Beverly
    Wilmington in Delaware or search through the land,
    But if you want a spree that a saint can only see,
    You must join a jolly party in the Hallelujah Band.

The final verse winds up as follows:

We satisfied the inner man then cleared the crumbs
    away,
We danced and sung, declaring we had spent a happy
    day,
Then had a game at Kiss in the ring, and kissed each
    other's wives,
And vowed it was the jolliest day we'd spent in all
    our lives.

Despite its many thousands of converts, the Salvation Army was frequently subject to ridicule, and its members were booed and even assaulted. Such disorders occurred even while the missioners sought to feed the poor and the hungry, setting up soup kitchens which dispensed large bowls of soup and chunks of bread, sold to the poor for a penny, given outright to the penniless.

The Salvation Army first spanned the Atlantic in 1879. An English family named Shirley, members of the army from Coventry, came to Philadelphia, where Mr. Shirley was employed as a factory foreman by day and spent his nights emulating the teachings that he had acquired from General Booth's forces in England. He, along with his wife and daughter, went into Philadelphia's saloons and slums; the women sang hymns written to popular American tunes. To the melody of the well-known "Shew Fly, Don't Bother Me" the ladies sang verses of their own starting "Satan Don't Bother Me." Their audiences were delighted (according to reports) and called the women the "Hallelujah Females."

Within a year their "business" had expanded to such an extent that General Booth decided the time had come to send a sizable expedition to the

United States to augment the work of the Shirleys. Two gentlemen and six ladies were dispatched forthwith, the contingent being under the direction of Commissioner George Scott Railton. As soon as they arrived in New York they sought to find a public hall or a church in which to hold an initial meeting. Since none was available, Railton accepted the invitation of the owner of a notorious music hall, who offered the use of his facilities. The group was both cheered and jeered as the meeting progressed. At its conclusion, they were joined by a well-known Broadway character named James Kemp, known around his neighborhood as "Ashbarrel Jimmy" because he lived on the contents of trash cans. Jimmy became the Salvation Army's first convert in America. He advanced up the ladder to lieutenant, and then to captain, not a bad showing for an old trash-can man.

It was not long afterward that those famous theatrical satirists, Edward Harrigan and Tony Hart, realized that the Salvation Army afforded entertaining subject matter for inclusion in one of their music hall presentations. These had been going on since the late seventies; the background was always that of the Irish immigrants of New York, and the gibes were poked at everybody from policemen and the army to young Irishwomen posing as members of New York's high society.

In 1882, in a musical entitled *The McSorleys*, Harrigan wrote the words and Dave Braham, Hart's father-in-law, composed the music for "Salvation Army, Oh." A rollicking ditty in six-eighths time, the piece pokes fun at both political and biblical characters. For example, referring to the New York gubernatorial election:

> Oh, Cleveland and Folger they went out to fight,
> And Cleveland hit Folger with all his might;
> The winner he lives in Buffalo,
> And the loser's join'd the salvation army, oh!

And again:

> Ol' Jonah he lived away down in a whale,
> In a little back room very close to the tail;
> Don't give it away, for he's out on bail,
> And he sings in the salvation army, oh!

And the chorus:

> Away, away with rum and gum!
> Here we come, hear the drum!
> A reg'lar proper lum tum-tum,
> As we join'd the army, oh!

Gum? Why rum and *gum*? Not even the officers of today's army have any clue to that one.

Despite the fun that irreverant characters poked at the army, it conducted a deadly serious and solidly constructive business, feeding, healing, and restoring the faith of human beings in themselves. William Booth and his wife and children, the leaders of the flock, had the deep conviction that meaningful songs could be a stimulus for conditioning people to respond to their appeals. All of Booth's sons and daughters became song writers. Bramwell Booth, the oldest son, wrote the popular "My Faith Looks Up To Thee, My Faith So Small, So Slow." Ballington, a younger son, was best known as a song writer for "The Cross Is Not Greater Than His Grace." A daughter Emma, attained song writing success with "I'm Climbing up the Golden Stair to Glory."

The most musically prolific member of the family was the youngest son, Herbert, whose songs were published in 1890 under the title *Songs of Peace and War*. Eighty-six pieces—nearly all by Herbert—were included in the volume. One wonders when he found time to serve as a leader in the army. Many songs of the Booths and their associates appear in *The Song Book of the Salvation Army, The Bandsman and Songster*, and other publications of the music which helped to ascribe a unique quality to the Salvation Army.

Yet some of the army's song writers did not hesitate to commandeer a well-known popular song and write new words to the music. For instance, the melody of one of the best-remembered songs of the famous Henry Clay Work of Chicago, "Ring the Bell, Watchman," written in 1861, was used in 1878 by the army's Captain William J. Pearson for possibly the most widely used of his many songs, "Song of the Salvation Army." An odd example in the choice of tunes occurs in the verses composed by a Scottish officer named Robert Johnson, who wrote his "Storm the Forts of Darkness" to the melody of "Here's to Good old Whiskey, Drink it down!"

Tin-pan alley found that the Salvation Army had its own peculiar type of attractiveness, not for followers or converts, but for those people who enjoyed popular songs. And for them, the Salvation Army girl had sex appeal. The best-known of these young ladies, something over fifty years ago, was "Salvation Nell." Nell's background dates to 1908, when a play written by Edward Sheldon and carrying the title of *Salvation Nell* first saw the lights of Broadway. Opening in November of that year with one of the leading actresses of the day, Minnie Maddern Fiske in the title role "Nell" enjoyed a run of just seventy-one performances.

Salvation Nell

There's a girl of sweet sev-en-teen,— Al-ways has a cute tam-bou-rine,—

Heav-en-ly grace — Heav-en-ly face — Neath a bon-net with "Sal-va-tion" writ-ten on it;

Ev-'ry fel-low liv-ing in town— Thinks — she's migh-ty swell— Ev-'ry night

Chorus

they gath-er a-round — Sweet Sal-va-tion Nell— She keeps say-ing

"Fol-low On - ward! Bro-thers!" And they al - ways fol-low Sal-va-tion Nell

She gets them shout-ing "Hal-le-lu-jah! Hal-le-lu-jah! Hal-le-lu-jah!

Doc-tors, law-yers, but-chers and bak-ers And some spor-ty old fel-lows, as well,—

— They've been sin-ners for years— Yet they burst out in tears,— And join the Ar - my

join the Ar - my Just to be a-round Sal-va-tion Nell.—

2. Ev'ry married woman in town,
Bought an army bonnet and gown,
Each one was dressed, Just like the rest
Like ducks wading they all started in parading,
Then they said "we're fooling the men"

But it's sad to tell
Husbands all deserted them then
For Salvation Nell
CHORUS

Despite her comparatively brief appearance before the theater-going public, she proved to be a "natural" for the song writers, even after she had been retired from the legitimate stage for a few years. An enticing girl, Nell was re-created in 1913, in sheet music form, by lyricists Grant Clarke and Edgar Leslie, and veteran composer Theodore Morse. Her pose on the song cover, tambourine held high above her head, is something between that of a bewitching Spanish senorita and a belly dancer, but she wears the Salvation Army headdress, a close-fitting little bonnet with ribbons tied under the chin—possibly for protection from the men who stretch out their arms in her direction.

> There's a girl of sweet seventeen,
> Always has a cute tambourine,
> Heavenly grace, Heavenly face
> Neath a bonnet with "Salvation" written on it;
> Ev'ry fellow living in town
> Thinks she's mighty swell
> Ev'ry night they gather around
> Sweet Salvation Nell.
>
> CHORUS: She keeps saying "Follow Onward! Brothers!"
> And they always follow Salvation Nell.
> She gets them shouting; "Hallelujah! Hallelujah!
> Hallelujah!"
> Doctors, lawyers, butchers and bakers
> And some sporty old fellows as well,
> They've been sinners for years
> Yet they burst out in tears
> And join the Army, join the Army,
> Just to be around Salvation Nell.[1]

During World War I the popularity of the Salvation Army mushroomed. As Salvation Army huts sprang up in every camp where soldiers were stationed, and as Salvation Army girls dispensed doughnuts by the millions, the men of the armed services were won over en masse, possibly not to the evangelistic espousals of the redeemed, but to the practical aspect of a work which boosted the morale of those who were fighting for their country.

In 1918 the U.S. Army's Ordnance Department, with headquarters at the U.S. Proving Grounds in Aberdeen, Maryland, presented a farce with music, *Who Stole the Hat*. One song in the show was so outstanding that it was published for general and wide consumption. The number was called

---

[1] "Salvation Nell." W/Grant Clarke & Edgar Leslie M/Theodore Morse. Copyright 1914 Used by Permission Edgar Leslie.

"My Salvation Army Girl." Composed by a well-known tin-pan alleyite, Al Piantadosi, with words by Jack Mason, it was unstinting in its praises:

> We've heard of all the noble deeds, since
>   this here war began,
> Now every one has done his share, to cheer
>   each mother's son,
> But there's a pal we never heed,
> She's a friend "when a friend's in need."

> CHORUS: It's my Salvation Army Girl,
>   That has helped our heroes through,
>   With doughnuts and coffee in hand,
>   Feeding our boys in "No Man's Land,"
>   So let's help her along, she's the one who
>   "Carries On,"
>   She's stuck to our boys on the firing line,
>   And she'll be with them when they cross
>   the Rhine,
>   My own Salvation Army Girl.

The song writers again responded to the widespread popularity of the Salvation Army in the field. A pair of them, Jack Caddigan and Chick Story, brought out "Salvation Lassie of Mine" in 1919, just a few months after they had scored a big success with their eulogy to a Red Cross nurse, "The Rose of No Man's Land." The title page portrayed a sweet faced "Lassie" in army regalia, posing before a Salvation Army hut on which were the words "All welcome," and into which a group of soldiers was streaming.
The chorus:

> A sweet little Angel that went o'er the sea,
> With the emblem of God in her hand,
> A wonderful Angel who brought there to me,
> The sweet of a war furrowed land,
> The crown on her head was a ribbon of red,
> A symbol of all that's divine,
> Tho' she called each a brother, she's more
>   like a mother,
> Salvation Lassie of mine.[2]

In the same year there appeared another song—the only secular song ever to be recognized with the official seal of approval of the Salvation Army.

2 "Salvation Lassie of Mine." Words and Music by Jack Caddigan and Oliver Story. Copyright 1918 and renewed 1946. Copyright assigned to Jerry Vogel Music Co., Inc. 121 West 45th Street, New York, N.Y. 10036. Used by permission of the copyright owner.

Endorsed by Commander Evangeline Booth, the smart little marching number, entitled "Don't Forget the Salvation Army," or "My Doughnut Girl," and developed by a four-man team of writers, the verse began:

> Pennies, nickels, dimes and quarters,
>   hear them ring.
> Oh what joy and oh what bliss those
>   coins can bring
>
> . . . .
>
> CHORUS: Don't forget the Salvation Army,
>   Always remember my doughnut girl.
> She brought them doughnuts and
>   coffee
> Just like an Angel, she was their
>   best pal. . . .
> As brave as a lion but meek as a lamb,
> She carried on beside the sons of
>   Uncle Sam,
> So don't forget the Salvation Army,
> Remember my doughnut girl.[3]

And with one notable exception, this was probably the last time that the Salvation Army was used to advantage by tin-pan alley. The exception occurred in 1951, when some of the short stories of Damon Runyon were skillfully woven into a musical comedy, *Guys and Dolls*, with a comely Salvation Army girl as the ingenue. The great Frank Loesser contributed his greatest score to help make the show an overwhelming success. Nowhere did he win his audience more completely than in the song delivered by a happy (and slightly intoxicated) Salvation Army girl, "If I Were a Bell." Fulfillment comes to her when she is able to convert en masse all of Runyon's loveable crapshooters.

Today, the Army is better fortified than ever, and it continues to use its music to great advantage. Only listen on some street corner in the holiday season to a small dedicated Salvation Army group singing with lusty fervor "Oh Boundless Salvation." True, many passers-by are indifferent as they come abreast of the devoted lads and lasses. But many others are stirred by the earnestness of the singers and aware that coins dropped into the kettle will aid some unfortunate who is one of the army's recognized charges.

---

[3] "Don't Forget the Salvation Army." W/Elmore Leffingwell and James Lucas; M/Robert Brown, William Frisch © 1919 All rights for the USA and Canada controlled by Broadway Music Corp., c/o Walter Hofer, 221 West 57th St., New York, New York. Used by permission. All rights reserved.

General Booth never waved a sword, but for more than a century the forces he developed have waged a battle to win the compassion of the world. The war goes on, and the staunch men and women of the Salvation Army are undaunted. They continue to "Storm the Forts of Darkness."

The Gibson Girl

FROM THE LATE 1880's to the time of World War I, a handsome, brawny six-footer had the ability to captivate more American males than anyone else in his time—unless you might consider Uncle Sam as his competitor. Lest this should appear to indicate some gross misbehavioral pattern, it must be stated immediately that no homosexual implications are to be construed—far from it! The rugged gentleman was an artist by the name of Charles Dana Gibson, and the spell which he cast over American men, old and young, was achieved through his portrayal of the faces and forms of the most delectable women to grace the popular books and periodicals of the turn of the century.

A few decades ago a new magazine, *Esquire*, achieved almost instant popularity, substantially because of the luscious females discovered within its covers as portrayed by George Petty, young ladies who were christened forthwith the Petty Girls. Later, a Peruvian, Alberto Varga, introduced a somewhat different breed of his own in the same magazine, and the Varga Girl was adopted as the pet of the eager male. In recent years *Playboy* magazine has captured the imagination (not too much was left to it) of young gentlemen with its monthly Playmate.

But none of these bits of fluff could develop the outright devotion of the male population that the Gibson Girl inspired. Tall and straight, not too willowy, robust but not rotund, her modified Venus figure and her majestic bearing made her the idol of the country's mankind; and she remained on her pedestal, with none to challenge her eminence, for more than twenty-five years.

Gibson did not confine himself to the portrayal of beautiful girls. He was a portraitist of rare distinction and a cartoonist without peer in his time. In fact, the first drawing that he sold, at the age of nineteen, to the old *Life* magazine, was a little comic sketch of a small dog baying at the moon, some years before a pretty girl was to grace his sketch pad. *Life*'s editor, John Ames Martin, decided that the dog was worth four dollars to him, and paid Gibson cash on the spot.

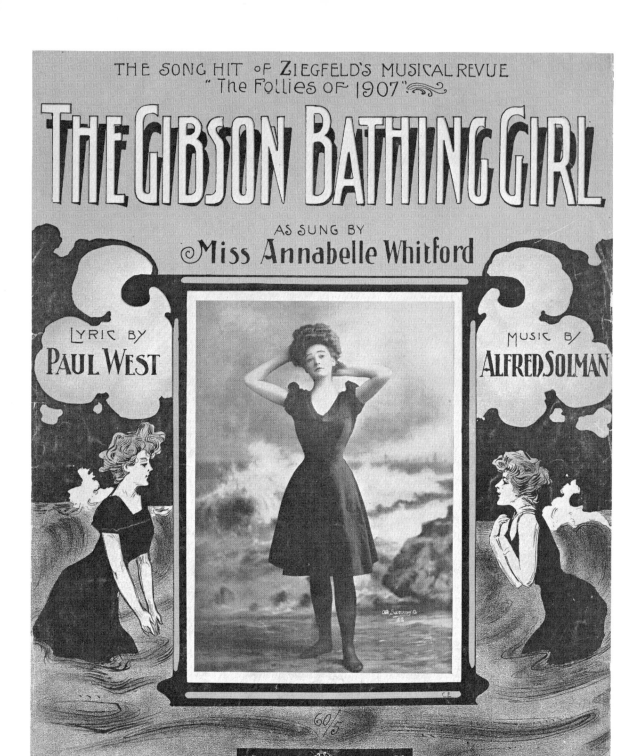

The Gibson Bathing Girl.

I am one of the queens Of the best ma-ga-zines Long by Charles Da-na Gib-son made fa-mous, We have shown you the charms Of our shoul-ders and arms, And we real-ly don't think you can blame us; But we hat-ed to hide Oth-er beau-ties be-side, And we fumed at the ar-tist's o-mis-sion, So one day we a-rose In re-volt at long clothes, And pre-sent-ed this tear-ful pe - ti-tion:

Refrain

Mis-ter Gib-son! Mis-ter Gib-son! Why can't we take a swim? Paint us, please, with dim-pled knees, And plen-ty of round-ed limb! Mis-ter Gib-son! Mis-ter Gib-son! Just give your brush a whirl! And they'll say on the beach, "There's a peach, a peach of a Gib-son Bath-ing girl!"

2. There are mermaids, they say,
Swimming round in the bay
And the rocks by the sea they look grand on.
But we Gibson girls smile,
We can beat them a mile,
For they havn't a leg to stand on
As we stroll by the shore,

Loud the breakers may roar,
But the brokers roar more to get to us,
And they gaze on us long,
As we murmur the song,
That we sang to the artist who drew us:
CHORUS

Within a few years his exceptional ability had catapulted him into the ranks of the most popular pen-and-ink artists of his day. By the time his Gibson Girl became an accepted feature of the current illustrated magazines and novels in 1890, he was making hundreds of dollars a month.

At the outset, however, she appeared under an assumed name. *Life* magazine called her, for a while, Penelope Peachblow. When she appeared in the prestigious *Century* magazine, not in person, but in a description of a beautiful girl in a story by a popular authoress, Nathalie Harris, she was described as a Goodrich Girl. And nobody knew then, nor do they know today, what, or who, a Goodrich Girl was. It was impossible, however, to pretend much longer that the lovely women created by the artist could be disguised as anything except Gibson Girls. And so they became, first on a nation-wide, then on a world-wide scale.

Dana Gibson, after a while, developed a few stock characters among his women. There was the daughter of the rich American family, destined to be presented at a European court and to be dangled as a reward to any nobleman with an intriguing title. There was the beautiful young widow, who had men of all ages panting in her wake. There was the demure but confident bathing girl in her knee-length skirt and long black stockings. And many, many more.

In the days when every popular personality was a target for the song writers, it was but natural that the Gibson Girl should get some musical treatment. The first edition of the *Ziegfeld Follies*, a 1907 production, featured a stunning actress named Annabelle Whitford, who stopped the show when she appeared in a bathing suit of the period, a complete coverall except for the arms and a bit of exposed neck, to sing "The Gibson Bathing Girl." And the following year, when the customers demanded larger doses of Gibson, the composer of the "Bathing Girl" was a cosponsor of *The Gibson Girl Review*, which reintroduced his first number and added several others, such as "The Gibson Sailor Girl" and "The Gibson Widow."

Alfred Selman composed these songs, and Paul West wrote the lyrics. The widow's first husband was a Gibson Man—and Gibson men were as handsome as any girl could desire. But unfortunately—as the lady tells it—" 'Twas too sweet to last. That is why I'm lonely here today."
And then the chorus:

> I am the Gibson widow
> Sighing with a Gibson woe!
> Crying Gibson tears, Sad with Gibson fears!
> Lonely for my Gibson beau!

> I've a lot of Gibson money,
> I spend it on the Gibson plan,
> For I am the Gibson widow
> And I'm waiting for another Gibson man!

As for the bathing girl who helped to put the *Ziegfeld Follies* on the map, she was a self-opinionated creature when lyricized by Mr. West, breaking out at once into:

> I am one of the queens of the best magazines
> Long by Charles Dana Gibson made famous
>
> . . . .
>
> One day we arose in revolt at long clothes,
> And presented this tearful petition:
> CHORUS: Mister Gibson! Mister Gibson!
> Why can't we take a swim?
> Paint us, please, with dimpled knees,
> And plenty of rounded limb!
> Mister Gibson! Mister Gibson!
> Just give your brush a whirl!
> And they'll say on the beach,
> "There's a peach, a peach
> Of a Gibson Bathing Girl!"[4]

Gibson himself married one of the great beauties of his day, Irene Langhorne from Virginia, who served as his model for a number of years after their marriage.

In 1905, when he was nearly forty, Gibson determined to learn how to work in oils, and he set out for Europe, casting aside the pencils that had made him world-famous to devote several years to the arduous task of becoming a painter. As he sailed off, his friend and associate, Robert W. Chambers, a popular author of the day, many of whose works had been made even more popular because Gibson illustrated them, bade him farewell in a tender article in *Collier's Weekly*: "Since the world entire has become his audience, I doubt that there are many men in the world, personally unknown to millions, who are as personally beloved by those millions as Dana Gibson. . . . I do not exactly know what we Americans shall do without him."

When World War I came to the United States Gibson was in the forefront of the many popular artists who volunteered their services with inspiring posters urging men to enlist, families to buy Liberty Bonds and to economize on the consumption of food, and girls to confine their dates to the men in the armed forces.

[4] "The Gibson Bathing Girl." © copyright E. B. MARKS MUSIC CORPORATION used by permission.

An article in *Arts and Decoration* in 1922 by Perriton Maxwell summed up the public's feeling about Gibson with this evaluation: "After all, Gibson is—Gibson; the man who evoked with a pen-point a distinctive, original type of young womanhood and lived to see her acclaimed the ideal American girl. . . . the man who for thirty years has held his supreme position in the sphere of reproductive art as a vital, unique force."

No more popular American artist ever lived. His caricatures, his portraits, and his war posters alone would have ensured his enduring fame. But he will always be best remembered for his gorgeous girls, who still remain, in the view of many, as America's most enchanting and enduring examples of female pulchritude.

"September Morn"

In 1912 a medal of honor was awarded by the art committee of the French Academy to a picture which in the judgment of today's society would have elicited no controversy whatever, at least as far as its subject matter was concerned. The picture portrayed a teen-age girl taking a quiet bath in a quiet body of water in a position which would indicate fresh young innocence. Paul Chabas was the artist and he called his masterpiece—for such might be the title of any work of art to be awarded such an important medal—"September Morning."

The news of the award reached the United States and its art dealers. Now it is always something of a scoop when an American dealer can acquire a piece of importance in the current art world and display it in its windows. "September Morning" was coveted by Braun and Company, a firm of art dealers on West 46th Street in New York. Through the proper channels they secured the loan of the picture and in May, 1913, gave it a prominent place in their window.

It would probably have created no disturbance at all had it not been for an indiscreet action on the part of Mr. Anthony Comstock, the head of New York's Society for the Suspension of Vice. Mr. Comstock happened to be walking along 46th Street one day, and as he glanced in the windows of Braun and Company, he stopped short in his tracks. There was "September Morning" practically face to face with him but as oblivious to the encounter as Mr. Comstock was extremely aware of it. Normally Mr. Comstock would hardly have been one whit disturbed at viewing such beauty, except for one very evident fact—the young lady was devoid of any clothing whatsoever.

Mr. Comstock, thereupon marched into the store and stalking up to James Kelly, the salesman who was in charge, ordered: "Take her out at once, the picture of the girl without any clothes on." But, Kelly explained: "That is the famous 'September Morning.' " Mr. Comstock was in no mood for argument. "There is too little morning and too much maid," he rejoined, "take it out." Kelly refused and told Comstock that no visitor had the right to make this his business, whereupon Mr. Comstock threw back the flap of his coat displaying his badge of office. This was most upsetting to James Kelly, and he hauled in the picture.

When the proprietor, Mr. Ortiz, returned to the store and Kelly informed him of the occurrence, Ortiz ordered "September Morning" back into the window, where it remained for several days. Ortiz appeared adamant. "We will keep it on display if we have to spend the value of our entire stock in contesting the points with Mr. Comstock," he said.

The story made the newspapers immediately and created an upheaval. In Chicago, as a paper pointed out, Alderman "Bath House John Coughlin" announced that the picture was shocking and that he would not permit it to be displayed there publicly.

Mr. Comstock took refuge in his own decision with the statement that he was investigating the complaint of a school teacher that such pictures were being displayed in shops in the neighborhood. He said: "It is not a proper picture to be viewed by boys and girls. There is nothing more sacred than the form of woman, but it must not be denuded. I think everyone will agree with me that such pictures should not be displayed where school children, passing through the streets, can see them."

This kind of business had the effect which Mr. Comstock had hoped it would and the picture was taken from the window three days later. It was not removed because of Anthony Comstock. In fact it had been kept on for several extra days in the window for no other reason than that it had incurred Mr. Comstock's displeasure. But the newspaper reports had the effect of drawing thousands of people to view the painting. They came in such droves that the entrance to the interior of the store was blocked to potential customers, and this was the principal reason why the picture had to be removed from view.

But Ortiz continued to fight for his rights. William Hammerstein, the producer, was inspired to design a living picture form in the opening performance at Hammerstein's Roof Garden on June 2. The living picture was to have been "September Morning," and Mr. Ortiz had Hammerstein

September Morn.

(I'd Like To Meet Her)

Song

WORDS BY
STANLEY MURPHY

MUSIC BY
H. I. MARSHAL

5

JEROME H. REMICK & CO.
NEW YORK   DETROIT

Oh You September Morn

There's a girl-ie caused a sen-sa-tion, Late-ly she's be-come the rage   She is known to ev-er-y na-tion, Now we've got her   on the stage,   She don't care a bit for style,

In the Spring or Fall,   All she wears is just a smile,   No-thing else at all!

Chorus

Oh —— you beau-ti-ful Sep-tem-ber Morn,   Oh —— come love   me for I'm

all —— for-lorn,   Oh —— I want to call you mine,—   You —— splash me

and I'll splash   you, the wa-ter is fine!   No —— use wait-ing for a sil- v'ry

moon,—   If —— we're going to hug and kiss— and   spoon,—   Be my lit-tle

Ve-nus, I'll be your A-don-is,   Lead-ers of the fash-ion will have no-thing on— us Oh you

— Sep-tem-ber Morn.————

2. The youth was wise as he could be
And said, "Now plainly I can see,
September Morn's the girl for me,
She's economic, Goodness knows,
She never has to pay for clothes,

She doesn't even wear a rose;
Old Mother Nature dress'd her up just right,
So listen to me sing with all my might,
CHORUS

served with an order to show cause why he should not be restrained from reproducing a living model of the famous painting.

It was not surprising that tin-pan alley took up immediately this very controversial and entertaining subject. One song, published by the eminent firm of Jerome H. Remick & Co., with a picture of the painting on the cover, was entitled "September Morn (I'd Like to Meet Her)," and the story was that of Braun and Company's display, set to words and music, which started off:

> A youth upon the avenue
> Was feeling blue and lonesome, too!
> He didn't have a thing to do.
> When suddenly he noticed there,
> An awful crowd, who stop'd to stare
> Up at a posing maiden fair;
> The vision sent his poor brain in a whirl,
> And so he sang while searching for the girl.[5]

Not only that, but there was even a musical comedy of *September Morn* produced in Chicago, despite the rantings of "Bath House John Coughlin." The title song, "Oh, You September Morn" commences:

> There's a girlie caused a sensation,
> Lately she's become the rage
> She is known to every nation
> Now we've got her on the stage,
> She don't care a bit for style,
> In the Spring or Fall
> All she wears is just a smile,
> Nothing else at all![6]

Incidentally, the show did not take the town nor the nation by storm, but the subject was kept alive in various parts of the country.

In August the post-office department sent orders to New Orleans to ban from the mails reproductions of "September Morn." This announcement apparently was made following the arrest of Harold Marx, proprietor of an art store which had displayed Paul Chabas' picture in its window several weeks before. The police had ordered the picture out of the window, but Marx had disobeyed the order and was then charged with exhibiting in-

---

[5] "September Morn, I'd Like to Meet Her." W/Stanley Murphy, M/Henry I. Marshall © 1913 Jerome H. Remick & Co., Copyright Renewed. All Rights Reserved. Used by Permission of WARNER BROS. MUSIC.

[6] "Oh You September Morn" from "September Morn." Words by Arthur Gillespie, Music by Aubrey Stauffer Copyright 1913 and renewed 1940 Copyright assigned to Jerry Vogel Music Co., Inc. 121 West 45th St., New York, N.Y. 10036. Used by permission of the copyright owner.

decent pictures. But before the controversy was very old, his postcard reproductions began to appear, and the New Orleans postmaster, Leon Hardt, sent one to the department in Washington which issued the stern edict.

If such an edict were to be enforced today, what would become of our children? No *Playboy*? No sneaking in to "R"-rated movies? The kids would be forced to spend all their leisure hours before the T.V. sets, suffering through politicians making love to the public. What a dreary country this would be. It seems we owe Mr. Comstock some sort of medal of honor for first bringing to the attention of the people the knowledge that vice is in the mind of the beholder and not in the subject that he beholds.

5
GROWING PAINS

Oklahoma

The population of some states of the Union is almost homogeneous. Northern New England is practically pure Yankee. Iowa, Kansas, Nebraska are, with few exceptions, solidly white, agriculturally oriented. Idaho, Wyoming have the stamp of the wind-burned, sun-burned descendants of pioneers who live the same rugged lives their fathers did.

But in most of the other states there is an amalgam of humanity which illustrates the acceptance of America as a melting pot. In the great Southeast, the Caucasians and the Negroes are each dependent on the others as complementary groups to serve the states' economic functions. In lower California a great influx from Mexico has joined the white and black Americans and the Orientals to form a polyglot society.

In only one state, Oklahoma, have the native Americans, the Indians, who were the initial ingredients of the melting pot, survived in quantities sizable enough to challenge the later inpouring of white men. Both groups of Oklahomans were to become, in their day, grist for the songsters' mill, as we shall see.

In the field of literature—in fiction and in poetry—there had long been a certain glamor about American Indians. The noble savage, the shy squaw, the bright-eyed papoose—the thought of these native Americans, leading their picturesque, if primitive, lives long before white explorers discovered them, had captured the imagination of novelists and poets.

But unfortunately, the sentiments of novelists and poets have little effect on the course of history, and in the nineteenth century the red men were subjected to humiliating pressures from their white brothers. As the expanding United States ruthlessly took measures to appropriate the lands where the Indians—and the buffalo—roamed, they went about relocating tribes. Most of those living in the southeast (Florida, Georgia, Alabama, Mississippi) were rounded up in the 1820's and 1830's and resettled in Arkansas Territory, which at that time embraced the land to the west of Arkansas which is today Oklahoma. There some of the tribes endeavored to set up primitive forms of government.

In 1827 the great Cherokee Nation adopted a regular constitution modeled on that of the United States. The following year, the Cherokees elected a principal chief, John Ross, a Scotch-Cherokee of one-eighth Cherokee blood. He was an extraordinarily able executive, and he held his office for nearly forty years, counseling his people during the strenuous period of the Civil War and later participating in the treaty-making sessions of Indians and officers of the federal government. When he died in August 1866, grieving friends Francis de Haes Janvier and J. W. Jost wrote a dirge which went in part as follows:

> Dead! The mighty Chief is dead!
> Fallen, fallen is the Nation's head!
> Eyes unused to tears, today . . .
> Weep in sorrow o'er his clay.

And then, impressively, the song was translated into Cherokee.

The writers of popular music did not realize the strong interest in the Indian until the beginning of the twentieth century. True, there were exceptions. In 1848 half a dozen pieces about the Indians of New York State made their appearance. They shared a joint title page which pictured a handsome chief in full regalia. One particularly touching ballad was "The Song of the Red Man" by an unknown author, with music by A. P. Knight (reproduced in *Grace Notes in American History*, Norman, 1967). In the 1840's and 1850's an occasional instrumental number about Indian warriors or a sentimental musical poem about an Indian maiden would be presented.

These writers, however, were not pioneers on the subject. The first musician to use an Indian as the basis for an important work was Stephen Storace, an Englishman and friend of Mozart, whose musical play, "The Cherokee," was staged in London in 1794. Storace's lyricist, J. Cobb, put together a fanciful tale of a young Cherokee from the eastern seaboard who dreams of himself as a London dude. The performance was so highly successful that the songs made their way to this country and were published in Boston and elsewhere before 1800. The English managed to develop some amazingly ribald verses about Cherokee Indians, which would probably be suppressed today despite the First Amendment, but which circulated in England without repression.

One hundred years after Storace, a well-known American song writer introduced what was probably the first popular song to mention Oklahoma. The writer was Paul Dresser, brother of Theodore Dreiser, the novelist, and composer of "On the Banks of the Wabash" plus dozens of other melodious numbers. "Three Old Sports From Oklahoma," written in 1894, was definitely not one of his greatest works. It was introduced in a farce called *A Green Goods Man*, and the lyrics were farcical indeed:

> Three old sports from Oklahoma,
> Bunko Bill and Reuben the Jonah,
> Red haired Mike who lives in Tacom,
> Looking for trouble, Whoop, Hooray.
> We're stronger than Sampson. One day in November,
> We held up a train of cars, engine and tender,
> The brakes were all broke, and as we remember
> We took up a collection, Whoop, Hooray

> CHORUS: Three old sports from Congress quite evident,
> When she's in session we're Washington residents,
> Shake ev'ry morning with Grover the President,
> Regular cuckoo sports are we.

Shortly after the start of the 1900's, all of a sudden the song writers were unleashing a superabundance of numbers about Indian girls. "Iola," "Red Wing," and other captivating maidens were presented musically to the public, who snapped up the songs by the hundreds of thousands.

Squarely in the center of Indian Territory, which would form part of Oklahoma within a few years, was a tract of two hundred thousand acres assigned by a presidential order of August 15, 1883, to the Kickapoo tribe. Within another several years the government was desperate for additional land for the many settlers who were eyeing the Southwest greedily for potential homesites. Among the most desirable locations was the land occupied by the Kickapoos, whose population had dwindled to less than three hundred. Lengthy negotiations between the tribe and the government were concluded in 1893. They allowed each member of the tribe eighty acres and stipulated that the United States was to give the Kickapoos $64,500 for the balance, or somewhere around forty cents an acre.

This was a bit more than the Indians of Manhattan got from old Peter Stuyvesant about two hundred and fifty years earlier, but it can hardly be said that the government was extravagant. At that figure the United States

My Pretty Little Kickapoo

Heap big brave loved lit-tle kick-a-poo, oo, — Pret- ty cop-per col-ored maid-en, —

To her tent one night he went to woo, oo, — And his heart with love was la- den;

Camp fires are out the big chief sleeps, As to her tent he soft-ly creeps, Chant-ing her name,

Heart all a-flame, whis-per-ing love words as he came, Pale moon is shin-ing in the sky,

Soft-ly the eve-ning breez-es sigh, Stol-en the kiss, sweet-er the bliss, As he whis-pers this: "My

Chorus

Pret-ty lit-tle kick-a-poo, I do love you, My pret-ty lit-tle kick-a-poo, I will be true; —

when the sun sinks in the west, sinks to rest, 'Neath the sil-ver moon I'm dream-ing,

Dream-ing of the gleam-ing of your big brown eyes, Shin-ing like the stars that twin-kle in the skies

Dream-ing you love me as I love you, My pret-ty lit-tle kick-a- poo."

2. Softly sighs the little Kick-a-poo, oo,
   Heap big brave you love me dearly,
   From my tribe I'll fly away with you, oo,
   For I love you so sincerely;
   As o'er the rolling plains they went,
   He softly says "I'll build a tent,

Build it for two, Just me and you, my
   little bright eyed Kick-a-poo.
There in the land of buffaloes,
You'll be my redskin prairie rose,
Winter and spring, kisses I'll bring,
While I softly sing: "My
CHORUS

had practically nothing to lose and everything to gain by opening the land to homesteaders (along with outlaws and adventurers). On May 23, 1895, one hundred and seventy-five thousand acres were available to the hordes that packed the borders of Kickapoo territory, scrambling when the guns were fired at twelve noon, to stake claims in every available section of the former reservation.

Among the many tribes then residing in Indian Territory, were numerous luscious Indian maidens who, the composers believed, were timely subjects for the pianists and singers of the day. But these writers were not inclined to give the girls ordinary names like Mary or Lizzie; rather, they usually endowed each maiden with the name of the Indian nation to which she belonged.

Though the Kickapoos were a thinning nation, they were not forgotten—not even by the song writers. In 1904 one of the best-known teams in the field of popular music, Andrew B. Sterling and Harry Von Tilzer (who used to claim that his published compositions ran into the thousands), wrote "My Pretty Little Kickapoo," a boy-and-girl love song with a heavily con-trived Indian atmosphere. To introduce it to vaudeville audiences, they were able to secure the services of a talented young bother and sister, Harry and Eva Puck, who, as child actors, won the hearts of their public and held them for another twenty-five years, emerging in 1927 as a delightful comedy team in that great American musical, *Show Boat*. The Pucks were pictured on "Kickapoo's" title page, and apparently had no difficulty in making the song a success.

The Seminole tribe had at one time occupied thousands of choice acres in northern Florida; but the land was coveted by the government, and shrewd treaties drove the Indians first to swampy grounds to the south, and then westward to Arkansas—later Indian Territory. The Seminoles, like the Kickapoos, were eventually divested of most of this land by treaty with the United States government, and were forced to see homesteaders take it over.

> Heap big brave loved little Kickapoo, oo,
> Pretty copper colored maiden,
> To her tent one night he went to woo, oo,
> And his heart with love was laden;
> Camp fires are out, the big chief sleeps,
> As to her tent he softly creeps,
> Chanting her name, heart all aflame,
> Whispering love words as he came,
> Pale moon is shining in the sky,

Softly the evening breezes sigh,
Stolen the kiss, sweeten the bliss,
As he whispers this:

CHORUS: My pretty little Kickapoo, I do love you,
My pretty little Kickapoo, I will be true;
When the sun sinks in the west, sinks to rest,
'Neath the silver moon I'm dreaming,
Dreaming of the gleaming of your big brown eyes,
Shining like the stars that twinkle in the skies,
Dreaming you love me as I love you,
My pretty little Kickapoo.

Again a little Indian girl was introduced to remind American pianists of her great nation. Egbert Van Alstyne, a prolific composer who had a short while previously scored a hit with his "Navajo," in 1904 brought out a bright march and two-step called "Seminole." It is a spirited piece, with the beat of the tom-tom running through it and a melody which can be whistled after it is heard a couple of times. On the title page is the picture of a stunning Indian girl, drawn by Gene Buck, a gifted composer himself, who some years later held the glamorous position of president of the American Society of Composers and Publishers.

In the northern part of the Territory lived the Pawnees, who had been expelled from their native Nebraska in 1876. The two thousand transferred to their new home had been beset by smallpox and other diseases that decimated their ranks and cut the population in half. Most of the 280,000 acres occupied by the Pawnees was gobbled up in 1893 as part of the "Cherokee Outlet." The poor Pawnees were no hand at negotiations and spent much time in making such demands as the gift of twenty-eight beeves for a Thanksgiving feast, the distribution of sets of harness, and the right to have social dances. After such serious problems had been disposed of, the last transaction involved the sale by the 830 members of the tribe of 169,000 acres for white settlement. For these lands, the Pawnees received something less than fifty cents an acre.

In 1906 another well-known composer, Silvio Hein, wrote "Pawnee" as an intermezzo two-step. Hein was one of the most gifted writers of the day, the composer of a number of successful musical comedies. "Pawnee" was a jingly little piece in two-fourths time, with a hint of Indian background— as imagined by the white man—in its simplified G-minor melody. On the colorful title page is a lovely young woman, shading with her hand her big brown eyes as she peers into the distance, while a group of tepees nestle among the pines behind her.

But the subject matter of the music inspired by Oklahoma was not confined to Indians. Admitted to the Union in 1907, the state itself found many local composers eager to sing its praises, and others from the East ready to romanticize the colorful new lands. One such easterner was Stanley S. Sherman, who wrote "In Oklahoma" in 1909. Cowboys, tall in the saddle, were then competing with cute Indian cuties and brave Indian braves for musical popularity. Sherman's song was—as the legal profession might term it—"boilerplate."

> Way out in Prairie land, in Oklahoma grand,
> I won my Mary's hand out on the range,
> Pony, he liked her too, told me her heart was true
> Whispered, "You're lucky, Lou" Wasn't that strange?

> CHORUS: Way out in Oklahoma, no more I'll ride alone,
> Girlie in San Antoine, says "Fix a home."
> Under the prairie sky, Pony, sweetheart and I,
> It's there we'll live and die, in Oklahoma.

Songs praising Oklahoma, by men and women who had settled there, were making their appearance for several years before statehood. In 1904, Mrs. Priscilla V. B. Webster wrote her "Oklahoma." With lyrics slightly reminiscent of parts of Stephen Foster's nostalgic ballads, she declares:

> There's a land in the southwest that's as fair as
> fair can be,
> 'Tis the land where the wheat and cotton grow.
> There the sun it shines so bright, and the air it
> feels so light,
> 'Tis no wonder why the people love it so.

Nineteen hundred five marked the entry of another musical Oklahoma booster, again with the title "Oklahoma," to which were added the words, "A Toast." The author-composer, Harriet Parker Camden, wrote:

> I give you a land of sun and flow'rs and summer the
> whole year long:
> I give you a land where the golden hours roll by to
> the mockingbird's song,
> Where the cotton blooms 'neath the southern sun; where
> the vintage hangs thick on the vine;
> A land whose story is just begun, this wonderful land
> of mine.

CHORUS: Oklahoma! Oklahoma! fairest daughter of the West.
           Oklahoma! Oklahoma! 'tis the land I love the best.
           We have often sung her praises, but we have not told
               the half;
           So, I give you "Oklahoma;" 'tis a toast we all can
               quaff.

The following year James A. McLauchlin wrote and scored for a vocal quartet "Oklahoma-Land of the Fair God." The five verses, detailing Oklahoma's numerous natural advantages, would today serve as a superb brochure for a company advertising acreage for sale. Some samples:

Here the rich soil of the Indian is producing in
       abundance
Maize and corn, cane and potatoes, watermelons and
       tomatoes;
Prairie hay, oats, and alfalfa thrive for horses,
       sheep and cattle,
While the fat hogs, quail, and turkeys invite to
       the feast.

Here the coal mines and the oil-wells give employment
       and immense gain,
With the broad fields of white cotton and richest
       golden grain.
Here the men are the bravest and the women the fairest,
And the children the smartest, 'tis America's best.

Here the farmer and the merchant and the laborer prosper,
Ev'ry calling of honor our great state will foster ...
Let the Gov'nor and the Pres'dent, legislators and judges,
Give a square deal unto each man, and all honor to God.

When statehood was achieved in 1907, Mrs. I. C. Robinson wrote the words and music for "Oklahoma, the New State." Once more the inspiration of Stephen Foster made itself felt.

The sun shines bright on the Oklahoma plains,
And the flowers are blooming and gay,
The broad fields groan with their weight of golden grain,
And the white man has come here to stay ...
The sunflow'rs grow all along the dusty road,
And bow to the great God of day,
Beautiful fields with their great heavy load,
Of sweet potatoes and hay,
We plan another star, on red, white and blue,

Oklahoma the last and best . . .
No matter where I go . . .
No place suits me as well as the new state,
Oklahoma, the great southwest.

The year 1908 brought "Hurrah for Oklahoma! Patriotic Song and Chorus," by Rev. S. J. Oslin, who felt impelled to mix patriotism with sermonizing:

Hurrah for Oklahoma! the fairest of the states.
The youngest in the nation, and numbered forty-six . . .
We've statewide prohibition; we've said, "Saloons must go!"
Best is our constitution for "equal rights" to show.

With officers and people who hand in hand doth (*sic*) pull,
And earnest bands of Christians with righteousness are full,
We'll win for Oklahoma the honors due the brave!
Her star is in "Old Glory" and over us she'll wave.

In 1914 another song writer, M. J. Kennedy, entered the field with the same old title—"Oklahoma." But Mr. Kennedy, before looking ahead to the future, wished to remind his patrons of their debt to the past, so he indulged in reminiscences.

A contest was projected in eighteen eighty-nine,
Uncle Sam tho't just and fair to all,
'Twas then that men arrayed themselves in line to make
        the run,
With horse and cart and any way to go,
Even footmen were the racers, some joining in for fun,
To acquire some land or farm for future home.
They came from near and far, over fifty thousand strong,
To add to our flag one more glorious star . . .
Education is provided for by ample funds in land,
For boys and girls of ev'ry zone.
To compete as men and women in the battle life demands,
To be good Americans when grown.
Ancient legends of the red man we ev'ry one respect,
Great deeds are well recorded, done of yore.
Equality before the law, with special rights to none,
Oklahoma welcomes one and all.

By today's standards, these songs may seem unsophisticated. But they were honest, and they expressed the sentiment and the pride that consumed these early Oklahomans who wanted the world to know how good was that part of the country in which they lived.

If only the Cherokees, and the Kickapoos, and the Seminoles, and the Pawnees, had had a better break! Who can say how many more men like John Ross, and that other well-loved Oklahoman of Indian extraction, Will Rogers, might have been added to the list of names which meant so much to the great Southwest of yesterday?

Texas

A 1943 Cole Porter song says it all in six words: "See That You're Born in Texas." But to Texans, even though they may concur in the thought that anyone who fails to heed this admonition is a second-rate human being, one great song about their state is not sufficient—not *nearly* sufficient.

As a matter of fact, there was music about Texas even before it became a state of the Union in 1845. Texans had seceded from their first mother country, Mexico, on March 2, 1836. Four days later their San Antonio fortress, the Alamo, was overwhelmed by General Santa Anna and his Mexican army, and the Alamo's garrison of 183 men was annihilated.

As the hectic month neared a close, a formal constitution was adopted by the Republic of Texas, the Mexicans routed, and Santa Anna captured. In September General Sam Houston, the war's hero, was elected the first president of the new republic. Before the American public was aware of the conflict's early end, "The Texian War Song" had been written by one Charles Irwin and had been set to music by F. A. Wagler. With apparent reference to the massacre in the Alamo, Irwin wrote:

> We ask not for mercy, Be witness, O Heaven,
> No mercy they've shown us and none shall be given.

Other songs in support of the Texans followed quickly, "The Texan Song of Liberty," and the "Texian Hymn of Liberty." The first "dedicated to General Houston" by the lyricist, Mrs. M. A. Holley, said:

> The Texan chiefs are with the slain, martyrs
>   to liberty;

and then:

> Brave Houston leads a gallant band....
> Rush, freemen to the promised land,
> And Texas shall be free!
> Santa Anna (*sic*) savage fiend, no more
> Our lovely fields shall drench with gore;
> The monster never met before
> So brave an enemy.

The "Texian Hymn" by Stephen C. Parmenter went:

> Though the blood of Texians shall crimson
>   ev'ry plain,
> The rights that God has given us forever
>   we'll maintain

A composer linked Texas with another exciting part of the West in 1844. In that year the Democratic convention had declared that the country's title to "The whole territory of Oregon" was "clear and unquestionable." With a chip on its shoulder and an eye to the proximity of Canada to the north, the convention adopted the slogan "54–40 or fight." The heady promise of a huge expansion westward and the imminent inclusion of a tremendous area to the southwest led to the composition in 1844 of the "Texas and Oregon Grand March" by Anthony Philip Heinrich. But Oregon was obliged to wait fourteen years after Texas before being admitted as a state of the Union in 1859.

"The Yellow Rose of Texas," written by a modest fellow whose initials, J. K., remain the only clue to his still undiscovered identity, appeared in 1858 as a tribute to a beautiful girl of mixed blood. Responding to what may have been a bit of boasting by a writer from a sister state, J. K. announced firmly that "the yellow rose of Texas beats the belles of Tennessee."

The state song, "The Eyes of Texas," was first sung in a minstrel show performed by University of Texas students in 1903. The president of the university, William L. Prather, had, as a college youth, heard General Robert E. Lee, then president of Washington College, declare to the student body, "Young gentlemen, the eyes of the south are upon you." Prather, in turn, said at a gathering of *his* students, "The eyes of Texas are upon you." This pronouncement caught the fancy of a youth named John Lang Sinclair, who used it as the title of a song for a minstrel show. He set it to the music of an 1894 Princeton piece, "Levee Song," better known thereafter as "I've Been Working on the Railroad." The verbal "triple play," Lee to Prather to Sinclair, resulted in one of the most inspiring of all our state songs.

After 1900 Texas was a sure-fire subject for many a star on the vaudeville and musical stage. Only a few need be mentioned. To start, let's dwell briefly on Richard Carle. Carle was not only a great comedian; he was a skillful lyricist. From 1891 on, and for almost forty years, his dry and unctuous style delighted his audiences, first in the theater and later in the movies. He wrote lots of entertaining songs for lots of amusing shows, among them *The Maid and the Mummy, The Mayor of Tokio, The Spring*

Chicken (in which he convulsed his audience with "I Picked a Lemon in the Garden of Love"), *Jumping Jupiter*, and *The Tenderfoot*.

For *The Tenderfoot*, produced in 1903, Carle played the comic lead and contributed the lyrics of all the songs. One of the most endearing of these is "My Alamo Love," in which a lovesick boy tells of his advances to a San Antonio cutie.

> Once all alone in San Antone
> I found myself one June day,
> Depress'd and blue I wandered through
> The town from morn till noon day;
> I chanced to go to the Alamo,
> And fell in love at sight,
> With a senorita named Pepita,
> Vision of delight!

> CHORUS: I met my love in the Alamo when the moon
> was on the rise,
> Her presence quite be dimm'd its light,
> so radiant were her eyes!
> No star in Heaven's firmament can her bright
> smile outshine,
> There's no one like that Alamo love of mine!

> This dainty maid was not afraid
> When I, at first, addressed her,
> She smiled a bit and fancied it,
> As to my heart I pressed her;
> But when I said "Come let us wed"
> She coyly cooed "Not I"
> And tho' she threw me down, 'tis true
> I'll love her till I die!
> CHORUS

One of the great song-and-dance minstrels of the turn of the century was Eddie Leonard. (His real name was Tooney.) Leonard started out playing the cymbals and serving as all-around handy man for the Primrose and West minstrel troupe. They had about decided to release him when he composed and introduced—against his manager's orders—a song he had just written, "Ida" (sweet as apple cider). It was a sensational success, and propelled Leonard into orbit.

A solid favorite among theatergoers, he performed most of the time in blackface, but made exceptions when the occasion demanded. One such exception was his rendition of "Texas Dan," a feature of his 1905 vaudeville skit, *Lifting the Lid*. As a white-faced minstrel, in a beautiful white suit, with ruffled shirt and tall white stovepipe hat, the strutting Leonard would stop the show with his hit number, written by two prolific words-and-music men of the period, William Jerome and Jean Schwartz.

> Who's dat comin' down the street, Texas Dan
> Patent Regals on his feet, Texas Dan
> See that headlight in his tie,
> Certainly just hurts my eye,
> Dazzles ev'ry passer by, Texas Dan,
> For style and form he's more than warm.

> CHORUS: Texas Dan, Gamblin' Man,
> Takes a milk bath ev'ry day,
> And a sun-bath up and down Broadway,
> Texas Dan, Sportin' man,
> The sun keeps shinin' all the time for Texas Dan.

Poor Eddie Leonard! He could not cope with the changes that the years brought to vaudeville routine, though he tried desperately to modernize his acts. In his palmy days in New York he used to stop at the Hotel Imperial, which always assigned him the same room. When he finally realized that the end of his performing days seemed to be approaching, he checked in once more at the Hotel Imperial and requested the same room, hoping the old familiar setting would change his luck. But the impulsive gesture was too late; he was found dead in bed the next morning.

Then there was Louise Dresser, one of the great beauties of the stage. Miss Dresser was born Louise Kerlin. She adopted her stage name after Paul Dresser, who wrote "On the Banks of the Wabash," introduced her one day as his sister and helped her find work as a roof-garden singer. In 1906 she married Jack Norworth, a clever young actor and composer ("Shine On, Harvest Moon" was one of his all-time greats), who took her to New York and got her a singing role on Broadway. She "clicked," and for the next thirty years she prospered in the field of entertainment.

Though she grew heavier in the later years of her long career, as a girl she was a knockout. Her lovely face appeared on the title page of "Sombrero," which she presented in 1905. The product of a pair of musical work horses, James O. Dea and Neil Moret, the sentimental ballad unfolds:

> Way down by the silv'ry Rio Grande,
> There lives Sombrero, a cowboy brave,
> Far out in that golden prairie land,
> He rides where pampas plumes serenely wave,

With jingling spurs he comes to town,
Where in the plaza's shade, each lovely maid,
With soulful glance from eyes of brown
To win his heart so true and strong will sing
    this song

CHORUS: Sombrero, Sombrero, won't you greet a Senorita,
    Say we'll never part,
    Sombrero, Sombrero, truly you have
    "Rounded up" my heart.

In 1905, Philadelphia was the scene for the gathering of the sovereign Grand Lodge of the World of the International Order of Odd Fellows. The Oak Cliff Lodge of Dallas, Texas, had a contingent in attendance and arranged to have a song written for the occasion, which their Degree Staff quartette presented. The words of "The Texas Star," the quartette's offering, were written by the director of the Oak Cliff Degree Staff Orchestra, John R. Guyer, and he fitted them to a tune which everybody knew, "The Old Oaken Bucket." They follow (in part):

How dear to our hearts is the great State of Texas,
The place where fraternity prospers so well;
Where neighborly love and fraternal affection,
With truth and close friendship eternally dwell.
Its wondrous resources, its health laden breezes,
Its comforts of life seem to us so complete,
That all who have tasted its sweets can but love it
And know of its greatness with story replete.

CHORUS: The Lone Star of Texas,
    The Grand star of Texas
    The Bright Star of Texas,
    It shines for us all.

And in the belief that Odd Fellows everywhere would like the opportunity to obtain the words and music of this anthem, a notation on the title page read: "Any member of the I.O.O.F. can secure a copy of this song by sending 2 cents postage to the International Conservatory of Music, Kansas City, Dallas, and Atlanta." Apparently circulation figures were never reported.

Sixty and more years ago the names of cities in Texas attracted the song writers. Songs about American towns have always struck a chord, ever since a pleasant number, "New York, O What a Charming City!" was introduced to the American public in the 1830's. Looking toward the other end of the spectrum, many will recognize, "Big D" (Dallas, of course), from Frank Loesser's great 1956 score of *The Most Happy Fella.* But around 1907 the Texas towns that people sang about—Galveston and San Antonio, for instance—were far less sophisticated than Big D.

The words and music of "Galveston" were written by George A. Norton.

> Sunrise across the Texas prairie land,
> Ranch house with life is all a-glow,
> Big herd of cattle makes a picture grand,
> Cowboys a riding to and fro.
> "Pals," said a puncher to his comrade there,
> "I won't go on the run today,
> I've got a letter from my lady fair,
> She says to come back right away"
> Just ninety miles to ride, Then I'll be by her side, In

> CHORUS: Galveston, Galveston, That's the place for me, by gum,
> With my pal, my best gal, Easy life and lots of fun,
> Galveston, Galveston, With my blanket, nag and gun,
> I leave today, on my way, To dear old Galveston.[1]

So back to San Antonio, where all the ruckus started. In 1907, "San Antonio" was written by one of the greatest teams of the decade, Harry Williams and Egbert Van Alstyne. Van Alstyne was almost forty at the time. He had been born in a small Illinois town, and at a tender age was considered a musical prodigy; when he was seven he was playing the organ in Sunday School. After winning a scholarship at the Chicago Musical College, he toured as pianist and director with stage shows and eventually went into vaudeville with Williams. In 1900 they got to New York where Van Alstyne eked out a living for the two as pianist for a music publisher. After their first successful song, "Navajo," in 1903, they were started up the ladder. One hit followed another, "In the Shade of the Old Apple Tree," "Cheyenne," "Won't You Come Over to My House?" and "I'm Afraid to Come Home in the Dark."

"San Antonio" was a typical cowboy number of the period; almost any pseudocowboy or pseudo-Indian song in the century's first decade was a winner, and "San Antonio" ran true to form.

> Just as the moon was peeping o'er the hill,
> After the work was through,
> There sat a cowboy and his partner Bill,
> Cowboy was feeling blue.

---

[1] "Galveston." W/M George A. Norton © 1907 Cooper Kendis & Paley Music Pub. Co. Copyright Renewed All Rights Reserved Used by Permission WARNER BROS. MUSIC.

Bill says "Come down Pal, Down into town, Pal,
Big time for me and you,
Don't mind your old gal, you know its "cold" Pal
If what you say is true.
"Where is she now" Bill cried
And his partner just replied

CHORUS: San Antoni Antonio
She hopped upon a pony
And ran away with Tony
If you see her just let me know
And I'll meet you in San Antonio.[2]

In 1909 a lady from Rotan, Texas, decided to make her own musical contribution to her native state. Her song is called "Texas, Pride of the South." and her feelings are expressed candidly:

You may talk about your blue bloods of Virginia,
And your thorobreds of old Kentucky too,
And your aristocracy of Pennsylvania,
Texas has a few,
I was born and raised in dear Old Texas,
Pride of all the U.S.A.
I never wish to roam for Texas is my home
And here I'm going to stay.

CHORUS: Texas, Texas Pride of the South
How we love you honor you too
Lone star, bright star waving on high
I was born and raised on Texas soil,
In Texas let me die.

One comparatively recent tribute to the Lone Star State should be mentioned before we gallop off into the musical sunset. That, as many readers might have guessed, is "Deep In the Heart of Texas," where, we are told, the stars are big and bright, bigger and brighter, no doubt, than in Louisiana, New Mexico, and other contiguous but lesser sister states. The song was written in 1941 by June Hershey and Don Swander and first published, not in Texas, but in Hollywood, which has bright stars, too, shaped differently (thanks be) than those of Texas. Still and all, Texas has a right to be proud —proud of its history, of its long line of heroes, of its picturesque cities, and of the music inspired by its mighty image. Naught remains to be said but "Yippee!"

[2] "San Antonio." W/Harry Williams M/Egbert Van Alstyne © 1907 Remick Music Corp. Copyright Renewed All Rights Reserved Used by Permission of WARNER BROS. MUSIC.

San Antonio

Just as the moon was peep-ing o'er the hill —— Af-ter the work was through

— There sat a cow-boy and his part-ner Bill —— Cow-boy was feel-ing blue —

— Bill says "Come down Pal, Down in-to town Pal, Big time for me and

you,—— Don't mind your old gal you know it's "Cold" Pal, If what you say is

true — "Where is she now" Bill cried——And his part-ner just re-

Chorus

plied ———— San An-to-ni An-to-ni-o— She hopped up on a po-ny and ran

a-way with To-ny If you see her just let me know and I'll meet you in San An-to-ni-

o. ————

2. You know that pony that she rode away,
That horse belongs to me
So do the trinkets that she stow'd away
I was the big mark E
I wont resent it, I might have spent it
Plunging with Faro Jack

If she's not happy there with her chappie
Tell her I'll take her back.
No tender foot like him
Could love her like her boy Jim.
CHORUS

DEDICATED TO Mr. AND Mrs. E.I. LONG.

ARIZONA PROSPECTOR

WORDS BY
C. Ellsworth Snider

MUSIC BY
THEODORE F. MORSE

Price 50¢

PUBLISHED BY
Arizona Music Publishing Co.
New York.

Copyright 1901, by C. Ellsworth Snider.

Arizona

THE 1901 TITLE PAGE of "Arizona Prospector" is illustrated with a photograph of a stolid gentleman clad in dark work shirt and sturdy trousers held up by broad suspenders and carrying a pickax slung over his right shoulder and a dinner pail in his left hand. The verse goes, in part:

> There's a little cabin in the valley,
> Hardly large enough for three . . .
> There lives a prospector, wife and child.
> He owns a little claim just over the way,
> Where with pick and drill he labors each day;
> How happy is he when his day's work is done,
> And he starts back to his little cabin home. . . .
> His darling child sees him coming
> Ev'ry evening down the foot-hill,
> Calls to mama and starts running
> To meet him and carry his dinner-pail. . . .

> CHORUS: Oh! Who would not a prospector be,
> In the sun-kissed land of Arizona,
> If were only blessed with a wife and dear baby like this,
> To make life so happy and free.

Since the song, written by C. Ellsworth Snider and the well-known popular composer Theodore F. Morse, is "dedicated to Mr. and Mrs. E. J. Long," it must be deduced that the rugged prospector on the cover is Mr. Long himself, though considerable research fails to unearth any record of the career of this presumably worthy gentleman. No doubt he lived an honorable life, swinging his pick with the best of them, and, even though he may not have uncovered a Golconda, panned enough precious metal to keep the wolf and the coyotes from the door of that little cabin in the valley.

In those early days of the territory, before the responsibilities of statehood made song writing about the great Southwest a seriously sentimental procedure, Arizona did not seem to cultivate popular composers. Her white citizens were too fully occupied trying to accommodate themselves to pioneer living and to learning to get along with the Indians who had preceded them as settlers by quite a few hundred years.

White men first ventured into the country in the sixteenth century. Spain laid claim to it and managed to hold on while she had a firm hold in Mexico; but she lost that in 1822, when Mexico established her independence, and in 1824 the "Territory of Arizona and New Mexico" was formed.

Soon the Americans began to drift in over what was to become the Santa

Arizona Prospector

A-way down in a South-ern clime, the land of flow-ers gold and sun-shine, There's a

lit-tle cab-in in the val-ley, hard-ly large e-nough for three —— Free as the birds and midst

flow-ers wild, There lives a pros-pec-tor wife and child, He owns a lit-tle claim just

o-ver the way, where with pick and drill he la-bors each day; How hap-py he is when his

day's work is done, and he starts back to his lit-tle cab-in home; Well he knows who will be

out to meet him, with kind words, and kiss-es to greet — him.   His dar-ling child

sees him com-ing ev-'ry eve-ning down the foot-hill.   Calls   to ma-ma and starts

run-ning to meet him and car-ry his din-ner pail — You may talk a-bout the pal-ac-es

and man-sions, The pleas-ures and lux-ur-ies of the wealth-y, There's none more brigh-ter

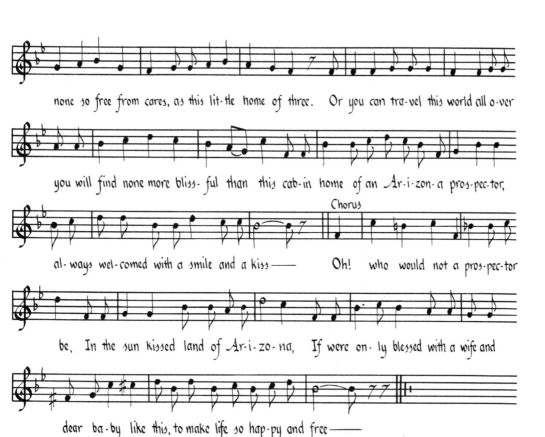

none so free from cares, as this lit-tle home of three. Or you can tra-vel this world all o-ver you will find none more bliss-ful than this cab-in home of an Ar-i-zon-a pros-pec-tor, al-ways wel-comed with a smile and a kiss —— Oh! who would not a pros-pec-tor be, In the sun kissed land of Ar-i-zo-na, If were on-ly blessed with a wife and dear ba-by like this, to make life so hap-py and free ——

Fe trail. When the war with Mexico ended, most of Arizona and much other southwestern territory was ceded to the United States, which, in 1853, paid Mexico $10,000,000 for another 45,000 square miles to round off a section which reached south to the present border of Mexico with Arizona and New Mexico. Our minister to Mexico at that time was James Gadsden; the land acquired was known as the Gadsden Purchase.

Silver and copper were first mined in 1856, and gold was discovered along the Gila River in 1858. A thousand persons converged on the region and formed Gila City, but the initial excitement soon proved to be a real flash in the pan, and Gila City became Arizona's first ghost town.

In 1861 the area was declared Confederate country, and the following year President Jeff Davis proclaimed Arizona a territory of the Confederacy. Little fighting took place there, however. In 1863 the government in Washington created a Federal Territory of Arizona, and after the war, settlers arrived in sharply increasing numbers.

Law and order were problems for several decades, but the intentions of the settlers were good, and bad men got their just deserts, frequently on the end of a noose. In 1885 polygamists and bigamists were prohibited by law from holding office. At about this time a unified school system was organized, and the largely unlettered state began to become lettered. It did not yet become musical, although an occasional bit of music relevant to some aspect of the state would appear from time to time.

In 1903, Miss Mabel McKinley, a niece of the late President, wrote, under the nom de plume of Vivian Grey, a pseudo-Indian ballad called "Anona." As one of the first in the field of songs about beautiful Indian maidens— "Red Wing," "Iola," "Silver Heels," and others were to follow—"Anona" was a welcome innovation.

> In the western state of Arizona lived an Indian maid;
> (Note: Statehood came, actually, nine years after the
> song was written.)
> She was called the beautiful Anona so 'tis said.
> Graceful as a fawn was she, just as sweet as she could be,
> Eyes so bright, dark as night,
> Had this pretty little Arizona Indian maiden
> All the chiefs who knew her came to woo her,
> For her pined. To marry she declined.
> At last she changed her mind,
> But 'twas not a chief so grand, who won her heart and hand,
> But a warrior bold, who wooed her with a song:

> CHORUS: My sweet Anona, in Arizona
> There is no other maid I'd serenade;
> By camp-fires gleaming, of you I'm dreaming,
> Anona, my sweet Indian maid.

> When her father heard that his Anona loved this youthful
> brave,
> Straightway he said he would disown her; things looked
> grave.
> She must marry "heap big chief;" sweet Anona hid her grief,
> Ran away, so they say,
> And got married to the man she loved without delaying.
> Then her father sought her; never caught her,
> Till one day, when two years passed away, they both came
> back to stay.
> Then the chief declared a truce, when they named their
> young papoose,
> After him, and to his grandchild he would sing:
> CHORUS:

Toward the southern part of the state much of the male population was employed in the copper industry. Bisbee was the focal point of Arizona's copper at the turn of the century, and one of the most productive facilities was the Copper Queen mine. With the conviction that there was nothing farfetched about introducing the Copper Capital to the piano, an instrumentalist named Frank Winstein composed in 1904 the "City of Bisbee March," displaying on the music's title page an up-to-date photograph of the little city rising from the copper-bearing hills about it. The march is "respectfully dedicated to the Copper Queen Co."

Bisbee was a boom town in those days. Its citizens were arrogant; the city was called a "white man's camp." Orientals had to leave town before night-fall, and Mexicans were not allowed to work in the mines. Dance halls flourished; in the numerous saloons women were prohibited from serving as entertainers or bartenders. In 1908 the town was swept by a disastrous fire from which it recovered slowly and painfully. A dramatic, spontaneous ballad, a "corrida," was composed on the occasion of the catastrophe by Señor Francisco Chavez, one of the best-known Mexican entertainers in the state. The opening lines, literally translated, went:

> The year, nineteen hundred and seven and who would have thought
>   it possible?
> At about eleven o'clock at night half of Bisbee went to burn.
> Americans and Negroes and a part of Mexicans
> Were running frantically with cans of water in their hands.
> And all the firemen didn't know what to do———
> They said, "The water has given out. Now Bisbee is going to burn."

The singer ends his "corrida" as follows:

> This song is composed, was composed by surprise,
> I would sing it over again for a glass of beer.
> To all my friends I give notice, if they don't know,
> This song was composed by Señor Francisco Chavez.

Arizona attained statehood in 1912, and soon her proud inhabitants were writing songs of praise. Probably the best known is one with words by Margaret Clifford and music by Len Fleming. Mrs. Clifford wrote with feeling:

> 1. Come to this land of sunshine,
>   To this land where life is young.
>   Where the wide, wide world is waiting
>   The songs that will now be sung.
>   Where the golden sun is flaming
>   Into warm, white, shining day,
>   And the sons of men are blazing
>   Their priceless right of way.

2. Come stand beside the rivers
   Within our valleys broad.
   Stand here with heads uncovered
   In the presence of our God.
   While all around, about us
   The brave, unconquered land,
   As guardians and landmarks
   The giant mountains stand.

3. Not alone for gold and silver
   Is Arizona great.
   But with graves of heroes sleeping,
   All the land is consecrate!
   O come and live beside us
   However far ye roam
   Come help us build our temples
   And name those temples "home."

CHORUS: Then Hurrah for Arizona
         Her climate, schools and Law,
         For her copper, Gold and Silver,
         Hurrah, Hurrah, Hurrah!

The song grew in popularity in the state, but not everyone was pleased with the melody. So, in 1915, a new air was composed by Maurice Blumenthal. Mrs. Clifford decided, at the same time, to write a chorus more stirring than the somewhat stilted four lines of the original, so she restylized the chorus as follows:

Sing the song that's in your hearts,
Sing of the great Southwest,
Thank God for Arizona
In splendid sunshine dressed.
For thy beauty and thy grandeur,
For thy regal robes so sheen,
We hail thee, Arizona,
Our goddess and our queen.

In 1917 another musical lady, Mrs. M. F. Homer, felt the inspiration of the muse and was sentimentally affected by the state's area of striking beauty. The result was a beautifully descriptive ballad, "Arizona My Land."

Arizona, though so youthful, yet few lands with you compare.
Your desert fast is springing into fields and gardens fair,
Bringing forth a bount'ous harvest. Many products choice and rare,
Grown from your fertile soil.
Mines of silver, gold, and copper, which are 'mong the world's foremost,

Flocks of sheep and herds of cattle, fine as any land can boast.
With these and other riches, greatly blest you give the most,
For the least amount of toil.

CHORUS: O my Arizona Land, where there's ne'er a day that's dreary,
Weather always bright and cheery, unsurpassed your balmy clime.
O my Arizona Land, air so pure on you reposes,
Fraught with scents of pines and roses, in perpetual summer-time.

You have scenes of rarest beauty where the giant cactus reigns;
While 'mong your extensive forest, one of yore as stone remains.
 [This alludes, of course, to the famous Petrified Forest.]
Luring are your wondrous canyons, mountains cool, and sunny plains,
Beneath azure skies so clear.
You are always bathed in brightness, giving landscapes brilliant hues,
And the colors of such splendor, blended in your sunset views;
So very clear your stars shine, so much mellow light diffuse,
That heaven seems more near.
CHORUS

After such overpowering encomiums, what more can be said?

6

THE MUSCLE MEN

"The Victors"

Football? The Greeks had a word for it; they called it *harpaston*. It was played in ancient Sparta on a rectangular field with lines marking the center, sides, and goals, where contestants passed and kicked the ball (the inflated bladder of a boar) and even carried it over the goal line. The number of players seems to have been unlimited, and there is no mention of officials.

Rome's football game was called *follis*. Down through the centuries it retained its popularity. When the Latin language was superseded by Italian, *follis* was renamed *calcio*. The Florentine nobles of the sixteenth century were *calcio* buffs; princes would "choose up" for sides, and the *sconciatori* (halfbacks) were, says a contemporary manuscript, "powerful men, big, fierce, muscular, and of great skill."

In medieval England the English version, "Ballown," was so popular that for centuries the kings tried to suppress it by royal edict. In 1457 the Scottish parliament "decreeted and ordained that . . . the Fute ball and Golf be utterly cryit doune, and nocht usit."

Not only did the English rulers fail in their efforts to eliminate football at home, they could not control the spread of the game to their colonies. In *Relation of Virginia*, published in 1609, it is stated: "They vse beside football wch women and young boys doe much play at. They make their gooles like ours only they never fight nor pull another doone." And so, nearly four hundred years ago, football came to America. But it was a far cry from football as we know it today; indeed, it was little like the game that was introduced on a limited scale to American colleges in the 1840's.

As first played at Princeton, groups of students kicked on a pig bladder, inflated by strong breath, between Princeton's east and west college buildings. Any number of students could play, and the teams were formed indiscriminately. For example, students whose names began with the letters A to L might meet those whose names began with M to Z. Whichever side was able to kick to the wall scored a goal and won the game. The only hard and fast rule observed was that any part of the body *except* the hands might be used to propel the ball. As a rule, there was more kicking of shins than of pig bladder.

Harvard followed Princeton in instigating similar clashes. Her matches were staged between freshmen and sophomores, and soon got to be known as "football." But the free-for-alls or rushes, as they were called, became too rough for the likings of the Harvard faculty, who ordered a discontinuance of the skirmishes in 1860. Whereupon a procession of undergraduates marched to a site upon which one of Harvard's great halls stands today, dug a grave, pronounced a funeral oration, and buried the ball, erecting over it a monument reading: "*Hic Jacet Football Fightum. Obiit* July 2, 1860."

The enormous popularity of intercollegiate football today had its inconspicuous origin in 1869, when Rutgers challenged its neighbor, Princeton, to a series of three matches, the winner to be the college which could capture two of the three. The home team laid down the rules. On November 9 the first game was played in New Brunswick under Rutgers rules. Result: Rutgers six goals, Princeton four. A week later Princeton was host and rules maker too. Result: Princeton eight goals, Rutgers none. The deciding game was prohibited by the two faculties, so 1869 produced no intercollegiate champion.

Costumes for 1869 players must have been desultory; there were no uniforms for another seven years, and the sole identifying feature was a scarlet turban, worn by each of the Rutgers players. The captain of the Princeton team recalled years later that a low fence along one side of the field, serving as scanty seating facilities for the spectators, was crashed into by two opposing warriors pursuing the bounding ball. A section of the fence disintegrated, and the hapless spectators were tumbled to the ground. He even remembered that Princeton had a locomotive cheer, probably the first of its kind, though college yells had been in vogue a few years earlier on occasions of intercollegiate boat races. These had consisted, in the main, of nine rahs, followed by the name of the school, and became so universal that college students were soon dubbed by the public "rah rah boys."

In 1871 a student entering Yale from Rugby promoted a game between the classes of 1873 and 1874. Much like the rugby played in England, the rules were nevertheless modified a bit. The success of the enterprise led to the organization in 1872 of the Yale Football Association, which played its first intercollegiate game that fall against Columbia. The following year Harvard, Rutgers, and Princeton all showed an interest in attempting, with Yale and Columbia, to formulate a set of rules under which intercollegiate football might be played. The suggested rules did not suit Harvard, which courteously declined to attend the rules conference; but the other colleges got along fine. They all agreed on teams of twenty men each, free kicks and fair catches, no carrying or throwing of the ball, and no dribbling on the kickoff.

Three games were played that fall. Yale, and then Rutgers, beat Columbia; Princeton defeated Yale. So much for the first college football season.

By 1880 colleges in the South and Middle West had become engrossed in the sport. Soon systems of signals were developed. Yale used sentences, Princeton letters, Harvard and Pennsylvania a combination of the two. Eventually these gave way to numerical signals, some quite complicated. It has never been substantiated that the burly, and not too clearheaded, fullback of one team called in desperation to his quarterback, "To hell wid your mystic signs and symbols. Gimme de ball!"

Popular music with college themes had been known in this country as early as the 1830. Songs dedicated to college graduates were commonplace in the 1850's, but songs about college sports did not appear until much later. The college football song first emerged in the late 1890's, and burst on the nation in all its glory in the early years of the twentieth century. Thanks to the enormous popularity which the sport achieved, many of these early songs are among the best-remembered of our garden-type variety of musical literature.

As stirring as any later contestants for musical honors is the University of Michigan march, "The Victors," written by Louis Elbel in 1898, and played and sung today with the same enthusiasm which inspired it seventy-five years ago.

> Hail to the victors valiant,
> Hail to the conq'ring heroes
> Hail, hail to Michigan,
> The champions of the West!
> U of M, rah rah,
> U of M, rah rah!
> Horrah hoorah, Michigan, Michigan,
> Rah rah rah!!

UNIVERSITY of MICHIGAN
FOOT BALL TEAM ~ '04

MARCH.

THE VICTORS

BY

LOUIS ELBEL

BAND, ~ ORCHESTRA ,   MANDOLIN, ~ GUITAR.

PUBLISHED BY ~ ELBEL BROS. SOUTH BEND, IND.
COPYRIGHT ~ FOR - ALL COUNTRIES

The Victors

Hail to the vic-tors val-iant Hail to the conq-ring her-oes Hail Hail to

Mich-i-gan the cham-pions of the West

U of M Rah Rah U of M Rah Rah Hoo Rah Hoo

Rah Michigan Michigan Rah Rah Rah Hail to the vic-tors val-iant Hail

to the conq-ring her-oes Hail Hail to Mich-i-gan the cham-pions of the West.

Other Michigan songs, written some years later, were never able to dislodge "The Victors" from its place in the affection of students and alumni. One, written in 1910, with words by C. Arthur Blass and music by Julius Wuerthner, starts out with a color scheme.

> Old Yale may have her blue,
> And Harvard crimson hue,
> Chicago her maroon and white,
> And Penn her red and blue,
> But give us those old colors,
> So dear to every heart,
> The maize and blue of Michigan
> From which we ne'er shall part.

> CHORUS: Hail dear old Michigan,
> The maize and blue we'll honor and adore . . .

Harvard, whose students sang about their school in the 1840's, seems to have delayed until the early 1900's for its first specific football song, "Three Times Three for Harvard." The title page carries a photograph of a tangle of men on the field in a game watched by many thousands of spectators in tightly packed stands, while a leader with megaphone directs the cheers of the student body. The 1902 song by two Harvard men, Richard Inglis and William H. Smith, has a rousing melody in six-eighths time, hardly matched by the banal words.

Three times three for Johnny Harvard
For we all are Harvard men.
We'll drink a health to Harvard
Round and Round again.
Deep the crimson in our glasses,
Then ev'ry heart be gay and free
Here's to the team that surpasses
And for Harvard "Three times three."

Another Harvard march and two-step, written in 1904 by two undergraduates, James V. Dignowitz and Parker H. Daggett, pointed at the Yale game.

Up boys! Let us have a cheer for the good old
        crimson,
Hats off! Wave your colors high,
For Harvard's day has come.
Harvard! We will win the game
Mid the banners gay,
Upon the field, old Yale must yield
To Harvard's sway.

Yale's old classic was her great Boola song, so well known that it needs no repetition here. The melody had been adapted from an 1890 song, "La Woola Boola," by the great Negro song writers, Bob Cole and Billy Johnson. In 1901 a Yale man, A. M. Hirsh, wrote the immortal untranslatable words, dearer to most Yale graduates than their sheepskins. Cole Porter wrote in 1911, "Hail to Yale," with words far less inspirational than such later paeans of praise as "You're the Top," "You Do Something to Me," and "My Heart Belongs to Daddy."

But Yale had other favorites, too, such as "Touchdown," written in 1905 by W. Kyle Sheffield, with words by Paul H. Sears. These could be shifted around for the big game of the moment, depending on whether the opponent was Harvard or Princeton. For the Harvard game, the words ran like this:

As cheer meets cheer across the field
With Harvard's team the Eli's clash.
The sons of Yale will never fail
The Crimson line to tear and smash.
Old Eli's Blue the Crimson hue
Will obscure without fail
Now all to-gether,
A touchdown for Eli Yale.

The greatest of the Princeton songs by far was "The Princeton Cannon Song March," written in 1906 by two undergraduates, J. F. Hewitt and A. H. Osborn. With a melody as familiar as Michigan's "Victors" or Yale's "Boola," the chorus goes:

Crash through the line of blue,
And send the backs on round the end,
Fight! Fight! for ev'ry yard,
Princeton's honor to defend.
(spoken) Rah! Rah! Rah!
Rah! Tiger Sis Boom Ah,
And locomotives by the score,
For we'll fight with a vim
That is dead sure to win
For old Nas-sau.[1]

This was not Princeton's earliest football song. Back in 1902 an undergraduate named Kenneth Clark had adapted an early melody of the great blues writer of Memphis, Will Handy, and called it the "Ramble Song." Clark followed this three years later with a "Princeton Jungle March."

Another football-conscious eastern university was Cornell, whose undergraduates contributed several songs to the cause. "The Big Red Team" by Romeyn Barry and C. E. Tourison had a title page depicting the great team of 1905, and a chorus which went:

Cheer till the sound wakes the blue hills around
Make the scream of the north wind yield
To the strength of the yell from the men of Cornell,
When the big red team takes the field,
Three thousand strong we march, march along,
From our home on the gray rock height,
Oh! the vict'ry is sealed when the team takes the field,
And we cheer for the red and white.

George F. Pond wrote "We March to Victory" in 1908, and the piece was

1 "The Princeton Cannon Song." A. H. Osborn & J. F. Hewitt Copyright 1906 by Shapiro Bernstein & Co., Inc. 666 Fifth Avenue New York, N.Y. 10019 Copyright Renewed and Assigned USED BY PERMISSION.

featured by the Cornell glee club and the band and mandolin clubs. The words were inconsequential, the only mark of note being that the writer felt intimate enough with the school's founder to call him by his first name.

> For we are here today for Ezra,
> For Cornell so great and grand.

The songs most honored by the men of the University of Pennsylvania had no reference to football, except for one back in 1907, which became popular for a time. It was "Fight for Penn," with words by a student, Norman L. Harker, and music by Paul Eno, director of the combined music clubs. Here again their paternal ancestor, Benjamin Franklin, was brought in on a first-name basis.

> Do or die, that's the cry, Spirit of old Penn,
> Victory, now for thee, Cheer our Father Ben,
> See our team is winning as of old,
> Now they score and win the fray.

A 1905 graduate of Dartmouth, John Thomas Keady, was responsible for the words of that college's big football number, "As the Backs go Tearing By," sung to a spirited tune by Carl W. Blaisdell.

> As the backs go tearing by
> On the way to do or die,
> Many sighs and many tears mingle with the [Harvard] cheers,
> As the backs go tearing by,
> Making gain on steady gain,
> Echo swells the sweet refrain,
> Dartmouth's going to win today, Dartmouth sure must win today,
> As the backs go tearing by.

Farther west, the University of Illinois used to sing "The Illinois Siren Song," written in 1908 by T. H. Guild. Part music, part college yells, it is the first football song to admit to a coeducational environment.

> ... the banners of the Blue and Orange, waving high
> The loyal men and maidens trooping gaily by;
> Thousands then the bleachers filling
> Rise with one grand impulse thrilling,
> And "Illinois" is thunder'd in a mighty cry,
> As the team comes forth to victory ....
> Send 'em a singing out with a ringing shout,

(shouted) Give em a Hullabaloo!
(sung)   Hilarious yell of joy,
> Smite the foe with fear, with every good bold cheer ...
(shouted) Che-he! Che-ha!.
> Now the Siren! Ready! One, two three!
(siren)   W-w-w-w-wow! Illinois!

Scarcely any football song sung or whistled today is better known than a sixty-year-old number written by two forgotten university men, Paul Beck and W. T. Purdy. They were the team who in 1909 wrote "On Wisconsin!" which is still one of the great favorite tunes in football music. The stereotyped words blend into the melody.

> On Wisconsin! On Wisconsin!
> Plunge right thru that line!
> Run the ball 'round Minnesota,
> A touchdown sure this time.
> On Wisconsin! On, Wisconsin!
> Fight on for her fame.
> Fight! fellows! Fight! And we will win this game.[2]

One of the greatest football universities in recent years is Ohio State, whose games draw attendances in the neighborhood of eighty thousand. These enormous crowds chant the stirring words of a song written in 1915 by a student of that period, W. A. Dougherty, Jr. to a tune familiar to every Ohio alumnus and most residents of the state.

> Fight that team across the field,
> Show them Ohio's here,
> Set the earth reverberating
> With a mighty cheer
> (spoken) Rah! Rah! Rah!
> Hit them hard and see how they fall;
> Never let that team get the ball,
> Hail! Hail! The gang's all here,
> So let's beat that [Northwestern] now.

The southern colleges gave no quarter to those of the North or West where football fever was concerned. Take little Virginia Polytechnic Institute, for example. In 1919 a pair of youngsters, Mattie E. Boggs and W. P. Maddux, wrote a lively marching song called "Tech Triumph," the words of which are:

> Just watch our men so big and active,
> Support the Orange and Maroon! Let's go Techs!
> We know our ends and back are stronger,
> With winning hopes, we fear defeat no longer,
> To see our team plow thru the line, boys,
> Determined now to do or die;
> So give a Hokie, Hokie, Hokie, Hi!
> Rae, Ri, old V.P.I.!

2 "On Wisconsin." W/Carl Beck M/William T. Purdy © copyright 1909 by Flanner-Hafsoos Music House, Inc. copyright renewed and assigned to Edwin H. Morris & Company, Inc. by Mrs. Purdy. Used by permission.

By far the best-known tune of those used by the southern schools is the "Washington and Lee Swing." Dating back to the winter of 1906–1907, a South Dakota student named Mark W. Sheafe, who was their director of the mandolin and glee club, picked out the air of the chorus on his mandolin and taught it to the other musicians in the club. He called the tune simply "The Swing."

The following fall there was appointed a committee to write songs for the annual football game with Virginia Polytechnic Institute. Among those submitted was a set of words to "The Swing" by a Brooklyn boy, C. A. ("Tod") Robbins. The words and music were embraced by the student body and adopted as the university's official athletic song, which became known as "The Washington and Lee Swing." So infectious was the melody that soon other colleges picked it up, revising words to suit each particular purpose.

Later on, Thornton W. Allen, a New Jersey man, who attended the university for the 1909–10 season, and who directed the band and the orchestra, wrote words and music for verses which were fitted into the chorus but which never attained the enormous popularity of the chorus itself. And while the words of the chorus are not dynamic, the music bears them along.

> When Washington and Lee's men fall in line,
> We're going to win again another time;
> For W. and L. I yell, yell, yell, yell, yell,
> And for the University I yell, I yell like h——
> So fight, fight, fight, for ev'ry yard!
> Circle the ends and hit the line right hard!
> And roll the enemy upon the sod (on the sod)
> Rah! Rah! Rah![3]

The great gridiron rivalry between the United States Military Academy and the United States Naval Academy commenced in 1890, when the two football teams met each other for the first time. It was many years later, however, that the songs which we associate most closely with these struggles were composed. The Army's great marching song, "The Caissons Go Rolling Along," was the work of Edmund L. Gruber in 1921; he wrote both the words and the music. The Navy's stirring "Anchors Aweigh" was intended originally as a class march. It was customary to have a song written in honor of each graduating class; and the tune for "Anchors Aweigh" was composed by Lieutenant Charles A. Zimmerman, bandmaster of the Naval Academy

[3] "Washington and Lee Swing." W/M C. A. Robbins, Thornton W. Allen, M. W. Sheafe Copyright © 1910, T. W. Allen & R. G. Thack Renewed 1938 ROBBINS MUSIC CORPORATION Used by Permission.

Band, for the class of 1907. The words were written by a midshipman, A. H. Miles. When we hear these two gallant marches played at the annual classic meeting of the two teams of our service academies, we feel a sense of exhilaration, and of pride too, in the young men chosen to defend our country.

Music has always been an integral part of the excitement of college football. And in the foreseeable future no gridiron battle between college teams will be complete without a strong sideline complement of lusty voices raised in the rousing songs of Alma Mater.

The Fighters

Prize fighting over the past hundred years owes whatever aspects of gentility it may have to a man whose name is never mentioned. That man was John Sholto Douglas. Rare indeed would be the fighter, manager, or promoter who could indicate any recognition of Douglas' significance to the devotees of the "manly art." But the announcement of Douglas' official title would dispel all the fogginess as to why his name should be, for the prize-fighting fraternity, a household—or rather, a ringside—word. For Douglas was an English peer, the eighth Marquis of Queensberry. He was a devotee of sports and principally of boxing, and for a hundred years boxers have fought by the Marquis of Queensberry rules.

Despite widespread belief, the Marquis didn't write the rules himself. The code was compiled by a member of the British Amateur Athletic Club, John Graham Chambers, whose name now means no more to sports followers than does that of Douglas. It was customary in England in those days (back in 1867) for writers of subjects relating to sport to seek the patronage of a member of the peerage and to use his name as sponsor. Chambers having requested Queensberry's endorsement, and Queensberry having graciously acquiesced, the new rules, superseding the old London Prize Ring Code, were blessed with Queensberry's name, though his only contribution toward their promulgation was a nod of consent to Chambers.

An Englishman may have written the rules by which championship bouts are governed, but the influence of England upon prize fighting stops there. For from Queensberry's time on, nearly every heavyweight titleholder was an American, or, if we feel that hyphenating is in order, an Irish-American. For a few years after the Civil War, before prize fighting acquired a legal status in the United States, English sluggers were in the ascendant. But in the late 1870's the first of the great American fighters began to stir excitement among supporters of the ring. The young man with a future was named John Lawrence Sullivan, better known after a few years of professionalism as "the great John L."

Sullivan was a Bostonian. He was born in 1858 to immigrant parents in the suburb of Roxbury, headquarters of the great Irish population of Boston, and he came by his profession honestly; his father's father had been a well-known Irish wrestler. His parents saw him graduate from high school and enter Boston College, his mother dreaming that her son might aspire to the priesthood. But John had quite different ideas; he left the college after a little over a year's study, in which he devoted himself for a great part of the time to elocution and drama. He entered several amateur boxing tournaments for relaxation while he apprenticed himself to a plumber so as to learn an honest trade. Unfortunately for his employer, the foreman picked a quarrel with his apprentice, who soon had broken his boss's jaw and ended his own plumbing career with a dismissal the following day.

From plumbing he went to a position as a tinsmith and then to baseball, where he grew to enjoy the idea of playing and being paid for it (as a semi-professional ballplayer he drew up to a hundred dollars a week). But soon he was embarked on the career that would lift him to a pinnacle of fame. At the age of nineteen he was induced to accept the challenge of a Boston boxer named Tom Scannel. Scannel had a local reputation and on that particular night was offering to take on all comers and stop each of them within three rounds. Big John rolled up his sleeves, threw a powerful right to the jaw, and knocked Scannel senseless.

Sullivan's friends were quick to grasp his potential as a fighter, and they arranged match after match for him. Strong as a horse, eager as a beaver, and savage as a wildcat, his string of victories brought demands for his appearance in boxing rings around the country. Shortly before his twenty-first birthday the "Boston Strong Boy" signed an agreement to meet the heavyweight champion, an Irish-born fighter named Paddy Ryan, known affectionately as the Trojan Giant. The Giant was three inches taller and twenty-five pounds heavier than Sullivan, but his advantage stopped there. The battlers met in Mississippi City on February 7, 1882, in a bare-knuckles fight to the finish, for twenty-five hundred dollars a side. Thousands of boxing enthusiasts traveled south to see the great match. It was exciting, but it soon became a one-sided affair as Sullivan pounded away at the champion with deadly accuracy. The end came in the ninth round, when Sullivan's sledge-hammer right sent Ryan to the floor and to oblivion.

For ten years John L. was king of the ring. No complete record of his knockouts was kept, but there were at least fifty, according to unofficial reckoning. For several years he toured the country, offering the sum of one thousand dollars to anyone who could last four rounds against him. For such bouts he prescribed gloves; and their nearly universal adoption thereafter may be attributed to the boxing glove requirements stipulated during Sullivan's tour.

Sullivan was one of the most popular heavyweights who ever held the title. He enjoyed acknowledging the plaudits of the crowd with a short statement such as, "I will fight any man breathing. Always on the level, yours truly, John L. Sullivan."

In 1887 he went to England, where he received the most enthusiastic, tumultuous welcome that British sportsmen ever extended to an American athlete. Crossing over to Ireland, he was acclaimed a national hero. Back in London he was introduced to and shook hands with egregious, fun-loving Albert, Prince of Wales. The handshake became the basis of a song which was sung on the vaudeville stage all around the United States and which included the wisecrack: "Let me shake the hand that shook the hand of the Prince of Wales!"

Some years earlier, in fact just after Sullivan had beaten Ryan for the heavyweight title, E. J. Bowen had composed "Sullivan's Grand March." Under the picture on the cover, showing a grim-faced, mustachioed John L., appears the dedication, "To the champion, John L. Sullivan."

He held his title for nearly ten years, during which period he laced his professional career with appearances in vaudeville and in a play *Honest Hearts and Willing Hands*, and in informal exhibitions. Meanwhile, he indulged himself with the bottle and other worldly pleasures so freely that in 1888 he was confined to his bed for three months.

A little more than six months after recovering from his serious bout with his weaknesses, and after rigorous training had reduced his bulk from 240 to 205 pounds, he was in the ring again in Richburg, Mississippi. This time he was in a bare-knuckle fight to the finish with Jake Kilrain, who was wearing a heavyweight championship belt awarded him by the publisher of the *National Police Gazette*. Sullivan, who wore his own $10,000 diamond-studded championship belt, had traveled to New Orleans. Wherever the train stopped en route there was a crowd to cheer the great John L. In the New Orleans depot he was mobbed, and his carriage was pulled by hand to his hotel. The fight was advertised extensively, but the time and place were never mentioned, for prize fighting, despite its enormous popularity, was illegal in every one of the country's thirty-eight states.

When the match, held on July 8, 1889, on the property of a wealthy lumberman began the temperature was 104 degrees in the shade. It didn't go lower during the seventy-five rounds of the battle. As the seventy-sixth started, after two hours and sixteen minutes of fighting, Kilrain's seconds threw in the sponge. The last great bare-knuckles fight had ended.

After the fabulous John L. was counted out in his match with Gentleman Jim Corbett in 1882, he walked to the ropes, raised his arms, and said, "I fought once too often but I am glad that the championship remains in America. Yours truly, John L. Sullivan."

Seven years later a new star shone in the boxing firmament. The star's name was James J. Jeffries. An Ohioan by birth, the big farm boy had moved to California and at fifteen had taken a job as a boilermaker. Before long he was signed on as a sparring partner by Jim Corbett. One of Corbett's handlers had introduced Jeffries to Corbett with the remark, "He's as strong as a horse," to which Corbett, looking at the youth from the country, replied, "They should have sent the horse."

Jeffries was strong, all right—one of the strongest men who ever entered the prize ring. At twenty-one he weighed two hundred and twenty pounds, stood six feet two inches in height, had a chest like a barrel and the muscles of a weight lifter. He was amazingly agile for his size; he could run a hundred yards in eleven seconds and clear a bar in the high jump at nearly six feet.

Jim's work with Corbett ended when the champion fought to defend his title against Bob Fitzsimmons in March, 1897. But Corbett went down for the count in the fourteenth round, and Fitzsimmons was the new pugilistic idol.

It took two years more before Fitz was ready to face Jeffries, who had been taking on rugged assailants in his climb up boxing's ladder. During that period Fitzsimmons had allied himself with a theatrical troupe which traveled around the country. Jeffries was the first man he faced after winning the championship, and Fitzsimmons picked him because he wanted to work cautiously while he got himself back into perfect fighting form. He did not realize what a murderous opponent he was up against.

Jeffries in two years had learned to adopt a style of his own that became known as the "Jeffries crouch." With his legs bent in a half crouch, his stomach well protected, his head tucked in, and his left arm extended and ready to batter an approaching rival, he was nearly impervious to damage. Meanwhile his offense was always deadly dangerous; his powerful arms had to travel only a few inches to commit near-murder. Never flashy, always plodding ahead, the longer a fight lasted the more strength he appeared to develop.

He was ready for the big match with Fitzsimmons when the great day, June 9, 1899, dawned. But he was so skeptical of his ability to defeat the skillful champion that on the morning of the fight he placed a five-thousand-dollar bet, through his trainer—on Fitzsimmons. Jeff figured that, if he lost, he would have an additional sizable nest egg, and if he won, the championship would bring him in so much more for future bouts that the temporary impairment of funds would be recovered many times over.

> Chorus: Who's dat man wid-a hand like da bunch-a banan!
> It's da Jim-a-da-Jeff
> Oh! da Jim-a-da-Jeff,
> From da West wid-a chest like da brudder Sylvest,
> It's da Jim-a-da-Jeff,
> Oh! da Jim-a-da-Jeff.
> Who give-a da Jack Jonce one-a little-a tap?
> Who make-a him take-a one big-a long nap?
> Who wipe-a da Africa off-a da map?
> It's da Jim-a-da-Jeff,
> Oh! you Jim-a-da-Jeff.

The Old Fox, as Fitzsimmons was called, fought a shrewd fight for the first half dozen rounds, but his best punches could not hurt Big Jim. Jeffries kept jabbing away with short solid punches until he made the champion groggy, and finally in the eleventh round a blow to Fitzsimmons' chin ended the uneven match.

In his dressing room he was visited by old John L. Sullivan. The gray-haired former champion was stone-broke, and cautioned Jeffries not to waste his assets nor be careless about his physical condition. "Now that you've got the championship, don't throw it away like I did," warned John L.

Jeffries didn't require the warning. He was no spendthrift; he was still the stolid, conservative country boy. He hated crowds and kept to himself as much as possible. A poor speaker and a terrible actor, he consented to be starred in one stage play and flopped miserably. Soon he began to hate his championship status. Once he said, "All I got out of it was embarrassment. They wanted to put me on exhibition like a prize pig."

JIM·A·DA·JEFF

KIMBALL BROS.

212

Jim-a-da-Jeff

A-way out-a West where dey rais-a da prune,— A great big-a man he run-a da farm;

—— An' he push-a da plow— an' he hum-a da tune,—An' he do-a no-a bod-y da harm.

—— But a man from da East come a-long wid da mon,—An' he talk-a to him a-

bout da stage;— Den he pack-a da grip,—An' he take-a da trip,—An' now-a he-a

Chorus

great-a big-a rage.—— Who's dat man wid da hand like da bunch a ba-nan! It's da

Jim-a-da-Jeff,— Oh! da Jim-a-da-Jeff.— From da West wid-a chest like da brud-der Syl-

vest;— It's da Jim-a-da-Jeff,— Oh! da Jim-a-da-Jeff.— Who take all da man-a-dat-a

put on da mitts?— Who take-a da Cor-bett, da Shar-key, da Fitz?— Who make-a dem all

look-a like-a two bits?— It's da Jim-a-da-Jeff, Oh! you Jim-a-da-Jeff.——

2. This man have a wife, she da pride of his life,
She-a one-a very little a gal;
An' she say-a to him "Now-a look-a here Jim,
You-a do-a just-a what-a I tell.
You commence right away to get into condish,

An' you punch-a bag-a day and night;
An'-a den pretty soon,
When you meet-a da coon,
You knock-a him-a clear-a out-a sight."

But he was always willing to fight. For five years, during the period that has been called the "Golden Age of the American Ring," he took on all deserving challengers and disposed of one after the other. A year before he retired undefeated in 1905 he met Jack Johnson, a powerful Negro heavyweight, in a San Francisco saloon. The story goes that Johnson challenged Big Jeff to a fight for the championship. Jeffries is supposed to have replied, "I won't meet you in the ring because you've got no name. . . . But I'll go downstairs to the cellar with you and lock the door from the inside. The one who comes out with the key will be the champ." Johnson walked out.

The day of retribution came five years later. Johnson had beaten the best of all the available heavyweights and had been crowned champion, a situation which was nearly unbearable to many thousands of prejudiced white fans, who grimaced at the thought that a Negro—the first of his race—held the title. Tremendous pressure was put on Jeffries to return to the ring and recover the championship which he thought he had relinquished for good. He succumbed to popular appeal and agreed to fight Johnson on the fourth of July, 1910, in Reno, Nevada.

The sporting set was delighted and awaited Jeff's predicted victory with impatience. One of the country's song writers, a woman named Dorothy Forrester, brought forth a paean of praise for the former champ. In "Jim-a-da-Jeff," written in the popular Italian-style dialect of the day, she admonished Jim to

> Commence right away to get into condish,
> An' you punch-a da bag-a day and night,
> An'a den pretty soon, when you meet-a da coon,
> You knock-a him clear-a out-a sight.
> Chorus: Who's dat man wid-a hand like da bunch a banan!
> It's da Jim-a-de-Jeff, oh! da Jim-a-da-Jeff,
> . . . .
> Who give-a da Jack Jonce one-a little-a tap?
> Who make-a him take-a one big-a long nap?
> Who wipe-a da Africa off-a da map?
> It's da Jim-a-da-Jeff

Unfortunately for Jeffries' many followers, things didn't work out as planned. In the years since retirement Jeff had ceased active training and taken up active eating. Given a white beard, he could have been mistaken for Santa Claus. The thirty-five year old Jeffries topped the scale at more than two hundred and ninety pounds, and a lot of fat would have to be melted away before he could face as savage a fighter as Jack Johnson. His trainers managed to help Jeff take off sixty-five pounds, but they couldn't give him back his youth. The black man's advantages were apparent to all when the opponents faced each other in the ring.

Nevada had its share of hot afternoons, and this July day was too hot for old Jeff. Johnson jolted him and taunted him unmercifully and called, "Come on now, Mister Jeff, let's see what you got."

What Jeffries had was the will, but not the power. In the fifteenth round Johnson floored him three times in quick succession. Never before had Jeffries been knocked to the canvas floor. As he was smashed down for the third time his seconds called a halt to the slaughter. A great fighter, probably the greatest of all time, had made his last public appearance. In his later years he would say over and over, "Jack Johnson didn't beat me. Age did." The habits of the country boy didn't change much. Jeffries added $117,000, his share of the purse, to his other savings. He invested his money wisely and died a rich man at seventy-seven.

Jack Johnson sought a life of pleasure. In 1913 he was found guilty of violating the Mann Act and fled the country. He lost his title a few years later, returned to the United States, served a prison term, and was killed in an automobile wreck in North Carolina.

The Olympics

The first *recorded* set of Olympic games occurred in 776 B.C., but there is evidence that they had predecessors almost five hundred years before that date. Some of the old stories of the pre-Olympics bear retelling.

The earliest concerns the Greek hero Heracles and his troubles with Augeas, the king of Elis. The king grew annoyed with Heracles and, to punish him, gave him the task of cleaning the vast stables in which a great herd of horses was kept. Heracles, a legendary strong man, made a wager with the king that if he accomplished the assignment, his pay would be 10 per cent of the herd. The stables were cleaned very quickly by a simple method; the mighty Heracles diverted the river Alpheus from its course so that it ran right through the stables—a neat trick for most people, but apparently a simple task for our brainy muscle-man. Augeas refused to pay the bet, whereupon Heracles killed him and took over his throne, his herd, and all of his property. To celebrate his noteworthy deeds, he instituted the first Olympic games about 1253 B.C.

A later entertaining story has as its leading characters another king of Elis, Oenomaus, and his stunning daughter, Hippodamia. Her father is reported to have offered the damsel to any young suitor who could successfully kidnap her and make off in his two-horse-power chariot. Time after time, the king arranged that this was not going to happen, because he would pursue the young suitor in another chariot with faster horses, and after catching up with him, would drive a spear through his body. Thirteen young men were eliminated in this fashion. The fourteenth, Pelops by name, had learned of the king's ability to keep his daughter unmarried and decided to play his own game. He bribed the king's charioteer to loosen the axle on the king's vehicle, with the result that after the pursuit had started, the chariot lost its axle, the king lost his life in the crash, and Pelops won the girl. Among the ceremonies at the marriage was the installation of a set of games at Olympia in the year 884 B.C.

Nearly 2800 years after this legendary event, Baron Pierre de Coubertin, a young French nobleman interested in sociology and education, was traveling around the western world to further improve his knowledge in these fields. He became particularly impressed with the Anglo-Saxon interest in sports and determined that international understanding might be strengthened by a partnership between education and athletics.

Some years before, the French and German governments had begun to excavate the ancient Greek site of Olympia and had uncovered some of the historic remains of the early Olympics. Attempts were made to reintroduce the games on an international basis, and in 1892 Coubertin presented a plan to the Athletic Sports Union in Paris for a revival of the Olympic games. As a result the National Congress on Amateurism assembled in 1894, and the dignitaries from the nine countries represented voted to recommence the Olympic games in 1896, holding the first modern Olympiad in Athens.

So began a new era of the games. After the series in Athens, they came to Paris in 1900, St. Louis in 1904, Athens again in 1906, London in 1908, and Stockholm in 1912.

Of all the sports, the most important and exciting was the marathon race. This too has a history. About 500 years before the common era, the king of Persia, Darius, sent an army to overrun and enslave Athens, and its ally Eretria. After Eretria had been captured, the Persian army returned to Marathon, approximately twenty-six miles from Athens. In those days Athens was friendly with Sparta, and the Athenians sent a courier, Pheidippides by name, to enlist the aid of Sparta. Pheidippides was an Olympic champion; he ran, climbed mountains, and swam rivers for days without rest before he reached Sparta and persuaded the Spartans to come to the aid of the Athenian army. Before the Persians could advance on Athens, the

Greek general, Miltiades, attacked them at Marathon, and, aided by his Spartan allies, drove the invaders from the plain. The Persians rushed headlong to their ships. Athens was saved.

The general now sought out Pheidippides and told him to break the news to Athens as quickly as possible. He ran the twenty-six miles from Marathon to Athens, arrived home, shouted "Rejoice; we conquer!" and dropped dead. Small wonder that the twenty-six mile marathon race was the climax of modern Olympic games. Small wonder, too, that the games began to build up an enormous amount of excitement once they were started again.

By far the most exciting marathon race in the history of the modern Olympics occurred in 1908 when the great little Italian runner, Dorando Pietri, a candymaker from Capri, was favored to show his heels to the rest of the field. Seventy-five men from seventeen countries were entered in the race. The pack was to start at Windsor Castle and push past Eton College, following dirt roads and footpaths, and eventually, after passing under the Great Western Railway lines and between the prison and Hammersmith's infirmary, enter the stadium through a special gate which would bring the runners within sight of the finish. To start the race the contestants lined up in four rows, with Dorando in the fourth row. At two thirty in the afternoon of July 24, 1908, at a signal given by her royal highness, the Princess of Wales, the starting gun was fired by Lord Desborough; and the runners, according to the official record of the games, "dashed off at a lively pace."

Dorando kept well up near the front, taking over second place at the end of eighteen miles, and keeping right behind the leader for the next six miles, after which he spurted out ahead. But the effort was too exhausting for the little Latin, and by the time he approached the entrance to the stadium, where nearly 100,000 spectators were waiting for the runners to appear, he was almost unconscious. As he reached the stadium's cinder track, he turned and collapsed. Feeling that he might die in the presence of the enormous crowd, doctors and attendants rushed to him and pulled him to his feet. They would have liked to remove him in an ambulance, but the Italians in the audience were so excited and so hopeful that their hero would still finish first in the race, that sympathetic British officials lifted him to his feet and half-carried him across the finish line, despite the fact that such assistance would result in an automatic disqualification. A few seconds later, a nineteen-year-old American, Johnny Hayes, burst into the stadium and trotted unconcernedly across the line, followed thereafter by two dozen more of the pack.

Dorando

I feel-a much-a bad, like a-ny-thing;— — All the night I nun-ga can-na sleep— It's a my pi-zon Pas-quale, He say we take da car And see Do-ran-do race a-"Long-a-ship;"— Just like da sport I sell da bar-ber shop,— And make da bet Do-ran-do he's a win.— Then to Ma-dees-a Square,—Pas-quale and me go there, And just-a like-a dat, da race be-gin.—— Do-ran-do! Do-ran-do! He

Chorus

run-a, run-a, run-a, run like a-ny-thing. One-a, two-a hun-dred times a-round da ring. I cry, "Please-a nun-ga stop!"— Just then,— Do-ran-do he's a drop!— Good bye, poor old bar-ber shop.—It's no fun to lose da mon, When de sun-of-a-gun no run,— Do-ran-do,— He's good-a for not!——

2. Dorando, he's a come around next day,
   Say "Gentlemen, I wanna tell-a you,
   It's a one-a bigga shame,
   I forgot da man's a-name
   Who make me eat da Irish beef-a stew;
   I ask-a him to give me da spagett,

   I know it make me run a-quick a-quick,
   But I eat da beef-a stew
   And now I tell-a you,
   Just like da pipps it make me very sick."
   CHORUS

After the completion of each Olympic event the flag of the country represented by the winner is flown from the tallest flagpole in the stadium, while the flags of the second and third place contestants are raised to lower standards. When, after the marathon, the Italian flag was hoisted to the top of the highest pole, the American athletes restrained their indignation, sure that the error would be corrected. Soon there was a bit of reshuffling of the banners; with Dorando officially disqualified, down came the flag of Italy, and the Stars and Stripes, which had been raised on one of the lower poles, was transferred to that of the winner.

For two and one-half hours after the race the little Italian lay between life and death, with an anxious crowd hovering over him. When he was told that the warmhearted queen of England had awarded him a special gold cup for his gallant effort, his spirits revived and the next morning he appeared completely restored to health.

By this time the name of Johnny Hayes was on everyone's lips; the world wanted to learn more about this apple-cheeked youngster, this unheralded victor who was suddenly catapulted into the athletic hall of fame. Johnny, they discovered, had been employed at the age of sixteen, as a clerk at Bloomingdale's department store in New York. For three years he had served there in a modest capacity, but after store hours he turned to his second occupation, long-distance running. A cinder track had been installed on the roof of Bloomingdale's, and each night found Hayes training there. Samuel Bloomingdale seems to have been a physical fitnesss buff; he sanctioned a Bloomingdale Athletic Club, of which Hayes was the captain.

It seems that Hayes was much better groomed for his greatest race than most people realized. Under the colors of the Irish-American Athletic Club, he had taken part in a number of lesser marathons in the United States, never winning but, as an eighteen year old, placing second in a marathon race in Boston. For his trip to London, he was given a leave of absence with full pay. It is possible that Mr. Bloomingdale was not surprised when he heard of the stunning win of his young employee. He ordered the store decorated in Johnny's honor, tendered him a reception upon his return home, and, as a fitting tribute, promoted him to the position of manager of the sporting goods department.

The song writers of America made much out of the events of the Olympic games and their activities that year. By far the most popular song to relate the story of the games came from the pen of Irving Berlin, a young waiter who had published his first song only three years before. The nineteen-year-old Berlin felt a kindred spirit with the nineteen-year-old Hayes and was inspired to write one of the most amusing songs of his whole career, "Dorando." In it he relates the story of an Italian barber who was so sure that Dorando would win the marathon that he wagered his barbershop on the result. Berlin's Italian dialect seemed hardly forced at all when he wrote:

> Dorando! Dorando!
> He run-a, run-a, run-a, run like anything
> One-a, two-a hundred times around da ring.
> I cry, "Please-a nunga stop!"
> Just then, Dorando he's a drop!
> Good bye, poor old barber shop.
> It's no fun to lose da mon,
> When de sun-of-a gun no run,
> Dorando, he's good-a for not![4]

Another group of song writers, Michael J. Patterson, Joseph F. Coufal and Frederick Mead, paid tribute to the whole American Olympic team in a song released at the same time as Berlin's, with a picture of "Little Johnny Hayes" on the cover, and entitled "Hail to the Boys of the U.S.A.," whose chorus went:

> Hail to our ath'letes,
> Hail to our victors,
> "Little Johnny Hayes"
> Beat them forty ways.
> And so did Melvin Sheppard too.
> Don't forget Martin Sheridan
> Bacon, Smithson, and Flanagan;
> For they all deserve the credit
> And they're certainly goin' to get it,
> Our Boys of the U.S.A.

The Americans ran away with the 1908 games and repeated their success four years later at Stockholm. Again the song writers waxed jubilant. They had no American marathon champions to rave about, but in the dashes, the middle distances, the jumps, the shot-put, the hammer throw, the pole vault, first place was claimed in each instance by an American.

The best-known Olympic song of 1912 was written by Leon Sekoson and Paul Eugene and was called "Hats Off! To Our Olympian Athletes." The lyricist tried to incorporate the name of every top American participant in the field in his verses, one of which recounted:

---

[4] "Dorando." by Irving Berlin © Copyright 1909 Irving Berlin © Copyright Renewed. Reprinted by permission of Irving Berlin Music Corporation.

221

Take Davenport and Babcock, McDonald Rose and Ry'n;
Jim Meredith and Matt McGrath, Craig, Richards
    and Horine,
There's Reidpath Tewanima, Jim Thorpe and
    peerless "Mel,"
The Adams boys Strobino, and Berna from Cornell,
And all our noble athletes who won or lost so well!
They all deserve our praises, Now everybody yell!

As for the music, the composer's bosom must have been swelling with pride, for in the melody of the chorus he included snatches of "The Star-Spangled Banner," "Yankee Doodle," "Marching through Georgia," "Oh Where and Oh Where Has My Highland Laddie Gone," "Auld Lang Syne," and a final burst from George M. Cohan's "You're a Grand Old Flag." Those were the days when athletic competitions all went our way, before the Russians posed a challenge to our supremacy. But who can predict the Olympic heroes of the future—the Italians? the Israelis? The Iranians? The United States and Russia will have their jobs cut out for them.

7

THE
TRAGIC ERA

"The Hall-Mills Case"

September 16, 1922, was mild and sunny. The two bodies lay on their backs, side by side on the ground, the woman's head resting on the man's arm, the man's face covered with a Panama hat. The woman had been shot in the head three times, and her throat had been cut from ear to ear. The man had been shot through the brain; the bullet entered his head near the right temple and emerged at the back of the neck on the left side. They had been dead for about twenty-four hours.

The fifteen-year-old girl who found them was terrified; her escort was badly unstrung but not too unnerved to rush away from the frightful sight with his companion, across the field to the home of an acquaintance, to whom he blurted out the story of the gruesome discovery.

An immediate telephone call to the police brought the sort of action which some headquarters are wont to take; not for another twelve hours was a New Brunswick patrolman ordered to investigate the report that the bodies of a man and a woman were lying under a crabapple tree near De Russey's Lane. Picking up a fellow officer en route, patrolman Edward Garrigan made his way toward the scene of the crime. The young couple who had found the bodies met them and led them on, until Garrigan and his associate thought they had better make the final approach alone. The sight that came to view, down in the tall grass, was the prelude to an investigation which culminated in one of the most famous murder trials in the history of America.

The dead man was the well-known and highly respected rector of New Brunswick's Protestant Episcopal Church of St. John the Evangelist, the Reverend Edward Wheeler Hall. The woman was a member of the church choir, Eleanor Reinhardt Mills. Neither Hall's wife nor Mrs. Mills's husband had, according to testimony given subsequently, any inkling of the intimate relationship of the dead couple until the contents of letters lying on the ground between the bodies were disclosed. They were startlingly revealing, as, for instance, this bit scrawled by Eleanor Mills: "There isn't a man who could make me smile as you did today . . . . I have the greatest of all blessings, a noble man . . . eternal love. My heart is his, my life is his, all I have is his . . . . I am his forever."

Just a few months earlier, the Reverend had sent Mrs. Mills a single rose, accompanied by a note: "This red, red rose is but a symbol of love, devoted, faithful, true." And then Mr. Hall waxed poetic:

> For love is like a rose, dear heart, fresh as the
> early morn.
> God took the beauty of the skies, the glory of the
> dawn,
> The fire of passion, the calm of evening, the golden
> glow
> And, with the mystery of the stars, he made the love
> we know.
> So in this rose you find me, dear, the love it can
> impart;
> Love, loyal, true, and absolute, the offering of my
> heart.

Pretty warm sentiments from the spiritual leader of a congregation, when addressed to a woman who was not his conjugal partner!

Hall's funeral was conducted at his church by a bishop. Sidestepping a eulogy, he read instead a carefully worded statement by twenty-nine ministers who attended the funeral and who declared, "We do not hesitate to maintain our confidence in his character." At Mrs. Mills's services, held the following morning, those attending were surprised to learn that a wreath, placed on the casket, had been sent by Mrs. Hall.

And now began a great and futile investigation, lasting almost five months, pursuing a course which enveloped one suspect after another and finally terminating in a dead end.

The gentleman who led the police officials, legal talent, newshawks, and a large interested public through a maze of clues into a frustrating cul-de-sac was Azariah Beekman, prosecutor of Somerset County. He was inveigled by one false scent after another. Everybody had his own idea about who had committed the crime. Many of the newspapermen were convinced that it was the work of Willie Stevens, one of widow Hall's two brothers, a shaggy-haired, walrus-mustached little man, who was reputed to be somewhat dim-witted and who was known to own a .32-caliber revolver; the deadly bullets were .32 caliber also. The catch was that it was learned later that Willie's weapon had not been in working order for a year before the murders.

De Russey's Lane was close to the border line of Somerset and Middlesex counties, and the Middlesex prosecutor, Joseph E. Stricker, felt he had a right to an investigation of his own. He brought Mrs. Hall and Willie Stevens, with great secrecy, into his office, where he questioned them at length. As they left the courthouse, the newsmen flocked around them eagerly, thereby arousing Willie's anger. "I want you fellows to understand that I don't want to be referred to as 'Willie' any more!" he yelled, "I'm not a half-wit . . . and I'm not a sissy."

A week later Willie was spirited away from the Hall residence, where he lived, and taken back to the Somerset County Courthouse. There he was grilled for another six hours before being returned home by a member of the county police, who apparently had learned nothing which could help them.

Two more days passed, and now the police were off on a new lead. Pearl Bahmer, the fifteen-year-old girl who had first discovered the bodies, along with her escort, Raymond Schneider, and two other youths named Hayes and Kaufmann, were brought to prosecutor Stricker's office and subjected to a twelve-hour grilling. Eventually a weird story was elicited from the sixteen-year-old Kaufmann. According to him, on the night of the crime the three young men were following Pearl and a drunken companion of the girl's. Hayes, said Kaufmann, took a pistol from his holster, but was cowed when the older man wheeled and confronted him. The boys then withdrew. However, when the prosecutor turned his attention from Kauf-mann to Schneider, he panned what appeared to be pay dirt. Schneider had a second chapter to add to Kaufmann's story, namely, that Hayes had killed the victims under the mistaken idea that they were Pearl Bahmer and her father.

A charge of murder was thereupon lodged against one Clifford Hayes, who was soon lodged in the Somerset County Jail—but not for long. Two days later Schneider renounced his statement, and Hayes was freed. (Schneider was later convicted of perjury and received a two-year sentence.)

Further interrogation of Mrs. Hall and her brother by the prosecuting attorneys of the two counties led to no further disclosures, and on October 23 the attorney general of New Jersey took the case out of the hands of the county officials.

Three days before, Beekman had released a story told him by a new and mysterious witness: she had claimed that she had seen the murder committed. Beekman had held back details, however, and before they came out another report was circulated to the effect that three Negroes, or three white men with blackened faces—possibly, rumor had it, members of the Ku Klux Klan—had been seen jumping from an automobile parked near De Russey's Lane. This story held the attention of the newsmen briefly, but they discarded it as soon as Beekman's new witness shed her anonymity. She proved to be a fifty-year-old widow named Jane Gibson, a swarthy lady who lived with her weak-minded son on a sixty-acre farm near the scene of the crime. Because one of her rural activities was hog raising, the newsmen immediately christened her the "Pig Woman."

Mrs. Gibson's tale was a fascinating one. On the night of the murder she had been aroused by the barking of one of her five dogs. Going to the door, she saw a shadowy figure leaving her cornfield and deduced that the stranger was stealing her corn. She mounted a mule and followed the suspect to a spot in the field near the crabapple tree. There she discerned the outlines of four people "silhouetted" against the sky. A shot rang out, a figure slumped to the ground, a woman screamed, "Don't! Don't! Don't!" and Mrs. Gibson backed her mule away, but as she did so, she heard another volley of shots, and a second person fell to the earth. A few seconds later one of the remaining persons placed her hands on the shoulders of her companion and shouted, "Henry!" Quite a story; but the description of the individuals was so vague that it would have been well-nigh impossible to make a grand-jury presentation without more positive identification. "Henry" could have been Mrs. Hall's second brother, but it could just as well have been any of a million Henrys throughout the land, if, indeed, it was not a figment of the "Pig Woman's" imagination.

A week after this amazing disclosure Mrs. Hall decided to "meet the press." This she did with dignity and composure, denying the truth of Mrs. Gibson's story and stating that she had no vindictive feelings against the murderers, whoever they might be.

Shortly thereafter New Jersey's deputy attorney general, in charge of the case, revealed that Mrs. Gibson had identified the murderer. She had excitedly pointed out to a detective a commuter boarding a train to New York. He was a prominent citizen of New Brunswick, a member of a New York stock brokerage firm, a cousin of Mrs. Hall. His name was Henry da le Bruyère Carpender, and he lived just two doors from the Halls.

Meanwhile, a neighbor of Mrs. Gibson's, Nellie Lo Russell, who had read the "Pig Woman's" story in the papers, wrote to Mrs. Hall that the two women were together at Mrs. Russell's shack on the fatal night and that Mrs. Gibson could not possibly have witnessed the murder when she said she did. Mrs. Russell later signed a lengthy affidavit to that effect.

So the facts of the case remained shrouded in a deep fog, and the Somerset County grand jury, which heard stacks of conflicting testimony, adjourned, after listening to sixty-seven witnesses, without an indictment. The black-clad Mrs. Hall, who had sat through the proceedings stoically, arose and walked silently away, her head held high. The mysterious case was closed. Or so it seemed—for three and a half years.

And then on July 3, 1926, a piano tuner named Arthur S. Riehl, who ten months earlier had married Louise Geist, a former maid of the Halls, filed a petition in Trenton for an annulment of their marriage. Chapter two of the Hall-Mills murder case had begun.

In his petition Riehl declared that his wife had told him that she knew Dr. Hall had planned to elope with Mrs. Mills, that she had so informed Mrs. Hall, that on the night of the murder Mrs. Hall and her brother Willie had been driven to the abandoned farm near the spot where the bodies were found, and that Mrs. Riehl had been paid five thousand dollars for informing her mistress about the Reverend and for thereafter keeping her mouth shut. Moreover, the one-time maid had informed her husband that a pistol was always kept in the Hall library drawer and that Willie was a good shot.

As a front-page news story in William Randolph Hearst's New York *Daily Mirror* of July 16 and the week that followed, the lurid tale created such a wave of excitement throughout the country that New Jersey's governor, A. Harry Moore, determined to reopen the case and turned it over to his legal authorities.

Mrs. Hall consulted her attorney. Mrs. Riehl called her husband's allegations "a pack of lies." The *Mirror* screamed for action. On July 28 Mrs. Hall was charged with the double murder and placed in the Somerset County Jail. On July 30 she was released on fifteen thousand dollars' bail. On August 12 two new arrests were made. Charged with murder were Willie Stevens and Henry de la Bruyère Carpender. Henry Stevens was added to the list of the accused one month later. On September 17 the quartet was indicted by the Somerset County grand jury. Mrs. Hall's bail was increased to forty thousand dollars; the three men remained in jail.

This seemed to be the right time for a topical song on such a matter of

The HALL-MILLS Case

Song

By

Virginia Curtis

MADE IN U.S.A

Published by Shapiro, Bernstein & Co.
MUSIC PUBLISHERS
COR. BROADWAY & 47th STREET
REG. U.S. PAT. OFF. New York

The Hall-Mills Case

In a lit-tle town in old New Jer-sey—— Lived a man whose name was Doc-tor

Hall——— There he preached the Gos-pel to his peo-ple——— And they learned to

love him one and all——— He was lead-er of his con-gre-ga-tion———

And they tho't he lived a per-fect life——— Nev-er did they once dream for a

mo-ment——— He could be un-faith-ful to his wife.———

2. But there was a mother whom he courted
   One who had no right to share his love
   Every Sunday she sang in the choir
   While he preached of Heaven up above.
   No one knew that she would often meet him
   No one knew their secret trysting place
   And they did not heed the ten commandments
   Till they met their Master in disgrace.

3. Then one night these lovers met each other
   And they strolled along De Russey's Lane
   Then next day the world was horror stricken
   When they found them where they both were slain
   We may never know what fate befell them
   When they heard the trumpet's final blast.
   But it seems that Justice was upon them
   And their sin had found them out at last.

national interest, and shortly one made its appearance. Written by Virginia Curtis and published by the eminently respectable firm of Shapiro Bernstein & Co., "The Hall-Mills Case" quickly acquired popularity. The title page showed a stylized rural scene, which might have represented either de Russey's Lane or the setting of Mr. Hall's church. Vignettes of the Reverend (who looked like a sufferer from a thyroid condition) and Mrs. Mills (whose eyes avoided the photographer) were prominently displayed. The first verse ran:

> In a little town in old New Jersey
> Lived a man whose name was Doctor Hall
> There he preached the gospel to his people,
> And they learned to love him one and all.
> He was leader of his congregation,
> And they tho't he lived a perfect life,
> Never did they once dream for a moment
> He could be unfaithful to his wife.

A few of the vital details followed, and the song ends on this moral note:

> We may never know what fate befell them,
> When they heard the trumpet's final blast,
> But it seems that Justice was upon them,
> And their sin had found them out at last.[1]

The spectacular trial opened on November 3, 1926, and lasted a month. (Carpender's trial was scheduled to be held after that of the other three.) The star witness for the prosecution was Mrs. Gibson, the "Pig Woman," who was carried into court on a sickbed, and who repeated, with embellishments, the story she had given to the prosecuting attorney four years earlier. She identified the people seen in de Russey's Lane as Mrs. Hall and her two brothers. But her veracity was discredited when the defending attorneys uncovered the fact that, whereas she was known to her acquaintances as Mrs. Gibson, her real name was Easton, and Mr. Easton was still alive, though he never made an appearance in court. Much of the remaining evidence of the prosecution turned out to be hearsay, and the defense lawyers were impressive in elaborating on the sterling qualities of the socially prominent Mrs. Hall and her two brothers.

The jury was out five hours. When they returned, they rendered a verdict of "not guilty" for the three defendants. The following morning the presiding judge, Charles W. Parker, dismissed whatever charges remained

---

[1] "The Hall-Mills Case." Virginia Curtis Copyright 1926 by Shapiro, Bernstein & Co., Inc. 666 Fifth Avenue, New York, N.Y. 10019 Copyright Renewed and Assigned. USED BY PERMISSION.

against them and against Carpender, and the final curtain was drawn on the great Hall-Mills murder case.

At the hospital where the "Pig Woman" lay ill, the news was broken to her by her physicians. That evening a Jersey City reporter called the hospital. He wanted to know how Mrs. Easton had reacted to the jury's verdict. "She's sleeping like a baby," responded the floor nurse.

"Why Don't They Set Him Free?"

A SHOT RANG OUT, then two more in quick succession. The tall man at the table near the stage slumped forward and, collapsing suddenly, tumbled to the floor. His assailant, holding on high the fatal pistol, walked through the stunned crowd to the elevators and descended to the sidewalk to join his wife. And thereupon was touched off the spark which was to blaze into the most spectacular courtroom trial of the twentieth century. For the man lying dead in a pool of blood was the world-famous architect Stanford White, and his murderer was the wealthy Pittsburgh playboy Harry Kendall Thaw, who just the year before had married Evelyn Nesbit, late of the "Floradora Sextette."

Evelyn, of course, was the cause of it all. A frail, appealing beauty, she had from her early teens proved almost irresistibly attractive to men. Artists such as Charles Dana Gibson sought to recreate on paper her winsome charm. Other males struggled to win her attention. Among these, two proved preeminently successful. They were, as may be supposed, Thaw and White.

The trial of the century hinged around one point—was Thaw insane when he killed White? Certainly he had been wildly jealous of his wife's premarital relations with his rival, but was he *insanely* jealous? And had his reason left him completely on the night of June 25, 1906, when in the roof-garden theater he disposed of his rival so dramatically?

Stanford White had met Evelyn Nesbit when she was quite young, certainly no more than sixteen or seventeen. And soon an "intimacy" started. Thaw did not come into the picture until a year or two later. Whether Thaw himself or his money appealed to Evelyn is difficult to determine; at any rate, he soon had the little chorus girl in his entourage, which at times included her mother, possibly for the sake of appearances. Thaw and Evelyn traveled through Europe together while he continued to press for her hand in marriage. She seemed reluctant to consent and finally told him why; she felt that her affair with White had made her unfit to marry Thaw. But he persisted and finally overcame her hesitancy; they were married in Pittsburgh in April, 1905.

After the marriage the knowledge of his wife's early affair with White preyed on Thaw's mind. Moreover, he never felt sure that the intimacy between the two was really at an end. He became convinced that White was continuing to seduce innocent young girls, a practice that Thaw decided must be ended permanently. He was also sure in his own mind that White had designs on his life. Thus, reasoned Thaw, there was only one thing to be done; White had to be eliminated.

On the sidewalk outside Madison Square Garden in New York, with the pistol still in his hand, Thaw, the deed accomplished, walked toward Evelyn, who had heard the shots and who gazed at the weapon in horror and cried, "Good God, Harry! What have you done?"

Thaw replied quietly, "All right, dearie. I have probably saved your life."

A fireman on duty outside the building approached Thaw and took his pistol. He was joined in a short time by a policeman. As the unresisting killer was arrested, he remarked to the policeman: "He deserved it. I can prove it. He ruined my wife and then deserted the girl."

After a night in a police station Thaw was transported to the Tombs, the city prison, where he was lodged in a cell in murderers' row. Six months later he was on trial for his life, defended by the finest criminal lawyers that his family fortune could secure; they were opposed by New York's popular district attorney, William Travers Jerome.

During the period between the arrest and the trial the newspapers had reviewed every possible detail in the lives of the dead man and his slayer. For a number of weeks that summer the *Evening Journal* requested and published letters and opinions from its readers in answer to the question: "Was Thaw justified in killing Stanford White? If so—if not—why? Send your reply, not over 100 words, written on one side of the paper only." The first day's tally resulted in a response of guilty, 31; not guilty, 69. The final listing in August read: guilty, 2,054; not guilty, 5,119.

Thaw's wealthy mother directed her own campaign to seek sympathy for her son. She employed a press agent to portray Thaw as a chivalrous knight avenging the flower of young womanhood from attacks by a beast of prey. She even backed a play written on the theme of the murder, which ended with the killer in his cell proclaiming: "No jury on earth will send me to the chair . . . for killing the man who defamed my wife. That is the unwritten law made by men themselves, and upon its virtue, I will stake my life."

Thaw's trial, after a brief postponement, commenced on January 23, 1907. It was not until February 1, after more than one hundred prospective jurors had been rejected, that the panel was completed. For over two months they sat in the jury box while the high-powered lawyers battled grimly over each witness. They retired to consider the verdict on the afternoon of April 10. At 4:30 two afternoons later they returned to the courtroom to report that they were in hopelesss disagreement—seven voting for first-degree murder, five voting Thaw not guilty by reason of insanity.

Nine months later the second trial commenced, and a little more than three weeks later it was all over. The second jury found Thaw not guilty on the ground of insanity. The trial was over, but the judge had to be reckoned with. He lost no time in presenting a prepared statement, in which he declared that he found the defendant "a person dangerous to the public safety" and ordered him sent to the state asylum for the criminally insane at Matteawan.

There Thaw remained for over five years. One day in August, 1913, a carefully worked out plot enabled him to escape from the asylum, jump into an enormous black limousine, transfer from the limousine to a Packard touring car, and tear off toward the Connecticut state line at seventy miles an hour.

Two days later he was in Sherbrooke, Canada, a town of eighteen thousand, where the people cheered him as he drove through the streets in an open carriage. For three weeks an American delegation of lawyers, headed by Thaw's old nemesis, William Jerome, fought to have him deported and finally compelled the Canadian minister of justice to accede to their demands and order Thaw back over the line. So across the border to New Hampshire he went. But Jerome's victory was still far from achievement. Thaw turned out to be as much a hero in New Hampshire as he was in Canada. For fifteen months Jerome struggled, and it was not until December, 1914, that Thaw was ordered returned to New York—by no less an authority than the United States Supreme Court.

It is not surprising that some of these spectacular happenings were recreated by the song writers of the period. For example, there appeared in 1913 a song entitled "For the Sake of Wife and Home," with words by Ross Edwards and music by Fred Leopold. The title page bears a picture of Harry Kendall Thaw, with the inscription "Theme Suggested by the Thaw-White Tragedy." Here is the first verse:

Why Don't They Set Him Free?

'Twas a crowd-ed roof gar-den on a sum-mer's night in June, Cho-rus girls up-on the stage

sang a mer-ry tune, A shot rang out, a-las! a soul had left this life, One man had killed an-

oth-er one, be-cause he'd wronged his wife; The ju-ry found him guil-ty, he has suf-fered now for

years, He thought he did his du-ty, and re-venged her sobs and tears, For love he lost his

lib-er-ty, did what his heart cried "do," He's suf-fered long e-nough, he should have his life a-new:

Chorus

Why don't they set him free? — Give him his lib-er-ty? — Just be-cause he's a mill-ion-aire —

— Ev'ry one wants to treat him un-fair, Mon-ey does not stop true love, — His

act proved sin-cer-i-ty — He did not shoot to seek mere fame, Just to de-fend — his

dear wife's name. Why don't they set him free? — Give him his lib-er-ty? —

2. Money can't buy you happiness no matter how
   you try,
   When your loved one is away, life is one long
   sigh,
   The law can do great things, when its power
   starts,
   But with its strength so mighty it can't mend
   poor broken hearts.

The people say the world is fair, why then if
this is true,
Why don't man treat a man as man in all
ways not a few,
For if a man defends his home he does it as
his right,
Because one man was brave, now he has a
life time fight:
CHORUS

A happy little family as loving as could be
While fortune smiled to banish care and strife,
She told him all her secrets and he kissed her tenderly
And vowed he would protect her with his life.
Then came the fatal meeting, her friend of bygone days,
Whose selfish love had left its sting of hate.
Forgetting all save honor, the other in his rage
A pistol shot; they stop him, but too late.

And in the same year Shapiro Bernstein & Co. of New York, one of the country's largest publishers of popular music, brought out "The Great Harry K. Thaw Song, Why Don't They Set Him Free?" with the cover carrying another photograph of Thaw, this time apparently in his cell at Matteawan. The melody was composed by Harry C. Loll, and the words were by Thomas J. Blue, who went into detail about the affair on "the crowded roof garden on a summer's night in June" and who, reaching the chorus, asked plaintively:

Why don't they set him free?
Give him his liberty?
Just because he's a millionaire
Ev'ryone wants to treat him unfair
Money does not stop true love,
His act proved sincerity
He did not shoot to seek mere fame,
Just to defend his dear wife's name
Why don't they set him free?
Give him his liberty?

Well, he got it eventually. In July, 1915, he was declared sane and acquitted of all charges. His first act after being released was to file for divorce from the wife in whose behalf he had committed murder nearly ten years before.

The Iroquois Fire

IN LESS THAN A SIX-WEEK PERIOD there occurrred two of the most devastating fires in the country's history. One resulted in a horrible loss of life, the other in a crippling destruction of the heart of a city. The first erupted in Chicago, the second in Baltimore.

It seems that disasters—fifty, sixty, one hundred years ago—always impelled song writers to seek words and music to record the catastrophic events. For them, the newspaper reports were insufficient; the stories had to be sung as well as read. A by-product of the Baltimore fire was a song written by Joseph DeVito. The title was "In That City of Wealth and Fame." Here are some of the words which accompanied a bland melody:

> When I arrived in Baltimore to meet my old friend Jack,
> A sudden sheet of flames broke forth, the crowd aghast
> stood back;
> I quickly joined the Volunteers, the flames we tried to
> stay,
> No dead or injured found so far, but danger great that
> day.
> CHORUS: Sighs with tears and pain are heard both far and wide,
> Some were injured, others died, in the city of wealth
> and fame.

The words of "The Iroquois on Fire," following the Chicago conflagration, were much more poignant. Written by Zella Evans, this song made no effort to spare the feelings of those who had to listen to it:

> The Iroquois playhouse, lo, so beautiful and grand
> Was crowded with a merry throng that day
> That fatal day that sorrow brought throughout the
> far wide land
> When changed to death and terror was the play.
> Now sparkling eyes and laughing lips, oh see the
> sudden change;
> The lips grow pale, the eyes in terror stare
> As o'er the crowd roars suddenly the flaming
> avalanche,
> And hideous death, terrible death is there.
> CHORUS: The sad wild scenes I saw that day I never shall
> forget
> A mother cries to God above to save her darling
> yet,
> While men were fighting fierce and wild 'gainst
> unrelenting fate,
> Their doom is sealed, their fight for naught
> and every help too late.

Another, written by Morris S. Silver, with music by Thomas R. Confare, and entitled "The Burning of the Iroquois," describes the catastrophe, and then proceeds:

> Just picture in a cottage at the close of this sad day
> A frantic husband waiting for his wife and children gay,
> Although they came not to the door to greet him with a
> kiss,
> He dream'd not for a moment then that aught had gone
> amiss.

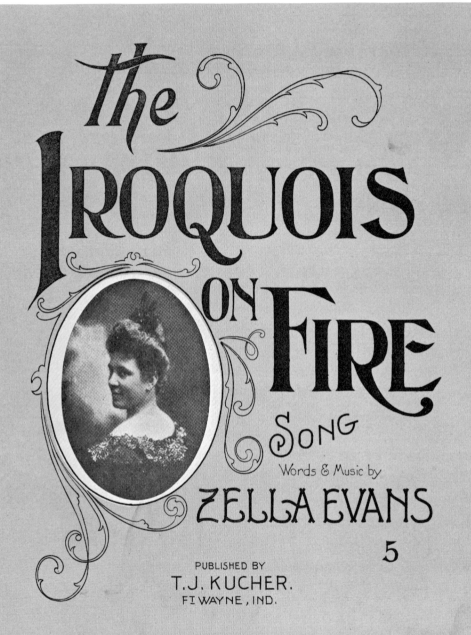

The IROQUOIS ON FIRE

SONG

Words & Music by

ZELLA EVANS

5

PUBLISHED BY
T. J. KUCHER.
FT WAYNE, IND.

The Iroquois On Fire

The I-ro-quois play-house, lo, so beau-ti-ful and grand Was crowd-ed with a mer-ry

throng that day —— That fa-tal day that sor-row brought through-out the far wide land,

When changed to death and ter-ror was the play.— Now spark-ling eyes and laugh-ing lips oh

see the sud-den change: The lips grow pale the eyes in ter-ror stare.— As o'er the crowd

roars sud-den-ly the flam-ing a-va-lanche, And hid-eous death ter-ri-ble death is

Chorus

there. —— The sad wild scenes I saw that day I nev-er shall for-get,— A

moth-er cries to God a-bove to save her dar-ling yet,— While men were fight-ing

fierce and wild 'gainst un-re-lent-ing fate,— Their doom is sealed their fight for naught

and eve-ry help too late.—

2. The cry of fire changed at once the scene of mirth and glee
To untold horror which no men can paint,
When anguish and despair made minutes to eternity,
When after prey, the flames more gained and gained.

So many young and blooming lives were crushed beneath the feet,
And of its sunshine robbed so many homes.
For ever they are gone from us but some day we shall meet,
They wait for us above in heaven's dome.
CHORUS

In vain he listens for their steps, he little knows
    their fate,
"Where can they be," he wonders, "and what's keeping
    them so late?"
At last he learns the awful news, 'tis more than he
    can bear,
The ones he loved so dear have gone, his heart breaks
    in despair.

CHORUS: Sad are the hearts that are weeping and lone,
    Mourning for loved ones tonight;
    Sorrow has entered many a home
    Where all was once cheerful and bright.
    Faces familiar will never return,
    Misery clouds ev'ry joy.
    Parents, children and wives
    And husbands lost lives,
    In the burning of the Iroquois.

To reconstruct the disaster, we turn back to the afternoon of December 30, 1903. It was a Wednesday, a matinee day; and, since the schools had closed during the week between Christmas and New Year's, many school children were seeking theatrical diversion.

At the Iroquois Theater on Randolph Street an audience of eighteen hundred people had come prepared to be amused by the antics of Eddie Foy, one of the most popular comedians in the country, who was starring in a musical extravaganza entitled "Mr. Bluebeard." It was a flighty show with a big cast including lots of pretty girls, and a ridiculous plot. Like the other theaters of that day, the Iroquois had a balcony and a gallery, which, combined, held half the people who packed the house. As usual at matinees, the great proportion of the audience was made up of women and children.

The second act had just gotten under way and on the decorated stage eight men and eight girls were singing "I'll Meet You in the Pale Moonlight." They finished the first verse; the second was never sung. Suddenly on the right-hand side of the stage—the audience's left—there was a flash of fire. Sparks from calcium lights, operated from the flies to illuminate the stage, caught a bit of the flimsy material of an inner curtain, and it flared up immediately.

For a second everything was hushed. The musicians stopped playing; the singers broke off in the middle of their song. The first bit of fear ran through the audience and with the first outcry people jumped to their feet and started to break for the exits.

At that moment a strange figure dashed onto the stage. It was Eddie Foy, costumed as a clown. When he heard the commotion he had been completing his make-up in the wings and was now wearing part of his theatrical apparel, with just half of his make-up on. Facing the audience from the center of the stage he shouted: "Keep quiet, don't get excited." He called to the orchestra leader, Herbert Dillea: "Start an overture, for God's sake! Play and keep on playing." Dillea did his best. The musicians commenced the overture, realizing all the while the terrible danger facing them. One by one, they gave way to their fears; one by one, led by the bassoonist, they stole off. Eventually, when nearly all of his players had deserted him, Dillea himself broke down and shot over the orchestra pit and under the stage, leaving behind him a burning cello and bass viol.

Meanwhile, the stagehands labored unsuccessfully to bring down the asbestos curtain. One side slid down easily, but the other was caught on wires in the wings. The curtain buckled and failed to close off the stage. The fire spread rapidly up the flimsy scenery and almost instantaneously, it seemed, enveloped the gallery and the balcony. For most of the people in these sections there was no escape. The stairs were frightfully narrow, and as the crowd rushed toward them, they became so blocked with the mass of humanity that it was impossible to force a way to the exit.

The people in the orchestra were more fortunate. With more plentiful and more spacious exits, the men, women, and children in the orchestra seats escaped unscathed.

From the stage, the wings, the dressing rooms, the members of the cast and the stagehands fled precipitously. A troupe of girls, known as the "flying ballet," were in position up in the flies, ready to make their appearance on invisible wires high above the orchestra. Miraculously, all but one were rescued. The principal dancer of the group, Nellie Reed, a teen-age ballerina, was so badly burned that she expired soon after being carried to a hospital. No other member of the troupe of 150 was lost. It was not possible to determine the exact number of people who perished, though a close estimate set the figure at seven hundred.

Prolonged testimony before a grand jury brought out a number of factors which, together, helped to account for the great loss of life. The theater had been so crowded that people were sitting on the steps of the balcony and the gallery. Inadequate fire apparatus was available on the stage and throughout the theater. Exit doors which should have been opened, remained bolted, and two iron gates across emergency stairways were padlocked. Stairways were far too narrow to be used by a panicking audience. Lights in the theater, which should have been switched on to assist the people to see as they bolted, remained off, and the theater was dark save for the flames.

But there were, for all the panic and the horror, a number of miraculous escapes. A twelve-year-old girl, Winnie Gallagher, was caught in the midst of struggling terror-stricken people on the main floor. Only a few rows from the stage, she managed to fight through the churning mass of men and women, and made her way to the street. By the time she reached open air her clothing had been torn to shreds. A young newsboy, seeing her plight, took off his overcoat, wrapped it around her, and led her to the central police station.

Across an alley separating them from the theater were the law and dental schools of Northwestern University. Workmen had been employed in the school building, painting, cleaning, redecorating. They seized one of the long planks which had been used as they worked, and stretched it across the alley to a door which opened up on the theater gallery. The plank was strong. Over this narrow crawl-way, one hundred feet above the pavement, some scores of women and children crept to safety.

After the fire had been extinguished, articles cast aside by the terrified people were collected by firemen and policemen. Ten basketfuls of money and jewelry were picked up from the orchestra floor. Five bushel baskets of purses, gloves, and handkerchiefs were found, and two barrels were filled with lost and castoff shoes.

The cast of "Mr. Bluebeard" lost all of their possessions. A few weeks earlier they had passed through a serious fire in a Cleveland theater and had escaped, fortunately, without injury or loss of their belongings. But this time they were in real trouble. Not only were a score of them held as witnesses to the disaster, but many had no funds with which to pay their hotel bills. Even though the producers of the show had provided transportation for the cast to New York, the home territory of most of them, their personal baggage was retained by hotel proprietors who would not release it until these bills were paid.

They were rescued from a distressing situation by Mrs. Ogden Armour, a leader in Chicago's social activities, who contributed $500 to help settle the hotel bills of the girls in the chorus. Having thus been "bailed out," one hundred members of the cast were able to board a New York train four days after the fire.

By one of those quirks which sometimes link prophecy with actual occurrence, there was recalled a fanciful article which had appeared in the *Chicago Times* on February 13, 1875, more than twenty-five years before the Iroquois fire. In this story, written to captivate its readers, the *Times* related that "scores of houses are saddened this beautiful winter morning by the fate which overtook so many unsuspecting people in Chicago last night ... there are smoking ruins down in the heart of the city—ruins of one of the finest theaters in Chicago, which fell a prey to the devouring element last night. There are mourning households and rows of dead bodies in the morgue." The object of this allegorical report was to criticize the construction of the theaters of the period and to warn that unless adequate exits and other avenues of escape were provided, a fire in a theater could result in the loss of lives of hundreds of people.

The Iroquois fire taught the United States a costly lesson. It was not learned thoroughly, as witness later holocausts in a night club in Boston, a circus in Hartford, and in hotels across the country. Fire may have been one of the great boons to mankind, but it remains one of our greatest hazards.

The Titanic

A cold dark night, a sea of ice,
A ship out on the ocean,
All fitted out by man's device,
She rode in perfect motion.
A jar, a crash, a fearful clash,
A sound like awful thunder,
The dying groan, the living moan,
As the splendid ship went under.

CHORUS: Out on the sea, when the ship went down,
Out where the life-boats rocked,
Husbands were parted from loving wives,
Captain and sailors they gave up their lives.
Wireless rang with the awful news
By which the whole world was shocked.
Out on the sea, near Eternity
Where the angry waters frown,
"Nearer My God" they sang,
Just as the ship went down.[2]

JUST AS THE SHIP WENT DOWN

The above illustration used by courtesy of Chicago Record-Herald.

A SONG OF THE SEA

Words by
EDITH MAIDA LESSING

Music by
GIBSON AND ADLER

PUBLISHED BY
HAROLD ROSSITER MUSIC COMPANY
CHICAGO, U.S.A.

Just As the Ship Went Down

A cold dark night, a sea of ice, A ship out on the o-cean, All fit-ted out by man's de-vice, She rode in per-fect mo-tion. A jar, a crash, a fear-ful clash, A sound like aw-ful thun-der, The dy-ing groan, the liv-ing moan, As the splen-did ship went un-der.

Chorus

Out on the sea, when the ship went down,— Out where the life-boats rocked,—— Hus-bands were part-ed from lov-ing wives,— Cap-tain and sail-ors, they gave up their lives Wire-less rang with the aw-ful news, By which the whole world was shocked.—— Out on the sea near E-ter-ni-ty, Where the an-gry wa-ters frown,— "Near-er my God" they sang, Just as the ship went down——

2. The sky grows black, the icebergs crack,
And Death hangs o'er the water,
But "Women first!" the orders rang,
For mother and for daughter.

A cry, a shriek, but who can speak?
For then the waters parted,
The sea was cleft; and what was left,
For the living broken hearted?
CHORUS

The greatest disaster in the history of the seas was unfolded not only in news stories around the world but also by the song writers and composers, who lost no time in further publicizing the tragedy which befell the great steamer *Titanic* on the night of April 14, 1912. The words of the song quoted above were the work of Edith Maida Lessing, and the music was written by Bernie Adler and Sidney Gibson. Almost simultaneously, within a few days of the tragedy, other songs as well as descriptive piano solos were brought out by the music publishers. And why not? The sinking of the *Titanic* was the most shattering occurrence to smite the American people since the assassination of President William McKinley eleven years earlier.

It was puzzling that several of the songs stressed one sentimental report that was never confirmed—the last piece rendered by the ship's doomed band. One song writer after another pointed out that this final—all too final —number was "Nearer My God to Thee." The full title of one of the most popular of such songs was "The Band Played 'Nearer My God to Thee' as the Ship Went Down." The title page indicates that the piece was written "in memory of the heroes of the ill-fated *Titanic*." The chorus of the song, with words by Mark Bean and music by Harold Jones, goes:

> There the brave men stood, as true heroes should,
> With their hearts in faith sublime,
> And their names shall be fond memory
> Until the end of time.
> And the band was bravely playing,
> The song of the Cross and Crown:
> "Nearer My God to Thee"
> As the ship went down.

Still another song, written by Mrs. C. W. Hea and composed by L. F. Malkemus, entitled "Death Song of the *Titanic*," had this chorus:

> Down sank the great *Titanic* into the yawning sea,
> But the heroes sang as the ship went down,
> "Nearer my God to Thee, nearer to Thee."

The strange thing about the subject of these songs is that there is no indication, in stories of the disaster, that the band *ever* played "Nearer My God to Thee." Some said that bandmaster Henry Hartley and his men were playing ragtime as the ship's last moments approached. Others, whose memory was meticulously supported by the testimony of a trained observer, junior wireless operator Harold Bride, recalled the last piece played was an Episcopal hymn entitled "Autumn," the original version of which appeared in a Geneva psalmster in 1551 and which goes in part:

God of mercy and compassion!
Look with pity on my pain . . .
Hold me up in mighty waters,
Keep my eyes on things above.

The origin of the "Nearer My God" myth is unexplained, but the myth itself climaxes a story of the fallibility of man's proudest achievements.

The saga of the *Titanic* is a gruesome fantasy, hardly believable. The great ship, over 880 feet long, weighing over 46,000 tons, a product of the greatest British shipbuilders, left Southampton for New York on her maiden voyage April 10, 1912, (alas, she was to die a maiden!).

The largest ship then afloat, and the most luxurious, she was considered unsinkable, with double bottoms and a watertight compartmentalized hull. Her quiet sailing from Southampton was not entirely uneventful. As she moved slowly out of her dock, the surge of water sucked the adjacent steamer *New York* from her moorings and surged her toward the great liner. The veering *New York* was controlled barely in time to avoid a nasty collision. But from that disturbing occurrence until 11:40 on the night of the fourteenth all was serene, and even beautiful, on board.

All during the day wireless messages reporting icebergs in the vicinity of the *Titanic*'s path had been coming in from other ships, the *Caronia*, the *Californian*, the *Baltic*. At 11:30, just minutes before the fateful collision, a new message came from the *Californian*: "Say, old man, we are stuck here, surrounded by ice." To which the *Titanic*'s first wireless operator, Phillips replied: "Shut up, shut up. Keep out. I am talking to Cape Race; you are jamming my signals." The *Californian* shut up.

Ten minutes later the lookout in the *Titanic*'s crow's-nest grabbed the telephone and called the bridge: "Iceberg! Right ahead!" The quartermaster at the wheel swung the bow to port, but the ship could not respond rapidly enough.

All that was felt by most passengers was a slight shock, as if, one of them said, "somebody had drawn a giant finger along the side of the ship." Another thought it was like a heavy wave striking the ship. No one, not even Captain Edward Smith, could suspect that the *Titanic* was mortally wounded, with a three-hundred-foot slash in her hull.

But in a matter of minutes the frightfulness of the situation was apparent, and within half an hour the *Titanic*'s wireless was crackling CQD, CQD, the call for assistance; then, shortly afterwards, SOS, a new call, and, as a matter of fact, the first SOS in history.

At 12:30 A.M. the order was passed to prepare to lower the lifeboats. Life preservers were fastened on the passengers, and the women and children were stowed in the boats, most of the women protesting violently at the separation from their husbands. But there was no panic, and hardly any disorder; for the most part the instructions of the crewmen directing operations were obeyed meticulously. Unfortunately, there were not nearly enough boats; and many of those were cast adrift before they could be filled. The resulting loss of life was to be appalling. Seven hundred people were saved; more than fifteen hundred were lost.

When the final accounting was made, it was found that only five women on the first-class passenger list went down with the ship. One of these was Mrs. Isidor Straus of the well-known New York family, owner of Macy's department store, an elderly gentlewoman who refused to be parted from her husband. A touching song, in Yiddish, entitled "The *Titanic's* Disaster," shows on the title page the spirits of Isidor Straus and his wife in a last embrace ascending from the doomed vessel and crowned with laurel leaves bestowed upon them by a hovering angel. Another casualty, a young woman named Evans, gave up her place in a boat to an older lady and went down with the ship.

The *Titanic's* officers had repeated over and over: "This ship cannot sink. We need just wait until another vessel comes along and takes us off." The passengers felt confident in these assurances, and so husbands did not clamor to follow their wives into the boats, sure in the knowledge that they would be reunited, either on a rescuing steamer in midocean or on the New York docks. And yet the lifeboats had to be lowered, even if the first ones were only partly filled. One opinion expressed was that the captain should have stated bluntly: "This ship will sink soon. Only women and children may go into the boats." Then the question would remain, Would the captain have the authority to enforce such an order? As it happened, some husbands who had stepped into lifeboats with their wives were commanded to leave them and return to the ship's deck.

A few men had miraculous escapes. One who had not expected to survive was the *Titanic's* second officer, Charles Herbert Lightoller. He had remained on board with most of the crew and dived at the last moment, before the ship went under. Sucked down and held against one of the blowers and carried under water for what seemed a long distance, he was suddenly thrust up again by what he described as a "terrific gust," the blower forcing him clear of the foundering vessel. Close by him was an upturned collapsible boat, to which he swam and on which he climbed with about twenty other men, one of whom was Harold Bride, the second wireless operator. The men managed to cling to their perilous perch throughout the night; then, as dawn broke, they were sighted by passengers in one of the lifeboats, who took them off.

Each lifeboat had its own incidents. One, which was about to cast off with its full complement of sixty passengers, was threatened when a swarm of third-class passengers made ready to jump into it. The officer in charge, aware that it would sink if overloaded, yelled "Look out!" and fired one shot, then three more between the lifeboat and the ship's side. The crowd recoiled, and the crew swung the lifeboat out and managed to launch it.

Another boat, whose oars were manned by women, struggled until dawn, when the passengers saw a light on the far horizon. It was the *Carpathia*. To attract the steamer's attention and in desperation, a passenger seized one woman's straw hat and set it afire, waving this odd torch above the billows. Fortunately it was observed, and the *Carpathia* edged its way through the icebergs surrounding the little boat and took the women off.

After another lifeboat containing mostly women and children was put off, four Chinese were found stowed away between the seats. Among the passengers in this boat was one who was to be examined extensively upon his return to England, J. Bruce Ismay, managing director of the White Star Line, owner of the *Titanic*.

Formal inquiries were undertaken in the United States and in England. They sought to determine the cause of the tragedy and point fingers at those who shared the responsibility for the collision. They drew a pattern of the ships in the area of the *Titanic* when she was struck and probed the reasons why no prompt rescue attempts were made by the vessels closest to her. The *Californian* was singled out for particular scrutiny, for she was reported to have been less than twenty miles away. But after her earlier message warning of icebergs, she was strangely silent. According to one authority her radio operator had been on duty for over eighteen hours, his ship had been stopped by ice for the night, and there was no apparent reason for him to continue at his wireless set any longer. He turned in at 11:20 P.M. and fell asleep twenty minutes before the crash; those twenty minutes spelled the destiny of hundreds of victims.

Bruce Ismay was questioned at great length about whether he had left the ship when there were still people who had not been put into the boats. Ismay replied that he had heard numerous calls for women but that he did not see any on deck when he left.

There was much discussion about whether Ismay's conduct had been unbecoming, in that he chose to save his own life while many passengers, including scores of females in the second and third cabins, had not left the ship. He was severely castigated by one member of Parliament, who held the firm opinion that the managing director, like the captain, had no right to save his life at the expense of the life of a single passenger.

The counsel for the White Star Company, another member of Parliament, took violent issue with his fellow M.P., insisting that no other life would have been saved had Ismay stayed on board the *Titanic* and that the director did not get into the lifeboat until it was being lowered away.

The claims and counterclaims, the accusations and refutations were continued officially on both sides of the Atlantic. But in the end nothing was resolved, except that the British queen of the seas had followed twelve years later her old monarch, Queen Victoria, to the grave. As Solomon Small, author of the song "The *Titanic*'s Disaster," referred to earlier, put it:

> Indeed, such a tragedy
> No one had foreseen.
> Drowned are all the joys,
> Only sorrow remains.

8
RELAX
IS ALL

The Merry-Go-Round

THE VERY WORD captures fond childhood memories. What reader can fail to recall the wonderful youthful excitement of circling round and round on a gleaming white or black or brown steed, to the accompaniment of sweet, even if a trifle off-key, music? How much innocent joy could be purchased for a nickel, with the ever-present hope of a second ride for free, if you snared the brass ring? And how often, year after year, would such a thrilling experience lure young folks back to the joys of carrousel rides?

A team of song writers, Joseph Puschett and Harold Orlob, turned out, in 1907, a catchy number called "With Mary Ann on a Merry-Go-Round." They wrote:

> There are various ways for a lad to make plays,
> When he wants to impress his young lady,
> There's the old-fashioned trip on the old-fashioned
> ship
> And the nook near the brooklet that's shady.
> Quite a few up to date think an Auto is great,
> And for "toot-sing" it's simply a hummer,
> But my girl's satisfied, when we go for a ride
> On the Merry-go-round in the summer.

> CHORUS: You may have your trolley,
> Shoot the chutes with Molly,
> Sail a boat with Polly
> On the moonlight plan,
> But in the good old summer
> Ev'ry ride's a hummer,
> As 'round I go on the Merry-go-round with Mary Ann.

With Mary Ann on a Merry Go Round.

There are va-ri-ous ways for a lad to make plays, When he wants to im-press his young la-dy,—— There's the old fash-ioned trip on the old fash-ioned ship And the nook near the brook-let that's shad-y.—— Quite a few up to date think an Au-to is great, And for "toot-sing" it's simp-ly a hum-mer,—— But my girl's sat-is-fied, when we go for a ride On the Mer-ry-go-round in the sum-mer.——

Chorus

You may have your trol-ley—— Shoot the chutes with Mol-ly—— Sail a boat with Pol-ly On the moon-light plan,—— But in the good old sum-mer—— Ev-'ry ride's a hum-mer—— As 'round I go on the Mer-ry-go-round with Ma-ry-Ann.——

2. Pretty Mary prefers nightly round trips for hers,
Of the ride seeming ne'er to grow weary,
She's confessed with a smile,
"For a very long while I have moved in the
best circles, dearie."
As her hand deftly clings to the small jingling
rings,

I determine that soon I will bring her
Just another small band, when she gives me
her hand
And 'twill be one of gold on her finger.
CHORUS

In the same year there appeared another song with the same theme, this one by Bob Adams. While possibly not as popular as the first, it had some of the best stage folk to plug it for him. Miss Blanche Ring, probably as well known as any comedienne of the beginning of the century, permitted her picture to appear on the cover of Adams' song "On the Merry-Go-Round," and she sang:

> On the merry, merry-go-round . . .
> Ain't it dandy, ain't it fine,
> Breezing round in the good Summer-time
> To the tune of Sweet Rose O'Grady,
> And keep on the Sunny Side,
> If you get the Brass Ring, boys!
> One, two, three,
> You can ride, ride, ride.

These songs may give the indication that the carrousel was something of a novelty in 1907. But the Carrousel, or Merry-go-round, is steeped in history which extends back many hundreds of years. It is reported that in ancient Mexico a form of carrousel was in use by the Aztecs. In a weird ceremony, after erecting a pole eighty feet high, they suspended natives on ropes, by their heels, their heads downward, and swung them around at terrifying speed.

In the twelfth century, Arab horsemen played a game in which they threw at each other fragile clay balls, filled with scented water. Spaniards and Italians, participating in the crusades, saw the sport, and brought it back to their own countries. They called it "carosella" or "garosello," which meant "little war," and changed its character so as to exhibit the art of good horsemanship and to display the fine garments worn by the horsemen.

Frenchmen became intrigued with the game at the start of the seventeenth century. French royalty participated in a "carrousel" in 1605, and again in 1608 and 1612, the last date being the occasion of a royal wedding, when some 550,000 crowns were lavished on the occasion. Fifty years later a still more splendiferous entertainment of similar nature took place in the square between the Louvre and the Tuileries. The Arc de Triomphe du Carrousel in the square is still a tourist attraction.

Germany, Russia, and Great Britain all found the carrousel an agreeable pastime. The term "merry-go-round" was first introduced in a poem by George Alexander Stevens, published in 1729, describing the St. Bartholomew Fair in England:

Here's Whittington's cat and the tall dromedary,
The chaise without horses, and Queen of Hungary:
Here's the merry-go-rounds, come who rides,
  come who rides, Sir?

In America in past years, there have been many names used for the old carrousels. They were known as flying horses, whirligigs, Kelly's goats, steam riding galleries, and carry-us-alls.

In 1825 the Common Council of Manhattan Island granted one John Sears a permit to "establish a covered circus for a Flying Horse Establishment," at the same time withdrawing a petition by P. Paguet for a similar type of operation. It is presumed that Paguet had been exhibiting his Flying Horses before that date and somehow ran into difficulties with the authorities.

The 1840's and 1850's witnessed extensions of the merry-go-round's popularity, as noted in journalistic accounts of the period. Not only Manhattan, but the New Jersey coast resorts offered carrousel rides. A large tent covered the merry-go-round; the cars—to be replaced later by wooden animals—were suspended from beams under the roof. The pleasant entertainment was a one-horse-power operation, with the horse, a docile beast, circling round and round in the carrousel's innards and carrying along with him the cars which were attached to his harness.

The new era for merry-go-rounds in America was now at hand. It dawned in 1860 with the arrival in Philadelphia of a German gentleman named Gustav A. Dentzel. Dentzel's family had had extensive experience in carrousel building, and he soon made use of his unique knowledge. He constructed a small carrousel in his cabinetmaker's shop on Brown Street. Testing it, he found Philadelphians enthusiastic. Repainting the sign above his shop to read, "G. A. Dentzel, Steam and Horsepower Carousell Builder —1867," he worked zealously to improve his product.

His early carrousels had no wooden horses, only seats like park benches, which hung from chains attached to sweeps projecting from a center pole. Dentzel himself pulled the riders around. Years later, one of his carvers, Daniel Muller, told of the transfiguration from benches to horses. Muller said his father, a pioneer carver, found an old book with prints of wooden animals, cut a pattern, hewed the horse from a block of wood and carved it into shape. That was the end of the benches; equines were thenceforth the work horses of the merry-go-round.

Dentzel's first adventure of any size was a carrousel which he erected in

1870 at Smith's Island, an amusement resort in the Delaware River opposite the foot of Market Street, Philadelphia. So popular were the rides that he decided to put the merry-go-round on tour. He dismantled it and set it up in Atlantic City, which was just beginning to acquire a reputation as a vacation spot.

From Atlantic City he continued southward, setting up shop in Richmond, Virginia. Now, these merry-go-rounds revolved to band organ music and the makers tried to use the most popular tunes of the day to attract customers. But in Richmond, when Dentzel started his carrousel revolving, he couldn't get riders. Instead he found boys throwing stones at him. When he appealed to the police to help him, they advised him, "Mister, if you want business, don't ever play 'Marching thru Georgia' in the South." From that time on Dentzel was careful to avoid controversial music for his organs.

While Dentzel was thriving in Philadelphia, other entrepreneurs were exploring the possibilities of similar successes elsewhere. Charles I. D. Looff had come to New York from Germany in 1870 and had worked as a wood carver in a furniture factory in Brooklyn. An energetic man, he would rise at early dawn and in his home, before he went to work, would carve and paint wooden animals.

When he assembled them on a frame and platform he had erected at Coney Island, he found his merry-go-round to be such a success that he extended his operations. A second carrousel was made for a Coney Island beer garden, and a third for Young's Pier in Atlantic City. As Looff's business grew in size, so did his merry-go-rounds. One that he constructed in 1895 for installation in Riverside, Rhode Island, had sixty-two horses and four chariots—almost enough for a Roman holiday.

Philadelphia and Manhattan had their day in the carrousel field, but the town which came to be known as the merry-go-round center of America was North Tonawanda, near Buffalo, New York. It was here that a young Scotsman (there had to be some competition for the Germans) named Allan Herschell started a machine plant in 1872. Eleven years later he and his partners built their first "steam riding gallery," a carrousel operated by a steam engine. A second and a third followed. Herschell, after selling a half interest in the third to one Christ Krull, took the carrousel to New Orleans, where it was successful despite many mechanical breakdowns. He dutifully reported his experiences to his partners, who ungraciously telegraphed their reply: "Throw same in canal and return to North Tonawanda, plenty of work at foundry." Herschell, in a rage, kept himself incommunicado for two months.

A mechanic named Bert Stickney who, in 1885, helped to set up and operate this carrousel at the World Exposition and Cotton Centennial in New Orleans, recalled later: "It took a cowboy to ride it and it beats all that people were so crazy to ride that we had a devil of a time to keep them from overloading the machine which had 24 prancing horses and four chariots.... We lighted the machine with gasoline torches which smoked, filling the canvas top with gasoline fumes .... The boiler burned soft coal, generating about as much smoke as it did steam. When the wind blew the smoke toward the machine, some of the people who had paid a perfectly good nickel to ride were a sweet looking sight."

For over forty years North Tonawanda maintained its leading role in the merry-go-round field. It was a magnet for carvers and woodworkers, whose skill in producing wooden horses and other beasts was vital to the success of the unique carrousel industry. Almost everyone in North Tonawanda, it seemed, was carving horses. And such delightful, such willing, such good-natured horses! They seemed to have a slight smile and an eager look. Their ears stood upright, their forelocks were parted, and their manes brushed. What accommodating mounts for eager young riders! However, Herschell never developed a monopoly. Competent carvers continued operations in the country's metropolitan areas.

European exports found their way to this country too. For example, in 1905 the Pavilion of Fun in Coney Island featured what was probably the most magnificent carrousel in the world, built originally for Kaiser Wilhelm II of Germany, whose imperial seal adorned one of the chariots. The carrousel featured not only handsomely carved horses, but ducks, cupids, pigs, and even gondolas for nonequestrians.

One successful firm in Brooklyn was established by two immigrants from eastern Europe, Solomon Stein and Harry Goldstein. Expert wood carvers, each had started individually, early in the twentieth century, to produce ladies' wooden combs, a staple article at a time when a woman's long hair was carefully arranged on her head after much brushing and combing.

But after a few years and a number of visits to Coney Island with its popular merry-go-rounds, Stein and Goldstein came, jointly, to the conclusion that wooden horses were less difficult to carve, and more profitable to produce, than combs. Their first sample horses were highly attractive, and in no time at all they were devoting full time in their cramped tenement shop to the new venture. Goldstein was a restless man who rocked back and forth as he carved, whereas Stein carved quickly and authoritatively. The two partners carved the heads and left the rest of the animal to the other carvers.

In 1912 they found an experienced carrousel man, Henry Dorber, who built the machinery necessary for the manufacturing of carrousels. He became a third partner, and the trio's business expanded rapidly. They billed themselves as "the Artistic Carousel Manufacturers," and advertised "3 to 6 abreast jumping horse carousels," the largest machines made anywhere in the world.

Eventually all sorts of animals claimed places on the carrousel—serpents, peacocks, bears, storks, elephants, kangaroos, giraffes, even mermaids and centaurs.

The popularity of carrousels continues today, though not to the extent of a generation ago. Yet it still manages to crop up occasionally in popular music. One of the cutest songs in *The Band Wagon*, Arthur Dietz' and Howard Schwartz' 1931 revue, was "I Love Louisa," in which a youthful Fred Astaire sang:

When we ride on the merry-go-round
I kiss Louisa.

And in 1935 when Lily Pons starred in Jerome Kern's movie, *I Dream Too Much*, one of her great songs was "The Jockey on the Carousel." But now people look for other pastimes. It is hard to imagine any maiden who would today have as good a time for such a small investment, as Mary, whose young man sang:

My girl's satisfied, when we go for a ride
On the Merry-go-round in the summer.

"As We Go Down the Pike"

SO ON APRIL 30, 1803, by a stroke of the pen and an investment of fifteen million dollars the United States doubled its size. It had, the day before, been a country of 827,000 square miles. Its western border, which had been marked by the Mississippi River, now swung far out; the Mississippi would thenceforth become the midriff of the new giant; the United States would now extend to the Rocky Mountains. The world's balance of power was on the way to being transformed by two great men, Napoleon Bonaparte, who was anxious to sell, and Thomas Jefferson, who wanted to purchase. A huge territory, named for King Louis the Ninth of France, was the fifteen-million-dollar tract involved; the Louisiana Purchase was Jefferson's greatest accomplishment since the drafting of the Declaration of Independence twenty-seven years before. And a new metropolitan plant, named Saint Louis, was about to bloom and to dominate for decades the enormous area which Jefferson acquired.

The stunning supertransaction could not be ignored by the contributors to the popular music of the day, and one, Michael Fortune (the accreditation includes "music by an amateur") wrote the verses of a song entitled "The Acquisition of Louisiana," which went, in part, as follows:

> Tho' Tyrants may boast of their pow'r and dominion,
> Their greatness exists in a Courtier's opinion,
> Tho' Sycophants gaze on the splendor of Crowns,
> And pay adoration to Despots on Thrones:
> We admire the calm Sage, who presides o'er a nation
> Of Freemen (no boasting) each man in his station.
> Without arms, without dread,
> Or a drop of blood shed
> Great Jefferson adds to the wealth of a Nation.

One hundred years later Saint Louisans, residents of a city whose size then exceeded the combined population of New York, Philadelphia, Boston, and Baltimore at the time of annexation, were giving thought to some sort of fitting centennial celebration to mark the "Acquisition of Louisiana." The Louisiana Purchase Exposition was the result of the deliberations of the governor of Missouri, newspaper editors, bankers, and business leaders in numerous fields.

They couldn't quite get it into shape by 1903, the centennial year, but its panorama of technical wonders, material progress, peoples from every continent in their native costumes, and enticing entertainment for visitors of all ages, was displayed in its full splendor in 1904. In that year, after the official opening by President Theodore Roosevelt, the exposition attracted millions from all over the world.

Every modern invention of consequence was on view, every new development of conveniences that made life more enjoyable—the newest luxury in automobiles (the Simplex, the Rambler, the Haynes-Apperson), with the place of honor held by a car which had been driven nonstop from St. Louis to New York and back in fifteen days and two hours; the great steam engines, powerful enough to transport passengers across the entire continent in four days; the most comfortable trolley cars, the backbone of every city's transportation system.

Small wonder that the exhibits were thronged with sightseers, who gaped at the splendor of the national pavilions of China, Brazil, Germany, and Siam; at the great galleries of famous works of art; at the Palace of Varied Industries, which displayed Ingersoll watches and Waterman fountain pens; at the eight-gang steam plow and the automatic manure spreader; at the N. K. Fairbank Company's Fairy Soap Bubble fountain in the agricultural building, where the world-famous Fairbank Company's Gold Dust Washing Powder ("let the Gold Dust Twins do your work") was touted in booklets distributed by live little replicas of the dusky twins.

Small wonder, too, that when Andrew B. Sterling and Kerry Mills wrote "Meet Me in St. Louis," it became in no time at all just about the most popular song of 1904. According to the title page, it was sung "with great success" by Lew Dockstader, Lottie Gilson, Nora Bayes, Bonnie Thornton, Ethel Levey, and a dozen more celebrities of the vaudeville stage. The first verse and chorus go:

> When Louis came home to the flat,
> He hung up his coat and his hat,
> He gazed all around, but no wifey he found,
> So he said "where can Flossie be at?"
> A note on the table he spied,
> He read it just once, then he cried,
> It ran, "Louis dear, it's too slow for me here,
> So I think I will go for a ride."

> CHORUS: "Meet me in St. Louis, Louis,
> Meet me at the fair,
> Don't tell me the lights are shining
> any place but there,
> We will dance the Hoochee Koochee,
> I will be your tootsie wootsie,
> If you will meet me in St. Louis, Louis,
> Meet me at the fair!"

There were six verses and choruses in all, each a paragon of the kind of popular ditty which captured the attention of the gallerygoers of the day. Here is number six:

> In church sat a man near the door, asleep, he was starting to snore,
> The Minister rose, and he said, "We will close singing, Meet
> on the Beautiful Shore."
> The man in the back then awoke, he caught the last words that
> he spoke;
> He said, "Parson White, you can meet me alright, but The
> Beautiful Shore is a joke."

CHORUS: Meet me in St. Louis, Louis, meet me at the fair,
Don't tell me the lights are shining any place but there;
I'll be waiting at the station, for the whole darned
congregation,
Meet me in St. Louis, Louis, meet me at the fair.

The greatest of all the Fair's attractions was the "Pike." The Fair's officials had not wished to tout another "Midway," which term, they felt, would remind visitors of the well-known sucker seducer of the great Chicago Exposition of 1893, featuring the scandalous—for those days—"Streets of Cairo" and eye-popping belly dancers.

So St. Louis hit on a name far more staid. Chicago's "Midway" was succeeded by St. Louis' "Pike." St. Louisans themselves were not certain about the term's significance. Some related it to Pike County, from which many Missourians migrated to California. One newspaper of the period merely said, "There is no Midway here—it is called 'The Pike,' in honor of Missouri." The showmen on the mile-long street were known as "Pikers," and visitors to it were invited to "Take a Pike."

The "Pike" had something for everybody—spectaculars, panoramas, moving pictures, a scenic railway, Hagenbeck's Circus, an infant incubator, and replicas of modes of life around the globe, including India, Paris, Cairo, Jerusalem, Japan, Spain, Switzerland, Rome, China, Turkey, Siberia. It reflooded Galveston; it re-created the world; it reactivated the Wild West. It even reached far into the future; one of the weirdest of the shows was called "Hereafter." There was a fire-fighting exhibition and an Irish industrial exhibit; there were glass weavers and an Eskimo village; there were the Tyrolean Alps and Boyton's Deep Sea Divers.

A feature of the two previous American expositions had been Hagenback's Wild Animal Show. No fair was complete without such an exhibit, so Carl Hagenbeck and his sons in Hamburg, reputed to be the biggest wild-beast merchants in the world, shipped more than eight hundred choice specimens to St. Louis and established once more their popularity.

Captain Paul Boyton, the inventor of the chute-the-chutes at Coney Island, lent the St. Louis Exposition one of his prize possessions, a twenty-five-foot piece of the original Blarney stone, available for kissing by anyone who needed the inspiration for long-tale telling. There had been a phony cobblestone at the Chicago World's Fair, but this time, the showman said, the piece of stone was the genuine article—no "sham-rock!" And there was that old stand-by, the Temple of Mirth.

But the good people of St. Louis were determined that nothing off color would be permitted to offend the sensitivity of the delicate ladies and innocent children who would descend on this elaborate playground. In 1902, when the Fair was still in the planning stage, the Board of Lady Managers passed a resolution expressing their "earnest desire" that there be "no indecent dancing or improper exhibits in the Midway" (this was in pre-"Pike" days), a request which was promptly passed on to the concessionaires by the director of concessions and admissions. Moreover, read the concession contracts, concessionaires were not permitted to employ "spielers," "criers," or other noisemakers to tout their wares.

Declared the *St. Louis Globe-Democrat* in October, 1902, regarding St. Louis's Pike-to-be: "Her midway is to be watched over with all the tender solicitude that is bestowed on a Sunday School picnic. Nothing that is not ennobling, elevating, soul-inspiring is to be . . . . (word missing). The proceedings are to be opened every morning with prayer and closed with the Doxology at sunset. At least, that is the beatific vision presenting itself to the enraptured fancy of the Fair authorities. But you just wait till that fair gets in full swing and—well, you will see what you will see.

"What do you suppose those concessionaires are giving up 25% of their receipts for, anyway? Beside, however circumspect a man may walk before the eyes of his church and in the bosom of his family, when he goes away from home he wants . . . to be taken for a devil of a fellow. When he goes to see a midway he wants to see the real thing and not a sanctified substitute therefor."

For such a fairgoer, the Pike managed to include two very well attended girlie shows, bearing the names "Gay Paree" and "Streets of Paris." Despite the prohibitive clauses in their contracts, these shows employed barkers to whip up trade, inveigling the crowds with promises of performances by beautiful wild women from New York, Chicago, Paris, and the Orient. The response of the curious male sightseers was gratifying to the promoters.

The Irish village featured a handsome minstrel with an exquisite tenor voice. His name was John McCormack, and he came to St. Louis fresh from his success as the winner of highest honors at a famous Dublin music festival. Within five years he was destined to become one of the brightest stars of the Metropolitan Opera Company in New York.

The Pike's great Wild West show combined the personnel of the Rough Riders of the World and the Wild West Indian Congress, who together numbered two hundred people. These were augmented by some four hundred animals—quite a production! Among the hired help was a twenty-six-year-old Oklahoma cowboy named Will Rogers, who was billed as "The Mexican Rope Artist." Rogers, like McCormack, was on his way up the ladder of fame; he became one of the greatest drawing cards in Florenz Ziegfeld's annual *Follies*, where his skill with a lariat was matched only by his delightful cracker-barrel humor.

In anticipation of the treats in store for fairgoers, two ladies named Mary Lee Berry and Ida Kroger wrote, in 1903, a song, "As We Go Down the Pike," recalling the pioneers of a century before and the delights that awaited the visitors to the coming Exposition. The lyrics, penned by Miss Berry, reminisced:

> It's near one hundred years ago,
> A gallant party strode
> They travelled far the wildwoods through,
> And made a "Turnpike Road,"
> The dear old Pike comes up to view,
> And at its very sound,
> Fond mem'ry mingles old and new
> That makes my heart rebound.

> CHORUS: And now the Fair will jolly be,
> When you and I can "bike"
> And take the girls we love the best
> A-down the World's Fair Pike.

Other song writers, too, extolled the pleasures of the Pike. Felix F. Feist and Harry Bennett collaborated on a jolly waltz entitled "Strolling 'Long the Pike," in which they pointed out:

> It's not like the Bowery, or dear Coney Isle,
> There are things to be seen that will cause you to smile.
> As you stroll along the Pike,
> You'll see many things you like,
> But without any dough my advice is, don't go,
> For a stroll along the Pike.

Since those carefree, sentimental times, many a new world's fair has come and gone—San Francisco, New York, Brussels, Montreal, Osaka, Munich. But none has inspired song writers to dedicate their compositions to the host city; and even today when we think nostalgically of the splendor of the great expositions that have come and gone, there is only one song which will capture their festive spirit:

> Meet me in St. Louis, Louis,
> Meet me at the Fair.

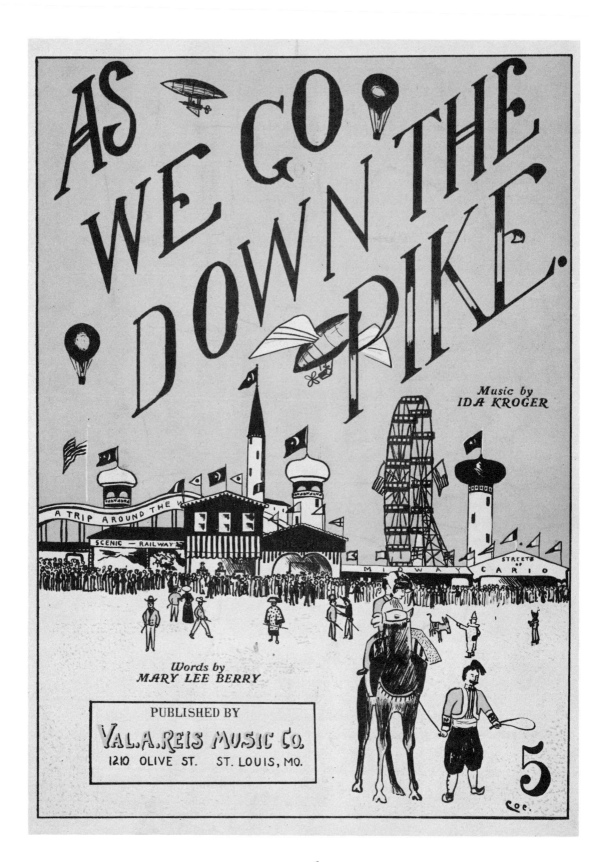

As We Go Down the Pike.

No "Mid-way"! at the Fair —— But 'tis what we all would like—— But we will saun-ter here and there A-long the love-ly "Pike" —— It's near one hun-dred years a-go— A gal-lant par-ty strode —— They trav-elled far the wild woods through and made a "Turn-Pike Road" —— The dear old Pike comes up to view—— And at its ve-ry sound. —— Fond mem'-ry min-gles old and new That makes my heart re-

Chorus

bound —— And now the Fair will jol-ly be—— When you and I can "bike" —— And take the girls we love the best A-down the World's Fair Pike —— And oh, the fun that we will have—— Will be your hearts de-light —— —— And boys and girls will ev-er bless The "Mid-way" turned to "Pike."——

2. I wander back to days of yore
To days I always like
When with my sweetheart by the hand
We strolled along the Pike
The Fair will have its foreign sights
And things that all will like
But naught will tingle through my blood

Like tramping down the Pike
One fondest mem'ry dear to me
In dreams by day and night,
Will be the time when I can take my sweet-
 heart down the "Pike"
Chorus

Rube Goldberg

Lyrics by Rube Goldberg? Nonsense! Melody by Rube Goldberg? Absurd! But wait—proof will be forthcoming with cartoon illustrations.

Rube Goldberg, one of the greatest American cartoonists of all, almost wasn't. Despite the fact that Rube had begun to draw at four, and had followed this up at the age of twelve by taking art lessons—from a sign painter —at 50 cents a lesson, his family had other ideas of a profession for a young man. Rube, a San Franciscan by birth, was propelled by his father into the engineering school of the University of California at Berkeley, and there he labored until he received his degree as a mining engineer in 1904. During his university career he had managed to find time to contribute drawings to the college newspaper; one cartoon won a prize—a trip to Yosemite. But he was resigned to the wishes of his family, and he went to work for the city engineer, designing water mains and sewers. The first time he had the opportunity to look down the two-thousand-foot shaft of a mine, he had the feeling that he and the career of a mining engineer were not compatible. Two months later, his job grew too onerous for him, and he quit. He craved an occupation which might satisfy his latent talents as an artist, and he started hunting. Soon opportunity knocked.

The son of the *San Francisco Chronicle's* city editor had been at the university with Rube, and had shown his father some cartoons that Goldberg did for the *Pelican*, the campus paper. So when Goldberg applied to the *Chronicle* for work, he was not completely unknown at the paper. He got a job at once as an office boy in the art department at eight dollars a week. In his spare time he drew pictures, hoping the art department would accept them. For three months this kept up with a uniform result; picture after picture was consigned to the wastepaper basket.

One day he received an exciting assignment; an editor's son was participating in a track meet, and Rube was sent by the sports editor to cover the meet and to sketch a picture of the race in which the boy was running. Rube laid out pencils and paper on his desk for the drawings that were to be produced later and went to the track. After the race he dashed back, ready to portray the event in black and white, only to find the other men gone, his materials put away, and his desk nailed tight—courtesy of his associates in the department.

Goldberg acted promptly. Paying a quick visit to a nearby hardware store, he purchased a hammer and nails, and nailed up every other desk in the room. He could hardly have anticipated the result of his precipitate reaction to the prank played on him. The next day when his department reopened, the men were astounded and delighted by the nerve he had shown. From that time on he was accepted as an equal by the older men. Now he was one of them, and the following day his first cartoon appeared.

After a short time he left the *Chronicle* for the *Bulletin*, which raised his salary to thirty dollars weekly. He was working for the *Bulletin* at the time of the calamitous San Francisco earthquake, and he tried to lighten the heavy mood of the city with his cartoons, which were now daily features of the sports pages. But despite his increasing popularity, Goldberg was not satisfied; he longed for an opportunity to join the staff of a really great metropolitan paper, and he determined he would try to "crack" New York. So thither Goldberg sped in 1907 at the age of twenty-three to call on news-paper editors. As Goldberg himself later summarized it: "Big fire started, water mains did not work, city burned up and Goldberg had to flee."

The first five papers which he visited were uninterested; being thrown out of five offices may not have broken any records, but the fact remains that it was not until his sixth try, twelve days after he had reached the Big City, that he found a sympathetic ear. The name of the ear's owner is not known, but he was on the staff of the *Evening Mail*, and that was the paper that en-gaged the services of Reuben L. Goldberg at the staggering salary of fifty dollars a week.

It must have been something of a struggle for Goldberg to get his bearings in a place as enormous as New York. He himself says it wasn't until his thirteenth day in town that he learned that the Sixth Avenue El and the Brooklyn Bridge were two different structures.

At first he did not appear to be making progress, though his cartoons were a regular feature of the sports page. Some of his friends feared that his name was holding him back, and they urged him to caption his drawings with a different signature. But Goldberg rejected the suggestion firmly; he de-termined to make his name one which the public would not only accept, but respect; and he toiled harder than ever.

In those days the top of the sports page of the *Evening Mail* was enhanced by seven columns of cartoons, which attracted the readers' attention as a rule even before they scanned the page for the baseball and racing results. Within three months after Goldberg had been hired he was doing the seven-column spread, and recognition was coming his way. His readership grew to im-mense proportions when he started his first series, which he called "Foolish Questions."

Like so many success stories, this one was the result of an accident. Rube needed a subject one day to fill a blank space in the cartoon on which he had been working. On impulse he drew a grotesque picture of a man who had just fallen from the window of the Flatiron Building, New York's best-known skyscraper in the early 1900's, with a woman inquiring sympathetically, "Are you hurt?" To which the man replied, "No, I am taking my beauty sleep." Goldberg labeled the picture "Foolish Questions." He didn't think much about it, but was astounded when letters began to pour into the office and the phone rang incessantly. It seemed as if everybody in New York wanted to suggest a subject for his next foolish question, and it dawned on Rube that he had a theme for a highly successful series of cartoons. He was not one to let such an opportunity slip by, and he made the most of it. For years "Foolish Questions" was a feature of his syndicated material; in fact, he never had a more popular feature in his entire cartooning experience.

In gratitude for Rube's contribution to the sports page's popularity, the *Mail* jumped his salary to $65 a week, and six months later a second increase brought it to $75. Before he was thirty, Goldberg was earning $25,000 a year. In 1915, Hearst wanted him and dangled a $50,000 salary between Rube's eyes. The *Mail* was in no mood to part with such a valuable asset, and $60,000 was their response; Goldberg stayed where he was.

He continued to produce one series after another, and half a dozen were enormously successful; "I'm the Guy," "Boob McNutt," "Mike and Ike, They Look Alike," "Lala Palooza," were prime examples.

Goldberg, who was so shy that he might gulp when he met someone, was nevertheless avid for New York's night life; Broadway and 42nd Street were among his favorite haunts. One evening he was enjoying a vaudeville show on the old Hammerstein Roof Garden, when his attention was captured by a remark in a comic repartee: "I'm the guy that put the salt in the ocean." He returned to his desk to start an "I'm the Guy" series. The grotesque little fellow who was the series' central figure would emerge in the third frame of a four-frame strip, from some unexpected place or in some impossible act—coming up from a flowerpot or riding a bicycle upside down on the ceiling. For example, the strip would illustrate a fisherman making a great haul, then sitting down to a feast and getting a bone lodged in his throat. Up from some incredible place would emerge a little old man, who, when asked by the fisherman who he was, would reply, "I'm the guy that put the bones in fish." Later on, the strip developed into a play on words. For instance, a soldier attacking a fort would sit down to compose a poem, as follows:

> I sing of the smoke of the battle,
> My country is there with the punch.
> We'll capture them yet though I sorely regret
> That we do not stop fighting for lunch.

Up pops the little old man on the wall of the fortress, and is challenged by the soldier, "Little defender, who are you?" Back comes the reply, "I'm the guy that put the bard in bombardment." Pretty crude, you think? Goldberg's readers wouldn't agree; they ate it up.

"Boob McNutt" was a poor slob who could never do anything right, loved by a beautiful girl named Pearl who always had her hands full keeping Boob out of trouble. Then there were the inventions of Professor Lucifer Gorgonzola Butts. These were developed in accordance with Goldberg's law: "The more extremes to which a gadget-maker goes in irrational complexity, the more people will go for it." Goldberg's series of marvelous inventions were delightful. He developed the most complicated contraptions (with parts A, B, C through M, N, O, P) to perform the simplest of tasks, such as sharpening a pencil or catching a mouse or scratching your back or getting an olive out of a long-necked bottle.

Most readers, particularly males, who pick up a newspaper will turn first to one of two subjects, the comics or the sports. And both of these fields have inspired the writers of popular songs. Baseball songs have been written for more than a century; songs about horses, football, rowing, racing have been sung as far back as the memory of our oldest inhabitant can reach.

As for the comics, most of the old-time, and some of the newer, comic strips had songs describing the antics of their heroes—"Little Nemo," "Foxy Grandpa," "The Newlyweds and their Baby," "Barney Google," "Little Abner." And naturally, "I'm the Guy" and "Boob McNutt."

In fact, the "I'm the Guy" strips inspired two songs, one with "Ravings by Rube Goldberg" and "Noise by Bert Grant," according to the song's title page. This pictures Goldberg's "Guy," a bald-headed little fellow with a grotesque white mustache resembling a headless seagull in full flight. The song made its appearance in 1912, during the height of the strip's popularity. The narrator is blatantly immodest about his affluence, his connections, and his unique qualifications:

> The Kaiser shines my shoes, the Czar pours
>   out my booze,
> And the King of England cuts my hair....
> I'm the guy that put the notes in the music
> I'm the guy that put the horns on deer,

I'm The Guy

When they hear me talk,— when they see me walk,— Peo-ple turn a-round to say "Who's

that?—— All the peo-ple cry,— all the lad-ies sigh,—'Till they know ex-act-ly where

I'm at —— The Kai-ser shines my shoes,— the Czar pours out my booze, And the King

of Eng-land cuts my hair,—— I eat a bale of hay— For break-fast ev'ry day,—

Chorus

I'm here, I'm there, I'm most-ly ev'ry-where.—— I'm the guy that put the salt in the

o-cean —— I'm the guy that put the bones in fish,—— I'm the guy can't tell a lie,

I'll al-ways live, I'll nev-er die. In the wish-bone, I'm the guy that put the wish——

I'm the guy that put the smoke in the chim-neys —— I'm the guy that put the leaves on

trees —— What's that? Who am I? Don't you know? I'm the guy, I'm the guy that bites the

2. I wear stylish clothes,
   I'm the guy that knows,
   Why a chicken goes across the street.
   I'm the only man knows how old is Ann;
   And I place each copper on his beat.
   My shoes are diamond soled, my bed is made of gold,
   Twenty thousand servants bring my meals.
   I'm chased by pretty girls and Dukes and Lords and Earls,
   And I'm the final court of all appeals.

   CHORUS: I'm the guy that put the sand on the beaches
           I'm the guy that put the crust on pies,
           I'm the guy that's far and nigh,
           I take a bath and come out dry,
           I'm the guy that puts the wings on little flies
           I'm the guy that put the hump on the camel
           I'm the guy that put the cough in croup
           What's that? Who am I? Don't you know?
           I'm the guy, I'm the guy that put the noise in noodle soup.

3. When I take a car, going fast and far,
   No one dares to ask me for my fare
   Ev'ry one who knows says: "look, there he goes."
   Gee, there's nothing to it, I'm a bear
   I've got a million wives, who'd sacrifice their lives,
   Just to make things comf'table for me
   I live on fancy things, prepared by Queens and Kings,
   I go to ev'ry show admission free.

   CHORUS: I'm the guy that put the hole in the doughnut
           I'm the guy that put the feet in shoes,
           I'm the guy that knows just why the little stars are in the sky,
           I'm the guy that gives the papers all the news.
           I'm the guy that put the notes in the music,
           I'm the guy that put the horns on deer,
           What's that? Who am I? Don't you know?
           I'm the guy, I'm the guy that put the foam on lager beer.

I'M THE GUY
COMIC SONG
RAVINGS BY
RUBE
GOLDBERG
NOISE BY
BERT GRANT
5
JEROME H. REMICK & CO.
New York Detroit

What's that? Who am I? Don't you know?
> I'm the guy.

I'm the guy that put the foam on lager beer.[1]

At the same time, a younger, little-known team of writers, Clarence Gaskill and Charles Shisler, wrote a song on the identical theme and dared to compete with Goldberg himself. Entitled "Look at Me, Bing! Bang! I'm the Guy," their hero proclaimed:

> I'm the guy that put the wart on the pickle,
> I'm the guy that put the laugh in tickle....
> Did you ever stop and wonder where they get
> > the noise for thunder,
> Look at me, I'm the guy[2]

In 1917, Rube decided that he could write the music as well as the words for a popular song, so he composed a simple melody for a set of verses which he called "Cartoons in Tunes." The verses were "Sillysonnets." Here's an example illustrated, on the title page, by a poet declaiming to his pet cat, (said poet to be cut down to size in the fourth and last of the pictures on the cover by the rejoinder of a perfect stranger):

> I know not why the stars do shine,
> I know not why I call thee mine,
> I know not why the birdies sing—
> (Stranger) In fact, you don't know anything![3]

In 1926 Goldberg cooperated with three collaborators to produce a song about Boob McNutt:

> Boob McNutt! That's the guy I mean with the
> > empty bean....
> Someone in Miami had sold some lots to him,
> Poor Boob couldn't find them because he
> > couldn't swim,
> And now, his hair he is tearing,
> Because his neighbor now is a herring.[4]

Again Rube designed the title page with a cast of zany characters; in fact, the title page is funnier than the song.

---

[1] "I'm the Guy." W/Rube Goldberg M/Bert Grant © 1912 Remick Music Corp. Copyright Renewed All Rights Reserved Used by Permission of WARNER BROS. MUSIC.

[2] "Look at Me, Bing Bang, I'm the Guy." W/M Clarence Gaskill and Charles Shisler © 1912 M. Witmark & Sons Copyright Renewed All rights reserved Used by Permission WARNER BROS. MUSIC.

[3] "Silly Sonnets." W/M Rube Goldberg Copyright © 1917, Renewed 1945 LEO FEIST INC. Used by Permission.

[4] "Boob McNutt." © 1926 by Mills Music Inc. © Renewed 1954 by Mills Music Inc. Used by Permission.

As Goldberg grew older he displayed other talents. At an average salary of $150,000 a year over a fifteen-year period he accumulated enough substance to enable him after a time to indulge in less remunerative practices. He wrote magazine articles; he acted in a movie with Jack Benny. In his late seventies he became a sculptor and fashioned small comic figures as whimsical as his cartoon characters. His delightful little book with quaint illustrations, entitled "How to Remove the Cotton from a Bottle of Aspirin," was dedicated to the man who said "A straight line is the shortest distance between two points, but I'd rather go in a circle." What a loss when he left us for good in 1971.

Look Out for Jimmy Valentine

IN THE FIELD of the short story in America, the classics by O. Henry have never had a peer. The imagination, the character delineation, the sudden twist, the surprise ending, have long been acclaimed as marks of a master literary draughtsman.

One of the most delightful among many intriguing tales is "A Retrieved Reformation," written in 1903 for the *Cosmopolitan* magazine and appearing in 1909 in the volume, *Roads of Destiny*. Few would suspect that the hero of this fascinating little gem was lifted from a real-life individual by the uninspiring name of Henry Hyatt. Perhaps his pen name, or more appropriately *one* of his pen names, might awake a faint response in the memory of some of our middle-aged citizens—Jimmy Valentine.

Jimmy Valentine, *alias* "Slim" Jones, *alias* William F. Jones, *alias* The Duke, *alias* Dr. W. W. Goelet, *alias* Francis P. Whyte (which was probably his real name) was just about the greatest gentleman burglar who ever "cracked" a safe without the use of explosives. The hearing in his left ear was so acutely sensitive that when he pressed it tightly against a safe he could hear the tumblers in the time locks drop.

Hyatt became known to O. Henry when the two were serving terms together in the penitentiary in Columbus, Ohio—Hyatt for burglary, O. Henry for embezzlement of funds from a bank where he had been a teller. The writer was captivated by the adventures of his romantic fellow convict, and later, when he saw fit to recount some of them, he conceived the name of Jimmy Valentine as one appropriate for such a charming personality. He did not foresee the chain reaction which was to follow, and which will be dealt with later on. First things first.

Francis P. Whyte, nephew of former governor William Pinckney Whyte of Maryland, was born in Hyattsville, Maryland on July 29, 1871. His mother died in childbirth, his father's death occurred a few years later, and the boy landed in an orphanage, a dreadful place where he was thoroughly unhappy. He became known there as "Slim" Jones, and grew to be a tall, gaunt boy who hated the orphanage with a passion. At thirteen he escaped, and with his animal instincts sought to survive. He lived in the streets, slept anywhere, and stole to fill his stomach. This life was interrupted when one night he was awakened roughly from his bed, a pile of sacks near Hollins Market in Baltimore, by a policeman who accused him of being a member of a gang of toughs. Jones, for so he was now known, drew a sentence of six months in the house of correction in Jessups, a term eventually shortened by twenty-five days because of his good behavior.

But he was not to enjoy his freedom long. One Sunday morning he attempted to assuage his hunger and thirst by taking a quart of milk and a bag of rolls which had been left inside the screen door of a porch. As he walked quietly away with his haul he ran into the officer on the beat who took him in custody. This time the charge was "breaking and entering, larceny and receiving." Judge Dennis decided that "Slim" would be best off by spending his next two and one half years in the Maryland State Penitentiary.

Here it was that Jones met up with the man who was to be the greatest influence in his life, a gentleman crook named Henry ("Si") Sage. Sage was at that time past sixty, well educated, and a linguist who spoke French and Spanish with fluency. Sage took young Jones in hand. Besides instructing him in mathematics and the art of reading, he proceeded to teach him everything he knew about safes and bank vaults, their locks and their mechanisms. Jones was the most adept of pupils. He had always taken fine care of his body and particularly his hands, which were carefully groomed at all times. Now this care served him in good stead, for Sage instructed him how to use those hands to make a living.

Upon Jones's release, he sought out Sage, who had been freed previously, at the old Eutaw House in Baltimore. The meeting had been prearranged by Sage for an important purpose; he wanted Jones to help him rob a bank. Little time was lost before the pair proceeded to Westminster, Maryland, where they opened the bank's safe and came away with $50,000. Sage was scrupulously fair; he split the loot down the middle, took his $25,000 and went west, where he bought a chicken ranch, orange grove, and grape vineyard. He prospered and entered into church work. Nevertheless, as his end approached he lamented, "All that has come to me is built on a false foundation." He died sad and broken.

Jones—or Hyatt (why not give him his right name?)—had different ideas. He believed in living high, wearing fine clothes, attending concerts, reading good books, traveling extensively. He was confident that his erect stature, his smart clothing, and his smooth talking would enable him to get wherever and whatever he wanted, solely through his unique ability to pilfer, rob, burglarize. He never carried a weapon, never shed blood, never used explosives. His hands, his ears, and his eyes were all the tools he required, save, at times, for a jimmy. So he spent freely, for whenever he ran out of money he robbed again. In his later years he estimated that his total "take" ran well over a million dollars.

He visited distant points: South America, India, England. In London he attempted to rob a jewelry store, but ran afoul of a British bobby. As a result, he spent two more years in England than he had anticipated, residing during this extended stay in a Portsmouth prison.

When England deported him they turned back to him his original wardrobe, but not enough money to satisfy him. This posed no problem. Landing in Newport News, Virginia, he ferried to Norfolk, registered, with presentable baggage, at one of the best hotels and went to work that night. With the aid of a twisted umbrella rib he turned the key in the lock of a bedroom door, and, without disturbing the couple sleeping there, made off quietly with the gentleman's wallet and the lady's jewels. The next morning he left for parts north.

For three years he spent a portion of his time in Philadelphia, whose citizens were very generous to him. His methods were ingenious. Attending a concert, he would strike up a conversation with a prosperous looking gentleman, who would, after a while, introduce Hyatt to his wife, who would in turn, after another while, invite him to dinner and introduce him to other residents of Philadelphia's Main Line. As Hyatt became familiar with the room arrangements of each house, he found it a simple matter to return to his host's home after dining there—several hours later, as a rule—by way of a second-story window instead of the front door, always operating alone.

Another part of that period he spent in Ohio, but not of his own volition. He was apprehended there and served a couple of years in the penitentiary at Columbus. After his release he decided to head for the West.

This proved to be a mistake, for he was arrested after an attempted bank robbery in Wyoming, and involuntarily spent two years there, until released from prison in 1902. After this unfortunate episode, Hyatt made a strenuous attempt to go straight. In Denver he became acquainted with an evangelist, Reverend William Edward Biederwolf, on whom he made such a favorable impression that he was engaged as the Reverend's publicity director at a salary of fifty dollars a week.

A few months of this were enough for Hyatt and he resumed his westward trek. As he walked down a Los Angeles street he was approached by an elderly man, who greeted him with "Good old Slim!" It was his old friend Henry Sage. Sage told Hyatt how he had gone straight, invested his money, and remained honest for the rest of his life. Hyatt was impressed and moved, but he pushed on.

In San Francisco he secured a position as manager of a popular lecturer, Benjamin Fay Mills. Through a follower of Mills's, he met a beautiful divorcee, named Corinne. They developed a mutual attachment to each other, and soon she was living as Hyatt's common-law wife. Corinne was psychic, so she claimed; when she went into a trance she could perceive matters hitherto unknown to her. Of course, she had to "concentrate" on Hyatt, who was at that time using the name of Dr. Walter W. Goelet; and such concentration revealed to her that her man had been in prison not long before. Hyatt had to own up, fearing the worst, but Corinne forgave him, and eventually decided to help him plan new burglaries. Prior to her divorce she had been well acquainted with some of the leading families in the area and she gave him plans of their homes. Berkeley, Oakland, Alameda and San Jose were soon plagued by episodes of important robberies, one after the other. All went well for Hyatt until one night he was careless enough to drop his wallet as he reached for a jimmy. In the wallet was a photograph of Corinne, and through this Hyatt was tracked down by Berkeley's astute chief of police, Gus Vollmer. Vollmer struck a deal with the burglar; return the important pieces of jewelry, he said, and the dreaded long-term would be lightened. Fortunately for Hyatt, the fence to whom he had turned over the jewelry still had the greater part of it. For its recovery, Hyatt was let off with a four-year term in San Quentin, instead of an expected sentence of fifteen years. When he was released, he learned that Corinne had been committed to a sanitarium after he was taken away and had died there. Another chapter was closed.

Hyatt became a "wandering burglar." He robbed in New Mexico and Texas. Then in San Francisco he became a publicity man for the Women's Federated Clubs, who were battling for the right to vote in California. So skillfully did he conduct their campaign that just before their votes-for-women amendment was carried in 1911, they made Dr. W. W. Goelet (né Hyatt) their honorary vice-president. But success cost him his job, and he set off for the East again, earning his way with a relapse into the skillful-finger and sensitive-ear profession.

As was indicated at the beginning of this story, he had been apprehended in Ohio in the late nineties and found his way to the penitentiary in Columbus, where he made the acquaintance of, and told his adventures to, O. Henry.

Among the readers of "A Retrieved Reformation," shortly after its appearance in *Roads of Destiny*, was a playwright named Paul Armstrong, who envisioned theatrical possibilities for the story. No sooner said—Armstrong converted it into *Alias Jimmy Valentine*, which opened at the Wallack Theater in New York on January 21, 1910. Laurette Taylor, who was shortly afterwards to become the "Peg of My Heart Girl," was in the cast; so was young H. B. Warner (fifteen years later he portrayed the role of Jesus in the supercolossal silent movie, *The King of Kings*). *Valentine* had a run of more than one hundred and fifty performances, a solid showing for those days.

At the height of its success, it came to the attention of one of the most popular song writers and vaudeville entertainers of the day, Gus Edwards. Edwards had come to New York from Germany at the age of nine, started working in a cigar factory before he had reached his teens, and did a bit of singing for lodge meetings on the side. At thirteen he gave up cigars and went into the music profession hook, line, and sinker, plugging songs for sheet-music publishers and selling their wares in theater lobbies. He fought for a place on the vaudeville stage, where he appeared on the same bills as the great singing comediennes Lottie Gilson and Maggie Cline.

After a bit he became a headliner himself, and by now he had his own songs to promote, for his production as a composer was becoming voluminous. He had an amazing number of hits—"Goodbye, Little Girl, Goodbye," "Tammany," "In My Merry Oldsmobile," "School Days," "By the Light of the Silvery Moon." His collaborators were the top lyricists of the day—Will D. Cobb, Vincent P. Bryan, Edward Madden. It was Madden to whom Edwards turned when he decided to do a Jimmy Valentine number. At this period in his career he was at the top of the heap of vaudeville performers. His great act was called "Gus Edwards' Song Review," and his troupe of thirty included a dozen youngsters, pre- or barely teen-agers, clever teeny-boppers who, for the most part, would find their own names in

6

Jimmy Valentine

When the stars a - bove are blink-ing   And the house is dark and still—

And a sound comes clink, clink, clink-ing   From the near - by win - dow sill—

If you see a fig - ure crouch - ing   In the ghost - ly pale moon - shine——

And the bulls-eye gleams thro' your start-led dreams   Then it's Jim - mie Va - len - tine——

Chorus

Look out,   look out,   look out for Jim-mie Va - len-tine   For he's a pal of

mine   A sen-ti-men-tal crook   With a touch   that lin-gers   In his sand - pap-ered

fin-gers He can find the com-bi-na-tion of your pock-et-book   Look out,   look

out,   for when you see his lan-tern shine   That's the time to jump right up and shout

Help!   He'd steal a horse and cart   He'd ev-en steal a girl-ie's heart   When Jim-mie

2. Through a mask two eyes gleam brightly
   As they rove in search of loot,
   While a voice remarks politely
   "If you move an inch I'll shoot,

I'm a souvenir collector
So you have no cause for fright"
Then he bows away with your last week's pay
And he wishes you good-night.
CHORUS

headlights one day. For example, his boys included Walter Winchell, Eddie Cantor, Georgie Price, and George Jessel, all of whom appear on the covers of some of Edwards' songs of the period, such as "If I Was a Millionaire," and, more important for our purpose, "Look Out for Jimmy Valentine," which Edwards and Madden wrote in 1910.

The title page shows a miniature gentleman burglar, probably Georgie Price, tiptoeing onto the stage with flashlight and pistol (an error here; Hyatt never carried a pistol) while Edwards sits and sings at his on-stage piano and the other kids go through the motions of looking scared.

The melody was one of Edwards' catchiest and the quality of Madden's lyrics was far above the average. Here is his chorus:

> Look out, look out, look out for Jimmy Valentine
> For he's a pal of mine
> A sentimental crook
> With a touch that lingers
> In his sand-papered fingers
> He can find the combination of your pocketbook.
> Look out, look out, for when you see his lantern shine
> That's the time to jump right up and shout
> Help!
> He'd steal a horse and cart
> He'd even steal a girlie's heart
> When Jimmy Valentine gets out.[5]
>
> 2. Through a mask two eyes gleam brightly
>   As they rove in search of loot,
>   While a voice remarks politely
>   "If you move an inch I'll shoot,
>   I'm a souvenir collector
>   So you have no cause for fright"
>   Then he bows away with your last week's pay
>   And he wishes you goodnight.

Around 1913, Hyatt became a steward on a British ship, enlisted in the British Merchant Marine, married a nurse, and had a child. When an old accomplice recognized him and in a burst of malice told Hyatt's wife about her husband's past life, she divorced him, taking the baby with her.

Nearly two seesaw decades later, at the age of sixty-one, Hyatt fell in love with a girl half his years, married her, and settled down in Philadelphia. Suddenly one evening on Market Street, he "got religion," overcome by the blandishments and affecting hymns of a little band of Salvation Army singers. From that night on Hyatt was a good boy. He lectured about the evils of a criminal life; he wrote a detailed autobiography, along with articles for newspapers in Philadelphia and Boston. These included a thirty-chapter series under the title of "I Have Stolen a Million." He turned over to the Salvation Army what money he had saved and lived the frugal and abstemious life of a respectable elderly citizen. Moving to Columbia, South Carolina about 1940, he prepared a twenty-seven page booklet published by Epworth Orphanage Press in Columbia, entitled "What Price Crime."

During his last few years, he served as sexton at the Episcopal Church of the Good Shepherd. When he lay on his deathbed in a Columbia hospital in 1945, he said to his friends, "I am not sick. Nothing hurts me. I am just dying from remorse."

The calm twilight of Henry Hyatt's life should draw the curtains on the drama of Jimmy Valentine's career. But these curtains have not closed, and possibly they never will. For, in spite of Hyatt's autobiography, the basis for this story, an unanswered question remains—was he *really* O. Henry's Valentine?

As a matter of fact, three other claimants to the title have been projected on the stage. One, as related by a fellow prisoner of O. Henry's in Columbus, Al Jennings, was a "habitual criminal" named Dick Price. Price had been in and out of prison since he was eleven years old. Jennings, whose book, "Through the Shadows with O. Henry," is a maudlin bit of sentimentality, drips with compassion whenever Price's name is introduced, and dubs him Jimmy Valentine without blinking an eye.

But the title is not earned, says Dr. Paul Clarkson of Clark University in Worcester, the leading authority on O. Henry. Writes Dr. Clarkson, "I would not believe Al Jennings under oath on a stack of bibles." Dr. Clarkson's candidate is another prisoner named Jimmy Connors, who was in the penitentiary for blowing a post office safe. His opinion is shared by Dr. George W. Williard, the prison's night shift doctor, who states dogmatically, "The moment I read O. Henry's description and character delineation of Jimmy Valentine in 'A Retrieved Reformation,' I said, 'That's Jimmy Connors through and through.'"

The third potential Valentine is one Maximilian Schoenbein, *alias* Max Shinburn, *alias* Baron Schindle, a nominee of William J. Brackley, a division manager of Pinkertons, the world famous detective agency. In 1966, Brackley wrote an article for the *Boston Herald*, in which he stated that Schoenbein's lurid burglarizing activities had inspired the writing of the play, *Alias Jimmy Valentine*. He made no mention of the O. Henry story, nor could he very well do so, as Schoenbein's criminal career does not include any "stretch" in Columbus where O. Henry was incarcerated. Dr. Clarkson had never heard of Schoenbein, nor of Hyatt. Says he, "The world is full of people stealing a ride on the tailgate of someone else's wagon."

To this day, no one has been able to state with authority whether Henry Hyatt's "Autobiography" is the McCoy, or whether it is the figment of an empurpled imagination. So who is our hero—or anti-hero? Hyatt? Price? Collins? Schoenbein? What matter now? To those with long memories and sentimental attachments, the gentleman burglar who was known as Jimmy Valentine will have a particular niche in the hall of the most famous romantics. And when you passs that niche as you stroll down the hall, look out! He will find the combination of your pocketbook!

The Funnies

NEWSPAPER POLLS have demonstrated that the first page turned to by a preponderance of a paper's readers is the one containing the comic strips. This preference for fun above serious matters probably holds good even for octogenarians, whose birth occurred in the same decade that the first weekly comic strips appeared in the *San Francisco Examiner* and two New York dailies, the *World* and the *Journal*.

Americans were not the originators of the use of comic characters in art form. About five thousand years ago the first cartoonists in the profession, the Egyptians, were circulating their sketches done on papyrus and limestone flakes. Around the beginning of the common era, the Romans were offering for sale satiric cartoons executed on tiles. In the 17th century England imported the comic character, Punch, from Italy and introduced his partner and better half, Judy; their portraits were sold at country fairs.

In America the man who first developed our cartooning skills was Benjamin Franklin, who was also attacked violently in other cartoons because of his stand on various political questions.

A little over a hundred years after Franklin discovered electricity, the editors of the *Examiner* discovered a cartoonist named James Swinnerton, who, in 1892, created on his drawing board a pride of small carnivora which he presented to his editors as, "The Little Bears and Tigers." Their appearance was that of kittens disguised as wild animals, and their antics were those of small children imitating grownups. Once a week their gambols and pranks could be enjoyed in black and white by readers young and old. They were cute, rather than funny; yet their regular appearance signified the real beginning of what was to emerge as a boon to the American funny bone—the Sunday comic supplement.

Four years after Swinnerton, another artist caught the attention of newspaper readers. He was Richard Outcault, who had been drawing humorous pictures for *Judge* and *Life*, and who turned out comic material about tenements and their youthful inhabitants for the *New York World*. Outcault had been an admirer of Harrigan and Hart, whose musical satires about Irish-Americans were all the rage. He adopted the locale for his work from the words of "Maggie Murphy's Home," a song in their 1890 play, *Reilly and the 400*. One verse of the song commences:

> I walk through Hogan's Alley
> At the closing of the day,
> To greet my dear old mother

So Hogan's Alley, and the little world around it, became the domain of Outcault's first experimental cartoon in the *New York World*. It appeared on February 16, 1896, and was entitled "The Great Dog Show in M'Googan Avenue." In the center of the melange of dogs, cats, and kids was a strange-looking little creature with jug ears and shaven head, wearing a garment resembling a nightshirt. The garment was yellow—the first attempt to put color into the "funnies." The cartoon created immediate attention, so favorable that a month later the *World* had a second cartoon featuring the queer little boy. By this time everybody was talking about the Yellow Kid, whose comments, instead of being printed in the usual cartoon "balloon," were expressed in full right on the wide yellow nightshirt. For example, in a cartoon appearing in the *World* in September, 1898, depicting the attack on a dogcatcher by the neighborhood boys, there appears this message on the Yellow Kid's shirt: "Say! He is de most popular bloke wot ever happened, I don't tink!... He don't ketch no Hogan's Alley sausage today."

By this time William Randolph Hearst of the *New York Journal*, could no longer bear to see the popularity of the Kid in a rival paper; so he went after Outcault with an offer that the *World* would not match and made off with his prize, coddling him until, after a few years, admirers of comic characters were seeking something new.

In 1897, while the "Yellow Kid" was still the yellow king, a composer named Gene Myers wrote a "Dance of the Hogan Alley Hoboes." On the title page, on which Myers acknowledges his indebtedness to "Mr. Out-cault's Yellow Kid," there is a likeness of the Kid himself. On his yellow shirt front is a set of sprawling letters reading: "Say if yer don't know dis here dans yer aint in it wid us."

The demise of the Yellow Kid did not signify the end of Outcault's career. In 1902 he found a new hero for another paper, the *New York Herald*. The new boy was Buster Brown, who, with his sagacious and faithful dog Tige, managed to get into and out of, a scrape a week for some seven or eight years before he too was forced to bow out. At the end of each weekly episode Buster was a sadder but wiser boy, who managed a semisolemn resolution to close the chapter. For example, after one adventure, when he tries to take a swim surreptitiously and gets his clothes stolen, he moralizes, "Resolved! That the loss of my clothes does not worry me. To lose one's self respect is the only serious loss. Clothes are nothing. Character counts, tis *everything*—your happiness, your *success*, and your eternity. . . . People would know more than they do if the carpet were as worn in front of the book case as it is in front of the looking glass. Buster Brown."

In Buster's heyday, he too was featured in a schottische by Roger Bernard, "Buster Brown's Barn Dance." Buster and Tige decorate the cover, and this time Buster has no resolutions to pronounce for the dancers.

By 1906 three big New York papers had developed full-color sections of comic strips for their Sunday editions. The *Herald*'s big drawing card was Winsor McCoy, who dreamed up the gentle character of "Little Nemo" and delighted myriads of children with his strip, "Little Nemo in Slumberland." In 1900 they had discovered Charles E. Schultze, who used the pen name "Bunny," and who created his lovable "Foxy Grandpa," but Hearst was able to wangle "Bunny" over to his *American* after "Grandpa" had become famous. The *Journal*, whose morning edition had become the *American*, had a plethora of big names, which included, in addition to Schultze, Outcault and a later arrival named Frederick Burr Opper, who was delighting old and young with his gawky, but touching, "Happy Hooligan." The *World* had George McManus, one of the finest pictorial humorists of all time, who hit pay dirt with "The Newlyweds and Their Baby," and half a dozen years later struck a new lode in "Bringing Up Father."

"Foxy Grandpa" became the hero of a musical comedy bearing his name, with a froth of a story and several catchy songs by Victor Vogel and Byron X. Stillman. The title song with a lively melody goes:

There's a chap that's just now famous,
Foxy Grandpa is his name,
You will find him at your elbow ev'ry day,
At home or at the theatre, club,
At ev'ry sort of game,
You're sure to meet old Foxy Grandpa gay.
When at a masquerade dance,
If there's one that makes you ask,
Who is that jolly old boy, all dress'd in blue?
Don't waste your time in guessing
Who is underneath the mask,
For when the mask's removed you'll find it's
    Grandpa fooling you.

CHORUS: It's only Foxy Grandpa. There is no use getting vexed,
The old boy keeps you guessing. What will he be up
    to next?
So join his merry laughter with a hearty Ha, Ha, Ha!
Because it's only Foxy, just your jolly old Grandpa.

Well, the music was pleasant, anyway.

A few years later an even more popular musical was brought out, with another set of characters plucked from the comic strips. This show was *The Newlyweds and Their Baby*. A collaboration of well-known song writers of the day combined to produce a dozen numbers, of which one was "Ev'ry Baby Is a Sweet Bouquet." With lyrics by Paul West and music by John W. Bratton, the chorus is as follows:

Your eyes are like the violets, my baby boy
Your cheeks are just as blushing as the rose,
Your skin is lily-white. Oh, you're such a pretty sight
From your forehead to your dimpled little toes.
Your hands are tiny flower petals, baby boy,
You seem to grow far sweeter ev'ry day;
Ev'ry time you smile that way, then I just can't help
    but say,
"Ev'ry baby is a sweet bouquet!"[6]

The advent of Happy Hooligan on the comic-strip scene was the introduction of a type of character new to the Sunday reader, an unlettered, penniless tramp with an unfailing facility for maneuvering himself into whatever situation might prove to be the most detrimental. Happy was always in trouble, and it was always unexpected. He was a born optimist through thick and thin; he built a dreamworld castle just before the roof fell in on him. We enjoy seeing him clobbered by his fellows, but at the same time we harbor sympathy for a well-intentioned unfortunate who was, in his day, one of the most lovable of all the funny characters on the comic pages of history.

A published edition of the song, "Happy Hooligan," written by Vogel and Stillman, the pair who gave us "Foxy Grandpa," has a title page by Opper, Happy's creator, showing the contented tramp riding the rails on the rear platform of a freight car relaxedly puffing at the remains of a cheap cheroot and oblivious to any possible catastrophe that may be lying in wait for him in the sweet bye and bye. Here is his song, vintage 1902:

> Happy Hooligan is a very funny man,
> Misfortune seems to follow him about,
> No matter where he goes, it is sure to end
>   in blows,
> And it's Hooligan that always gets knock'd
>   out!
> The police on their beat consider it a treat
> To pull him in, and no one goes his bail.
> He's told to change his ways. The judge
>   says, "thirty days!"
> And in a daze he's taken down to jail.

> CHORUS: He means to do good, but is misunderstood.
> He must have been born on a Friday!
> Tho' chuck full of pluck, he plays in
>   hard luck;
> His face and his clothes are untidy.
> So drink to this man, with glass or
>   with CAN,
> Poor Hooligan, lowly in station.
> In appearance a sight, his heart seems
>   all right
> He's the happiest man in the nation.

And now for Little Nemo. In all likelihood, McKay, his creator, derived the name from Captain Nemo, the hero of Jules Verne's *Twenty Thousand Leagues Under the Sea*. Little Nemo was the greatest dreamer in the history of the comic strip. Each Sunday a new dream was depicted, one more lurid than the next. In every incident Nemo's alter ego, a clown-faced, cigar-puffing pragmatist named Flip, appeared, usually managing to confound the little boy with fresh dilemmas. Nemo was always attired in gorgeous regalia, surrounded by pomp, luxuriating through it all. His troubles, though awesome at times, were never insurmountable; they were always resolved when Nemo awoke and the fanciful dream vanished. McKay was a master draughtsman; rarely did a more skillful artist turn his talents to the comic strip on a full-time basis, though occasionally one who worked in that field temporarily did emerge as a serious and respected painter in later years (George Luks and Lyonel Feininger may be listed as examples).

But to return to Little Nemo, his flights of fantasy were accompanied vicariously each Sunday morning by millions of little boys and girls, to whom he represented the pinnacle of breath-taking adventure. So universally approved was his image that the great Victor Herbert decided to do a Little Nemo musical comedy. When it opened in Philadelphia in 1908 it was a most lavish and expensive extravaganza. For two seasons it drew large audiences, first in New York, then on the road; but the investment of more than one hundred thousand dollars by Klaw and Erlanger, *Little Nemo*'s producers, was too staggering to permit the show to be a money-maker.

Herbert's songs were adequate, his instrumental numbers imaginative. One number which had a particular appeal for the youthful audiences was "The Happy Land of Once Upon a Time." The lyrics were by Herbert's old stand-by Harry B. Smith, who wrote:

> There's a land of childhood's fancies, that is
>   filled with old romance,
> 'Tis a realm of fairy tale and jingling rhyme.
> And the children of all ages, from the babies
>   to the sages,
> Love the happy land of Once upon a Time.
> Of those fascinating stories I remember best
>   the glories
> Of sweet Cinderella dancing at the ball.
> There was Jack who killed the Giant, so heroic
>   and defiant,
> And Riding Hood! I loved her best of all.
> CHORUS: Dear old friend(s) of the golden days,
>   Comrades in all of my games and plays,
>   Life was like a holiday, the world was in its prime,
>   In the happy land of Once Upon a Time.[7]

[7] "The Happy Land of Once Upon a Time." W/Harry B. Smith M/Victor Herbert © 1908 M. Witmark & Sons Copyright Renewed All Rights Reserved Used by Permission of WARNER BROS. MUSIC.

Among the childhood memories, the song writer recalls:

> The Brownies, quaint and funny, with their faces
> bright and sunny,
> They were like a jolly Christmas pantomime.

Strictly speaking, the Brownies were not funny-paper characters, but they were loved by the children, who had succumbed to their elfin charms ever since they first appeared in the pages of *St. Nicholas* magazine in the 1880's. Palmer Cox, the author and illustrator of the *Brownie* books, had written his stories in verse several times a year about his friendly little elves. Brownies were fun loving and good-natured, with widemouthed smiling faces, large ears and popeyes, little round stomachs, spindly legs, and long tapering feet. They never gave pain to anyone; they were meant to leave a pleasant impression and do good for goodness' sake.

In 1893, Effie F. Kamman wrote a charming little instrumental number, "The Dance of the Brownies." The title page is illustrated with sketches of a dozen of the quaint elves, disporting in grotesque, but entertaining, positions which, conceivably, none but a Brownie might assume.

In 1905, *The Isle of Bong-Bong*, a musical satire, contained in its score a song called "Brownies," with words by Will M. Hough and Frank R. Adams and with music by Joseph E. Howard. Here is a verse and the chorus:

> Oh when you hear the stairs and floors
> go creakin',
> Shadow shapes a-flittin' in the gloom,
> And creepy sounds around like mice
> a-skweakin,
> Who d'ye suppose is walkin' in the room?
> Most probably it's a dainty Brownie
> A-tryin' to scare you oo, oo, oo, oo,
> So snuggle in your bed so soft and downy,
> And don't you let him catch a sight of you.
> CHORUS: Keep still, hark, hark,
> Brownie elves are roamin' round tonight,
> Lay low, keep dark
> All the world is theirs till morning
> light.
> Sly pranks they're playin' round you,
> Look out, when once they've found you,
> Little Brownie Band beware.

One of the most lovable of all the quaint characters produced by cartoonists of that turn-of-the-century period was Sunny Jim. Jim started as a "commercial," but so quickly did he capture the heart of the country that soon he was the subject for numerous cartoons, and even a central character in a musical comedy. Sunny Jim was the creation of two young women, Minnie Maud Hanff and Dorothy Ticken, who developed him as an advertising gimmick for "Force," one of the first of the cold breakfast cereals. The appearance of the cheery-faced elderly gentleman was always accompanied by a few little couplets, the first set of which ran as follows:

> Jim Dumps was a most nervous man
> Who lived his days on a hermit plan,
> In his gloomy way he had gone through life
> And made the most of woe and strife,
> 'Till "Force" one day was served to him,
> Since then they've called him Sunny Jim.

Edward Ellsworth, who manufactured "Force," was a firm believer in the power of the printed word. Sunny Jim advertisements were run in 45,000 streetcars; 12,500 newspapers in the United States carried his picture and the rhymes that went with it. "Force" factories operated twenty-four hours a day, as Sunny Jim told youngsters that "Force" made them grow strong all over, in body, bone, and brain. "Force" was soon outselling all rival products. Jim became an international character; the company promoted a story that the cereal was being eaten for breakfast in thirteen languages. Ministers preached sermons about Jim; judges pointed morals from the bench referring to his sterling character.

A popular "Sunny Jim" march was written in 1902 by Floyd J. St. Clair. The title page has a wonderful picture of the gentleman strolling contentedly along the road, at peace with himself and with everything about him. To see him is to love him.

Many of the most popular comic sheet characters were invited to a ball in 1918, according to two songsters of the period, Jack Frost and Robert Speroy, who combined to write "At the Funny Page Ball." Old familiar names appeared, as did others which were of somewhat newer vintage—"Polly and Her Pals," "Mutt and Jeff," "Andy Gump," "Krazy Kat," "Abe Kabibble," "Old Doc Yak," and "Rosie and her Beau." Here are some of Frost's lyrics:

CHORUS: Both the "Newly Weds" they came to see the show,
Showing "Married Life" to "Rosie and her beau,"
Mister "Happy Hooligan" he had to act the fool again with "Oh! Min!"
Just then Bud Fisher called around for Mister "Mutt and Jeff",

At The "Funny Page" Ball.

The fun-ny pa-pers gave a ball last night,— And I de-clare it was a fun-ny sight;—

Old "Doc-tor Yak" sent in-vi-ta-tions To "Hap-py Hoo-li-gan" and all re-la-tions

He said, "The fun be-gins at half past eight,— I'll call for all in old "Three-for-ty-eight;"——

So e-ven "Bus-ter Brown" he thought he'd bust a-round, Gee! but it was great, I'll state. For

Chorus

"Pol-ly and her Pals" were sway-ing right and left, "Pa" was play-ing check-ers there with "Mutt and Jeff,"

"Ma-ma's An-gel Child" was pout-ing soon as she heard "An-dy" shout-ing "Oh! Min!" Then Mis-ter

"Kra-zy Kat" and "Iz-zy Mouse" be-gan to mix, "Hans and Fritz" they or-dered up a load of bricks;

"Abe Ka-bib-ble" act-ed mad and got real rough 'Cause the band re-fused to play the "Maz-zel-tov"

'Twas so en-tranc-ing while they were pranc-ing,— So gai-ly danc-ing at the "Fun-ny Page Ball."

2. Old "Baron Bean" was seen 'bout half past one,
He came on time, the fun had just begun;
I'll bet that he was in his glory
When he was asked to tell a funny story.

Old "Petey Dink" was buying black cigars
While talking to "that son-in-law of Pa's,"
Until the lights were dim they kept a-dropping in,
One and all swayed 'round the hall. For

Shortly after that most all the party left;
Ev'ry comic artist then took out his pen,
Promised his meal ticket he could come again.
'Twas so entrancing while they were prancing,
So gaily dancing at the "Funny Page Ball."

The funny papers gave a ball last night,
And I declare it was a funny sight;
Old Doctor Yak sent invitations
To Happy Hooligan and all relations

. . . .

Even Buster Brown he thought he'd bust around,
Gee! but it was great, I'll state.

CHORUS: Both the Newly Weds they came to see the show,
Showing "Married Life" to Rosie and her beau
Mister Happy Hooligan he had to act the fool again

. . . .

Ev'ry comic artist then took out his pen,
Promised his meal ticket he could come again
'Twas so entrancing while they were prancing
So gaily dancing at the Funny Page Ball.

The kids of that period didn't know Charlie Brown or Dick Tracy or
L'il Abner. But they basked in the bright haze which surrounded their own
giants—Foxy Grandpa, Hooligan, Nemo. Awesome names, all of them.

The Teddy Bear

The most lovable plaything in American history, one involving eventually millions of children, was created as the result of a fateful moment
when the president of the country, loaded gun sighted for the kill, lowered
his weapon suddenly without firing. The time was November, 1902, the
place the Little Sunflower River country of Mississippi, the president—well,
anyone who knows the sequence of our country's chiefs can come up with
the name of Theodore Roosevelt. Most important of all, the object which
the president declined to shoot was a small brown bear.

Now Teddy Roosevelt was a noted bear hunter. He had a number of
respectable-sized brown bears to his credit, and he had encountered and
vanquished the deadly grizzly. But when some of his Mississippi country
party captured a small brown bear cub and dragged it to the president so
that he could dispatch it with his rifle, Roosevelt drew the line. That kind
of trophy was not to his liking.

Like most stories about our presidents, this one was reported with alacrity by witnesses. One man who heard it decided to take his own form of action. The man was Clifford K. Berryman, cartoonist for the *Washington Post*, and he made the incident the subject of his next cartoon. "Teddy" is portrayed as a hunter who rejects the opportunity to kill a small frightened bear cub; the cartoon's caption is "Drawing the line in Mississippi."

It captured the public's fancy. The cartoon was reproduced millions of times, from coast to coast. It outpaced the weather as a topic of conversation. Politicians wove the incident into their speeches; actors included the subject in their lines, poets in their verses. And later came the song writers. But before the songs came, of course, the Teddy bear. So many people claim credit for creating the Teddy bear that it would require modern electronic equipment to unscramble them. A few are worth noting.

Apparently the first toy merchant to enjoy the Berryman cartoon was Morris Michton, the proprietor of a small shop in Brooklyn, who not only sold toys, but also, with the assistance of his wife, made a few stuffed animals. Michton had an idea. He and his wife designed a brown bear of plush, cut out the pattern and stuffed the body, giving it movable arms and legs. He set the toy in his shop window with a copy of Berryman's cartoon and a sign reading "Teddy's Bear." It was sold immediately. He made another; that one went into the window and was grabbed up in turn. After a few more experiences of this kind, Michton realized he had a good thing going. He took one important step; he wrote to President Roosevelt asking for permission to use the president's name on his bears. Roosevelt responded that he didn't know what good his name could be as a promotion for stuffed animals, but Michton was welcome to use it. So Michton went into production. He had limited facilities, and the total distribution of his bears was not large, but his contention that he invented the Teddy bear must be given the most serious consideration, particularly since Roosevelt's children were photographed with some of them, and since one of his original bears is on display at Sagamore Hill, now a memorial to TR.

The next claimant to the honors was a German named Steiff, a resident of Giegan, a small town in Württemberg. Steiff, a toy manufacturer, contended that his wife Margarete designed a toy bear which was displayed at the Leipzig Fair in 1902 *and* was given the name "Teddy Bear" by an American importer. Ah! but just when were Steiff's bears christened "Teddies?"

A Washington legend may help provide the answer. When the president's daughter Alice was married in 1906, the caterer was hard put to find a novel table decoration for the wedding banquet. Spying a toy bear in a shop window, he had a brainstorm. On each table there was put a little bear, dressed and equipped as a hunter or woodsman. One of the guests, wondering aloud what kind of bear it represented, declared that it should be known as a "Teddy Bear." The appellation was roundly approved, and a new and overwhelmingly successful plaything was ready for acceptance by the children of the world.

The popularity of the Teddy Bear brought unprecedented prosperity to the Steiff company and to Giegen. For years the whole town was busy making bears; Steiff bears were imported by all the important American toy distributors. At an opportune moment, Giegen paid proper tribute to the source of its wealth. In 1958, the centennial of the birth of Theodore Roosevelt, the Steiff company staged a year-long celebration. The featured event was a colorful parade, starring a life-size figure of the late president, in Rough Rider uniform, pince-nez and all, sitting astride a large stuffed toy horse, and towed on a float by men in cowboy costumes.

Long before this spectacular, another bear man had entered the fray. Presented for your consideration is Mr. Theodore Bear of Chicago. Mr. Bear's toy firm started out in Cincinnati around 1905 as Bear Brothers, and almost immediately introduced a little bear into his line. This animal was a kind of hybrid, with the body of a bear and the portrait of Mr. Bear as a face. Across the body was Mr. Bear's signature with the phrase "The Original Teddy." Moving to Chicago, the firm changed its name to Theodore Bear and Company and continued to make bears and bears for decades and decades.

By the fall of 1906, every self-respecting toy, doll, and game manufacturer was in the act. There were "Roosevelt Bears," "White House Bears," "Great American Bears." There was a "Teddy and the Bear" bank, Teddy Bear tea sets, hammocks, rubber stamps, water pistols, rocking horses, balloons; a Connecticut plush manufacturer advertised "Toy Bear Plush." At Madison Square Garden, New York, clowns and trick dogs were dressed as Teddy bears.

Some of the toy people, who had been used to seeing fads come and go, could not believe the Teddy bear would have staying power. In November, 1906, near the inception of the craze, one retailer was quoted as saying, "Bears will drop out of sight after the first of the year." Almost a year later he made another flat statement, "Bears are on their last legs." A month later

Bessie And Her Little Brown Bear.

A lit-tle brown bear in a toy—shop once Had been up on the shelf for a-bout two months, If that lit-tle brown bear had-n't been such a dunce, He'd been sold long a-go all-right,—— But he looked so—glum and he did-n't seem gay, Till a wee lit-tle girl in the shop one day, Said: I guess I'll take you home to play It was true love—at first sight— It was true love at first sight.

Chorus

Then Bes-sie wan-dered home, the lit-tle bear be-neath her arm, She vowed that she'd pro-tect him—from all kinds of harm; She showed him how to bend his arms and knees — She ev-en taught him how to hug and squeeze. Sit-ting on the kit-chen stairs right where the pale moon shone, The lit-tle bear kept say-ing—"won't you be my own" And the big round moon saw them kiss and spoon, Bes-sie and her lit-tle brown bear.

2. Once Bessie went out with her little brown bear
For a walk in the park and some nice fresh air,
But the bear for such things did not seem to care,
On a bench in the park they sat.

He spied a little girl that was dressed up in pink,
And his shoe-button eyes gave a roguish wink,
Then Bessie got wise and said: I think That'll be about all for that,
That'll be about all for that. Then

Chorus

he had to say, "That crazy bear is as popular as ever." That fall the Teddy bear was in Sears Roebuck's catalogue.

The song writers began to sense the subject's popularity in 1906. One of the earliest bear songs, and one which proved the most widely sung, was "Bessie and Her Little Brown Bear." It was the work of Albert von Tilzer and Jack Norworth, who were to team up two years later with one of the great smash hits of American popular music, "Take Me out to the Ball Game." Both were veterans in the field. Von Tilzer, a publisher as well as a composer, had scores of successes. Norworth was a gifted vaudeville comedian, the husband of Nora Bayes, one of the musical comedy stars of the period.

"Bessie's" verse tells the story of a little bear who sat on a shelf in a toy store, and couldn't be sold because he looked so glum, till:

> A wee little girl in the shop one day,
> Said: "I guess I'll take you home to play."
> It was true love at first sight,
> It was true love at first sight, Then

CHORUS: Bessie wandered home, the little bear beneath her arm,
She vowed that she'd protect him from all kinds of harm;
She showed him how to bend his arms and knees,
She even taught him how to hug and squeeze,
Sitting on the kitchen chairs right where the pale moon shone,
The little bear kept saying "won't you be my own"
And the big round moon saw them kiss and spoon,
Bessie and her little brown bear.[8]

The song had wide appeal, and soon reached the kind of pinnacle which is achieved by parodies of well-known poems and speeches. One sly one had Bessie riding with her companion on a motorcycle, and including the punch line, "Bessie and her Little Brown Bear Behind."

One of America's most attractive imports of this period was a beautiful Viennese light-opera singer, Anna Held. The well-known American producer, Florenz Ziegfeld, Junior, fell in love with her and induced her to come to this country and appear in some of his enterprises. One musical of his, presented in 1907, was *The Parisian Model*. Anna Held, the show's principal attraction, was the chanteuse for a bear song; and no one could have appeared more glamorous than Anna, as she helped to increase the

8 "Bessie and Her Little Brown Bear." W/Jack Norworth M/Albert Von Tilzer © 1907 All rights for the USA and Canada controlled by Broadway Music Corp., c/o Walter Hofer, 221 West 57th Street, New York, N.Y. Used by Permission. All rights reserved.

popularity of what was already the most popular plaything of any child's world. The song, written by two veterans of the musical stage, Vincent Bryan and Max Hoffman, was "Will You Be My Teddy Bear." The first verse:

> I'm so happy I don't know what to do,
> I've a sweetheart and I'm sure he is true,
> And though I tease him, we never fight,
> He's always with me day and night,
> When I rub against his pretty bear skin,
> It's like velvet when I cuddle to him,
> Then I declare, my Teddy bear,
> All my love with you I'll share.

> CHORUS: Come along with me, be my Teddy B.,
> Teddy, let me take you,
> I am so blue, come to me, do,
> Teddy, it is true, I'm longing for you
> Come and play with me, be my Teddy B.,
> I'll promise not to break you.
> I just want to tease you, Hug you tight and squeeze you
> Oh! Oh! Oh! Oh I love you so,
> Be my little Teddy Bear.[9]

A year later, Ziegfeld had Held starring in another operetta. Apparently bears were still important subject matter for musicals, and this time Anna had another one to sing about. "I've Lost My Teddy Bear" was a special number written by the best-known Negro song composers in the country, Bob Cole and Rosamond Johnson, and interpolated into a score with which they had no other connection. Anna's song was one of desolation, as the chorus indicates:

> I have lost my Teddy Bear,
> And I don't know where to find him,
> I have searched most ev'rywhere,
> If you see him please remind him,
> That I love him just the same;
> Please handle him with care,
> Have you seen him? (spoken: No!)
> Oh! what am I to do?
> I have lost my Teddy Bear.[10]

9 "Be My Little Teddy Bear." W/Vincent Bryan M/Max Hoffman © 1917 Jerome H. Remick & Co. Copyright Renewed All rights reserved Used by Permission of WARNER BROS. MUSIC.

10 "I've Lost My Teddy Bear." W/Bob Cole M/Bob Cole and Rosamond Johnson © copyright E. B. MARKS MUSIC CORPORATION. Used by Permission.

And the craze went on, unabated. It worried some people. A Michigan priest denounced the Teddy bear, stating that it destroyed the instincts of motherhood and led to race suicide. To which a New York girl replied, "Nonsense! They're the cutest, dearest, best-behaved little visitors we've ever entertained. I draw the line on their going to church, however." And a baby-carriage merchant announced, "Teddy bears may be a menace to motherhood in Michigan, but we are selling more baby barouches than ever before."

The song writers weren't worried either. One leading comic strip character of the day, Little Nemo, who became the hero of a musical show bearing his name, was attached to another important individual, the ever-present bear in a 1907 song introduced in *The Wizard of Oz*.

With music by Al Gumble and words by David Clarke, "Little Nemo and His Bear" had to appeal to almost everybody who enjoyed an occasional trip into fantasy land. Nemo sings:

> Let's play that you're my sweetheart
> And let me be your beau
> We'll build a great big castle
> And we'll love each other so
> Just you and I'll live in it,
> And you'll be my lady fair
> In this great big land of make believe
> Just Nemo and his bear.[11]

Theodore Roosevelt left the presidency in 1909, but the Teddy bears refused to leave the scene. Well over half a century later it was still a staple of the toy industry, like dolls and blocks and rubber balls. And apparently it will remain unique in its field. There is no indication of any competition from a Franklin Falla, a Lyndon Him and Her or a Richard M. Checkers. Nor will any of these late pets inspire poets to conjure up original verses about them, or even to parody an undying literary figure like Longfellow, as one hack did some seventy years ago when he quipped:

> The shades of night were falling fast
> As through an Alpine village passed
> A creature covered all with fur,
> A Teddy Bear whose contents were
> EXCELSIOR!

9
PROGRESS!
PROGRESS?

Atlantic City

If you find when you're ready you haven't a steady,
Just call up the best girl you know.
Choose a girl of high rating when you are out dating,
And say to her thro' the hello...

CHORUS: Meet me on the boardwalk, Dearie,
Meet me by the sea.
With your Sunday go-to-meetin's on,
That's the place to be.
I love my wife, but oh! you kid!
You sure look good to me.
Meet me on the boardwalk, dearie,
Down by the sea.

THUS WROTE Keller Mack and Frank Orth in 1909, when Atlantic City was approaching the zenith of its popularity as the most enjoyable resort on the eastern seaboard. There were miles and miles of beautiful beaches, but dozens of towns on the Jersey coast could offer similar inducements of smooth white sand and stimulating breakers. However, nowhere was there such a powerful attraction at Atlantic City's boardwalk, a promenade with shops, entertainment, restaurants, and with nearly forty years of historic development to bring Atlantic City to its stellar position as the vacation spot.

The germ of an idea that began it all occurred in the spring of 1870 to a railroad conductor named Alexander Boardman. From Camden, New Jersey, the old Camden and Atlantic Railroad used to carry holiday goers for a brief excursion to the seashore, where they would stroll on the beach or wade in the ocean's shallows and return to the train with their shoes full

Meet Me On The Boardwalk, Dearie,

If you're look-ing for pleas-ure and nice sun-ny wea-ther, Why not take a trip to the shore——

Where the wa-ter is bri-ny, the folks large and ti-ny, In bath-ing they go by the score—— If you

find when you're read-y you have-n't a stead-y, Just call up the best girl you know—— Choose a

girl of high ra-ting when you are out dat-ing, And say to her thro' the hel-lo——

Chorus

Meet me on the board-walk, dear-ie, Meet me by the sea,—— With your Sun-day go-to-

meet-in's on, That's the place to be,—— I love my wife, but oh! you kid! You sure look

good to me,—— Meet me on the board-walk, dear-ie, Down by the sea.——

2. On the boardwalk you meet her with smiles you will greet her,
   Then stroll for an hour or so,
   You chew 'til you're daffy on salt water taffy,
   Then sailing you ask her to go.
   Then take her a bowling,
   In a roller chair rolling,
   You treat her the best way you know.
   "Will I see you this ev'ning," you say when you're leaving,
   She says: "bet your sweet life kid oh."
   CHORUS

303

of sand. If they spent a night or two at the Chester County House on South New York Avenue, the sand from guests' shoes would spill onto the hotel's carpets, which would be scuffed and ruined in a short space of time. So when the hotelkeeper, a Pennsylvania Dutchman named Jacob Keim, got wind of Boardman's suggestion, he called him in for a conference, and the two men decided to assemble a small group to discuss the matter. The group, eight in all, agreed to petition the city council for a footwalk along the beach; and on May 9, 1870, the council resolved that the city should build a boardwalk between Massachusetts and Mississippi Avenues, a distance of a little over a mile.

No time was lost. A ten-foot-wide walk was constructed at a cost of $5,000, one-half the city's income, and the new venture was formally dedicated on June 26, 1870. Its instant popularity exceeded the town fathers' fondest hopes. In five years Atlantic City's population doubled; in another five, it had reached more than five times the number of inhabitants of preboard-walk days.

Built in twelve-foot sections which were taken up in the fall and stored over the winter, the boardwalk nevertheless received such heavy usage from the great crowds of summer promenaders that it was worn out by 1879. A new, wider boardwalk—fourteen feet this time—succeeded the first. Its ten-foot sections were again stored away during the winter months, like its predecessor.

By now, the city council was revising its thinking about the potential of its town's greatest attraction. Whereas heretofore any type of building within thirty feet of the walk had been prohibited, it decided in 1880 to permit business establishments to encroach within ten feet. The owners of the new boardwalk-oriented structures erected ramps to connect their buildings to the "Walk," and business boomed. Within three years, almost one hundred entrepreneurs were finding that their new boardwalk locations were prospering beyond their dreams. In addition to the stores, the boardwalk businesssmen were operating four small hotels, four guest cottages, fifteen restaurants, two piers, and fifty-two bathhouses renting rooms and suits.

But the boardwalk had no railings; and this led to accidents. Even the third boardwalk, a twenty-foot wide esplanade extending for two miles, which opened in 1884, was railless. This caused certain inconveniences, and worse. The town's daily newspaper said on August 15, 1895, "Nearly every day somebody falls off the Boardwalk. In nearly every instance, the parties have been flirting." (If "flirt" has become an obsolete word to today's readers, a dictionary definition is "to make love without meaning it.") One August day in 1886, such a large crowd assembled to see a stereoptican show that the decking gave way, and twenty-five people were catapulted to the sand.

In 1889 disaster struck. A September hurricane wrecked much of the "Walk" and destroyed dozens of buildings along it. With some sections of the city under as much as six feet of water, the council realized that the Boardwalk, to insure against further destructive natural forces, must be elevated significantly above the sand.

Most of the beachfront property owners agreed to a high, broader (twenty-four-foot) walk, but the city had no power to condemn lands, and when two property owners refused to consent to a right of way which would prevent boardwalk connections with any properties outside it, a tough problem faced the city council. They solved it by announcing that there would be no boardwalk opposite any structures on the ocean side of the new promenade. Two small piers were involved; and their owners, William W. Bowker and Richard H. Lee, shut off the boardwalk at their property lines, so that the walk was twice interrupted in its sweep along the beach. For ten years the battle raged; the establishments of the two battling owners became known as Fort Bowker and Fort Lee.

Meanwhile, the city was swarming with hotels and boarding houses. Shortly after 1890 their number had reached six hundred, with accommodations for a hundred thousand guests, while some hundred boats of all descriptions were available at the Inlet, on the northeast corner of the island, for visitors who were in the mood for sailing or ocean fishing.

Wider and longer grew the walk. In 1896 the city council passed a resolution making the name "Boardwalk" official. Another new one was dedicated (it cost $143,986.38), and the wife of Mayor Stoy completed its construction by driving a golden spike into it. The spike was then covered with a metal plate so that no one would make off with it. A congressman made a speech; military companies and fire companies paraded; fireworks were set off. The sequel: shortly after the ceremony the spike was stolen and never found again.

One of the most attractive aspects of the "Walk" was its view of the beach, and the bathers in their fetching costumes. The earliest costumes did not enhance the appearance of the ladies sufficiently to encourage leering. City regulations required that the entire body be covered; only faces and hands could be exposed. There was no such thing as sunbathing. The suits of the girls were voluminous contraptions of wool flannel, requiring some seven yards of cloth. Both the skirts and the undergarments, pants or whatever, descended to the ankles; stockings and canvas shoes completed the costume, with, at times, the addition of a fetching straw bonnet.

The first bloomer bathing suits were tried out tentatively around 1907, but the idea appealed to only a few women, and some of them demanded that they be supplied with skirts to wear over the bloomers. A handful of the younger girls now became very daring and discarded their stockings. The beach superintendent clamped down on this immodesty immediately, decreeing that no stockingless women would be permitted on the beach. That ended that—anyway until the 1920's, when a new generation of adventurous girls began rolling their stockings below their knees à la the Mack Sennett girls whom they saw in the movies; and then—horrors!—more and more bare legs appeared until by 1928 the authorities surrendered and forgot all about stockings, and the oglers had something to ogle over.

But even from the outset the women bathers had resorted to all sorts of schemes to intensify their charms. The all-embracing suits of the 1870's gave the women an opportunity to pad wherever desirable, so that breasts, arms, and calves frequently presented a pleasing plumpness which had been nonexistent before the bathing suits were stuffed at the appropriate places. As late as 1907 the city censors adopted an ordinance known as the "Mackintosh" law, requiring bathers to wear some sort of an enveloping garment over their bathing costume when using the public streets to reach the beach. The bluenoses died hard.

The boardwalk was originally designed for strollers, but not everybody wanted to stroll. Many wanted to be conveyed. For a while wheel chairs had been permitted on it, for the use of invalids, but soon healthy people clamored for similar privileges. So the famous rolling chairs came into being in 1887, conceived by one William Hayday, a hardware store owner who was convinced that people would find pleasure in using them. Within a few years the city realized that there was "money in them thar chairs," and, while collecting license fees on all sorts of businesses, slapped a license requirement on rolling chairs. At ten dollars per year per chair, the city began to find a tidy little income as the number of such boardwalk chairs ran into the hundreds.

So what else was new on the Atlantic City boardwalk? Well, saltwater taffy was. Two firms, Ritchie Brothers and Windle W. Hollis, started to make and sell taffy in their stores around 1880. A possible legendary story about the creation of the name arose in 1883. According to this story a high tide following a heavy storm splashed a lot of sea water over the candy

SAN ANTONIO
SONG
by
HARRY WILLIAMS &
EGBERT VAN ALSTYNE
COMPOSERS OF
"WHY DON'T YOU TRY"
"WON'T YOU COME OVER TO MY HOUSE"
"CHEYENNE"
5
STARMER
JEROME H. REMICK & CO.
NEW-YORK DETROIT

stock of a shopkeeper named David Bradley, whose store at St. James Place and the Boardwalk was located where the world-famous Fralinger store later sold taffy by the ton. The morning after the storm Bradley's first customer for candy was a small girl. After he had wiped the water off his stock, he handed the little girl a bag of taffy and remarked, "There, you have salt-water taffy, sis." The little girl relayed this to her parents who spread the word. The following year, according to reports, Bradley and his partner displayed the words "Salt-Water Taffy" on their sign. Apparently nobody thought of copyrighting the name, and it became a generic phrase, adopted by every candy store on the boardwalk.

The famous Atlantic City beauty pageants began in September, 1921, when the boardwalk and civic business interests sought to extend the vacation season an extra week by promoting a little extra excitement as the summer drew to a close. The first pageant had eight contestants; in 1924 the number of contestants had increased to eighty-three. Never since have so many girls participated in the pageant. Judging from the results, one old premise was refuted; the gentlemen who were the judges didn't prefer blondes. Of the first twenty-five contests, fifteen of the winners were brunettes, nine were blondes, and one was a redhead.

One of the best-known sights from the lower boardwalk was the Elephant in Margate, completed in 1882. Rumor has it that the Elephant, at one time used for a dwelling, later as a tourist attraction, was erected with a live elephant used as a model. It was chained on the beach while measurements were taken. The building was erected to scale, with a thirty-eight-foot-long body, and with legs twenty-two feet high and ten feet in diameter. Spiral stairs went up one of the legs; ascending from them to the howdah, sixty-five feet above the sand, a visitor had an observation room view up and down the beach and the boardwalk.

In 1903 a great storm played havoc with the elephant's front legs, and the poor beast sank to her knees in the sand. A house mover was able to raise her, fortunately, and he set her back fifty feet from her original location. Since then she has remained immobile.

The Atlantic House, the Ocean House, and three sister hostelries opened for business when the city first tried to claim a position as a vacation spot in 1854. These were not what are now known as "beachfront" hotels; wild, high sand dunes interposed their presence between the hotels and the beach. These old resort hotels, as well as the early boardwalk hotels, have long since gone; but some of today's familiar names were in use nearly one hundred years ago—the Dennis, the Traymore, the Shelburne, the Seaside.

In 1880 the Seaside introduced its own orchestra, with a well-known song leader as conductor. Septimus Winner was his name, and his magnum opus is still remembered today; it was "Listen to the Mocking Bird," which flitted through dozens of editions and was orchestrated and reorchestrated for concert orchestras around the country.

And the piers—what about the piers? Atlantic City's first pier, six hundred and fifty feet long, and located at the foot of Kentucky Avenue, had been built in 1881. At that early stage the science of sinking pilings in beach sand was not sufficiently developed, and a September storm demolished the fragile structure.

A Washingtonian, Colonel George Howard, then attempted a more extensive project. His pier extended eight hundred and ten feet into the ocean, near the site of pier number one. In January, 1884, its two outer pavilions were severely damaged when the schooner *Robert Morgan* rammed it before being driven ashore. It was rebuilt but was not a financial success, and in 1891 the pier was condemned and torn down.

James R. Applegate, a boardwalk photographer, was the next enterprising pier builder. His was a six hundred and twenty-five footer, extending out from Tennessee Avenue. A double-decker affair, it provided music and vaudeville, with a special enclosure where baby carriages could be checked for safety. In 1891, after seven good operating years, Applegate sold out. The new owners ran it for nearly forty years, suffering two disastrous fires during its frenzied existence but making money steadily nevertheless, as it increased its length to two thousand feet and entertained the sight-seers in huge pavilions which featured cakewalks and baby shows.

Of all the boardwalk's attractions, its famous piers were far and away the most fabulous. Many visitors patronized the auction rooms, the oriental bazaars, the taffy shops, the shooting galleries, the carrousels, that crowded the "Walk" for block after block; but *everybody* went on the piers. Some preferred Heinz's, built in 1898, where one could get free samples of nearly all the "57 Varieties." Thousands thronged daily, and nightly, onto the Steel Pier, opened the same year, when as many as 18,000 people were admitted on a single occasion. A 1,780-foot-long structure, it offered a limitless choice of entertainments—concerts, minstrel shows (with Dockstader and Frank Tinney), huge dances to the music of the great name bands, personal appearances of stars from the world of entertainment. There was the Steeplechase Pier, begun in 1899, purchased by George C. Tilyou of Coney Island fame in 1902, designed primarily for juvenile amusement with trick mirrors, revolving floors and barrels, and gusts of air shooting out from unexpected places. It was frequented with delight and/or embarrassment by fond parents with families in tow. There was Young's Million Dollar Pier, opened in 1906, which featured a twice-daily fish haul and an aquarium of the rare creatures of the sea, with motion pictures and various assorted amusements. In addition Young's Pier played host to a slew of national conventions and displayed their exhibits.

There was so much to inspire the composers of popular music. Back in 1905, George Schroeder wrote the "Atlantic City Promenade March and Two Step," to be followed the next year by J. M. Winne's "Atlantic City Two Step March," with a title page showing a beach scene of the well-covered bathers of the period. As late as 1945, Mack Gordon and Joseph Myrow brought out a rollicking song entitled "On the Boardwalk in Atlantic City." An unforgettable spot! Let's recall its early years with affectionate memories.

The Five and Dime

FROM THE moment Mr. Woolworth opened his first five-cent store, shortly after the United States celebrated its hundredth anniversary, the nickel took on new importance to shoppers. And when Woolworth and his competitors added a line of ten-cent items, the dime, too, came into its own.

To devotees of popular music, it is strange that for almost thirty years thereafter no song appeared to celebrate, or to poke fun at, this new phenomenon in retail merchandising. Not until 1907 did a popular lyricist and comedian named Dave Reed team up with Herbert Spencer, a composer, to develop a catchy song which they called, "She Couldn't Keep Away from the Ten Cent Store." As Reed put it:

CHORUS: couldn't keep away from the ten cent store,
    From the ten cent store,
    But as soon as I got in the water something tore
    And I knew that I was in a plight.
    Then she went and got a barrel from the ten cent store,
    From the ten cent store,
    That was ten cents more.
    It was eight P.M. when I came ashore,
    And I nearly killed the owner of the ten cent store.
3. I tho't that I would like to try
    A married life, so bye and bye
    The wedding day arrived and I was there to take the score.
    My lady said she would invite

A lot of lovely friends that night,
But all my joy was over when her lovely friends I saw.
'Twas a

Chorus: dizzy delegation from the ten cent store,
       From the ten cent store,
       From the ten cent store,
       Such a lovely imitation of a Chinese war.
       Oh I fancied I was in a fight.
       It was just like being married in a ten cent store.
       It was nothing more,
       And it made me sore.
       When a man yelled "Cash" why it cleared the floor,
       And they left a lot of presents from the ten cent store.

4. One day I went upon the scent,
   To see if there was any gent
Or what the great attraction was that took her to the store.
I didn't see a man in sight,
But can you fancy my delight
To meet a handsome blonde who said, she hoped I'd call some more.
Now I

Chorus: cannot keep away from the ten cent store,
       From the ten cent store,
       From the ten cent store.
       And I wish that I had gone a-scouting long before.
       But I'm married and it is not right.
       I will have to buy an int'rest in that ten cent store
       In that ten cent store
       Then I'll send my wife to the gay seashore,
       While I have an eye to business at the ten cent store.

       She was so economical she wouldn't spend a sou,
       She said a dime at any time was quite enough and not a crime,
       But goodness, Goodness, Agnes, how the ten cent pieces flew,
       For she couldn't keep away from the ten cent store . . .
       And a locomotive couldn't drag her by the door.
       Any time there was one in sight,
       There was always something needed at the ten cent store.
       If she spent one dime she would spend ten more.
       For she couldn't keep away from any ten cent store.[1]

[1] "She Couldn't Keep Away From the Ten Cent Store." W/Dave Reed M/Herbert Spencer © 1907 M. Witmark & Sons. Copyright Renewed. All Rights Reserved Used by Permission of WARNER BROS. MUSIC.

She Couldn't Keep Away From The Ten Cent Store.

I had a girl, a pret-ty pearl, The best that ev-er wore a curl, She was so e-co-no-mi-cal she

would-n't spend a sou; She said a dime at an-y time was quite e-nough and not a crime, But good-ness, God-

ness, Ag-nes, how the ten cent piec-es flew. For she could-n't keep a-way from the ten cent store,

From the ten cent store, From the ten cent store. And a lo-co-mo-tive could-n't drag her by the door.

An-y time that there was one in sight. There was al-ways some-thing need-ed at the ten cent

store, At the ten cent store, At the ten cent store. If she spent one dime she would spend ten more,

For she could-n't keep a-way from an-y ten cent store.

2. Upon a ship I took a trip,
   To Coney Isle to have a dip,
   I took my little lady as I'd always done before.
   We hired suits at Ten a throw
   That's all that she would let me blow,
   She said that they were just as good as those at twenty or more.
   For she

Today more than three thousand store fronts in the United States carry the Woolworth or the Kresge name; but like most supersuccessful enterprises, their beginnings were supermodest.

Frank Winfield Woolworth's first full-time job was in the leading store of Watertown, New York, in 1872. His first salary was exactly nothing a week, for which he qualified as errand boy, janitor, general handyman, stockroom boy, and relief clerk, on an 84-hour-a-week basis. After three months he was gratified to learn that his industry had gained due recognition; he became a salaried employee at $3.50 per week. In the short space of two years he attained advances to $6.00 weekly. When a competitive store made him the flattering offer of a head clerkship and the dazzling sum of $10.00 a week, Woolworth could not resist the opportunity. He grabbed at the position, not realizing the extent of his new responsibility, which included service as the establishment's night watchman and the necessity of living in the basement of the store. His constitution, though sound, was unequal to the task of coping with such a massive load; and, with his health impaired, he returned to his father's farm to recuperate.

In due time he was back in the retail business, as senior clerk in the store where he had started out as a wageless Jack-of-all-trades. But now he had the ability to project ideas of his own, the most important of which was the revolutionary introduction of a "5¢ counter." The customers approved, and Woolworth planned boldly to open a five-cent store of his own.

On Washington's Birthday in 1879 a little store front in Utica flashed a freshly painted sign, "Great 5 Cent Store." The young proprietor stood smartly behind the counter, awaiting his first customer. The door opened, and in walked a lady bearing in her hand an advertising circular which Woolworth had distributed that morning. She pointed to an item reading "fire shovels 5¢ each." Woolworth wrapped up the shovel and received his payment in fractional paper currency, which he dropped in the till, thereby completing the first sale made by a Woolworth store.

By all the proper portents, the Utica experiment should have been enormously successful. In this case, the portents were improper. The store's location was poor, and the rent was too high. Less than four months after it opened, Woolworth closed it up. But he wasn't insolvent; he had $225, with which he proceeded to open a second store—this one in Lancaster, Pennsylvania.

At the time of his early morning opening, the streets in Lancaster were crowded, yet nobody came into the store. Woolworth just couldn't understand it, but soon he learned the reason. He had opened—as luck would have it—on circus day, and everybody was out to watch the parade. So he spent a frustrating morning. By afternoon, the parade was over, and there was a sudden change in the situation. People flocked to the store in droves, and when he closed down that night he had taken in $127, more than he had ever sold in any one day in Utica.

Woolworth was on his way, and nothing could stop him now, particularly after he added a 10-cent line of merchandise to his stock the following year. He wasn't always a winner, as he proceeded to open new stores in Pennsylvania, New York, and New Jersey. Some were closed soon after the opening. But most of them were impressively successful, and he went on to greater and greater heights.

In 1909, when he had almost 250 stores, he decided the time was propitious to establish a chain in England. He sent two of his executives there to set up the first stores. They decided on Liverpool as the site of their initial experiment. The two clean-shaven young men descended on Britain, and their first discovery was that English businessmen were universally mustached, so they went and did likewise; and when the first Liverpool store opened, its managers were hirsute in all the right places. Initially the Liverpudlians appeared shy (this was a long generation before the Beatles) and did not seem attracted to an establishment which proclaimed itself a "3 pence and 6 pence store." But it wasn't long before they succumbed to its wares and its wiles. When a second Liverpool store was opened, it was the scene of a near riot. Barefooted, shawl-clad women mobbed the counters in such numbers that the counters themselves were pushed around the floor. Salesgirls fainted, and customers helped themselves to merchandise without the formality of paying for it.

In 1913, a half dozen years after "She Couldn't Keep Away from the Ten Cent Store" was written, Woolworth had supervised the creation of his personal $13,000,000 monument, the world's tallest skyscraper, christened, of course, the Woolworth Building. Towering fifty-five stories, eight hundred feet above the curb on Broadway, it was the most imposing landmark of the New York skyline until the late twenties when new steel giants reared their heads even higher.

A favorite story that went the rounds after the completion of the Woolworth Building relates the dialogue of two old Irish scrubwomen who came out of a downtown office building in lower New York late at night. They looked up at the enormous Woolworth edifice, and one asked the other, "Mary, how can any man put up a building like that? Where does he get the money?" "That's easy," replied Mary. "Your tin cints and my tin cints."

It was in Pennsylvania that the five- and ten-cent idea had proved itself a sound merchandising strategy. Other young entrepreneurs in addition to Woolworth had launched their careers there. Wilkes-Barre was the focal point. In the 1880's Frank M. Kirby, who had been a fellow clerk in the Watertown, New York, establishment with Woolworth, and who had been struggling for the trade of the Hungarian, Welsh, and Irish coal miners who drifted past his Wilkes-Barre shop without dropping in for a purchase, decided to put up a hand-lettered sign reading "Five-and-Ten-Cent Store. Nothing in this store over ten cents." The miners suddenly took notice of him, and trooped in to buy for their wives Kirby's dish drainers and egg beaters.

Another fellow across the street took notice, too. Sebastian Spering Kresge had come from a family of thrifty Pennsylvania Dutch farmers. But Kresge didn't want to farm; he was anxious to attend a technical school in the area. So he made a pact with his parents; if they would finance his school training he would turn over to them all his earnings, except those required for board and clothing, until he reached the age of twenty-one. He asked for one exclusion—the earnings on his first boyhood venture, which was a hive of bees. By the time he turned twenty-one his bees had grown to a colony of thirty-two hives, which augured well for a future chain-store operator.

When Kresge was striving to establish himself in Wilkes-Barre he was operating a small stationery store close to Kirby's. He struggled to make a business out of the sale of lead pencils, blankbooks, envelopes, and the New York morning papers. But when he saw how Kirby's revised merchandising policy was winning new friends among the buying public, Kresge decided that he, too, belonged in the five-and-dime business. So into it he plunged, and very successfully too.

Some years later Kresge, with many stores throughout the South, approached Woolworth and suggested a merger, which was declined. Kirby was engaged in building his own large organization until 1911, when, with ninety-six stores of his own, he agreed to merge with the still larger business of Frank Woolworth.

Meanwhile Kresge, who had tried to work with a partner for a short while, shook himself free in the late nineties. With a sign over the door of his downtown Detroit store reading "Nothing Over Ten Cents" he drew in an ever-increasing clientele. And he invaded an ever-increasing number of communities; within fifteen years he had 118 stores.

The three men had great respect for each other's ability. If a conversationalist ever hinted that one of them was abler or smarter than the other two, he would find himself attacked by the threesome simultaneously.

Kresge was always a doer, never an orator. He was a leading philanthropist; among his gifts was the Kresge Hall at Harvard's Graduate School of Business. At the dedication of this important building Kresge was called on for some remarks. The remarks turned out to be exactly six words: "I never made a dime talking!"

Twenty-five years after Reed and Spencer, the five-and-dime store formed the background for the hit number of a Broadway show, "Billy Rose's Crazy Quilt." Rose and Mort Dixon wrote the lyrics and Harry Warren composed the melody of "I Found a Million Dollar Baby in a Five and Ten Cent Store."

Today, ten cents won't take a lady shopper very far, and naturally the merchandising policies of the old "five and dimes" have broadened upward and outward. But the touch of those farsighted old pioneers remains; the finger of frugality beckons to the womenfolk, and the doors of the brightly fronted stores swing wide to admit an ever-widening stream of bargain hunters.

The Wondrous Telephone

Of all the great inventions, that ever yet was known,
There's one that lately has appeared, they call the Telephone.
Thro' it sound is carried, to the folks both far and near,
And not a word is spoken, but all the world may hear.

There surely is no knowing, what things may happen soon;
We may perhaps be talking, with the old man in the moon!
And everybody's secrets then, to us will all be known,
The whole world be united, thro' this wondrous Telephone!

THE WRITER of this 1877 song, Thomas P. Westendorf, could not have realized, as he let his fantasy run riot, that he was at the same time by way of being a minor prophet. Talk to the man in the moon indeed! What preposterous nonsense! It had been only a year since the first words were transmitted vocally over a wire running between two rooms in a house in Boston —an order from young Alexander Graham Bell to his young assistant, Thomas A. Watson, three floors below—"Watson, come here, I want you!" How unsentimental. How unearth-shaking. How prosaic; nothing to compare to "What hath God wrought" or "One small step for man..."

As a matter of fact, Bell's appeal was a shout for help. In the course of the experiment in which he was engaged, he had spilled some sulphuric acid on his trousers, and involuntarily called for aid from Watson. True, when he grasped the immense fact that his words had been audibly transmitted through a wire, he became highly emotional and as an afterthought exclaimed, "God save the Queen." Born in Scotland, he had been an American for only five years, and his toast to England's monarch was an involuntary gesture of speech.

Three months later, Bell exhibited his sensational discovery in Philadelphia at the Centennial Exposition. A group of distinguished scientists inspected his exhibit and one, Sir William Thomson of England, was invited by Bell to put the receiver to his ear. With such a captive audience, Bell was moved to oratory. "To be or not to be," he began and went on to spout the entire soliloquy of Hamlet. Sir William was thunderstruck. "My God, it talks!" he burst out.

Soon Bell was achieving telephone communications over a distance of several miles. In November he used the Eastern Railway lines to talk with Watson in Salem, twenty-six miles from Boston, and a few months later his voice was carried by wire from New York to Boston.

In 1877, Bell married and went with his bride to Europe. In England he tried to secure patents on his invention. He was helped by Sir William Thomson, now Lord Kelvin, who was delighted to demonstrate the use of the telephone in London by talking over the instrument to Bell, who was situated several miles away. Lord Kelvin, before a group of eminent scientists, pronounced into the phone these eloquent words: "Hi-diddle-diddle, the cat and the fiddle!" Then, turning and smiling to the audience, he said, "There he goes! The cow jumped over the moon!" What profundity! What erudition!

Bell felt that Queen Victoria should be treated to a firsthand demonstration of the modern marvel. An interview was arranged, and for the edification of the good queen, Bell arranged for a telephoned musical selection. A well-known social figure, Kate Fields, was chosen as the artist, and as her work of art she rendered "Coming Through the Rye." Her Majesty was much impressed.

By August 1, 1877, there were 775 telephones in use. In 1879 the New York telephone directory alone listed 252 names. By 1880, Salt Lake City had 100 phones. In 1883, New York, plagued by tens of thousands of miles of overhead wires, commenced laying its telephone wires in underground iron pipe, which was later discarded for asphalt and concrete. In the pipes were twisted cables of 100 wires each, wrapped in cotton. In 1900, New York had 56,000 phones; eight years later the figure had grown to 310,000, tended by more than 5,000 girls.

To think of the telephone industry today, it is necessary to toss around figures in the billions; but in those early days a million was a staggering figure. The Bell company, parent body of the industry, secured its first million dollars of capital in 1879; it acquired its first million dollars in earnings in 1882; it began to send a million messages a day in 1888; it installed its one millionth telephone in 1898.

The first White House telephone was placed in use during the first administration of Grover Cleveland in the middle 1880's. Cleveland himself hated the phone, and although he would occasionally answer it personally if it was ringing, most of the telephone conversations were carried on by the servants.

The first president to really utilize the potential of the telephone was William McKinley. In addition to considering telephone conversations diverting pastimes, McKinley foresaw their political value. During the Republican presidential convention in Chicago in 1896, McKinley sat glued to the telephone at his home in Canton, Ohio, and listened to the cheers of the crowd when his name was placed in nomination. Long-distance communications were now completed throughout most of the east and midwest; so the Republican nominee was able to direct through personal telephone conversation the activities of his campaign managers in thirty-eight states.

Not until the telephone began to acquire widespread popularity did the song writers seize it as a theme which could be exploited; and by the late 1880's they were beginning to recognize its potential as subject matter for the singer and the piano. The first appeals were to the sentimentalists, particularly those who were stirred by songs about youngsters. What could be more appealing than a child's gesture of love for a parent? So in 1888 we find a song composed by H. F. Sefton, with words by John Imrie, bearing the title "The Kiss Through the Telephone." It goes like this:

> The Telephone, in merry tone
> Rang "tinkelty tinkelty tink!"
> I put my ear close up to hear,
> And what did I hear, do you think?
> "Papa, hello! 'Tis me, you know!"
> The voice of my own little Miss.
> "You went away from home today,
> And never gave me a kiss!

It was a mistake, I was not awake,
Before you went out of the house;
I thought that a kiss would not be amiss
If I gave it as sly as a mouse!
So here goes, Papa, and one from Mamma,
And another when you can come home;
Just answer me this, is it nice to kiss
When you want thro' the dear Telephone?"

In 1889, Thomas Westendorf, he who had brought out twelve years earlier "The Wondrous Telephone," decided that he too would present a little girl who wanted to kiss papa. His song, almost a replica of that just described, was called "Kissing Papa Through the Telephone." His little girl, like the other child, was asleep when the old man stole off, so she rang him up, without fear of guilt that he might be involved in some important business transaction. Not at all; she is confident that:

He's so good and kind that he does not mind
If I should disturb him, and I know full well
He will smile and say when he comes today
That it made him glad to hear me ring the bell.

CHORUS: Ting a ling, ting a ling, hello!
Is that you papa? I am waiting here alone;
Ting a ling, ting a ling, hello!
I want to kiss you thro' the Telephone.

For years, the public responded to the popular song describing the sentiments of the small child. The telephone song with the most touching appeal of all was written by Charles K. Harris in 1901. Harris, one of the greatest song writers of the turn of the century, who gave us such all-time favorites as "After the Ball" and "Break the News to Mother," and who was a successful music publisher besides, tugged at the heartstrings of the country with "Hello Central, Give Me Heaven." The title page depicts a sweet-faced little girl whose stage name was Baby Lund speaking into one of the square wall boxes of the period, while a battery of long-distance operators are "plugging away" in the background. It is questionable whether any of them is acquainted with Heaven's telephone number, but Baby Lund has confidence. Pathetically she sings:

Papa I'm so sad and lonely,
Sobbed a tearful little child.
Since dear mama's gone to heaven,
Papa darling you've not smiled;
I will speak to her and tell her,

319

HELLO CENTRAL GIVE ME HEAVEN

BY CHAS·K·HARRIS

AUTHOR of "AFTER THE BALL" etc

SUNG WITH GREAT SUCCESS

BY BABY LUND.

PUBLISHED BY CHAS·K·HARRIS MILWAUKEE AUTHOR OF THE WORLD FAMOUS SONG "AFTER THE BALL" NEW YORK CHICAGO LONDON

"Hello Central, Give Me Heaven."

Pa-pa I'm so sad and lone-ly, Sobbed a tear-ful lit-tle child. Since dear
ma-ma's gone to hea-ven, Pa-pa dar-ling you've not smiled;— I will speak to her and
tell her,—That we want her to come home; Just you list-en and I'll call her—

Chorus

Through the tel-e-phone; Hel-lo Cen-tral, give me hea-ven, For my ma-ma's
there You can find her with the an-gels on the gold-en stair; She'll be glad it's
me who's speak-ing, call her, won't you please; For I want to sure-ly tell her,
We're so lone-ly here.

2. When the girl received this message,
   Coming o'er the telephone,
   How her heart thrilled in that moment,
   And the wires seemed to moan;
   I will answer just to please her,
   Yes, dear heart, I'll soon come home;
   Kiss me, mama, kiss your darling,
   Through the telephone:
   CHORUS

That we want her to come home;
Just you listen and I'll call her
Through the telephone:

CHORUS: Hello Central, give me heaven,
For my mama's there;
You can find her with the angels
On the golden stair;
She'll be glad it's me who's speaking,
Call her, won't you please;
For I want to surely tell her,
We're so lonely here.

The child seems to have found a sympathetic long-distance operator; touched by the little girl's despondency, she rises to the occasion:

When the girl received this message,
Coming o'er the telephone,
How her heart thrilled in that moment
And the wires seemed to moan
I will answer just to please her—
Yes, dear heart, I'll soon come home;
Kiss me, mama, kiss your darling,
Through the telephone:

But the music men were aware that the telephone could not be treated exclusively as a child's plaything. It was a universal commodity, to be requisitioned for all sorts of adult purposes, including, naturally, love. In 1899, Joseph E. Howard and his wife, Ida Emerson wrote a song in Negro dialect, which took the country by storm. It was "Hello Ma Baby." The tempo was true "cakewalk," a syncopated four-fourths beat which set feet to tapping and hands to clapping. The words were simple, the sentiment clear and unadulterated:

I've got a little baby, but she's out of sight,
I talk to her across the telephone.
I'se never seen my honey but she's mine, all right;
So take my tip, an' leave this gal alone.
Ev'ry single morning, you will hear me yell,
"Hey Central! fix me up along the line."
He connects me with ma honey, then I rings the bell,
And this is what I say to baby mine,

CHORUS: "Hello! ma baby, Hello! ma honey,
Hello! ma ragtime gal,
Send me a kiss by wire,
Baby my heart's on fire!

The Only Trolley Car Song

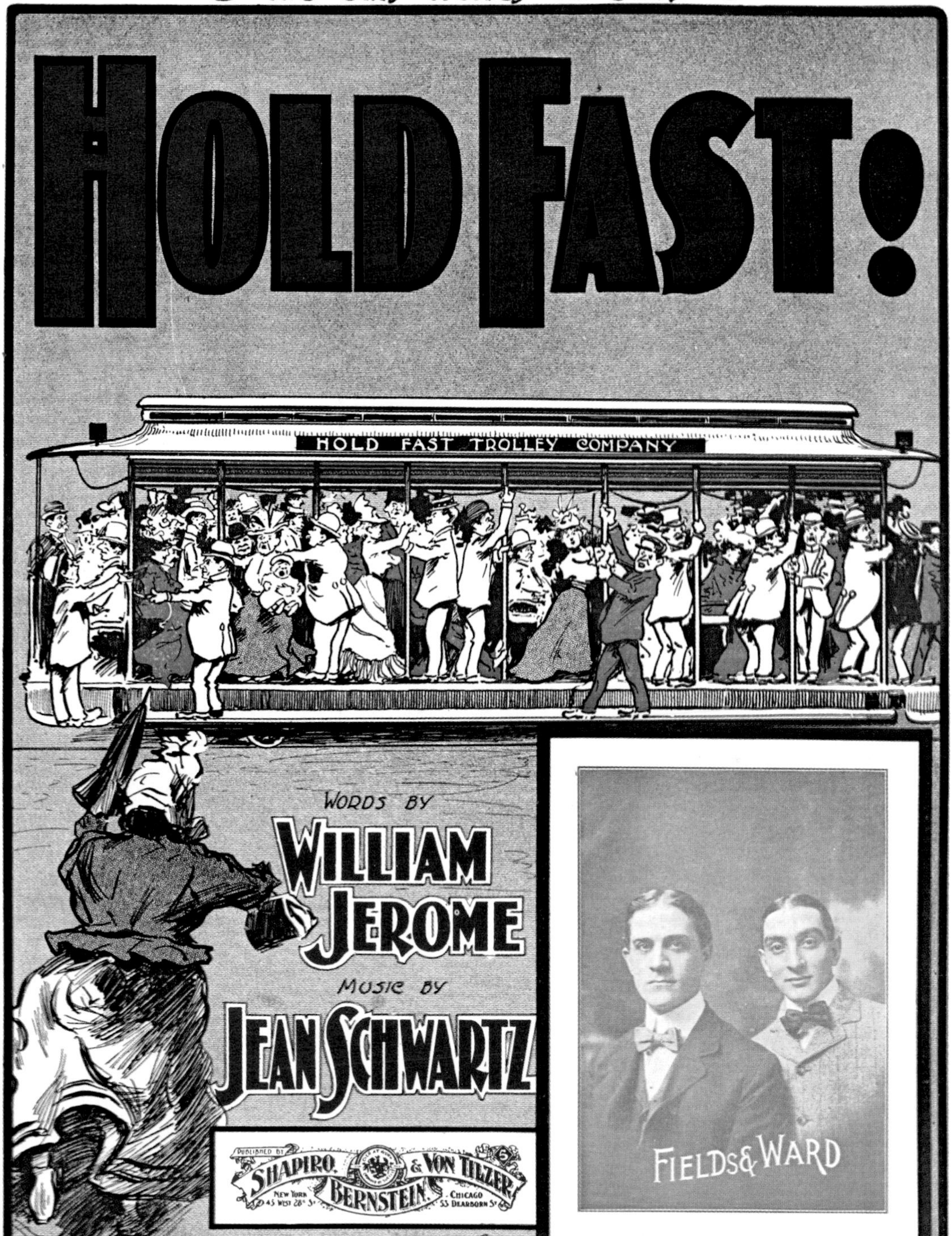

If you refuse me, Honey, you'll lose me,
Then you'll be left alone;
Oh, baby, Telephone and tell me I'se your own."

Numerous telephone songs made their appearance during the next few years—"Hello! Mr. Moon Man, Hello!," "Hello! All Right, Good-bye!," "Central! Give Me New York Town." It was not until 1915 that a new telephone song made good in a big way. The year 1915 saw the opening of cross-country telephone service, linking San Francisco with the east. It inspired two leading song writers, who were combining on the material for the famous *Ziegfeld Follies*, 1915 edition, to include in the review a song entitled "Hello Frisco!," which quickly became the sensation of the show.

Hello, Central, Hello Central, can't you see,
Kindly hurry, kindly hurry, just for me,
Please do get me San Francisco, someone's waiting all alone,
Frisco is her name, she's at the Golden Gate
Central, it's a shame for her to have to wait,
Please, long distance, do connect me, Get her on the telephone.

CHORUS: Hello Frisco, hello
(How do you do my dear I only wish that you were here)
Hello Frisco, hello
(How is the fair out there they tell me that it is a bear)
Don't keep me waiting, it's aggravating,
Why can't you hurry Central you're so slow
(I can hear you now, I can hear you now)
Hello, now can you hear,
(Dearie, I've bought the ring and I've arranged for everything)
You know I love you, dear
(We'll be together soon and then we'll have a honeymoon)
Your voice is like music to my ear,
When I close my eyes you seem so near,
Frisco I called you up to say "Hello."[2]

In the same year, when transcontinental service had begun to operate, the thoughts of a few song writers turned to the possibilities of telephone communication across the oceans. A second successful song made a 1915 debut; it was "Hello, Hawaii, How Are You?" and it was included in a sketch by a pair of leading comedians, Eugene and Willie Howard. With lyrics by Bert Kalmar and Edgar Leslie, and music by Jean Schwartz, the song was heard and enjoyed by millions. The theme: love can be expensive.

---

2 "Hello, Frisco!" W/Gene Buck M/Louis A. Hirsch © 1915 M. Witmark & Sons Copyright Renewed All Rights Reserved. Used by Permission WARNER BROS. MUSIC.

Captain Jinks one night on Broadway, all alone,
Read the news about the wireless telephone.
Pretty soon his thoughts began to stray,
Over seven thousand miles away.
Then he went and drew a whole month's pay,
To phone and say:

CHORUS: Hello, Hawaii, How are you?
Let me talk to Honolulu Lou,
To ask her this: "Give me a kiss, give me a
     kiss by wireless,"
Please state, I can't wait to hear her reply,
For I had to pawn ev'ry little thing I own,
To talk from New York through the wireless
     telephone;
Oh! Hello, Hawaii! How are you? Good-bye![3]

The composer of the catchy tune went on to other successes, among them
the music for "Hello, Central! Give Me No Man's Land" in 1918, a World
War I hit, for which Sam M. Lewis and Joe Young wrote the words.

But there was no more novelty to telephone conversations—at least, not
until the era of the astronauts. By then popular sheet music was in its dotage,
so one could look in vain for songs entitled "John Glenn, Hello," or "Kissing
Neil Armstrong through the Phone," or "Hello, Central, Put Me in Orbit."
The phone had had a longer life in the field of popular music than any other
invention—not even excluding the automobile.

The Flatiron Building

It was a piece of pie in the sky. It was a giant wedge, cleaving Broadway
and Fifth Avenue. It was the prow of a colossal earthbound battleship. It
was a V-for-Victory symbol, the conquest of the New York skyline from the
rule of the drab structures far below its ornate roof. It was the Flatiron
Building.

Today, a passer-by would not lift his eyes, much less strain his neck, to
take in the upward sweep of a twenty-story edifice. But at the turn of the
century, the skyscraper was one of the marvels of the age; and it commanded the respectful approval and even the universal awe of a population
unprepared for the barrage of wonders with which the years ahead were
destined to bombard them.

[3] "Hello Hawaii How Are You." © 1915 by Mills Music Inc. © Renewed 1942 by Mills Music. and
Edgar Leslie, Inc. Used by Permission.

Originally it was not the "Flatiron" Building at all; its given name was the Fuller Building, named for the George A. Fuller Company, its general contractors. But the shape of its site was so distinctive, so closely resembling the homely, useful article which every proper housewife wielded over the weekly laundered sheets, shirts, and chemises, that the nickname "Flatiron" was a "natural," and became almost at once the name by which the structure was known and recognizable to all.

To D. H. Burnham and Company, one of Chicago's most honored architectural firms, fell the assignment to convert the narrow triangular plot, with two two-hundred-foot sides and a one-hundred-foot base, into an eye-catching and profitable investment. Burnham had had no experience with skyscrapers in New York. Chicago had been more innovative in that respect.

Prior to the development of the skyscraper, the entire structure of a large industrial building was supported by the exterior walls; the design of the interior was not intended to add strength to the building itself. The skyscraper, on the other hand, had what was termed a "skeletal" construction; the external and internal loads and strengths were transmitted from the top of the building to the foundations by a skeleton or framework of metal.

Burnham was not the first architect to develop this form of construction. That honor went to another Chicagoan, William Le Baron Jenney, who effectively applied the skeletal approach to the Home Insurance Building at La Salle and Adams streets (in what is now the heart of Chicago's Loop). Construction was started in 1883 and completed in 1885. Originally a ten-story edifice, it proved to be so successful an experiment that two more stories were added in 1890. It remained useful until 1931, when a demolition crew pulled it down to clear the way for a much taller, grander structure.

Burnham's career for a while gave no indication of his later successes. A native of New York State, he moved with his family to Chicago in 1855, when he was nine. After the Civil War he became a clerk in a retail store. Tiring of this position after a few months, he entered Jenney's architectural office but was too restless to remain there long. A stint as a miner in Nevada brought him no financial gain, and he tried a new venture, politics, as a candidate for a seat in the Illinois State Senate. When his campaign proved unsuccessful, he seems to have decided to return to the field of architecture and became a draftsman.

In a short while he had formed a partnership with John Willhorn Root. The merger proved a fortunate one. Root had the necessary technical talent; Burnham was gifted with both executive and sales ability. The late

Frank Lloyd Wright, an admirer if not a follower of Burnham's conceptions, summed up his ability in the words "Uncle Dan was an impressario." Such gifted acumen did he possess, to such a scale did his enterprise carry him in the estimation of Chicago's industrialists, that when the business leaders planned a World's Fair in Chicago in 1893, Burnham was elected its chief of construction, and after the unexpected death of his partner was made chief consulting architect. A classicist at heart in construction, he tried, when the fair closed, to persuade Wright to join him in the exploitation of the classic style in buildings. Wright's response was, "I'm afraid it's too late now, Uncle Dan."

The Flatiron, when it was completed, was destined to make its viewers goggle-eyed. Declared the *Tribune Illustrated Supplement* on June 29, 1902: "Since the removal last week of the scaffolding . . . there is scarcely an hour when a staring wayfarer doesn't by his example collect a big crowd of other staring people. Sometimes a hundred or more, with heads bent backward until a general breakage of necks seems imminent, collect along the walk . . . and stay there until 'one of the finest' orders them to move on. . . . The Flatiron is not the tallest building in New York, but it is the slenderest—as a bright girl expresses it, 'the most aquiline'."

Said a writer in *Camera World* the following year, "We would not be astonished . . . if the whole triangular blade would suddenly begin to move northward through the crowd of pedestrians and traffic of our two leading thoroughfares, which would break like the waves of the ocean on the huge prowlike angle."

In July, 1905, Edgar Saltus described in *Munsey's* magazine, "The Most Extraordinary Panorama in the World." He was referring to his view from high up in the Flatiron Building when he wrote: "On one side is Broadway . . . the longest commercial stretch on the planet. On the other side is Fifth Avenue . . . the richest thoroughfare in the world. From the top floors of the Flatiron Building each looks meager, almost mean. In them are things that you would take for beetles, others that seem to you ants. The beetles are cabs; the ants are human beings." Another writer called the building "a city under a single roof." The president of the American Academy of Architects in Rome wrote from that city, "The only other building higher than your Fifth Avenue and 23rd Street building that I have ever heard of was the Tower of Babel."

The first skyscraper in New York, for nine years it remained unchallenged in its dominance of Manhattan's skyline. The sweeping view from

its upper floors commanded the calm greenery of Madison Square, the bulky Madison Square Garden—home of the circus and the smartest social events, like the horse show—the solid Fifth Avenue Hotel, the traditional gathering place for Republican politicians, and a sweep of Broadway almost up to Central Park.

Fifth Avenue had first stretched to the north only fifty years before the Flatiron arrived, but Broadway was much, much older. When New York was still New Amsterdam, and Dutch was its spoken tongue, a broad road extended up from the cluster of buildings huddled at the tip of Manhattan. In those days it was known as Breede Weg; the later transition could not have been more obvious.

For years before the turn of the twentieth century New York and its more popular spots, and even streets, had been celebrated in the popular-music field. Harrigan and Hart, the most famous team of popular song writers in the eighteen seventies and eighties, composed many songs about the Irish-Americans and the lower East Side, the section where they swarmed and bred new swarms of babies. In 1896, when Madison Square still retained most of its pristine beauty, a young composer named Edward V. Abram wrote "The Madison Square March and Two step," a catchy air which was quite popular for a time.

The striking-looking Flatiron Building was too important a part of the New York scene to be ignored by music writers. In 1903, J. W. Lerman brought out "The Flatiron March and Two-Step," a rollicking, jolly number with a swing that was suitable for brass band as well as solo piano. In fact, the piano score carried the information that the piece was published also for "Orchestra, Military Band, Mandolin, Guitar, etc." When one hears the melody, he can conceive of its appropriateness today at a mayoral inaugural in Lafayette Square or a between-the-halves selection at a New York Jets' gridiron conflict. A period piece—yes—but a piece that can come alive again on any occasion that marks the greatness of America's most fabulous city.

"The Song of the N.C.R."

THIS IS THE ERA of abbreviations, when to the average man the shortened name is more familiar than the original designation—Coke, Chevvy, Bud, HEW, the Cards, Doc, Shake, NAACP. At the beginning of the twentieth century, the average American was far more formal. A given name, an organization, a foodstuff or a potable liquid was stated fully and properly, so that no hint of slur or impertinence might appear. The closest thing to the

The Song of The N. C. R.

"For it's all of us together, our flag is never furled.
From Africa to Iceland, we're marching 'round the world."

Words by
W. D. Nesbit

Music by
Frederic Chapin

The N.C.R.

All round and round and round the world there sounds a sil-ver bell Wher-ev-er on the land or sea the folks have things to sell; It rings on the e-qua-tor and its e-choes rise and roll A-cross the si-lent plains of snow that lie a-bout the pole. It rings be-neath the south-ern cross, be-neath the po-lar star Does the jin-gle, jin-gle, jin-gle of the N. C. R.

Chorus

For it's all of us to-geth-er, our flag is nev-er furled. From Af-ri-ca to Ice-land, we're march-ing' round the world. Suc-cess on our ban-ner, we're heard both near and far, With the jin-gle, jin-gle, jin-gle of the N. C. R.

2. It rings where northern breezes toss the branches of the pine,
   It sounds throughout the golden west, in mill and mart and mine;
   It jingles in the sunny south of cotton, cane and palm,
   It gives unto the cultured east a more contented calm.
   There's never any discord, any sounds that harshly jar
   In the jingle, jingle, jingle, of the N.C.R.
   CHORUS

3. The Russian hails with joyous voice the great machine that thinks,
   The Frenchman sings the praises of the wheel that counts the clinks,
   The Hindu at the temple gates, the Arab on the sands,
   The Eskimo and Hottentot greet it with eager hands,
   On camel back, in burro pack, in stately ship, and car,
   We are going, going, going with the N.C.R.
   Chorus

4. Our President! Here's to him! He is with us hand and heart,
   No matter what the task may be he always does his part,
   His welfare plans have flowered in a thousand varied ways,
   May his good deeds come back to him through all the coming days.
   So, here's to him! He always rates a whole lot over par,
   The man behind the men behind the N.C.R.
   Chorus

5. So whether we go far and wide across the briny foam,
   No matter when or where or how we find that we must roam,
   We learn that each depends on each, that one must work for all,
   And all in turn must work for one, together stand or fall.
   And that is why in all the world, in countries near and far
   Sounds the jingle, jingle, jingle of the N.C.R.
   Chorus

6. And here's a health to (———) he's the man who boosts the sales,
   The man who shows the laggards it's no use to hide their trails;
   He talks the N.C.R. wherever he may chance to be
   And all the other fellows soon are talking in his key.
   The clock that every morning from his dreams gives him a jar
   Has the jingle, jingle, jingle of the N.C.R.
   Chorus

tolerance of an abbreviation appeared in an afterthought at the bottom of a personal letter—"PS." But to every rule and every custom there must be an exception, and in this case the exception was a company with headquarters in Dayton, Ohio, known around the world as the N.C.R.

Founded by a most unusual individual, the National Cash Register Company was a most unusual organization, in many respects half a century ahead of its time. Long before Henry Ford, John H. Patterson, N.C.R.'s guiding spirit, had concerned himself with the welfare of his employees, not only in the spirit of altruism, but with the conviction that a more contented workman turns in a better job for his company. Patterson's development of a consistent advertising campaign was started before anyone in today's great Madison Avenue firms was born. His first school for training a sales force was in session over seventy-five years ago.

In 1906 he encouraged the adoption of a company song, "The Song of the N.C.R.," which, like N.C.R.'s dynamic president, had no reticence when it came to self-aggrandizement:

> All round and round and round the world there
> sounds a silver bell
> Wherever on the land or sea the folks have things
> to sell;
> It rings on the equator and its echoes rise and
> roll
> Across the silent plains of snow that lie about
> the pole.
> It rings beneath the southern cross, beneath the
> polar star
> Does the jingle, jingle, jingle of the N.C.R.
>
> Our President! Here's to him! He is with us hand
> and heart,
> No matter what the tasks may be he always does his
> part.
> His welfare plans have flowered in a thousand varied
> ways,
> May his goodness come back to him through all the
> coming days.
> So, here's to him! He always rates a whole lot over
> par,
> The man behind the men behind the N.C.R.
>
> CHORUS: For it's all of us together, our flag is never furled,
> From Africa to Iceland, we're marching 'round the
> world.
> Success on our banner, we're heard both near and far,
> With the jingle, jingle, jingle of the N.C.R.

Like so many men who have risen above the herd, John H. Patterson had to face hard times and tribulations before he emerged in all his glory at the head of a business which amazed the world of the late nineteenth century.

Patterson was born in the 1840's and was just old enough to volunteer for the Union army in 1863. Discharged the following year, he enrolled in Dartmouth College, acquiring the sort of education which he described later on as "What I learned mostly was what not to do." He returned home to a succession of odd jobs—helping his father on the family farm, serving as a toll collector on a canal, operating a small coal and wood business. He was constantly aggravated by the slipshod manner in which accounts were kept and money transactions recorded, and so he devised his own system of bookkeeping. In his coal and wood enterprise, for example, he wrote on a slate the orders placed with him. Then he went out, bought the coal or the wood, and had it delivered, marking down on the slate the amount he paid, the amount he was to charge, and the profit. When his customer paid the bill, Patterson closed the transaction by wiping off the slate.

The business grew to such an extent that Patterson and his brother Frank leased two small coal mines and operated a mine store. The store did a large business but could not seem to show a profit. After a tour of inspection, Patterson put his finger on the trouble; many miners who bought at the store had made friends among the clerks, and a clerk would charge his friend only half the price of his purchase. So Patterson discharged the clerks and sought a method of checking the sales made by the new clerks who replaced them.

He found what he wanted in the form of a machine made in Dayton, which registered sales by means of keys which punched holes in a roll of paper. Patterson bought two, for fifty dollars apiece, and started his first use of a cash register. The year was 1882. The registers had been patented in 1879 by a Dayton saloonkeeper named James Ritty, who tried unsuccessfully to market the few he had made in his small shop. When Patterson made his purchase, the owner of the patent was the National Manufacturing Company, a seven-man organization with a twelve-thousand-dollar capital.

In the spring of 1883 the little company, which had managed to sell about fifty registers since its inception, improved its product with something called the "detail adder." They cast about for new capital and found the two Pattersons ready to "put up" twenty-five hundred dollars, acquiring fifty shares thereby. The company's next annual statement showed a loss and the brothers tried to unload their stock, succeeding in selling a little over half of it.

The following year John Patterson, aged forty, sold his coal business with all its ramifications for sixteen thousand dollars and looked around for a likely place to invest his capital. Once again he succumbed to the lure of the cash register. He called on George Phillips, the president of the National Manufacturing Company, who owned its controlling interest, and along with his brother acquired Phillips' stock for sixty-five hundred dollars. The next day he had a change of heart and offered to turn back the stock for two thousand dollars less than he had paid for it, but his offer was firmly declined.

On November 28, 1884, Patterson took over the operation of the National Manufacturing Company, in one room forty feet by eighty, and with a payroll of thirteen. His first act was to change the name of his business to the National Cash Register Company.

Patterson's most important problem was to produce sales. He solved it by a new method of luring salesmen. Up until that time, a company would hire salesmen indiscriminately, always on a commission basis, but pitting one man against another in the same territory, where the best man secured the most business and the poorer salesmen scrambled among themselves for the leftovers. Patterson was a pioneer in establishing exclusive territories for his salesmen, so that none encroached on another. Each of his men—and he had ten to start—was completely on his own, with no competitor from his company interfering with his method of canvassing his prospects.

And Patterson helped his salesmen with direct-mail advertising. He has often been called the "father of modern advertising," though this appellation may be challenged. But at least he had unique ideas about the approach to a potential customer. For example, soon after the sales force was organized, Patterson asked each man to send him a list of five hundred prospects in his territory. Five thousand merchants thus formed the nucleus of names for a gigantic—for those days—advertising campaign. Each day, over an eighteen-day period, a piece of advertising literature was mailed to each merchant. For eighteen days the prospect was bombarded with printed reasons for the need of a cash register in his store. Naturally, many merchants remained unconvinced; some grew hostile. One man, after suffering the reception of nine letters in the series, returned the tenth with a written notation, "Let up. We never done you any harm." But the way was made easier for the sales force, who followed up the advertising deluge with personal calls which brought tangible results.

John Patterson was a great man for writing his axioms in the form of crisp, succinct lists, which were circulated freely among his employees. Some were elementary, but Patterson was essentially a simple man and gave simple instructions. His sales manual, for example, contained a list of fifty "don'ts." Here are a few:

> Don't fail to seat the prospect properly.
> Don't point your finger or pencil at him.
> Don't put your feet on his chair.
> Don't slap him on the knee or poke him with your
>   finger.
> Don't chew gum or tobacco.
> Don't tell funny stories.

In his company paper, "The N. C. R.," which was probably the first house organ ever published, he had many other "don'ts" for salesmen, such as: "Don't advertise the register as a thief catcher." (Incidentally it was the "thief catcher" approach that brought the register's early sales.)

> Don't do all the talking.
> Don't answer a question except with the truth.
> Don't remain idle.
> Don't read these once, but twice. We want you
>   to make money and don't want you to fail.

In 1892 he wrote in "The N. C. R." this memorandum for his traveling salesmen:

> Travellers' Reminder: Have I packed my Coat, Waistcoat,
> Trousers, Socks, Shoes, Overshoes, Dressing-gown, Shirts,
> Undershirts, Nightshirts, Drawers, Suspenders, Collars,
> Cuffs, Postage-stamps, Flask, Nail-brush, Blacking-brush,
> Looking-glass, Razor, Court-plaster, Watch, Toothpicks,
> Cane, Umbrella, Pistols, Cigars, Drinking Cup, Glycerine,
>   etc.

In the early years of the N. C. R. John Patterson had severe labor difficulties. The morale of his employees descended to a low ebb. Three times in 1893 the factory was set afire, apparently by dissatisfied workers, and the following year many of the cash registers awaiting shipment were badly damaged by the use of acids applied surreptitiously. Patterson realized that his factory conditions must be radically improved and that the attitude of the employees had to be redirected from a spirit of antagonism to one of cooperation.

All his life John Patterson had been a man of impulse, and again he acted impulsively. He discovered that favoritism was practiced by some of his foremen; he put an end to it immediately. He was made aware of dirt in portions of his plant and of the refuse piling up in the factory yard; he cleaned out the unsightly spots and planted trees and flowers where broken crates and cinder heaps had offended the eye.

He was shocked to learn of the rapid turnover of his female employees. When he asked one departing girl why she had decided to quit, she said: "It's too dark and dirty and cold around here." Patterson commenced at once to improve the women's lot. He put in a lunchroom; he replaced the stools at the worktables with adjustable chairs with backs; he raised the girls' wages even though the company was not making a profit.

The plant was in a suburban area called Slidertown; after hours there was no form of recreation for the employees. The N.C.R. prepared a large plot of ground and invited the young sons of the factory workers to plant gardens after school. A head gardener, tools, and seeds were furnished; soon the first garden school for children in the United States was under way. Patterson found an enterprise for the youngsters in winter too; he started a Boys' Box Furniture Company, where the boys learned how to handle tools and market their products. The profits were their own.

A men's welfare work league came into being; a welfare hall was built in 1905, and later a large hall, called simply "The Schoolhouse," was constructed and filled to overflowing each weekday at noontime by employees for whom the company provided some form of entertainment. A kindergarten for one hundred children, cooking and sewing classes for girls, a library, a boy's brigade of one hundred, bands, gleeclubs, gymnasium classes, a bicycle club—all these were functioning actively before 1900. It need hardly be said that within the space of a few years employee relationships at N. C. R. changed from downright antagonistic to solidly enthusiastic.

"The Song of the N. C. R." brags of the product's world-wide distribution. This was no ill boast. Patterson began to do business in England in 1885, and in the same year he appointed sales agents in Switzerland, Germany, France, Belgium, and Holland. The year 1886 saw the start of their business in Sweden and Italy. In the 1890's the company was selling its registers in Austria, Denmark, and Russia. Some years later agencies were established in Greece, Roumania, Bulgaria, Turkey, Ireland and Spain, to be followed by others in China and Japan. Soon even Africa was involved with sales agents, not only in Egypt and Liberia, but "down under" in Sierra Leone and Nigeria.

At times the conversion of the cash registers' dollars and cents mechanism to the intricacies of foreign currencies produced special problems. One of the most difficult markets for calculating machines was India, whose monetary system included units of currency valued at hardly more than a sixth of a cent. The Indian rupee, with a valuation of thirty-nine cents, breaks down into sixteen annas, each of which in turn represents twelve pies. The registers made for India had to juggle rupees, annas, and pies with the same efficiency as if they were recording dollars and cents; and their success in such an intricate operation was an indication of the amazing multiplicity of the company's skills in adjusting to the problems of strange lands.

John Patterson was straightforward, frowning on nonsense or nonessentials, driving always along the course he charted himself, a road leading to ever-expanding use of his product. His external appearance reflected his personality. Firm of mouth, square of chin, with a well-trimmed mustache, and rimless spectacles accentuating his piercing eyes, this light, erect figure of a man would dominate any gathering of which he was a part. Widowed, with two small children, before he had reached middle age, he never remarried, but continued to live an abstemious life, in which industry was always the dominant factor.

Patterson's finest hour as humanitarian and citizen came in March 1913. On March 25 the "Great Rain" started in the Miami River area. Dayton, through which the river flowed, was built mostly on low ground; and to prevent the incursion of water during the spring flood season, dikes had been built outside the city. Patterson had studied the contour of the land for years before he built his plant on high ground. He realized that one day the spring waters would prove too strong for the levee. On March 27 Patterson rode about Dayton and along the river banks; then calling his executives together he told them Dayton would be flooded that day and his company must assume major responsibility for feeding and housing those who would have to abandon their homes. Impulsive as always, he suspended all N. C. R. company operations and within ten minutes had organized the citizens' relief association. Food, bedding, and hospital supplies were rushed to the factory. City and state officials, doctors and nurses were assembled there. A bread line stretched for two blocks. Supplies poured in on relief trains. The N. C. R. carpenters pounded together two hundred boats, one every seven minutes, and they were rapidly manned and sent out to rescue people from housetops and second-story windows. Twenty-five hundred people were fed daily in the dining room, and bedded down in the company's bedrooms and gymnasiums.

Wrote a correspondent of the *Outlook*, a national magazine:

> This ... was the very apotheosis of centralized one-man power. The National Cash Register is ... an expression of the somewhat eccentric genius of one man—an industrial captain. No novelist or playwright trying to picture the drama of modern business ever devised anything more ingeniously dramatic —this heroic use of efficiency.

After the waters had receded, Patterson was appointed chairman with "full authority" of a five-man citizens' relief committee, organized to clean up the muddy, broken town and to provide against the possibility of future floods. They set themselves a goal of two million dollars, and in one great, wildly exciting meeting the sum was subscribed, with Mr. Patterson and the N. C. R. contributing one third of the total.

A remarkable head of a remarkable company, he wrote down his thoughts and his practices, endlessly. He hated useless ostentation and lived simply, considering himself only a trustee of the money he earned. In one of his last memorandums, he wrote:

> J. H. Patterson is acting as manager of the N.C.R. for the people of the world.... He keeps only enough for his board and clothes and necessaries for himself and children. . . . On his last trip he can take nothing with him, as shrouds have no pockets.

The Panama Canal

FIFTY YEARS AGO, in a revue assembled by George White, the famous producer of girlie shows, and entitled enticingly, *George White's Scandals of 1921*, there was one especially flashy number, with dozens of females on the stage. It was a standard approach in those days; the girls had to be displayed in a series of fetching costumes which usually revealed more girl than dress. For this particular revue, White engaged George Gershwin to write its music, with a well-known lyricist named Arthur Jackson as his associate; and the song which set the scene for such an elaborate display of women and women's wear was called "When East Meets West." Here is how the chorus starts:

> When East meets West in Panama,
> And sea meets sea,
> Where Yankee brains and Yankee brawn
> Won victory...

George Gershwin was a very young man at that time. The song might have been more appropriate seven years earlier, but then George would have been a mere teen-ager not yet equipped to start on a musical career. And so, musically, there was no great fanfare on August 15, 1914, when the first vessel, the Panama Railroad ship *Ancon*, entered the Panama Canal from the Atlantic Ocean, and traversing lakes and locks for a little over seven hours, found herself afloat on the Pacific.

Among the witnesses to this unprecedented event was a colonel of engineers in the United States Army, George Washington Goethals. But Goethals was considerably more than a witness; the amazing construction job had been completed under his personal supervision. He was, to all intents and purposes, "Mr. Canal."

The year of completion was 1914, but the year when a white man was first able to realize the proximity of the two oceans at the isthmus antedated that by four centuries. On September 29, 1513, Vasco Núñez de Balboa, one of a hardy group of Spaniards who had come to explore and dominate the new world that Columbus had discovered, climbed to a high point on the south side of the isthmus and there beheld for the first time the vast Pacific Ocean, of which he formally took possession in the name of the king of Spain.

The Spaniards were the first colonizers in the New World; Panama had been seized for them by Balboa in 1511, after massacres had decimated groups of both Spaniards and native Indians. But the intrinsic wealth of the countries to the south of the isthmus, which sent to Panama their gold and silver, their jewels and pearls, for trade with the Spaniards, was too alluring not to attract other strangers from the old world. Most of these were pirates from England and France, who raided the coastal towns time and again over a period of nearly two centuries until the land was a waste and the commerce at a standstill. In 1821, Spain granted Colombia her independence, and in that same year Panama declared its own independence and requested inclusion in the republic of Gran Colombia, as the country was then called.

From time to time Spain, then France, and later the United States, had discussed seriously a means of connecting the two oceans at the isthmus. A canal was the obvious method, but a wagon road was considered also. There appeared to be no urgency to pursue these projects until, in 1848, gold was discovered in California. Then everybody wanted to get out there the quickest possible way. At that time there was no transcontinental railroad across the United States, so, except for the trail blazers, the gold rushers had to sail around Cape Horn. The Isthmus of Panama seemed an obvious short cut, but how to capitalize on its potential? The answer: a railroad. The French had contracted the previous year to build one, but were unable to raise capital for the project.

So the Panama Railroad Company was incorporated in New York with a capitalization of one million dollars and was awarded the concession which the French had forfeited. Surveys indicated that it would be feasible to build a fifty-mile road to avoid the most difficult terrain. Both time of construction and cost were badly underestimated. Five years' work and over seven million dollars went into the completion of the forty-seven-and-a-half-mile road, but when it was completed in 1855, the game was proved to have been worth the candle. Passenger rates were exorbitant: twenty-five dollars per adult passenger. The annual dividends to stockholders soared to 44 per cent in 1868; and before the road was acquired by the United States government in 1904, it had distributed dividends amounting in grand total to nearly thirty-eight million dollars.

By 1904 this country had fitted another string to its bow. The man behind the string behind the bow was president of the United States, Theodore Roosevelt. But before getting Teddy into the picture, a few steps have to be retraced.

In 1846 a treaty with New Granada—one of several names adopted by Colombia during its adolescence as a republic—gave the United States the right of way or transit across the Isthmus of Panama. This did not, however, restrict the plans of other ambitious countries. Great Britain wanted us to join her in developing a canal across Nicaragua, and France engaged in diplomatic correspondence with us to attempt to gain control of any mutually dug canal. But France went further, and in 1875 she persuaded the Colombian congress to approve a concession with her under which she would build a canal across the isthmus. The French company undertaking this enterprise bore the formidable name of *La Société Civile Internationale du Canal Interocéanique,* and its guiding spirit was the man who had successfully dug the Suez Canal, Count Ferdinand de Lesseps.

One of the conditions imposed by Colombia was that France would have to come to a satisfactory arrangement with the Panama Railroad. By this time the fortunes of the railroad were decidedly on the downgrade, and the French company purchased it for $25,000,000, acquiring its right of way. The magic name of de Lesseps, who was presented to the French public as president of the canal company, brought an outpouring of subscriptions from the thrifty French, and soon the company had $60,000,000 in its till, a sum which invited all sorts of extravagances.

Manufacturers were requested to send the company samples of surplus stocks that they had on hand. This resulted in some weird and lavish purchases. Ten thousand snow shovels were sent to Panama, a country where snow never falls; and after the company's demise, a ton of steel pen points was discovered, rust-encrusted and useless.

The extravagance, the many swindles, the enormous toll of lives from the scourges of yellow fever and malaria, and de Lesseps' inability to cope with the volcanic rock, the swamps, and the slide-prone clay banks, all contributed to the eventual collapse of France's great version of the "South Sea Bubble." Actually, de Lesseps had spent only two months in Panama, but the onus of the misfortune fell on his shoulders. The old man was tried in court for fraud, convicted, and sentenced to five years in prison, a sentence which mercifully was never carried out.

An incident of the Spanish American War in 1898 was a potent factor in focusing American interest on the canal. At the start of the war the battle-ship *Oregon* was off San Francisco at a time when she was badly needed in the Caribbean. She set off at once on a thirteen-thousand-mile journey around Cape Horn, arriving off Cuba in due course. However, the powers in Washington were aware that had there been a canal in Central America through which she could have steamed, the distance traveled would have been cut by two thirds.

In 1903 the United States paid the French owners of the canal $40,000,000 for all its interests in the project. By this time Panama had seceded from Colombia, elected its own president, and sent its first minister to Washington, where a treaty confirming our rights to complete the canal was quickly drawn up and executed.

President Theodore Roosevelt, who had been more than anxious for Panama's independence so that the canal project might be advanced, was indiscreet enough, when addressing an audience, to announce, "I took Panama." This statement rankled Colombia for years, and eventually in 1921 we paid her $25,000,000 as "compensation."

The United States now had a ten-mile-wide strip of fever-infested territory, a couple of thousand ruined buildings of various sorts and the responsibility of turning a failure into a success. Roosevelt gave the war department authority over the enterprise and appointed a commission to direct the work.

From the appointment of the first commission of seven men to the completion and opening of the canal, a period of ten years elapsed. A second commission of seven, three of whom served as an executive committee, succeeded the first. For the last seven years of the operation all were under the control of one man, Colonel Goethals.

Goethals already had a record of a number of creditable accomplishments. Bridges, locks, dams, pipelines, wells had tested his talents, and he surmounted one problem after the other. When he was sent to Panama in 1905, it was as a member of the fortification board of William Howard Taft, then secretary of war. At that time the chief engineer in charge of the work on the canal was John F. Stevens, whose forte had been railroad construction. Stevens was an able man, but the railroad was his first love. Of the problems in the depressing climate of the isthmus, he said, "There are three diseases in Panama. They are yellow fever, malaria, and cold feet; and the greatest of these is cold feet." Stevens himself succumbed to the third disease, paving the way for the appointment of Goethals by President Roosevelt,

VOCAL & INSTRUMENTAL NUMBERS
FROM THE NEW MUSICAL COMEDY

THE ROGERS BROS
"IN PANAMA"

GEORGE LYDECKER

Book by
SYLVESTER MAGUIRE
AND
AARON HOFFMAN

"IN PANAMA."

THE ROGERS BROS MUSIC PUB. CO
NEW YORK THEATRE BUILDING
Broadway bet. 44th & 45th Sts
NEW YORK
M. WITMARK & SONS, London.
Singing Rights Reserved.

Music by
MAX HOFFMANN
Lyrics by
EDWARD MADDEN

342

In Panama

I sing to thee land of dream-hours — sweet flow-ers — tra la — I sing to thy trees and thy

sweet Sum-mer breeze Pa-na-ma — Pa-na-ma — I dream of thy fair sen-o-ri-tas — who

greet us — a-far — The fair-est on earth is the land of my birth my be-lov-ed Pa-na-ma —

Chorus

Pa - na-ma Pa - na-ma — Sweet with flow-ers and dream la-den hours — in Pa - na

ma Pa - na-ma Un-der the shel-ter-ing Palm tree Land of milk and ho - ney skies so

blue and sun - ny I may roam, but home sweet home is Pa - na - ma —

2. Of other lands poets are singing with ringing guitar,
  Their hearts can not sing of the joy that you bring
      Panama, Panama
  In other lands lovers may dream of the gleam of a star
  They know not the dreams of thy tender moonbeams my
      beloved Panama.
  CHORUS

who, in February, 1907, asked him to take over two key jobs simultaneously: the head of the canal commission and the chief engineer.

Whether it was due to Roosevelt's colorful personality or to the public's confidence in Goethals, Panama became the subject of more and more publicity. Among the well-known figures who became Panama-conscious were two popular entrepreneurs of the musical comedy stage, Gus and Max Rogers. The Rogers Brothers had been known for half a dozen years as the exponents of the poor man's vaudeville extravaganza, whipping up at short notice popular type, lightweight musicals patterned after the burlesques of Weber and Fields. The brothers would locate their stories in popular surroundings. One year they would produce *The Rogers Brothers in Paris*, another year, *The Rogers Brothers in Ireland*, and so on. In 1907 they decided it was appropriate to write *The Rogers Brothers in Panama*, and this turned out to be one of their more successful ventures. The songs, written by Max Hoffmann and Edward Madden, were sappy, and their titles were banal—"In Panama," "Way Down in Colon Town." The latter told of the usual boy making love to the usual girl, but with a slight twist, as relates the second verse:

> Ah but she was a sad coquette
> When I stole a kiss and called her pet
> She boxed my ears with a castanet
> Way down in Colon Town.
> There's many a man bought jewels for her
> There's many a man fought duels for her
> But I'd go driving mules for her
> Way down in Colon Town.
> And when the hour had come to part
> She threw a kiss with an aching heart
> So I left my gal by the old canal
> And I heard her cry good-bye old pal.

The greatest obstacle to the builders of the canal was the continental divide, a series of peaks running the entire length of the Americas. Fortunately, the ridges, which in North and South America ascended for ten and twelve thousand feet, had shrunk to a few hundred in Central America, so that the problem of cutting through the divide at the isthmus, while difficult, was not insurmountable.

The highest point across the isthmus was at Culebra, a small settlement about eight miles from the Pacific Ocean. Here, Goethals knew, it would be necessary to make the deepest cut—two hundred feet—in the terrain. The size of this operation is indicated, even though its enormity may not be visualized, by the report that over one hundred and ten *million* cubic yards of earth and rock were extracted from the cut between 1904 and 1914. The Culebra Cut turned out to be just about the most difficult of Goethals' many harassing engineering problems. But he was a man who throve on harassment; the struggle to complete the deep cut, the disheartening slides of rock and mud which nullified in a matter of seconds the hard labor of months, the frightful turnover of personnel would have broken the back of many a man less impervious to hardships. Goethals took all in his stride, never evidencing a sign of discouragement.

The great difference between the original French approach and the American one was that de Lesseps had envisioned a sea-level canal, with ships sailing grandly and without impediment from ocean to ocean, whereas the Americans realized—a fact which the French had ultimately accepted— that a high-level lock-type canal was the only practical solution.

Goethals constructed a sea-level channel, running inland seven miles from the Atlantic Ocean. From there on, the water level was lifted by a series of locks to a height of eighty-five feet, where a ship proceeding through the canal would reach Gatun Lake, an artificial body of water developed by the damming of a river, the Chagres, which had been flowing from the continental divide toward the Atlantic Ocean. For nearly thirty-two miles the ship would make her way at this eighty-five-foot elevation to a point about ten miles from the Pacific Ocean. Then, passing through another lock, she would be lowered thirty feet into another artificial body of water, Miraflores Lake, on which she would travel a mile and a half to a last series of locks, which would take her down to the ocean level. Another channel, eight miles in length, would bring her to the Pacific itself.

The engineering feat achieved by Goethals' blood-and-guts effort was a stupendous one. Not only did it require his unique engineering qualities, but he had to demonstrate an ability to work with men as well as machines. For the physical labor required to operate efficiently in that torrid climate, with the latent threat of deadly tropical diseases, even though apparently tightly controlled, ready to strike suddenly at an unsuspecting toiler, was more than most men could stand. Nevertheless, there appeared to be no difficulty in securing necessary recruitments whenever the ranks thinned. When the United States had supplanted France as boss of the canal, total employment consisted only of a maintenance crew of 746 men. The working force jumped to 17,000 in a year, and at the peak of activity in 1913, almost 57,000 men were employed. The bulk of these were negroes from the West Indies, but Goethals saw to it that some 12,000 white Europeans were imported as unskilled laborers. At the outset, their capacity for hard work was double that of the West Indians, as was their pay scale; but as the years went on and the Spaniards, Italians, and Greeks lost some of their early enthusiasm, the work gap narrowed, though the pay differential remained.

And eventually the years of concentrated effort paid off for Goethals and for the United States. On September 26, 1913, the locks at the end of Gatun Lake were put to their first test. As the gates parted and the water rushed into the locks, the first little ship, the tug *Gatun*, stood ready for a canal trip through the locks to Culebra. The journey went smoothly, the locks working perfectly, and the tug steamed slowly down Gatun Lake, whistles tooting, flags flying, and a great crowd cheering her on from the sidelines of the locks. Water was now flowing the length of the canal, but the full-scale trip from ocean to ocean was to be delayed for almost a year.

However, the sight of the spunky little tug, rising in the Gatun locks, was enough to excite the country and even the world of popular music. Its historic appearance in the locks inspired the composition of "The Panama Canal March," by Will Wood in 1913 within a few weeks of the event. The title page is a reproduction of a photograph of the *Gatun* in Gatun locks, with crowds of onlookers lining both banks and with the caption, "First photo showing the waters of the Atlantic and Pacific running through Canal."

A year earlier, another composer, J. Bodewalt Lampe, had capitalized on the great popularity that Goethals had been amassing by writing a "military march and two-step" entitled "Hero of the Isthmus." The title page carries a photograph of the unsmiling engineer, flanked by drawings of two immaculate military men, swords crossed stiltedly above the photograph. The march is "respectfully dedicated to Col. George W. Goethals, Chief Engineer, Panama Canal." While the music doesn't capture the excitement of a big Sousa march, it cuts a nice dash in its breezy six-eighths time, and when scored for a brass band should have been enthusiastically received.

Certainly the "hero of the isthmus" deserved all the acclaim bestowed on him, which included, incidentally, after he had completed the biggest task of his useful life, his appointment as governor of the Panama Canal, and an elevation in army rank from colonel to major general. As he had done throughout his entire life, he took his new honors in his stride with dignity. He was, as the old college ditty put it bluntly, "a hell of an engineer."

10

FROM DIFFERENT ANGLES

Wall Street

IT WAS a handsome structure back in 1903. The classically inspired building had, in all probability, the first all-glass wall in New York. This wall had a highly practical purpose. Situated directly behind the imposing colonnade, which was the external mask with which the New York Stock Exchange faced its public, the glass wall captured the light of day and brought it unadulterated to the floor of the exchange.

In the 1890's the Western Union Telegraph Building adjoined the old Stock Exchange Building, whose site had been preserved in the erection of the new exchange. But now Western Union was to find a new location, and its old quarters were marked for demolition in the elaborate plans of the Stock Exchange, which aimed to engulf both structures in its impressive new accommodations. The great trading room now had an expanse of about 140 by 80 feet, with ample room for the multitude of floor brokers that swarmed within it.

The mind that conceived the elaborate new building was surrounded by a billiard ball head, from which protruded in the proper area between nose and chin a pair of fierce mustaches that would have done credit to any walrus. These accoutrements were the property of George B. Post, a seasoned designer of show places around New York, including the red brick Produce Exchange, built in 1881, and the Cotton Exchange with a round tower such as may be seen in some old-world cities.

The "March of the 1/8 Brigade," composed by R. Frank Rudell in 1903, when the new building became operative, was dedicated to "The Members of the Stock Exchange," the gentlemen for whom the one-eighth had the greatest significance, because the prices of stocks were subject to fluctuation

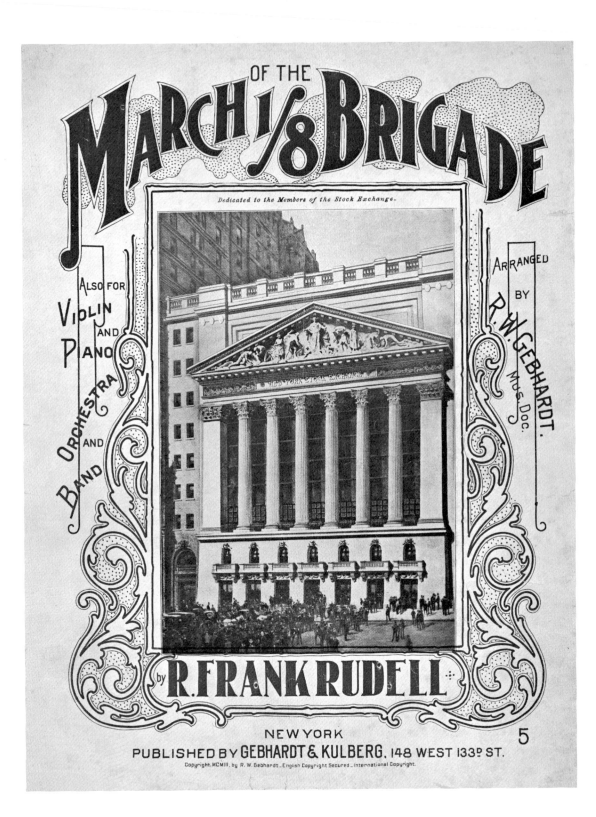

OF THE

MARCH 1/8 BRIGADE

Dedicated to the Members of the Stock Exchange.

ALSO FOR

VIOLIN AND PIANO

ORCHESTRA AND BAND

ARRANGED BY R. W. GEBHARDT. Mus. Doc.

by R. FRANK RUDELL

NEW YORK

PUBLISHED BY GEBHARDT & KULBERG, 148 WEST 133º ST.

Copyright, MCMIII, by R. W. Gebhardt _ English Copyright Secured _ International Copyright.

5

of one-eighth of a dollar, and quotations, both for the buyer and the seller, reflected such fractional changes in market value. The "1/8 Brigade" was a tight little group, limited to a few hundred, but it included a handful of powerful men who exercised unique control over some of the largest corporations in the United States, and who, by their actions and their manipulations, were able to reduce the country to a state of panic or inflame it to an orgy of speculation which could end only in a wholesale disaster.

But such escapades were not indigenous to the United States. Our so-called conservative British forebears were wont to sow their financial wild oats a century before the American brokers commenced to operate in a hesitant fashion in New York and Philadelphia. The term "stockjobber" was first used in 1688, when the English stock market began to function. At that time great numbers of new companies, both legitimate and bogus, were being organized, and there was much speculation in their shares and a boom in industrial stocks to be celebrated in 1693 by an English play which satirized the stockbrokers. Soon there came into use well-known brokerage terms which have ever since been part of Wall Street's language—"bull," "bear," "put."

The craze for speculation reached its zenith early in the eighteenth century with the organization of the "South Sea Company" in England and John Law's "Mississippi Company" in France. When, in the early 1720's, the fabric of these two companies had been stretched so tightly that they collapsed, the world's first money panic occurred, and the term "South Sea Bubble" became a synonym for an ill-fated speculative adventure. A few years later the Bourse of Paris was established, and the Frenchman's penchant for stock gambling was more carefully regulated. So Wall Street, and what it came to stand for, was in reality a European importation, which would be Americanized and refined as it grew older.

At the close of the American Revolution the First Congress authorized the issuance of stock to assume the $80,000,000 in war debts which the states had incurred. Banks were incorporated in Philadelphia and New York; and in 1791 Congress passed a measure—advocated by Alexander Hamilton—establishing a United States bank, an institution which lasted nearly fifty years. At once trading in bank stocks became active, as did trading in the stock which had been floated by the federal government. In 1792 there was an office at 22 Wall Street to handle sales of stocks; the men who were engaged in such dealings, on a commission basis used to meet under a buttonwood tree which stood in front of 68 Wall Street. That year, at Corre's Hotel, twenty-one of the most prominent brokers and three partnerships entered into an agreement not to buy or sell any kind of public stock for less than ¼ of 1 per cent commission. This pact, called the "Buttonwood Agreement" may be said to mark the beginning of a code of ethics for the transaction of brokerage business.

In 1801 there appeared in the *New York Evening Post* the first advertisement listing the prices of active stocks. Some of the quotations:

6 per cent funded debt [United States government]	98-¾ per cent
3 per cent funded debt	56-½ bid; 57 asked
8 per cent loan	112-½
United States Bank [a solid institution then]	143 bid; 143-½ asked
(Bank of) New York (Dividend off)	131-½
(Bank of) Manhattan	132

It should be of interest to note that at that time the banks were paying dividends of anywhere from 15 to 18 per cent.

By 1818 the exchange was dealing in twenty-nine different securities. These included the stocks of companies which had sprung up following the successful operation of the steamboat in 1807 and the plans for digging a series of canals to unite the cities of the Atlantic Coast with the areas to the west. The potentials of mining and of cotton growing excited investors, and there was much speculation in these fields. When the shares of the planned Morris Canal were offered to the public in 1821 they were oversubscribed twenty times.

As the volume of business accelerated, the actions of the members on the floor of the exchange grew more boisterous, and attempts were made to regulate them. A system of fines was imposed, with gradually improving results. In the 1820's penalties of $5 to $25 were levied on members who stood on chairs during trading hours, who knocked off another member's hat, or who threw "paper missiles."

Since 1794 the center of business life in New York had been the Tontine Coffee House on Wall Street, and for over thirty years the stockbrokers were accustomed to meet there. But in 1827 the exchange moved into the Merchants' Exchange Building on the site where the First National City Bank building now stands.

In the new location the speculators continued to make merry, though they quieted down from time to time. March 19, 1830, marks the nadir of their activity; on that day thirty-one shares of stock, with a value of $3,470.25, were traded. By way of contrast, records show that on June 26, 1835, an enormous volume of stock changed hands—7,875 shares (value no longer on record).

Six months later a great fire destroyed 648 buildings in downtown New York. The Merchants' Exchange Building was not spared; and again the Stock Exchange was forced to seek new quarters. The rebuilding process in the city was a laborious one, but by 1842 a new New York Custom House building had been completed, and the Stock Exchange found a home in it.

In the 1850's the floor of the exchange was a rather sedate-looking room. Each member of the board had his own seat. The brokers wore tall hats and kept them on during the hours when the exchange was open.

And still the volume of trading continued to grow. The November 24, 1856, issue of *Bankers'* magazine reported that aggregate transactions during the previous four weeks had amounted to nearly one million shares—somewhat less than the average number of shares traded in a half hour during the early 1970's.

At the outbreak of the Civil War the Stock Exchange board was a tight little group, conducting its affairs in secret with all quotations carried by hand from office to office. Ordinarily less than one hundred members were at their seats in the board room at any one time. Prospective new members were frustrated over and over by the persistent blackballing of names presented to the ruling fraternity.

As the war drew to a close, speculation grew so enormously that it was deemed both expedient and profitable to reduce the rate of commission from ¼ per cent to ⅛ per cent on speculative stocks. This increased the volume of trading still further. From eight in the morning until midnight the brokers would ply their trade; after hours it would be continued in the corridors of the Fifth Avenue Hotel. Eventually, in 1869, a revised system of governing the operations of the exchange was adopted, and some semblance of regulation made itself felt on the trading floor.

The nation's economy was on a financial roller coaster. It struggled through a gold conspiracy in 1869, when Jay Gould and Jim Fisk attempted to corner transactions in the precious metal, only to have their scheme thwarted by the prompt actions of President Grant and Treasury Secretary Boutwell. It bounced back from the panic of 1873, started by the failure of Jay Cooke, the promoter of the Northern Pacific Railroad, which precipitated seventy-nine stock failures of overinvolved firms. Another boom was soon on its way, interrupted by fresh panics in 1884 and 1893.

But then prosperity appeared to gain the upper hand, and the money and stock markets expanded until it became obvious that a new and larger Stock Exchange building was a necessity. And so George B. Post, he of the hairless pate and gorgeous mustaches, took over the project which eventually became the subject of our march, and which, in all its Grecian-inspired glory, decorated the music's title page.

The stock market was the subject of other music from time to time, including two or three pieces dedicated to the bulls and bears. In 1884 Joseph Poznanski wrote "The Bulls and Bears Galop," in 1894 there appeared a sinister little ditty called "The Man Who Broke the Brokers Down in Wall Street," and in 1901 R. M. Stults wrote "Bulls and Bears March and Two Step." The 1894 song, an unabashed parody of "The Man Who Broke the Bank at Monte Carlo," written by William Jerome and set to music by Dave Fitzgibbons, proclaimed:

> And when I walk along Broadway, I keep the sunny side;
> With lots of Yankee pride
> And a very English stride!
> The ladies' hearts go pit-a-pat,
> And people all take off their hats
> To the man who broke the brokers down in Wall Street!

But the "March of the 1/8 Brigade" must remain as a lone tribute—even with tongue in cheek—to the men who daily march, shout, wave, and fight the good fight on the floor of the New York Stock Exchange.

The Grand Army of the Republic

BY 1908 the ranks were thinning rapidly. The political threat that the veterans' organization had utilized for so many years, the power of a solid vote of four hundred thousand men and their followers, had wilted away, until only the respect for their past glory remained. But still they marched, thousands strong, at the Grand Army of the Republic's annual "encampment" in Toledo, Ohio, on September 3 and 4.

And the "Boys in Blue," as they were known ever since 1866, the year of the founding of the G. A. R., after the close of the Civil War, continued to live in the affections of the people. Songs were again sung about the aging veterans, a bit nostalgic now, but prideful too, as evidenced by one written by Duncan J. Muir for the occasion:

> Our soldiers again are marching
> To the rat-tat-tat of the drum,
> Up through the dusty village
> Our Vet'rans slowly come.
> They are old and bent and feeble,
> But their age-dimmed eyes today
> Flash as they did in the sixties
> When they gallantly marched away.

Our Soldiers Again are Marching

The G. A. R. Veterans of the "Sixties"

Song by

DUNCAN J. MUIR

5

THE S. BRAINARD'S SONS CO.

New York   Chicago

Our Soldiers Again Are Marching

Our sol-diers a-gain are march-ing To the rat-tat-tat of the drum, ———

Up through the dust-y vil-lage Our Vet'-rans slow-ly come,— They are old and bent and

fee-ble, But their age dimmed eyes to-day——— Flash as they did in the six-ties When they

gal-lant-ly marched a-way,——— Flash as they did in the six-ties When they gal-lant-ly

marched a-way.———

2. There were knapsacks on their shoulders,
And they marched with a warrior tread,
But now they are bearing flowers
For their comrades long since dead.
And so it will be wherever
There's a Vet'ran left to go
Marshalled by fife and drum beat
Where our heroes are lying low
Marshalled by fife and drum beat
Where our heroes are lying low.

So our soldiers again are marching
To the rat-tat-tat of the drum
Our pulses thrill as we hear it
Above the busy hum,
They are bearing their close-furled banner,
All tattered and battle torn,
The same that unfurled in the Sixties
To vict'ry was proudly borne,
The same that unfurled in the Sixties
To vict'ry was proudly borne.

The stirring music played "with martial spirit"—according to the notation under the author's signature—must have lifted the hearts of the elderly men who were closing ranks once more after forty years of battles fought on the political front rather than the field of war.

No group of lobbyists in this country ever wielded as much power for a single cause—namely, themselves—as did the G.A.R. At the height of their strength they were able, in half a dozen states, to place in Congress almost any man they wanted; and in the presidential campaign of 1884 one of their former commanders-in-chief was the Republican vice-presidential standard-bearer. Unfortunately for the Boys in Blue, that was the year when the Democrats nominated, for the first time, the astute governor of New York, Grover Cleveland.

The strength of the soldier vote was first apparent in 1864, when Abraham Lincoln was running for reelection, and when his followers were gravely concerned about the threat posed by his challenger, General George B. McClellan. They had believed the soldiers would cast an overwhelming vote for the general and possibly swing the election. Things did not work out that way. To the gratification of Lincoln, the army gave him 78 per cent of the military votes cast, which had a decided effect on the result of the election, for the nation as a whole gave Lincoln only 53 per cent of the popular vote, against 47 per cent for McClellan.

Lincoln had been able to exercise control over the various factions of the Republican party, but his successor, Andrew Johnson, lacked the skill required to prevent discord among the holders of diverse political points of view. Bitterest opposition to the new president came from the "radicals," who were determined to punish the southern whites and grant equality, political and economic, to the Negro. The radicals had, early in 1866, established a veterans' organization, the Soldiers' and Sailors' National Union League, through which they hoped to bring into the Republican fold the former members of the armed forces. But they were outmaneuvered by a new association which sprang up in Illinois under the skillful leadership of a handful of soldier-politicians with designs on furthering their own political ambitions. One was Richard J. Oglesby, governor of Illinois, who had won the rank of major general in the Union army, after a rapid rise and some severe wounds suffered in service. Another was General John Alexander Logan, a spellbinding orator and picturesque figure with beautiful flowing mustaches and long black hair, who had designs on a seat in the Senate. These two leaders were attracted by a plan, the concoction of an army doctor, Benjamin F. Stephenson, to organize a great benevolent veterans' society, which was to have the trappings of a secret order, with an oath of initiation, a ritual, passwords, grips, and signs. After various names for the organization had been suggested, the founders decided to call it the Grand Army of the Republic.

The first gatherings of the G. A. R. were in the rooms of Stephenson and a few of his associates. Stephenson accepted the position of commander, and on April 1, 1866, named his fellow officers and issued a charter for the society's first "post" in Decatur. A week later a second post was chartered in Springfield.

The secrecy of initiating a recruit was bound to impress him. The ritual contained no hint of any political purpose or pledge; it served only to recall wartime hatreds. Blindfolded, draped in a torn army blanket, the recruit knelt before a coffin, inscribed with the name of one of the victims of Andersonville, the Confederacy's most notorious war prison. On the coffin was a Bible and an American flag draped in mourning. The candidate, after an elaborate ceremony, took an oath, upon pain of punishment if he turned traitor, never to expose the secrets of the G. A. R. After promising to help his comrades in every possible manner and to "yield implicit obedience" to the local organization and to national headquarters, he was treated to some flowery remarks by the post commander which concluded with the conviction that if the soldiers held high positions in government, treason would "hide its repulsive head."

The ostensible purpose of the society was to seek special benefits for the men who had served the Union cause. Its declaration of principles indicated that the G. A. R. would strive to secure aid for needy or disabled veterans and provide for maintenance of the soldiers' families and for the education of their orphans. It would demand public recognition of the services and claims of the men; and above all it would insist upon allegiance to the United States and respect for its laws, "manifested by the discountenancing of whoever may tend to weaken loyalty, incite to insurrection, treason, or rebellion." What veteran could help but endorse such a plank? They flocked to sign up, first in Illinois, Indiana, and Ohio, then in every other state of the Union, one after another; they even enrolled memberships in the states which had seceded.

The first national convention, or "encampment," as it came to be known, was held in November, 1866, in Indianapolis. By this time the members of the G. A. R. had determined to call themselves the "Boys in Blue," and this nomenclature endured throughout the existence of the organization. The order announcing the convention even stated, explicitly, "All comrades are requested to wear the 'blue.'"

Directed skillfully by their commanders, the soldiers soon began to throw their political weight around. They were eagerly courted by the Republicans, and succeeded in including in the Republican platform of 1872 a plank stating that the nation had a sacred debt to the veterans, for whom they promised pensions along with the care of their widows and orphans. Heretofore these widows and orphans had received meager pensions, but the Boys in Blue were after more extensive returns. Their efforts were finally rewarded in 1878, when Congress passed a pension bill which directed a lump sum to be paid to each discharged Union soldier.

In every presidential campaign, the soldiers were recognized as voters with great potential for their candidates, and the Republicans capitalized on this by circulating songs appealing to veterans. In 1866, when Grant first ran for office, a pair of Ohio song writers, W. V. Lawrence and J. G. Dunlap, wrote a campaign song entitled "Boys in Blue," which they dedicated to the "Boys" and their supporters, and which went in part:

> Four years beneath that dear old flag,
> Now battle-stained and gory,
> Our leader marched, and toiled, and fought,
> And covered it with glory.
> With ballots now for bayonets,
> With Grant again to lead us,
> Those hearts that cheered through battles' storm,
> To victory now lead us.

> CHORUS: Ho! boys in blue, to duty true,
> Let not their threat'ning daunt you.
> Strike colors, foe, and learn to know
> No quarters we will *Grant* you.

In 1876 another song, this time in behalf of the new Republican candidate, Rutherford B. Hayes, was again dedicated to the "Boys in Blue." With music by one of the country's popular composers, H. P. Danks, and with words by S. N. Mitchell, the song, entitled "The Boys in Blue Will See It Through," declared:

> The Boys in Blue will see it through,
> And send to Washington
> The candidates who have been true,
> And have their laurels won;
> In Gen'ral Rutherford B. Hayes,
> We have an honest man.

357

James B. Garfield was the Republican standard-bearer in 1880, opposed by General Winfield Scott Hancock. Once more the G. A. R. endorsed the Republican in songs; in fact, a number of the campaign songs of that year were called the "Boys in Blue" series. One of them, "The Veteran's Vote," was composed by Charles Kunkel, a well-known musician from St. Louis. That city had a large German population, and the original words of the song were written in German, proclaiming, "*D'rum fuer Garfield ich muss sein.*" Translated, the chorus, denouncing Hancock, states:

> Once he wore the Union blue,
> Now he's donned the Rebel gray.
> I'm still to the Union true,
> Garfield is my man today.

Other music about and for the veterans was more sentimental, disregarding the political ambitions of the organization. In 1887, three years after their leader, John A. Logan, had failed in his bid for the vice-presidency of the United States, the annual encampment of the G. A. R. was the occasion for a song entitled "The Boys Who Wore the Blue." The "Boys" were sobering up now and contemplating their encroaching seniority:

> We're growing old, my comrades,
> Our faces once so fair
> Are seamed with many a wrinkle,
> Footprints of time and care.

> Chorus: Then give a cheer for those who're here,
> A tear for those who're past.
> Let hand clasp hand, and join the band,
> Our ranks are thinning fast.

And yet again, in 1895, a writer named W. C. Parker brought out "The Boys in Blue are Turning Gray," which he called modestly "A Song That Will Live Forever." This announcement was not quite accurate, but the words are touching, nevertheless:

> Peace to the fearless boys in blue,
> Who saved their country's sacred name,
> Whose dauntless deeds are graven deep
> On Honor's monuments of fame!
> Their ranks are daily growing less.
> The battle's din has died away;
> Their foes have vanished with the years;
> The boys in blue are turning gray!

The G. A. R.'s last encampment was held in 1949 in Indianapolis. Of the sixteen surviving members, only six were able to be present; the other ten old men were too infirm to attend. The Marine Corps Band serenaded them, and a commemorative stamp was issued for the occasion. Thousands of people lined the streets and cheered as the six aged gentlemen were taken, each in a separate automobile, to Monument Circle in the center of the city, while the television camera relayed the event to the nation. The Marine Band played "taps" to a misty-eyed crowd, and as the bugler's final notes faded away the six old men, honored by a military escort, were driven off again. It was as if they too had faded away.

The Unions

Ev'ry day that passes by, they increase and
    multiply,
The great knights, the noble knights of labor.
Let the millionaire reflect that their force
    cannot be check'd,
The great knights, the noble knights of labor.
In the Senate when they sit, all the frauds
    will have to git
Or they'll drive them from the country in a
    hurry;
Ev'ry dog has got his day; our mechanics want
    fair pay,
And in Union they will get it, don't you worry.

CHORUS: Oh, the great knights, the noble knights of labor
    The fine knights, the gallant knights of labor.
    'Till they treat our workmen fair, they will boycott
      ev'rywhere,
    The great knights, the noble knights of labor.

SO WROTE Will J. Hardman in 1886. Fifteen years earlier, nine journeymen tailors had met secretly in the American Hose Company hall in Philadelphia to start a new order. Their local Garment Cutters' Association had just dissolved because of lack of funds, yet the tailors had grand visions of a mighty new labor organization, a unified order which would make no discriminations against sex, color, religion, or nationality. It would be a secret society with an elaborate ritual, but it had no revolutionary doctrine and "no conflict with legitimate enterprise, no antagonism to necessary capital." It looked forward to the eventual "complete emancipation of the wealth producers from the thralldom, and loss of wage slavery." The tailors called their new organization the "Noble and Holy Order of the Knights of Labor." In order to protect the individual members from attack by their employers or by any antagonistic groups, secret rituals, such as those used by the Elks, Masons, and Odd Fellows were adopted. There were codes, ciphers, handclasps, and other rigamaroles destined to impress the members while concealing their identity on the outside. The number of craft unions in the order increased while their officials were rewarded with high-sounding titles like "Grand Master Workman" and "Venerable Sage." Within ten years the Knights had a membership of almost fifty thousand; by 1886 they were at their peak strength of seven hundred thousand. But before the end of 1887 they had lost all their effectiveness.

The workingman had had occasional favorable publicity in the nation's press; little of it in the nation's music. In 1877, Bobby Newcomb, a well-known singer and composer, had "come out" for the underdog in a sentimental song, "Don't Put the Poor Workingman Down." It went, in part:

> That money is root of all evil,
> Why all of us likely's found out,
> The richer class thinks that the poorer
> Should of pleasure know nothing about.
> The honest poor always will labor,
> They don't ask a title or crown.
> Why begrudge them sufficient to live on?
> Don't put the poor workingman down.

> CHORUS: Let capital shake hands with labor,
> Let the poor have the bread that they earn,
> For surely they need ev'ry penny,
> Is a lesson quite easy to learn.
> Remember the poor love their children,
> So give them a smile, not a frown,
> Live, and let live, be your motto.
> Oh! Don't put the poor workingman down.

During the 1880's the country suffered periods of hard times, causing widespread unemployment and a series of wage cuts in many industries. Thousands of workers resisted the cuts, and individual unions staged walkouts against their employers. Cotton spinners, miners, glassworkers, carpet weavers, and other skilled and unskilled operators struck their companies. Most of the strikes were crushed, but those in which the Knights of Labor participated were all, with one exception, successful.

Their greatest victory occurred in 1885, when they did battle with Jay Gould, the powerful financier who controlled the railroads of the southwest. That spring one of his roads, the Wabash, had begun to lay off employees who were members of the Knights of Labor. The Knights battled back. Those still employed by the Wabash were ordered out on strike, and they sabotaged Gould's other roads by stopping trains, uncoupling cars, and "killing" engines, with resulting violence and disorders.

The great Gould capitulated. He arranged to confer with the Knights, ended all discrimination against them, and endorsed the principle of labor unions. It was the Knights of Labor's greatest victory. Workers everywhere were singing:

> Toiling millions now are waking—
> See them marching on;
> All the tyrants now are shaking,
> Ere their power's gone.
> CHORUS: Storm the fort, ye Knights of Labor,
> Battle for your cause;
> Equal rights for every neighbor—
> Down with Tyrant laws!

So impressive were the victories that the laboring man seemed to be achieving, that the most popular team of singing comedians then on the New York stage, Edward Harrigan and Tony Hart, introduced a number called "No Wealth Without Labor" as part of their 1885 comedy, *The Grip*. With words by Harrigan and music by his regular collaborator, Dave Braham (Hart's father-in-law), the song went in part:

> The hand and the hammer are true loyal friends,
> Between them no quarrels arise;
> Oh, each on the other forever depends,
> To gain labor's sweet golden prize.
> The farmer, the blacksmith, and each working man,
> While toiling for comfort and joy,
> Remember the maxim, Oh, work all you can,
> No wealth without labor, my boy.
>
> CHORUS: Then cheer for the wage worker and toiler,
> He's the builder of home and joys,
> All riches must come after hard labor,
> There's no wealth without it, my boys.

Soon the Knights of Labor were to be in deep trouble. In 1881 six national unions and some local assemblies from the Knights of Labor founded the

"Federation of Organized Trade and Labor Unions of the United States and Canada." Although their resolutions included such problems as child labor laws, apprentice laws, abolition of prison labor, and exclusion of Chinese immigration, they were unable to replace the reigning Knights for their first five years of existence. But friction increased between the Knights and the craft unions which formed the core of the new federation's membership, particularly after the Knights refused to endorse the federation's move for the establishment of an eight-hour working day.

Such a move not only lent strength to the support of leaders of a new rival union, but it was the basis for another comic song, "I've Worked Eight Hours This Day," the words of which were included in an earlier book, *Flashes of Merriment* (University of Oklahoma Press, 1971).

In 1885 the railroad unions on some of Gould's lines struck again. This time Gould retaliated with strikebreakers and Pinkerton guards. When it developed that only one sixth of the forty-eight thousand employees on the Gould system had walked out, the tough railroad magnate refused them any concessions, and the union then ordered the men back to work.

Gould's success encouraged other employers to resist strikers. In the last half of 1886, one hundred thousand workers were involved in labor disputes and were for the most part wholly unsuccessful. Most disastrous was a strike called by the Knights against the Chicago stockyards, which collapsed when the union's leadership reversed its position and sent the men back to work. Within a year membership of the Knights of Labor had dropped by two hundred thousand. By 1893 their membership was down to about 10 per cent of their peak strength, and their effectiveness had completely evaporated.

The Federation of Organized Trade and Labor Unions had been leading a hand-to-mouth existence for five years, until a new face emerged on the scene. The face and small, compact figure was that of Samuel Gompers, a member of the Cigar Makers' Union. Gompers had come to America from England in 1863 at the age of thirteen and joined the union a year later. Always a realist, and always ambitious, he rose step by step, attaining the presidency of the International Cigar Makers' Union at twenty-nine. At thirty-three he was elected president of the Federation of Organized Trade and Labor Unions, an unsought honor, for the federation was at that time little more than a lame annual conference.

In 1886 the Knights of Labor, battling to maintain their position in the disintegrating labor field, decided to fight it out with the unions of the craftworkers for supremacy. These unions were not to be intimidated. In December they called a meeting at Columbus, Ohio. Along with representatives of the sinking "Federation" there were delegates of twenty-five labor groups, including the metalworkers, carpenters, cigar makers, typographers, and journeymen tailors. They banded together to form a new structure, the American Federation of Labor, and elected Gompers as its first president, a post he held until his death nearly forty years later.

The growth of the AFL was slow. Rivalry with the Knights of Labor was bitter, and attempts to heal breaches were unsuccessful. With a membership of about one hundred thirty-eight thousand at the outset, it took twelve years for that number to double. Along the way, the affiliates of the AFL were plagued with strikes, two of which were particularly disastrous.

In 1892 one of its strongest unions, the Amalgamated Association of Iron and Steel Workers, struck the Carnegie Steel plant in Homestead, Pennsylvania, in protest against a wage reduction. The company imported several hundred Pinkerton detectives to help them open the mill, and a pitched battle between strikers and Pinkertons ensued. When this proved of no help to the steel company, it called for assistance from the state, which sent in eight thousand National Guardsmen. Within five months from its inception the strike had completely collapsed, and its union had lost its power with the major companies in the steel industry.

Following the depression of 1893, the Pullman Palace Car Company was hard hit, and determined to lay off half its fifty-eight hundred workers in Pullman, Illinois, and cut the wages of the rest by 25 to 40 per cent. Business started to improve the following spring, and the company recalled two thousand workers, but made no upward adjustment in wages.

A committee of employees asked the company for consideration but was flatly refused, and three members of the grievance committee were discharged. During the hard months of the previous winter a great many pullman workers had been organized into locals of the American Railway Union. Now they struck Pullman. A sympathetic strike among union members tied up nearly every railroad in the middle west. But the 150,000 members of the American Railway Union were not powerful enough to withstand the might of federal troops sent to Chicago by President Cleveland on grounds that the strike had interfered with the delivery of mail. The one-sided struggle was quashed, the employees helpless after the turn of events.

One of the popular songs that emerged from the tragedy was "Ruined Through the Strike," with music by Stanley Clayton and words by Richard

Boyce. The title page pictures a train, with several cars off the tracks, while soldiers with fixed bayonets are everywhere. Published in Chicago in 1894, two of the verses, along with the chorus, follow:

> One day while with a crowd of men, and never meaning
>   harm,
> The soldiers fired into the crowd, and I—I lost an
>   arm!
> I lost an arm, but more than that, I lost my faith in
>   men,
> And never will I, in this world, possess that faith
>   again.
>
> And that is why you see me, sir! Disabled now, and
>   sad,
> With heart that's steeped in bitterness, and never
>   to be glad.
> I wonder sometimes, what is life, and where can be
>   my God?
> Perhaps I am to understand, when once beneath the
>   sod.

> CHORUS: We were ruined thro' the strike, O the weary tho't
>   of it;
> The long, weary strike, O the trouble brought of it.
> Waiting, hopeful of the morrow, that was but to
>   bring us sorrow,
> Pain and care is ev'rywhere. We were ruined by the
>   strike.

Samuel Gompers had not responded to a call from the trade unions that he call a general strike in sympathy with the Pullman workers. He had felt that the unions would be unwise to show hostility to the federal authority. Many labor leaders criticized him bitterly, but he withstood the charge of ultraconservatism and maintained his control of the Federation of Labor.

The Labor Day parade in 1896 was the occasion for a march written by H. C. Verner. The illustrated title page pictures columns of stiff-hatted, nattily dressed union men parading behind a cordon of heavy-set uniformed policemen, with billies thrown over the right shoulder. The chorus:

> Proudly we march on Labor day,
> With hearts so true, to guide the way.
> Steps light and free. Our banner's displayed,
> On "Labor Day Parade."

Dedicated to the fearless champion of organized labor

SAMUEL GOMPERS

President Am. Federation of Labor

STICK TO THE UNION. JACK.

TOM PLEADING WITH JACK.

THE STRIKE

UNION LABOR

SONG AND CHORUS

WORDS AND MUSIC
by JAMES L. FEENEY
Editor—International Bookbinder

JACK THE SCAB.

PUBLISHED BY THE TRADES UNIONIST PUBLISHING CO.
441-443 G STREET, N.W.
WASHINGTON, D.C.

Stick to the Union, Jack.

Tom and Jack were un-ion men, and side by side they toiled, In a fac-tory where the un-ion held full sway,— The firm de-ci-ded to re-sist the un-ion men's con-trol, And an-nounced a big re-duc-tion in their pay.— A meet-ing of the men was called, they vot-ed for a strike, Each man but Jack the un-ion's call did heed,— He proved un-faith-ful to his trust, a trait-or to the cause, But Tom his dear old friend with him did plead.——

Chorus

Stick to the un-ion, Jack, and it will stick by you, Don't des-ert the boys on strike, be loy-al, firm and true. Re-mem-ber now the vow you took, u-nit-ed we must stand, Stick to the un-ion, Jack, and lend a help-ing hand.

2. The men were idle many weeks, at last the strike was won,
And they all returned to work with spirits light,
But the one that proved a traitor, was shunned by every one,
For he had betrayed the cause he knew was right.

Deserted by his former friends, an outcast from them all,
His name disgraced he did regret the day,
He would not heed his friends advice, obey his union's call,
When Tom his friend so pleadingly did say:
CHORUS

Sam Gompers continued high in the saddle, as the twentieth century dawned. His picture graces the cover of a 1904 song written by James L. Feeney. Along with the likeness of Gompers are small vignettes illustrating the attitudes of union men; one sketch is entitled "The Strike," another "Jack the Scab." The song is "Stick to the Union, Jack," and is dedicated to "the fearless champion of organized labor, Samuel Gompers, President Am. Federation of Labor."

Here is the first verse, and the chorus:

> Tom and Jack were union men, and side by side
> they toiled,
> In a factory where the union held full sway.
> The firm decided to resist the union men's
> control,
> And announced a big reduction in their pay.
> A meeting of the men was called, they voted
> for a strike.
> Each man but Jack the union's call did heed,
> He proved unfaithful to his trust, a traitor
> to the cause,
> But Tom his dear old friend with him did plead:

> CHORUS: Stick to the union, Jack, and it will stick by you
> Don't desert the boys on strike, be loyal, firm
> and true.
> Remember now the vow you took, united we must
> stand,
> Stick to the union, Jack, and lend a helping hand.

Today, seventy years later, that song, and the other labor songs that preceded it, have an unworldly quality. Their words described a movement which was a far cry from the potent force which "Big Labor" has become. Pioneers like Samuel Gompers, calm, resourceful, pragmatic, served their purpose and enjoyed their day in the sun. The path they hewed has become a broad highway, traveled by many millions of hard-working, well-paid union men.

Tammany

TAMMANY was a seventeenth-century Indian chief, sachem of a tribe of Delaware Indians known as the Lenni-Lenape. William Mooney was an eighteenth-century paper hanger and upholsterer of New York City, a former soldier, charged at one time with deserting the American army during the Revolution. Fate willed that these two opposite-poled individuals should be connected irrevocably and eternally, for it was William Mooney who founded the Society of St. Tammany in 1789. The "saint" business was something of a mystery. In 1771 the late lamented chief made his debut as a saint in Pennsylvania (rumor had it that he was the first Indian chief to welcome William Penn in 1682) and was allotted a regular name day, May 1, later changed to May 12. He became the patron saint of the Pennsylvania troops in the Revolutionary War.

William Mooney, despite his shady army record, seems to have changed character completely. He became a fervidly patriotic American, and he conceived the new society as being "founded on the true and genuine principles of republicanism," holding as its objectives "whatever may tend to perpetuate the love of freedom, or the political advantages of this country." Lofty ideals, certainly. Mooney could not have foreseen how, eventually, his society would concentrate on "political advantages" and denigrate "love of freedom."

The society was a stratified organization, consisting of sachems, warriors, and hunters. Thirteen sachems represented the thirteen tribes of Tammany, corresponding to the thirteen original states. Chief of the chiefs was the Grand Sachem, specifically at Tammany's inception, William Mooney. In the early days, the president of the United States was made Great Grand Sachem, a chief cubed, as it were.

Every possible opportunity for a celebration was seized. There were numerous processions and parades, with members dressed like Indians. May 12, the fourth of July, and Columbus Day, October 12, were favorite days for extended celebrations. For twenty years numerous meetings were held at public houses, until the society, deciding that it needed a hall of its own, raised enough money to build one. The first Tammany Hall was erected in 1811 at Nassau and Franklin streets, New York City, the society reserving one room for its meetings on certain evenings, and renting out the rest of the building as a hotel.

The first man to make use of the Tammany Society politically was Aaron Burr. Burr was a candidate for president in 1800, at which time the New York vote was held to have a most important part. The presidential electors were chosen by the state legislators, so it was important that the men in the legislature be on the right side. Only substantial property owners, who represented but a small fraction of the population, were then enfranchised voters. Burr, with the aid of Matthew L. Davis, a Tammany sachem, set about to win them over. They were escorted into the wigwam, as Tammany Hall was called, and persuaded by one means or another to vote for legislators favorable to the Federalists, Burr's party. As a result, New York endorsed Burr for the presidency. He didn't prove to be the winning horse nation-wide; Jefferson had that honor, but Burr ran second, which gave him the vice-presidency.

From Burr's time until 1850 there was no single individual who exercised absolute control over Tammany. But in the late 1840's Fernando Wood, who had served a term in Congress, turned his thoughts toward the power vested in Tammany Hall. He wanted that power for himself, and set out to get it by negotiating with Tammany to nominate him for mayor. He won the nomination but lost the election.

He ran again, as Tammany's candidate in 1854, and this time he emerged the winner by 1,456 votes. Some of these were questionable, as for example those tabulated in the sixth ward, the "Bloody Sixth," where it was alleged that four hundred more votes had been cast than there were voters. Wood made a great show of enforcing those laws which would cause him to appear to the public as a man of strict integrity. He closed the saloons on Sunday; he arrested pickpockets; he clamped down on brothels and gambling houses; he kept the streets cleaner. These actions produced the desired result, he was renominated and reelected in 1856; the opposition claimed that ten thousand fraudulent votes had been cast for him.

Now began Wood's activities to make capital out of his position. He sold public offices to the highest bidder. He ordered street-cleaning contracts given to firms who would see that he shared in their fees. When 1,200 new ballot boxes were needed, Wood bought 4,000 at fifteen dollars apiece and received a hefty share of the profits.

But in another year Wood was ousted. He had almost doubled city taxes to a figure of nearly eight million dollars, a fair part of which Wood spent in ways profitable to himself. A too-long-patient citizenry assembled behind a rival candidate for the 1857 election and beat Wood by fewer than fourteen hundred votes. The winner, Daniel F. Tiemann, lasted for only one term; Wood reorganized his forces and was back in City Hall in 1859.

By this time a new power had begun to flex his biceps. William Marcy Tweed was a member of the city's board of supervisors, which appointed the registry clerks, who controlled the registry of voters and the balloting in their districts. The Tweed "Ring," as Tweed and his closest friends now became known, was formed originally by the Democrats on the board for the purpose of obtaining the appointment of inspectors of election.

Tweed had no use for Wood, and contrived to exclude him from influence with most of the registry clerks. Wood's reelection margin was small; Tweed had outmaneuvered him in the choosing of sachems for Tammany Hall and was to emerge as the most colorful of all the old-time bosses.

Tammany had made strenuous efforts to defeat Lincoln for the presidency in the 1860 election. Locally they were successful; Lincoln received 33,000 votes in New York City to Stephen A. Douglas' 62,000. Wood was still mayor then; and when it became apparent that the southern states were about to secede he sent an astounding message to the Common Council of New York City. He proposed that the city of New York likewise secede from the United States and establish Manhattan Island as a free and independent city state. He abandoned his position after Fort Sumter was fired upon, and climbed hurriedly on the Union band wagon.

Tammany Hall, now oriented against the mayor, issued its own patriotic proclamations and sent a Tammany regiment to join the Union forces. Both Wood and Tammany were defeated in the 1861 mayoralty election by a Republican, but the Tammany men were merely biding their time. Wood had now lost control, which was in the hands of Tweed and Peter B. Sweeney. On January 1, 1863, Tweed was made permanent chairman of the Tammany Society; and his star, now in the ascendant, burned brightly for almost ten years.

Soon he was given the title of "boss"; and as Boss Tweed he has been remembered. He had the physical attributes of a boss, too. Almost six feet tall, he weighed nearly three hundred pounds. A reddish brown beard and mustache ornamented his large-featured ruddy face. Most ordinary chairs were too small for the Tweed bottom, which required a resting place of gargantuan proportions.

When the "boss" chaired a committee, he acted the part of a despot. If, for example, he wished for approval of a matter, he would call only for affirmative votes, never asking for the negative response from its opponents. On one occasion, when he was chairman of a Tammany nominating convention, he declared the nomination of a certain candidate for judge unanimous, while the opposition protested violently. When Tweed declared the meeting adjourned, thirty delegates surged up to him to present a counternomination. Tweed's reply was direct and conclusive; he had the gas turned off.

By 1870, Tweed was an immensely rich man. In addition to his position on the board of election supervisors he was a state senator and deputy street commissioner. He had put his own man, A. Oakey Hall, in the mayor's chair, and with Hall's support controlled the awarding of contracts and the appointment of municipal servants. As for his "ring," it had been defined by an anonymous writer, who, when asked, "What is a Ring?", had defined it as "a hard band, in which there is gold all around and without end."

A popular composer and band leader of the period, C. S. Grafulla, capitalizing on Tweed's substantial following, composed in 1870 a quickstep, "Solid Men To the Front," which he dedicated to "Hon. William M. Tweed." A flattering portrait of Tweed, under a picture of Tammany Hall, graced the cover. The enormous diamond stud which the Boss was accustomed to wear had been omitted by the artist, who surrounded his subject with heroic symbols, including laurel wreaths, a liberty cap, a peace pipe, and the words "Local Sovereignty," "Chartered Rights," and "Good Faith Among Men." No rascal could have appeared more impressive than the noble-looking Tammany leader.

Tweed's end did come, however. Disclosures of enormous irregularities, unearthed by the *New York Times*, resulted in the formation of a large citizens' committee, which was able to force an investigation of municipal records. The extent of the corruption ran into tens of millions of dollars. Though Tweed had been reelected state senator in the fall of 1871, he was indicted for felony that December. Released on bail, his trial was held a year later, and he was sentenced to twelve years imprisonment. He served a year, then was released, only to be rearrested as the legislature authorized the institution of new civil suits. Held in the penitentiary on three-million-dollars bail, he was able to escape after several months. He fled to Cuba, then to Spain, where he was arrested and brought back to New York and to Ludlow Street jail, where he died in 1878.

Other powerful bosses—"Honest John" Kelly, Richard Croker, Charles Francis Murphy—followed Tweed; each wielded great power, but none exceeded Tweed's flamboyancy, and none had his overwhelming self-confidence.

Kelly shrewdly selected well-known reformers as sachems, such men as Samuel J. Tilden and Horatio Seymour, both later presidential candidates, but still managed to assess all officeholders a part of their salaries, which he used for his own ends.

Colorful Croker wound up his ten-year term by marrying, at seventy-three, a twenty-three year old Cherokee Indian girl, thereby bringing the first genuine Indian squaw into the wigwam.

A high spot in the career of Charlie Murphy was the culmination of his feud with Governor William Sulzer of New York. Tammany Hall nominated Sulzer in 1912 and helped him carry the state. But the governor refused to let Murphy dictate to him, and the unhappy result was the impeachment of Sulzer and his removal from office in 1912. Murphy thereafter regarded himself as not only a king-unmaker, but a king-maker, being instrumental in the nomination of James M. Cox for president in 1920, and planning the presidential nomination of Al Smith in 1924, a dream cut short by Murphy's sudden death in April of that year.

Song writers who selected Tammany as a theme were generally kind—possibly circumspect—when dealing with the subject. In 1905 a musical comedy, *In Tammany Hall*, was produced, featuring the rising young comedian Joseph Cawthorn. William Jerome and Jean Schwartz, one of the best-known words-and-music pair of their day, turned out the musical's songs, of which one of the catchiest was a lively waltz bearing the title of the show. Jerome wrote:

> The ballroom is crowded we're winners I guess,
> A night to remember, a great big success,
> Fifth Avenue jealous, I have to confess,
> The four hundred aint in it at all!
> The east-side is blazing with glory tonight
> The ladies are peaches, the music's all right,
> It's a good natured bunch, not a sign of a fight.
> It's a great night for Tammany Hall.

O. Henry and Franklin P. Adams teamed up to write the book and lyrics (A. Baldwin Sloane composed the music) of a 1909 musical called *Lo*, inferring that Lo was a poor Indian. But "Indians" brought Tammany to mind also, and one of the show's songs was called "Tammany on Parade." It went in part:

> March along to the rat-a-tat of the drums of Tammanee
> Hike, hike, hike along, Election day is growing nigh.
>
> . . . .
>
> Step, step, step along, the owners of the earth are we,
> Pay a lot of attention to those who march for Tammanee
> Tramp, tramp, tramp again and glory to the marching boys
> Hip! Hooray for Tammany, with a regular bunch of noise.[1]

By far the best-known of all the songs with this subject matter was "Tammany, a Pale Face Pow-Wow," written in 1905, with words by Vin-

Tammany

Hi-a-wa-tha was an In-dian, so was Nav-a-jo—— Pale-face or-gan grind-ers killed them man-y moons a-go—— But there is a band of In-dians, that will nev-er die,—— When they're at the In-dian club, this is their bat-tle cry:——

Chorus

Tam-ma-ny,—— Tam-ma-ny,—— Big Chief sits in his tep-ee, cheer-ing braves to vic-to-ry. Tam-ma-ny,—— Tam-ma-ny,—— Swamp 'em, Swamp 'em, get the "wam-pum," Tam-ma-ny.

2. On the Island of Manhattan, by the bitter sea,
   Lived this tribe of noble Redmen, Tribe of Tammany.
   From the Totem of the Green-light Wam-pum they would bring,
   When their big Chief Man Behind, would pass the pipe and sing:
   Chorus: Tammany, Tammany,
          Stick together at the poll, you'll have long green wam-pum rolls
          Tammany, Tammany,
          Politicians get positions, Tammany.

3. Chris Colombo sailed from Spain, across the deep blue sea,
   Brought along the Dago vote to beat out Tammany
   Tammany found Colombo's crew were living on a boat,
   Big Chief said: "They're floaters," and he would not let them vote.
   Then to the tribe he wrote:
   Chorus: Tammany, Tammany,
          Get those Dagoes jobs at once, they can vote in twelve more months.
          Tammany, Tammany,
          Make those floaters Tammany voters, Tammany.

4. Fifteen thousand Irishmen from Erin came across,
   Tammany put these Irish Indians on the Police force.
   I asked one cop, if he wanted three platoons or four,
   He said: "Keep your old platoons, I've got a cuspidor, What would I want
       with more?"
   CHORUS: Tammany, Tammany,
           Your policeman can't be beat. They can sleep on any street.
           Tammany, Tammany,
           Dusk is creeping, they're all sleeping, Tammany.

5. When Reformers think its time to show activity,
   They blame everything that's bad on poor old Tammany,
   All the farmers think that Tammany, caused old Adam's fall,
   They say when a bad man dies he goes to Tammany Hall, Tammany's blamed
       for all.
   CHORUS: Tammany, Tammany,
           When a farmer's tax is due, he puts all the blame on you.
           Tammany, Tammany,
           On the level you're a devil, Tammany.

6. Doctor Osler says all men of sixty we should kill,
   That would give old Tammany a lot of jobs to fill.
   They would chloroform old Doctor Parkhurst first I know
   After that they'd fix Tom Platt, because they love him so, And then Depew
       would go.
   CHORUS: Tammany, Tammany,
           When you chloroform to kill, don't forget old Dave B. Hill
           Tammany, Tammany
           Rope 'em, Rope 'em, and we'll dope 'em, Tammany

7. If we'd let the women vote, they would all get rich soon,
   Think how old man Platt gave all his money to a coon.
   Mrs. Chadwick is a girl, who'd lead in politics.
   She could show our politicians lots of little tricks, the Wall street
       vote she'd fix.
   CHORUS: Tammany, Tammany,
           Cassie Chadwick leads them all, she should be in Tammany Hall.
           Tammany, Tammany,
           Who got rich quick? Cassie Chadwick, Tammany.

8. Tammany's chief is digging out a railroad station here,
   He shuts off the water mains, on folks who can't buy beer,
   He put in steam shovels, to lay off the workingmen,
   Tammany will never see a chief like him again, He's the poor man's friend.
   CHORUS: Tammany, Tammany,
           Murphy is your big Chief's name, he's a Rothschild just the same.
           Tammany, Tammany,
           Willie Hearst will do his worst to Tammany.

cent Bryan and music by Gus Edwards, a felicitous combination of old pros. The music was as invigorating as an Indian war dance, and the words— well, here are some of them:

> Hiawatha was an Indian, so was Navajo,
> Paleface organ-grinders killed them many moons ago.
> But there is a band of Indians, that will never die,
> When they're at the Indian club, this is their battle cry:

CHORUS: Tammany, Tammany
> Big Chief sits in his tepee, cheering braves to victory.
> Tammany, Tammany,
> Swamp 'em, Swamp 'em, get the "wampum"
> Tammany.

There were eight verses, with appropriate choruses. Here's another example:

> Fifteen thousand Irishmen from Erin came across,
> Tammany put these Irish Indians on the Police force,
> I asked one cop, if he wanted three platoons or four,
> He said, "keep your old platoon, I've got a cuspidor,
> What would I want with more?

CHORUS: Tammany, Tammany,
> Your policemen can't be beat, They can sleep on any street
> Tammany, Tammany,
> Dusk is creeping, they're all sleeping,
> Tammany.

Peter Stuyvesant is said to have given the Indians twenty-four dollars worth of merchandise for Manhattan. Possibly the latter-day Indians in the Tammany wigwam felt that their pseudo ancestors were shortchanged. If so, there is no question but that their transactions with the New York City treasury completely reversed the procedure. To paraphrase the words of a great statesman, "Never has so gullible a government been so consistently robbed by so many unscrupulous scoundrels."

"Dr. Munyon"

IN THE EARLY YEARS of the twentieth century, the portrayal of a gentleman in a high collar, a straight bow tie, and a handsome pompadour, with right hand upraised and forefinger pointed to heaven, could bring to the minds of millions of Americans one well-known name, Dr. Munyon.

The United States Food and Drug Administration said that he was a quack and a humbug, and he was fined time after time for selling treatments for asthma, Bright's disease, catarrh, urinary troubles, and pain in the back. But this minor punishment apparently had no effect on the success of the doctor, who, if he could not clean out the systems of those who took his products, at least cleaned up financially.

He made millions, and he enjoyed both the use of his money and his marital and extramarital relations. His first three wives were legitimate. His fourth union was on a common-law basis and it was this fourth lady who got a good share of the doctor's accumulated wealth when he passed on.

If Dr. Munyon was a quack, he was one of the most solemn quacks who ever encouraged the public to invest in his wholesome remedies. He always dressed in black, and in every advertisement of his product he was shown with his right arm raised and the index finger pointing toward the sky. A typical advertisement of his products, showing the doctor in his customary stance, carried the words "by this sign we conquer" above the doctor's head, and below, "if the sign of the Cross were to be destroyed, the next best sign would be 'the index finger pointing heavenward'." Little wonder that the public was swayed by this overpowering message.

At any rate, Dr. Munyon proclaimed to his reading public, "Doctor yourself," and stated, "There is a Munyon pill for every ill." "No punishment is too severe for him who deceives the sick" was one of the doctor's favorite statements.

His remedies were homeopathic. He had wanted to call them "specifics," but another doctor had had the same idea before Munyon, so Munyon stuck to the word "cure." "Cure" was good enough for the folks who trusted in him. The fact that much of the "cure" had a sugar base, with infinitesimal quantities of medicinal agents, appealed to the taste buds of the healing public. The label bearing the doctor's picture on his rheumatism cure bears only the words "it will cure rheumatism." That was enough to sell it.

Eventually his advertising caught up with him. In case after case, the government chemists analyzed his "known asthma cure," which he stated would "permanently cure asthma," as consisting of sugar and alcohol. The shipment of Munyon's blood cure, when analyzed by the government chemists, turned out to be simply sugar pills. But Munyon stated that they would "positively cure all forms of Scrofula, Erysipelas, Salt Rheum, Eczema, Pimples, Syphilitic Affections, Mercurial Taints, Blotches, Liver Spots, Tetter and all skin diseases." In each case of misrepresentation Munyon, when charged, pleaded guilty and was fined $200. This left him with plenty of net profit, so he had no serious complaint to make.

He did a good job in Great Britain, too, principally with Munyon's pile ointment. The label offered unlimited promises of permanent relief for this

Dr. Munyon

SONG

WORDS BY
VINCENT BRYAN
MUSIC BY
E. RAY GOETZ

5

HARRY BULGER

JEROME H. REMICK & Co
NEW YORK   DETROIT

Doctor Munyon.

There is a doc-tor in this land and he is wond-'rous wise— His rem-e-dies cure ev-'ry ill

that na-ture can de-vise,— We real-ly ought to send for him, we need him I am sure— For

Chorus

we are troub-led with com-plaints that no one else can cure—— Doc-tor Mun-yon, Doc-tor

Mun-yon, what are we going to do—— we need you it's true,—— bring your med-i-cine

chest with you.—— If you'll fix up our com-plaints, the first thing to at-tack— Is to cure the

girl who wears her bon-net half way down her back

2. Good Doctor Munyon always tells his patients there is hope,
   There's not much hope for anyone that studies racing dope.
   We get a sure thing tip to play a horse at five to three
   The horse we play don't come in until after six you see
   CHORUS: Doctor Munyon, Doctor Munyon, what are we going to do,
         We need you it's true, bring your medicine chest with you.
         Cure the man who writes the tips the papers give us free
         Tho' they think they know what horse will win, they're
               crazy as can be.

3. Dress makers say that women's gowns will all be straight this fall
   They mean that fashionable girls wont show their hips at all
   Since this decree society is in an awful state
   For Newport will be very dull with all the women straight.
   CHORUS: Doctor Munyon, Doctor Munyon, what are we going to do,
         We need you it's true, bring your medicine chest with you,
         If the ladies won't wear hips, why ev'ry body knows
         You will have to cure the fat girls or they can't wear any
               clothes.

4. We ride upon our surface cars at six o'clock each night,
   We grab a strap, if we're in luck, there's not a seat in sight.
   The men who run the trolley roads tell us there's room to spare,
   And when we say we need more cars, we're crazy they declare.
   CHORUS: Doctor Munyon, Doctor Munyon, what are we going to do,
          We need you it's true, bring your medicine chest with you.
          Can it be we're going blind, oh, help us we entreat,
          For when we get on a trolley car, we cannot see a seat.

5. Good old John D was brought to court, they gave him quite a fine,
   For out of all his millions they have fined him twenty-nine,
   It worries him so much he only eats four meals a day,
   It was alright to fine poor John, but who can make him pay?
   CHORUS: Doctor Munyon, Doctor Munyon, what are we going to do,
          We need you it's true, bring your medicine chest with you.
          Give John D a sleeping powder when he goes to dine,
          For he'll have to be unconscious or he'll never pay that fine.

6. There are a lot of editors who fear the thoughts of war,
   Their papers want our battleships to shun our western shores,
   Tho' Uncle Sam can hold his own in any kind of scraps,
   These papers think we aught to crawl before the little Japs
   CHORUS: Doctor Munyon, Doctor Munyon, what are we going to do,
          We need you it's true, bring your medicine chest with you.
          Help these weak kneed editors and fixe their nerves up, please,
          For they seem to think that Uncle Sam can't fix the Japanese.

7. For years and years the Yankee girl as beauty's queen was crowned,
   A type of healthy womanhood no better could be found
   But since the Gibson girl is here we're worried it is true,
   She wears a blank expression, and her back is crooked too.
   CHORUS: Doctor Munyon, Doctor Munyon, what are we going to do,
          We need you it's true, bring your medicine chest with you.
          Fix those Gibson cripples and their monumental curls,
          Take the bends out of their backs, so they can walk
             like human girls.

8. They've got an innovation now in this land of free,
   A man who doesn't like his wife, finds his affinity,
   Affinities are nice young things that haven't any pride,
   But if this isn't stopped at once, 'twill cause race suicide.
   CHORUS: Doctor Munyon, Doctor Munyon, what are we going to do,
          We need you it's true, bring your medicine chest with you,
          Cant you fix a pill at once to cure all wives who scold,
          Or the men will find affinities and marriage will be cold.

9. Republicans can't find a president for nineteen eight,
   They're looking all around to get a good strong candidate,
   They say that Fairbanks is too thin, I'm told he drinks at that,
   And Secretary Taft won't do, because he is too fat
   CHORUS: Doctor Munyon, Doctor Munyon, what are we going to do,
          We need you it's true, bring your medicine chest with you,
          Can't you train somebody up to fit in Roosevelt's shoes,
          Or we'll make him run again because there's no one
             else to choose

unpleasant condition. When the *British Medical Journal* reported an analysis of the ointment, it estimated that one ounce of the cure cost one farthing (½ cent) to produce. It sold in England for one shilling (24 cents) a package, but the public loved him and continued to buy.

Munyon advertised not only in the newspapers and magazines, but he gave away song sheets with his picture on them. However, the song writers of the day were aware of his enormous power on the public. In 1907 two of tin-pan alley's top members, E. Ray Goetz and Vincent Bryan, wrote a song lampooning Dr. Munyon. It was a hit. They kidded the doctor unmercifully, indicating that his pills could cure every ill in the world. For example this verse about horse races:

> Good Doctor Munyon always tells his patients
>   there is hope
> There's not much hope for anyone that studies
>   racing dope,
> We get a sure thing tip to play a horse at
>   five to three
> The horse we play don't come in until after
>   six you see.

> CHORUS: Doctor Munyon, Doctor Munyon, what are we going to do
>   We need you it's true,
>   Bring your medicine chest with you.
>   Cure the man who writes the tips the papers give us free
>   Tho' they think they know what horse will win,
>   They're crazy as can be.

And another one about the trolley cars:

> We ride upon our surface cars at six o'clock
>   each night,
> We grab a strap, if we're in luck, there's not
>   a seat in sight,
> The men who run the trolley roads tell us there's
>   room to spare,
> And when we say we need more cars, we're crazy
>   they declare.

> CHORUS: Dr. Munyon, Dr. Munyon, what are we going to do,
>   We need you it's true,
>   Bring your medicine chest with you,
>   Can it be we're going blind, oh, help us we entreat,
>   For when we get on a trolley car, we cannot see a seat.[2]

2 "Dr. Munyon." W/Vincent Bryan M/E. Ray Goetz © 1907 Jerome H. Remick & Co. Copyright Renewed. All Rights Reserved. Used by Permission WARNER BROS. MUSIC.

Munyon always lived in style and he also died in style, at a luncheon table in the Royal Poinciana Hotel in West Palm Beach. If he had been able to die as he liked, probably just before his final collapse he would have raised his index finger toward the sky and uttered, "There is hope."

When America is Captured by the Japs

ONCE UPON A TIME there lived in America a man named Matthew C. Perry. He was a sailor; as a matter of fact, he was a commodore in the United States Navy. The United States wanted some favors of Japan. They desired permission for their sailing vessels to enter Japanese ports to replenish their stores and to take on water; their steamships needed coaling stations. But Japan kept saying no, no, not only to the Americans but to the Europeans who wanted to trade with them. Japan had always liked living alone; white foreigners were strictly taboo. So Commodore Perry was ordered to reorient the thinking of our closest oriental neighbors on the other side of the Pacific. He paid his first call in July, 1853, in big steam-powered, gun-toting vessels. The Japanese, who had never seen a steamship before, were mightily impressed, and within a year had signed a port-opening, trade-regulating treaty with the United States.

Half a dozen years later the two countries had ambassadors functioning in each other's capitals. The Japanese in Washington were well received. Probably the most popular man in the embassy was one of its official interpreters, Onojiro Tateishi, who seems to have ingratiated himself to such an extent that in 1860 a popular musician wrote a polka in his honor. "Tommy Polka," by Charles Grobe, one of the most prolific composers of the period, was dedicated to "Tateish Onogero" or "Tommy" as the interpreter was known to his American friends. A brief verse precedes the opening bars of the music:

> Wives and maids by scores are flocking
> Round that charming little man,
> Known as Tommy, witty Tommy,
> Yellow Tommy, from Japan.

The striking lithograph on the title page is a portrait of Tommy in handsome kimono surveying the artist warily but with a display of confidence and dignity.

Had Perry, the mighty conqueror, lived another half century, he would have witnessed miraculous changes in Japan's development. And the imagination of the American public was stirred by a song written in 1905 with the astounding title, "When America Is Captured by the Japs." How in the world could such a preposterous possibility enter our minds? To set the background, we must retrace our steps a few years.

Soon after Perry had made Japan aware of the strength of occidental civilization, the young scions of important Japanese families began to travel to England, France, the United States, and elsewhere to acquire groundings in the subjects in which each country was most outstanding. Law, commerce, military skills, all were grasped eagerly and efficiently by the bright young orientals. Soon they were putting this newly acquired knowledge to good use. A Diet, or Parliament, was established, a universal educational system was developed, and a form of military conscription was put into practice. It took only a few decades to make of the Japanese a fanatically nationalistic people, ready to fight and die for their emperor.

This they proceeded to do, exploiting the military weakness of China, then of Korea, and then in 1894 of China again, this time over the control of Korea, a country China had considered as a tributary. This last encounter followed a formal declaration of war by China. In a series of military and naval engagements Japan proved far superior to her adversary, who was finally obliged to sue for peace. Japan came out way ahead on the peace terms, which included the establishment of Korea as a free and independent country, and the ceding of Formosa (now Taiwan) and other islands to the victor.

But Russia was never far away from the center of the picture, and now she intruded more and more, threatening to assume a controlling position in Korea and laying a foundation for the takeover of Manchuria, China's great northern province, in which Japan had important commercial interests. Official communications between the two powers were exchanged early in February, 1904, but there was no real attempt at a peaceful solution. Diplomatic relations with Russia had been severed by the Japanese on February 5, a few days before the exchange of the formal notes. In fact, a day before Japan's official statement was made public, her navy was steaming toward Port Arthur, the headquarters of Russia's Asian fleet. War was to be declared by each country practically simultaneously on February 10, but the Japanese navy did not wait for that declaration to begin its engagement with the enemy. She landed several thousand soldiers at a Korean port, while her six battleships and ten armored cruisers, headed for the Russian naval base, opened fire, and sank three vessels of the Russian fleet.

The years 1904–1941, Port Arthur–Pearl Harbor. Strange that the tragedy at Pearl Harbor bore such a fatal resemblance to the battle of Port Arthur; in each case the surprise attack came first, the declaration of war later.

At any rate, the Japanese never relaxed the pressure on the Russian navy. Throughout the spring and summer they harassed their foe, while their army in Korea advanced steadily against the Russian positions. Port Arthur had been under siege for months, and in January, 1905, capitulated.

In February President Theodore Roosevelt offered his services to the belligerents in the hope of bringing them together to discuss peace terms. Russia would have none of this, not yet at any rate. Her reluctance proved costly; a great naval battle in the sea of Japan took place in May, and the Russians suffered a shattering defeat, losing twenty-two vessels and twelve thousand men out of a complement of eighteen thousand.

Fortunately for the combatants, Roosevelt persisted in his efforts to call a peace conference, and early in the summer of 1905, Japan and Russia agreed to send their representatives to Washington to work out the terms. The meeting took place in August at Portsmouth, New Hampshire, the climate in Washington—decades before air conditioning—being deemed too torrid for the effective conduct of negotiations.

By the end of August the details developed by the president had been approved by both belligerents, and the treaty of peace was signed on September 5. Roosevelt was a world hero. Messages of congratulations poured in, not only from the Czar of Russia and the Emperor of Japan, but from crowned heads and leading citizens of many countries.

Through it all Roosevelt was very calm. A voluminous writer, he was modest in accepting tributes. In a letter to his brother-in-law he said, "Don't be misled by the fact that just at the moment men are speaking well of me. They will speak ill soon enough. . . . Sometime soon I shall have to spank some little brigand of a South American Republic, and then all the well-meaning idiots will turn and shriek that this is inconsistent with what I did with the Peace Conference, whereas it will be exactly in line with it in reality."

As for the writers of popular music, they joined in the general acclaim for the president. Marches entitled "The Peacemaker"—with Roosevelt's likeness on the title page—"The Peace Conference," and "The Treaty of Peace," the last dedicated to "Our Honored President, Theodore Roosevelt," made rapid appearances.

Irving J. Morgan, a Philadelphian, was the first song writer on the peace scene. His song, "Roosevelt, the Peace Victor," bears this printed announce-

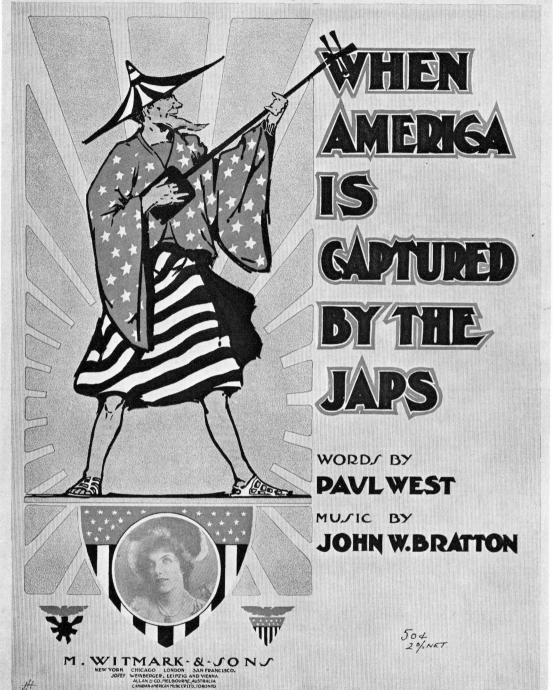

When America is Captured by the Japs.

Ev'ry day you read in pa-pers of the Jap-an-e-sy cap-ers, They have chlo-ro-formed the

Rus-sians and ju-jit-sued all their foes. They have taught us all a les-son, They've got ev-ry-bo-dy

guess-in' Now they've caught the fuss-ing fev-er, where they'll stop no-bo-dy knows. When they've

fin-ished up with Rus-sia They may take a whack at Prus-sia, Take the King of Eng-land pris-'ner and the

oth-er po-ten-tates, Then with cries of bat-tle fran-tic, sail a-cross the broad At-lan-tic, And be-

Chorus

fore we see them com-ing, grab the big U-nit-ed States. When A-mer-i-ca is cap-tured by the

Japs,—— We will car-ry fans and live on rice per-haps,—— When the yel-low fel-lows own us, We

will have to wear Kim-o-nos, Jer-sy Ci-ty will be strick-en from the maps,—— Doc-tor Park-hurst

then can soft-ly fade a-way,—— For the Japs won't un-der-stand a word he'll say —— And the

2. When the Japs begin to hustle they will worry Uncle Russel,
   And I pity Rockefeller, Gates and Mister Morgan then;
   For the only kind of money will be Japanese, it's funny,
   And instead of Morgan's dollars he won't have a single yen.
   Oh, the beef trust will be busted,
   The tobacco trust disgusted,
   We will eat no beef, we'll quit cigars and Opium smoke instead,
   And in place of beer and whiskey we'll drink saki till we're frisky,
   And Chicago men who eat with knives on chopsticks will be fed.
   When A—
   CHORUS: merica is captured by the Japs,
           Harry Lehr will have to go to work perhaps,
           Bakebean Boston, like St. Louis, Will exist, upon chop sooey,
           All the coons will play fantan instead of craps.
           In the papers we may find some news thats true,
           Some new jokes from old Japan for C. Depew,
           They will bring jinrickshaws for us,
           No more autos running o'er us,
           When American is captured by the Japs

3. When each railway guard's a Jappy we'll be satisfied and happy,
   For the trains will run on schedule and there'll be no strikes at all.
   On the Russians they've been proving They can keep a crowd a-moving,
   And perhaps we'll understand them when the station names they call.
   There'll be shop girl Japs at Macy's, Who won't look with frozen faces
   At the timid lady shopper, till she's too afraid to speak,
   Mary Ann and Katie Karney can go back to old Killarney,
   For the Japs will do our cooking and they'll stay at least a week,
   When A—
   CHORUS: merica is captured by the Japs,
           There will be no grafting senators, perhaps,
           We'll belong to Yokohama, Our next may'r will be Oyama,
           And the legislature won't be run by yaps.
           Oh, the women's hats won't bankrupt all the men,
           For like Jap girls they will go bare headed then,
           Men will never bet on horses,
           There will be no more divorces,
           When America is captured by the Japs.

4. Oh, our troubles all will cease when we get Japanese policemen,
   Who can capture crooks and burglars and be sometimes on the square,
   We'll have Japanesy cabman, Not the kind who up and grab men
   Or will hit you with blackjack if you won't pay double fare,
   We'll have Japs for railroad porters Who'll deserve our dimes and quarters
   If they carry our valises as they've carried on the war.
   And perhaps we will be happy when each motorman's a Jappy
   Who will pay us some attention when we hail a trolley car.
   When A—
   CHORUS: merica is captured by the Japs,
           They will write new comic operas, perhaps,
           They'll import new prima donnas, To achieve our coin and honors,
           And our tenors all will be wiped off the maps.
           They will make a rule that women shan't hold straps
           But always must sit right down upon our laps,
           Oh, the moth'r-in-law they'll banish,
           Make all bill collectors vanish
           When America is captured by the Japs.

ment: "This song is preeminently the first national song composed upon this subject, being written upon the inspiration of the moment and completed by nine o'clock on the day of the very first morning 'Peace' was publicly declared:—Aug. 30, 1905." The song goes in part:

> What's the Greatest Ruler's Name?
> It is "Roosevelt", we all claim;
> And he rules the Greatest Nation, 'neath the sun:
> Japs and Russians, all Hurrah!
> The Great Statesman, "Theodore"!
> Our beloved President at Washington!
>
> The Mikado, and the Czar,
> Are surprised at what we are;
> And they daily ask the question, "Can it be",
> That the great United States,—
> Is the Ruler of our Fates
> In these lands so far across the deep blue sea.

Nineteen five was the year for the introduction of popular songs, and even musical comedy, based on the newest popular subject, Japan. The great Negro words-and-music team of Bob Cole and J. W. Johnson presented a Japanese love song, "My Lu Lu San." The first verse indicated a *Madame Butterfly* theme.

> In the flowery kingdom of Japan,
> Close by the Inland Sea,
> Lived a cute little maiden named Lu Lu San,
> Pretty as the pictures on a Japanese fan,
> Oh! a dainty little maid was she.
> And there was a sailor on a Yankee ship,
> That sailed into port one day,
> Who lost no time when he saw Lu San,
> But he said to her right away:
>
> CHORUS: My Lu Lu San, You'll do Lu San
> Would you be true Lu San,
> True to a Yankee man?

Unlike Lieutenant Pinkerton, this Yankee seems to have stuck to the girl.

Then came Richard Carle, one of the great comedians of his time, to write the book and the lyrics of a musical comedy called *The Mayor of Tokio*. The music was the work of a seasoned hack of the period, William Frederick Peters. "Tokio" was the title of the best-known of the songs. Sung by a tourist from America, one of the verses goes:

Ev'ry breeze that scents the trees
Is very sweet but makes you sneeze
In Tokio, Dear Tokio.
And the rice is almost nice
But just a soupcon will suffice
In Tokio, Fair Tokio.
All the girls are sweet and charming
And the men are not so bad,
When they squeeze you in their oriental way.
But they stop if you say "Oh, Sir,
I'm a lady let me go Sir"
Not a bit like my native U.S.A.

But the song which captured the imagination of the crowd was one written by two experienced and imaginative writers named Paul West and John W. Bratton. Each had many successes to his credit. Bratton had composed "The Sunshine of Paradise Alley," "I Love You in the Same Old Way," and scores of others. West's output included "I Wants Dem Presents Back" and the lyrics for *The Merry Go Round*, a turn-of-the-century musical. Together they had written "My Boy Bill," and the songs in several musical comedies, among them *The Newlyweds and Their Baby*.

This time they seized on their fellow Americans' proclivity to take sides in a fight which was none of their business; it seemed that everyone in the United States was rooting for the Japanese, and when they showed their superiority the people of this country were delighted. So West and Bratton got together for a humorous fantasy called, "When America Is Captured by the Japs." Its rib-digging verses and choruses take not-so-subtle blasts at the annoyances and idiosyncrasies of the United States of 1905. They prophesy the end of the American multimillionaires. They see the downfall of the trusts, even burlesque's "beef trusts." They predict that opium will supplant cigars, and saki whisky. The idle rich of "The Four Hundred" will go to work (is that bad?). Bostonians will have to give up beans and cultivate a taste for chop suey. Chauncey Depew, the veteran statesman and famous teller of old jokes, will get new ones from Japan. Jinrickshaws will supplant automobiles. The trains will all run on time, and when the conductor calls the name of a station his diction will be understandable. The Japanese shopgirls will pay attention to the lady shoppers. We will have honest policemen. All in all, it will be a far, far better country. But here is Paul West:

Ev'ry day you read in papers
of the Japanesy capers,

They have chloroformed the Russians
And jujitsued all their foes.
They have taught us all a lesson,
They've got ev'ry body guessin'.
Now they've caught the fussing fever,
Where they'll stop nobody knows.
When they've finished up with Russia,
They may take a whack at Prussia,
Take the King of England pris'ner
And the other potentates,
Then with cries of battle frantic,
Sail across the broad Atlantic,
And before we see them coming,
Grab the big United States.

CHORUS: When America is captured by the Japs,
We will carry fans and live on rice perhaps,
When the yellow fellows own us,
We will have to wear Kimonos.
Jersey City will be stricken from the maps.
Dr. Parkhurst then can softly fade away,
For the Japs won't understand a word he'll say
And the showgirls, goodness gracious,
Will be driven out by geishas,
When America is captured by the Japs.

"Dr. Parkhurst" was the Rev. Charles Henry Parkhurst, a well-known Presbyterian clergyman, a caustic critic of public corruption.

Here's another sample:

Oh, our troubles all will cease when
We get Japanese policemen
Who can capture crooks and burglars
And be sometimes on the square.
We'll have Japanesey cabmen,
Not the kind who up and grab men
Or will hit you with a blackjack
If you won't pay double fare.
We'll have Japs for railroad porters
Who'll deserve our dimes and quarters,
If they carry our valises
As they've carried on the war.
And perhaps we will be happy
When each motorman's a Jappy
Who will pay us some attention
When we hail a trolley car.

CHORUS: When America is captured by the Japs,
Harry Lehr will have to go to work perhaps.
Bakebean Boston, like St. Louis,
Will exist upon chop suey . . . .
They will bring jinrickshaws for us,
No more autos running o'er us,
When America is Captured by the Japs.

What innocent fun, in a country blissfully free from foreign entanglements and foreign wars!

Enjoy the attractive little Japanese. Say boo to the hapless Russians. Sing your artless humorous songs. And sleep peacefully. The nineteen seventies, with their threatening catastrophes, their dread confrontations, are undreamed of, far over history's horizon, two generation gaps away. And halfway there, there will even be another Roosevelt. Who's afraid?

BIBLIOGRAPHY

Alderson, Bernard. *Andrew Carnegie: The Man and His Work*. New York, Doubleday, Page and Co., 1902.

Alsop, E. Bowles. *The Greatness of Woodrow Wilson, 1856–1956*. New York and Toronto, Rinehart and Co., 1956.

American Antiquarian Society. New Series. Vol. XIX, April 15, 1908, April 21, 1909, Worcester, Mass. Published by the Society.

American Medical Association. *Nostrums and Quackery*. Articles on the nostrum evil and quackery reprinted, with additions and modifications, from the *Journal* of the American Medical Association. 2d ed. Chicago, 1912.

Arizona: The Grand Canyon State. Compiled by the Workers of the Writers' Program of the Works Projects Administration in the State of Arizona. rev. ed. New York, Hastings House, 1940 (1956).

Automobile Manufacturers Association, Inc. *Automobiles of America*. Detroit, Wayne State University Press, 1968.

Avery, Catherine B., ed. *The New Century Classical Handbook*. New York, Appleton-Century Crofts, 1962.

Baldwin, Hanson W. *Sea Fights and Shipwrecks: True Tales of the Seven Seas*. Garden City, Hanover House, 1955.

Beath, Robert Burns. *History of the G. A. R.* New York, Taylor & Co., 1889.

Becker, Stephen. *Comic Art in America: Social History of the Funnies, the Political Cartoons, Magazine Humor, Sporting Cartoons and Animated Cartoons*. New York, Simon and Schuster, 1959.

Beesley, Lawrence. *The Loss of the S.S.* Titanic: *Its Story and Its Lessons*. Boston and New York, Houghton Mifflin Co., 1912.

Begbie, Harold. *The Life of General William Booth, the Founder of the Salvation Army*. Vol. II. New York, The Macmillan Co., 1920.

Bell, H. C. F. *Woodrow Wilson and the People*. Garden City, Doubleday, Doran and Co., 1945.

Benet, William Rose. *The Reader's Encyclopedia*. 2d ed. New York, Thomas Y. Crowell Co., 1965.

Bishop, Joseph Bucklin. *Theodore Roosevelt and His Time*. 2 vols. New York, Charles Scribner's Sons, 1920.

Black, Archibald. *The Story of Flying*. New York and London, McGraw-Hill Book Co., 1940.

Braithwaite, David. *Fairground Architecture*. London, Hugh Evelyn Limited, 1968.

British Olympic Association. *Fourth Olympiad: Being the Official Report of the Olympic Games of 1908 Celebrated in London under the Patronage of His Most Gracious Majesty, King Edward VII and by the International Olympic Committee*. London, 1908.

Bruno, Harry. *Wings over America: The Inside Story of American Aviation*. New York, Robert M. McBride & Co., 1942.

Buchanan, Lamont. *Steel Trails and Iron Horses: A Pageant of American Railroading*. New York, G. P. Putnam's Sons, 1955.

———. *The Story of Football in Text and Pictures*. New York, Stephen Paul Publishers, 1947.

"Building a Modern Railroad," *The Reading*. Philadelphia, Reading Lines, 1958.

Burleigh, Bennet. *Empire of the East*. London, Chapman and Hall, 1905.

———. *The Old Colony Railroad: Its Connections, Popular Resorts and Fashionable Watering Places*. Boston, Press of Read Avery & Co., 1875.

Butler, Frank M. *Book of the Boardwalk and the Atlantic City Story*. Atlantic City, The 1954 Association.

Butt, Archibald W. *Taft and Roosevelt: The Intimate Letters of Archie Butt, Military Aide*. Vol. I. Garden City, Doubleday, Doran & Co., 1930.

Carnegie, Andrew. *A League of Peace*. Boston, Ginn and Co., 1906.

———. *Autobiography*. Boston and New York, Houghton Mifflin Co., 1920.

———. *Problems of Today: Wealth—Labor—Socialism*. New York, Doubleday, Page and Co., 1909.

Carr, Albert Z. *John D. Rockefeller's Secret Weapon*. New York, McGraw-Hill Co., 1962.

Carson, Gerald. *One for a Man, Two for a Horse: A Pictorial History, Grave and Comic, of Patent Medicines*. Garden City, Doubleday & Co., 1961.

Caruso, Dorothy. *Enrico Caruso: His Life and Death*. New York, Simon and Schuster, 1945.

Casson, Herbert N. *The History of the Telephone*. Chicago, A. C. McClurg & Co., 1910.

Catt, Carrie Chapman, and Nettie Rogers Shirler. *Women Suffrage and Politics*. New York, Charles Scribner's Sons, 1926.

Chambers, Robert W. "Ave atque Vale, Gibson," *Collier's*, October, 1905.

Clarke, Thomas Curtis, and John Bogart. *The American Railway: Its Construction, Development, Management, and Appliances*. New York, Charles Scribner's Sons, 1892.

Cleveland, Reginald M., and S. T. Williamson. *The Road Is Yours*. New York, The Greystone Press, 1951.

Clymer, Floyd. *Treasury of Early American Automobiles*. New York, McGraw-Hill Book Co., 1950.

Coates, Thomas F. G. *The Prophet of the Poor: The Life Story of General Booth*. New York, E. P. Dutton and Co., 1906.

Condit, Carl W. *The Rise of the Skyscraper*. Chicago, University of Chicago Press, 1952.

Cone, John Frederick. *Oscar Hammerstein's Manhattan Opera Company*. Norman, University of Oklahoma Press, 1966.

Coon, Horace. *American Tel and Tel: The Story of a Great Monopoly*. New York and Toronto, Longmans, Green and Co., 1939.

Cosmopolitan magazine. Vol. LI (September, 1911), 507–11; Vol. LV (June, 1913), 126–27.

Couperie, Pierre, and Maurice C. Horn. *History of the Comic Strip*. Trans. by Eileen B. Hennessy. New York, Crown Publishers, 1968.

Cramp, Arthur J., M. D. *Nostrums and Quackery and Pseudo-Medicine*. Vol. III. Chicago, Press of American Medical Association, 1936.

Craven, Thomas, ed. *Cartoon Cavalcade*. New York, Simon and Schuster, 1943.

Crowther, Samuel. *John H. Patterson: Pioneer in Industrial Welfare*. Garden City, Doubleday, Page & Co., 1923.

Cutright, Paul Russell. *Theodore Roosevelt, the Naturalist*. New York, Harper and Brothers, 1956.

Daiken, Leslie. *Children's Toys Throughout the Ages*. London, B. T. Batsford, 1953.

Dairs, Robert H., and Arthur B. Maurice. *The Caliph of Bagdad: Being Arabian Nights Flashes of the Life, Letters and Work of O. Henry, William Sydney Porter*. New York, D. Appleton & Co., 1931.

Dale, Edward Everett. *Oklahoma: The Story of a State*. Evanston, Ill. and White Plains, N. Y., Row, Peterson and Co., 1940.

Daniels, Josephus. *The Life of Woodrow Wilson, 1856–1924*. Copyright 1924 by Will H. Johnston U.S.A., n.p.

Davis, Oscar King. *Released for Publication: Some Inside Political History of Theodore Roosevelt and His Times, 1898–1918*. Boston and New York, Houghton Mifflin Co., 1925.

Davis, Ronald L. *Opera in Chicago*. New York, Appleton-Century, 1966.

Day, Donald. *Big Country: Texas*. New York, Duell, Sloan & Pearce, 1947.

Dearing, Mary R. *Veterans in Politics: The Story of the G. A. R.* Baton Rouge, Louisiana State University Press, 1952.

Dictionary of American Biography. Vol. II. New York, Charles Scribner's Sons, 1928–36.

Dolan, J. E. *The Yankee Peddlers of Early America.* New York, Clarkson N. Potter, 1964.

Duffy, Herbert S. *William Howard Taft.* New York, Minton Balch & Co., 1930.

Dulles, Foster R. *Labor in America: A History.* 3d ed. New York, Thomas Y. Crowell Co., c.1966.

Durant, John. *The Heavyweight Champions.* rev. ed. New York, Hastings House, 1967.

Duval, Miles P., Jr. *And the Mountains Will Move: The Story of the Building of the Panama Canal.* Stanford University, Stanford University Press, 1947.

Eaton, Quaintance. *Opera Caravan: Adventures of the Metropolitan on Tour, 1883–1956.* New York, Farrar, Straus and Cudahy, 1957.

Encyclopedia Americana. international ed. Vol. VII (1918) 1968, Vol. XIX, 1970. New York, Americana Corporation.

English, A. L. *History of Atlantic City.* Philadelphia, Dickson and Gilling, 1884.

Ewen, David. *Complete Book of the American Musical Theatre.* New York, Henry Holt & Co., 1958.

Fast, Howard, *Goethals and the Panama Canal.* New York, Julian Messner, 1942.

Faulkner, Harold U., and Mark Starr. *Labor in America.* rev. ed. New York, Oxford Book Co., 1957, c.1949, 1944.

Fleischer, Nat. *The Heavyweight Championship: An Informal History of Heavyweight Boxing from 1719 to the Present Day.* rev. ed. New York, G. P. Putnam's Sons, 1961.

Folio of Popular College Songs. New York, Thornton W. Allen Co., 1938.

Foreman, Grant. *A History of Oklahoma.* Norman, University of Oklahoma Press, 1942.

Fox, William Sherwood. *The Mythology of all Races: Greek and Roman Mythology.* Vol. I. Boston, Marshall Jones Co., 1966.

Fraser, Chelsea. *Famous American Flyers.* New York, Thomas Y. Crowell Co., 1941.

Fried, Frederick. *A Pictorial History of the Carousel.* New York, A. S. Barnes and Co., 1964.

Fuld, James J. *The Book of World Famous Music: Classical, Popular and Folk.* New York, Crown Publishers, 1966.

Fulford, Roger. *Votes for Women.* London, Faber and Faber, 1956.

F. W. Woolworth Co.: 60 Years of Woolworth; Celebrating 60 Years of an American Institution. F. W. Woolworth Co., 1939.

G. A. R. Journal. Vol. XLII (1907–1911).

Gassner, John. *Best Plays of the Early American Theater*. New York, Crown Publishers, 1967.

Gatti-Casazza, Giulio. *Memories of the Opera*. New York, Charles Scribner's Sons, 1941.

Gerstle, Mack. *The Land Divided: A History of the Panama Canal and Other Isthmian Canal Projects*. New York, A. A. Knopf, 1944.

Gibson, Charles Dana, "A. B. Frost—A Personal Tribute," *Scribner's*, November, 1928.

Gilbert, Douglas. *American Vaudeville: Its Life and Times*. New York, Whittlesey House, 1940.

———. *Lost Chords*. Garden City, N.Y., Doubleday, Doran & Co., Inc., 1942.

Goldberg, Reuben L. *Rube Goldberg vs. the Machine Age*. New York, Hastings House, 1968.

Golden, Harry. *Forgotten Pioneer*. Cleveland and New York, The World Publishing Co., 1963.

Gracie, Col. Archibald. *The Truth about the* Titanic. New York, Mitchell Kennerly, 1913.

Greatest of Expositions (The). Official view of the Louisiana Purchase Exposition, published by the Official Photographic Company of the Louisiana Purchase Exposition, 1904, at St. Louis, U.S.A. St. Louis, Samuel F. Myerson Printing Co., 1904.

Grombach, John V. *The Olympics, 1960 Edition*. New York, Ballantine Books.

Hall, John F. *The Daily Union History of Atlantic City and County, New Jersey*. Daily Union Printing Co., 1900.

Hamilton, Edith. *Mythology*. Boston, Little, Brown and Co., 1940.

Harlow, Alvin F. *Old Wires and New Waves: The History of the Telegraph, Telephone and Wireless*. New York and London, D. Appleton-Century Co., 1936.

Harlow, Victor E. *Oklahoma History*. Oklahoma City, Harlow Publishing Corp., 1934 (1961).

Heilbroner, Robert L. "Epitaph for the Steel Master," *American Heritage*, Vol. XI, No. 5 (August, 1960).

Heimer, Mel. *The Long Count*. New York, Atheneum, 1969.

Herring, Donald Grant, Sr. *Forty Years of Football*. New York, Carlyle House, 1940.

Heston, Alfred M. *Absegami: Annals of Eyren Hanen and Atlantic City, 1609–1904*. Vol. I. Atlantic City, Alfred M. Heston, 1904.

Hilton, George W., and John F. Due. *The Electric Interurban Railways in America*. Stanford University, Stanford University Press, 1960.

Hope, Anthony. "Mr. C. D. Gibson on Love and Life," *McClure's*, September, 1897.

Hopkins, John. *The Marathon*. London, Stanley Paul, 1966.

Huneker, James Gibbons. *Steeplejack*. New York, Charles Scribner's Sons, 1922.

Hurst, P. G. *The Age of Jean De Reszke: Forty Years of Opera*. London, Christopher Johnson, 1958.

Hyatt, Henry. *Alias Jimmy Valentine Himself*. Philadelphia, Dorrance, 1949.

Intercollegiate Song Book. Southern and Western editions. New York, Thornton W. Allen Co., 1936.

Josephson, Matthew. *The Robber Barons: The Great American Capitalists, 1861–1901*. New York, Harcourt, Brace and Co., 1934.

Kieran, John, and Arthur Daley. *The Story of the Olympic Games, 772 B.C. to A.D. 1956*. Philadelphia and New York, J. P. Lippincott Co., 1957.

Kohlsaat, Herman H. *From McKinley to Harding: Personal Recollections of our Presidents*. New York and London, Charles Scribner's Sons, 1923.

Kouwenhoven, John Atlee. *Adventures of America, 1857–1900*. New York and London, Harper and Brothers, 1938.

Kresge, Stanley S. *S. S. Kresge Company and Its Builder Sebastian Spering Kresge*. New York, The Newcomb Society in North America, 1957.

Kunitz, Stanley J., and Howard Haycroft, eds. *The Junior Book of Authors*. New York, H. W. Wilson Co., 1934.

Kunstler, William M. *The Minister and the Choir Singer: The Hall-Mills Murder Case*. New York, William Morrow and Co., 1964.

Langford, Gerald. *Alias O. Henry: A Biography of William Sidney Porter*. New York, The Macmillan Co., 1957.

———. *The Murder of Stanford White*. Indianapolis, The Bobbs-Merrill Co., 1962.

Latham, Earl, ed. *John D. Rockefeller: Robber Baron or Industrial Statesman?* Boston, D. C. Heath & Co., 1949.

Lester, Robert M. *Forty Years of Carnegie Giving*. New York, Charles Scribner's Sons, 1941.

Lewis, Alfred Henry. *The Boss*. New York, A. S. Barnes & Co., 1903.

Lingg, Ann M. *John Philip Sousa*. New York, Henry Holt and Co., 1954.

Literary Digest, Vol. L (May, 1915), 1152–53.

Lodge, Henry Cabot. *The History of Nations*. Vol. VII. New York, P. F. Collier and Son, 1907, 1910, 1913.

Lord, Walter. *A Night to Remember*. New York, Henry Holt and Co., 1955.

Lyon, Peter. "Master Showman of Coney Island," *American Heritage*, Vol. IX, No. 4 (June, 1958).

———. *To Hell in a Day Coach: An Exasperated Look at American Railroads*. Philadelphia and New York, J. P. Lippincott Co., 1968.

McAdam, Roger Williams. *The Old Fall River Line*. Brattleboro, Vt., Stephen Day Press, 1937.

McClintock, Inez, and Marshall McClintock. *Toys in America*. Washington, Public Affairs Press, 1961.

MacCulloch, Campbell. "Stay Away from Hollywood, Advises Mary," *Good Housekeeping*, Vol. XC (October, 1930).

McFee, William. *Great Sea Stories of Modern Times*. New York, The McBride Co., 1953.

MacMillan, Norman. *Great Aircraft*. New York, St. Martin's Press, 1960.

Magoun, F. Alexander, and Eric Hodgins. *A History of Aircraft*. New York and London, Whittlesey House, 1931.

Mahony, Bertha E., Louise Payson Latimer, and Beulah Folmsbee. *Illustrators of Children's Books, 1744–1945*. Boston, The Horn Book, Inc., 1961.

Mangels, William F. *The Outdoor Amusement Industry: From Earliest Times to the Present*. New York, Vantage Press, 1952.

"Man Who Saw Millions in a Nickel, The," *Literary Digest*, May, 1919.

Marcosson, Isaac F. *Wherever Men Trade: The Romance of the Cash Register*. New York, Dodd, Mead & Co., 1945.

Marks, Edward B. *They All Sang*. New York, The Viking Press, 1934.

"Mary Pickford," *Current Opinion*, June, 1918.

Maxim, Hiram Percy. *Horseless Carriage Days*. New York, Dover Publications, 1936 (1962).

Mencken, August. *The Railroad Passenger Car: An Illustrated History of the First Hundred Years with Accounts by Contemporary Passengers*. Baltimore, The Johns Hopkins Press, 1957.

Milbank, Jeremiah, Jr. *The First Century of Flight in America*. Princeton, N. J., Princeton University Press, 1943.

Mollison, J. A., ed. *The Book of Famous Flyers: An Interesting Account of the History of Aviation from the Early Pioneers to Present-day Aces of the Air*. London and Glasgow, Collins' Clear-Type Press, n.d.

Moody, John. "Interesting People," *American*, April, 1914.

———. *The Railroad Builders*. New Haven, Yale University Press, 1921.

Moore, Charles. *Daniel H. Burnham, Architect, Planner of Cities*. Vol. I. Boston and New York, Houghton Mifflin Co., 1921.

Morton, Joseph W. *Sparks from the Camp Fire: Or Tales of the Old Veterans*. Philadelphia, Keystone Pub. Co., 1895.

Mullett, Mary B. "Mary Pickford: A Portrait in Rotogravure," *American*, Vol. XCV, No. 5 (May, 1923).

Municipal Art Society of New York. Burnham, Alan, ed. *New York Landmarks*. Middletown, Conn., Wesleyan University Press, 1963.

Myers, Gustavus. *The History of Tammany Hall*. New York, published by the author, 1901.

"My Own Story," *Ladies Home Journal*, July, 1923; September, 1923.

National American Women Suffrage Association. *Victory: How Women Won It*. New York, H. W. Wilson Co., 1940.

N. C. R. Magazine (The). Published by National Cash Register Co., Dayton, Ohio, November, 1904.

Neal, Harry Edward. *The Hallelujah Army*. Philadelphia and New York, Chilton Co., 1961.

Neil, Henry. *The Great Chicago Theater Disaster: The Complete Story Told by the Survivors*. Chicago and Philadelphia, Publishers Union of America, 1904.

Nevins, Allan. *John D. Rockefeller: The Heroic Age of American Enterprise*. Vol. I. New York, Charles Scribner's Sons, 1940.

New Jersey: A Guide to Its Present and Past. Compiled and written by the Federal Writers' Project of the Works Progress Administration for the State of New Jersey. New York, The Viking Press, 1939.

New York City Museum. Byron Collection. *Once Upon a City*. New York, The Macmillan Co., 1958.

New York Times. February 2, 1914; March 16, 1914; July 16, 1914; April 29, 1916; February 2, 1920.

Nicolay, Helen. *The Bridge of Water: The Story of Panama and the Canal*. New York, D. Appleton-Century Co., 1940.

Northrop, H. D. *World's Greatest Calamities: The Baltimore Fire and the Chicago Theatre Horror*. Philadelphia, National Publishing Co., 1904.

Oklahoma: A Guide to the Sooner State. Compiled by the Workers of the Writers' Program of the Works Project Administration in the State of Oklahoma. Norman, University of Oklahoma Press, 1941.

Olympic Cavalcade of Sports. New York, Ballantine Books, 1956.

Olympic Games (The). A book of records for reminiscence by the editors of *Sports Illustrated*, *Time* and *Life* Books. New York, 1967.

Padfield, Peter. *The* Titanic *and The* Californian. London, Hodder and Stoughton, 1965.

Parker, John. *Who's Who in the Theatre*. 9th rev. ed. London, Sir Isaac Pitman and Sons, 1939.

Parkhurst, E. Sylvia. *The Suffragette*. New York, Sturgis and Walton Co., 1911.

Partridge, Bellamy. *Fill 'Er Up!* New York, McGraw-Hill Book Co., 1952.

Perriton, Maxwell. "Charles Dana Gibson: Man and Artist," *Arts and Decoration*, May, 1922.

Perry, George Sessions. *Texas a World in Itself*. New York, Whittlesey House, 1942.

Phares, Ross. *Texas Tradition*. New York, Henry Holt and Co., 1954.

Pickford, Mary. *Sunshine and Shadow*. New York, Doubleday and Co., 1955.

Presbrey, Frank. *The History and Development of Advertising*. Garden City, Doubleday, Doran and Co., 1929.

Pringle, Henry F. *The Life and Times of William Howard Taft.* New York and Toronto, Farrar and Rinehart, 1939.

Ramsaye, Terry, ed. *International Motion Pictures Almanac, 1939–40.* New York, Quigley Publishing Co., n.d.

Reischauer, Edwin O. *Japan, Past and Present.* New York, A. A. Knopf, 1954.

"Remarkable Career of an American Merchant," *Bankers Magazine,* May, 1919.

Richardson, Rupert Norval. *Texas the Lone Star State.* Englewood Cliffs, N.J., Prentice-Hall, 1958.

Rogers, James C. *A Walk by the Sea: The Story of the Wonderful Atlantic City Boardwalk.* Philadelphia, n.p., 1926.

Roosevelt, Theodore. *An Autobiography.* New York, Charles Scribner's Sons, 1924.

Rothe, Anna, ed. *Current Biography: Who's News and Why.* New York, H. W. Wilson Co., n.d.

Rover, Constance. *Women's Suffrage and Party Politics in Britain, 1866–1914.* London, Routledge and Kegan Paul, 1967.

Rowsome, Frank, Jr. *The Trolley Car Treasury: A Century of American Streetcars, Horsecars, Cable Cars, Interurbans, and Trolleys.* New York, McGraw-Hill Book Co., 1956.

Saltus, Edgar. "The Most Extraordinary Panorama in the World," *Munsey's Magazine,* Vol. XXXIII, No. 4 (July, 1905), 381.

Smith, Cecil. *Musical Comedy in America.* Theatre Arts Books. New York, Robert M. MacGregor, 1950.

Smith, E. Alphonso. *O. Henry Biography.* Garden City, Doubleday, Page & Co., 1916.

Smith, William Alden. "The *Titanic* Disaster." Speech delivered in the Senate of the United States, May 28, 1912. Washington, Government Printing Office, 1912.

Sousa, John Philip. *Marching Along: Recollections of Men Women and Music.* Boston, Hale, Cushman and Flint, 1928.

Spaeth, Sigmund. *A History of Popular Music in America.* New York, Random House, 1948.

Stagg, Amos Alonzo. *Touchdown!* New York, Longmans, Green & Co., 1927.

Stagg, Jerry. *The Brothers Shubert.* New York, Random House, 1968.

Steen, Ralph W. *The Texas Story.* Austin, The Steck Company, 1960.

Steffens, Lincoln. *The Shame of the Cities.* New York, McClure, Phillips & Co., 1905.

Stevens, Doris. *Jailed for Freedom.* New York, Liveright Publishing Corp., 1920.

Stevenson, O. J. *The Talking Wire: The Story of Alexander Graham Bell.* New York, Julian Messner, 1947.

Stover, John F. *The Life and Decline of the American Railroad.* New York, Oxford University Press, 1970.

Sullivan, James E. *Marathon Running.* New York, American Sports Publishing Co., 1909.

Sullivan, Mark. *Our Times: The United States, 1900–1925.* Vols. II, III, IV. New York and London, Charles Scribner's Sons, 1929, 1930, 1932.

Taft, Mrs. William Howard. *Recollections of Full Years.* New York, Dodd, Mead and Co., 1914.

Tallmadge, Thomas E. *The Origin of the Skyscraper.* Report of the committee appointed by the Trustees of the Estate of Marshall Field for the estate of Marshall Field for the examination of the structure of the Home Insurance Building. Chicago, The Alderbrink Press, 1939.

Talmey, Allene. *Doug and Mary and Others.* New York, Macy-Masius, 1927.

Tarbell, Ida M. *History of the Standard Oil Company.* Vols. I & II. New York, McClure, Phillips & Co., 1904.

Tatlock, Jessie M. *Greek and Roman Mythology.* New York, The Century Co., 1923.

Taubman, H. Howard. *Opera Front and Back.* New York, Charles Scribner's Sons, 1938.

Tetrazzini, Madame. *My Life of Song.* London and New York, Cassell and Co., 1921.

Thaw, Harry K. *The Traitor: Being the Untampered with, Unrevised Account of the Trial and All that Led to It.* Philadelphia, Dorrance and Co., 1926.

Theatre Magazine. Vol. XIV, No. 129 (November, 1911), 156.

Thompson, Charles Willis. *Presidents I Have Known and Two Near Presidents.* Indianapolis, The Bobbs-Merrill Co., 1929.

Tracy, Lena Harvey. *How My Heart Sang: The Story of Pioneer Industrial Welfare Work.* New York, Richard R. Smith, 1950.

Tumulty, Joseph P. *Woodrow Wilson As I Know Him.* Garden City, Doubleday, Page & Co., 1921.

Turner, E. S. *The Shocking History of Advertising.* London, Michael Joseph, 1952.

Van Antwerp, W. C. *The Stock Exchange from Within.* Garden City, Doubleday, Page & Co., 1913.

Wagenknecht, Edward. *The Movies in the Age of Innocence.* Norman, University of Oklahoma Press, 1962.

Walker, John Brisben. "The World's Fair," *Cosmopolitan,* Vol. XXXVII (September, 1904).

Waters, Edward N. *Victor Herbert: A Life in Music.* New York, The Macmillan Co., 1955.

Waugh, Coulton. *The Comics.* New York, The Macmillan Co., 1947.

Weissman, Rudolph J. *The New Wall Street*. New York, Harper and Brothers, 1939.

Werstern, Irving. *The Great Struggle: Labor in America*. New York, Charles Scribner's Sons, 1965.

Weyand, Alexander M. *The Olympic Pageant*. New York, The Macmillan Co., 1952.

White, David M., and Robert H. Abel, eds. *The Funnies: An American Idiom*. New York, Free Press, 1963.

White, William Allen. *Woodrow Wilson: The Man, His Times and His Task*. Boston, Houghton Mifflin Co., 1929.

Who's Who in American Women. 6th ed. Chicago, A. R. Marquis Co., 1970–71.

Winkelman, Barnie F. *Ten Years of Wall Street*. Philadelphia, The John C. Winston Company, 1932.

Wood, James Ploysted. *The Story of Advertising*. New York, The Ronald Press Co., 1958.

Woodward, W. E. *The Way Our People Lived: An Intimate American History*. New York, E. P. Dutton & Co., 1944.

Woolworth's First 75 Years, 1879–1954: The Story of Everybody's Store. New York, F. W. Woolworth Co., 1954.

World's Work (The)—August, 1904. New York, Doubleday, Page & Co.

Wright, Richardson. *Hawkers and Walkers in Early America: Strolling Peddlers, Preachers, Lawyers, Doctors, Players, and Others, from the Beginning to the Civil War*. Philadelphia, J. B. Lippincott Co., 1927.

Ybarra, T. R. *Caruso: The Man of Naples and the Voice of Gold*. New York, Harcourt, Brace and Co., 1953.

Young, Barnard A. *Songs of the American Colleges*. Boston, Intercollegiate Music League, 1938.

Young, James Harvey. *The Toadstool Millionaires: A Social History of Patent Medicines in America before Federal Regulations*. Princeton, Princeton University Press, 1961.

INDEX

Abram, Edward V. (composer): 328
"Acquisition of Louisiana, The": 259
Adams, Bob (songwriter): 254
Adams, Franklin P. (lyricist): 372
Adams, Frank R. (songwriter): 289
Adler, Bernie (songwriter): 58, 246
"Aerial Polka, The": 55
Aeronautique Club of Chicago: 58
"After the Ball": 319
"Ah Me! Ancient Ballad": 110, 111
Albany Flyer (airplane): 62
"Album Leaf, An": 110
Alderson, Barnard (writer): 101
"Alexander's Ragtime Band": 45
Alger, Horatio: 27
"Alias Jimmy Valentine": 278
Allen, Thornton W. (publisher): 206
All Star Stock Company: 15
Alteridge, Harold R. (songwriter): 73
"America, Here's My Boy": 138
American Academy of Architects: 326
American Federation of Labor: 364
American Railway Union: 363
American Society of Composers and
    Publishers: 175
"America's Flying Hero": 63
"America's Sweetheart": 8
"Anchors Aweigh": 206
"Anona": 192
"Arizona My Land": 194–95
"Arizona Prospector": 188ff.

Armstrong, Paul (playwright): 278
Aronson, Rudolph (songwriter): 130
Arts and Decorations (magazine): 162
"Asleep at the Switch": 87ff.
Astaire, Fred (dancer): 258
"As the Backs Go Tearing By": 204
"As We Go Down the Pike": 263ff.
Atlantic City, N.J.: 301ff.
Atlantic City Beauty Pageant: 307
"Atlantic City Promenade March and
    Two Step": 309
"Atlantic City Two Step March": 309
"At the Funny Page Ball": 290ff.
"Automobile Spin, The": 67
"Autumn": 246

Baker, R. Melville (songwriter): 66
"Balloon Polka, The": 54
Baltimore and Ohio Railroad: 86, 98
"Band Played Nearer My God to Thee as
    the Ship Went Down, The": 246
"Band Wagon, The": 258
Bangs, John Kendrick (writer): 107
Bankers' Magazine: 351
Banta, Frank P. (composer): 65
"Barney Google": 269
Barry, Romeyn: (songwriter): 203
Barton, Roy (songwriter): 8
Bassett, Mrs. Annie (songwriter): 128
"Bath House John Couglin": 163, 166
"Bathing Girl": 160

Bay State Steamboat Company: 49
Bayes, Nora (actress): 48, 132, 260, 298
Beal, E. B. (songwriter): 74
"Be Good to California, Mr. President,
    California Has Been Good to You": 137
Bean, Mark (lyricist): 246
"Beautiful Jane in My Aeroplane": 61
Beck, James N. (composer): 86
Beck, Paul (songwriter): 205
Bela, Travnyik (composer): 57
Belasco, David (producer): 6, 7
Bell, Alexander Graham (inventor): 62,
    316
"Bells of Bard Street, The": 45
Bennett, Harry (songwriter): 263
Benny, Jack (comedian): 274
Berlin, Irving (composer): 23, 45, 94, 137,
    220
Bernard, Roger (songwriter): 285
Bernard, Sam (producer): 48
Berry, Mary Lee (songwriter): 263
Berryman, Clifford K. (cartoonist): 294
"Bessie and Her Little Brown Bear": 296,
    297
"Bessie and Her Little Brown Bear
    Behind": 298
"B-I-Double L-Bill": 127
"Big D": 184
Bigelow, Hosea (writer): 107
"Big Red Team, The": 203
"Billy Rose's Crazy Quilt": 316
"Biograph Girl, The": 7
Bioscope Studios: 6
Bischoff, J. W. (composer): 93
"Black Ghost, The": 66
Blaisdell, Carl W. (lyricist): 204
Blase, C. Arthur (lyricist): 201
"Bleriot Valse": 56–57
"Blondielocks": 7
"Bloody Sixth": 369
Bloomingdale, Samuel: 220
Blue, Thomas J. (lyricist): 236
Blumenthal, Maurice (composer): 194
Boggs, Mattie E. (songwriter): 205
"Bonita Caprice": 21

"Boob McNutt": 268
"Boola": 203
Booth, Evangeline (Salvation Army
    leader): 156
Booth, Sam (lyricist): 80
"Boston Strong Boy": 208
Bowen, E. J. (composer): 209
Bowers, J. Lee (songwriter): 70
Boyce, Richard (lyricist): 363, 364
"Boys in Blue": 352, 356, 357
"Boys in Blue Series": 358
"Boys in Blue Are Turning Gray, The":
    358
"Boys in Blue Will See It Through, The":
    357
"Boys Who Wore the Blue": 358
Braham, Dave (composer): 150, 361
Bratton, John W. (composer): 286, 389
Braun and Company (art dealers): 162
"Break the News to Mother": 319
Broadway Theatre (New York): 112
Brougham, John (songwriter): 118
Brown, A. Seymour (songwriter): 134
"Brunette Polka, The": 55
Brice, Fanny (comedienne): 132
"Bringing Up Father": 285
British Amateur Athletic Club: 207
British Medical Journal: 381
British Royal Flying Corps: 24
British Women's Social and Political
    Union: 143
Bryan, Alfred (songwriter): 134
Bryan, Vincent (songwriter): 67, 121,
    278, 299, 376, 381
Bryan, William Jennings (politician): 125
Buck, Gene (composer): 175
Budell, R. Frank (composer): 347
"Bulls and Bears Galop, The": 352
"Bulls and Bears March and Two Step":
    352
Bumble, Al (composer): 300
Burke, Joseph A. (lyricist): 135
Burlington Railroad: 86
Burnham, D. H., (architect): 325
"Burning of the Iroquois, The": 237, 240

"Buster Brown": 285
"Buster Brown's Barn Dance": 285
"Buttonwood Agreement": 350
Butts, Professor Lucifer Gorgonzola
  (comic-strip character): 269
Byrd, Richard E. (explorer): 64
"Byrd, You're the 'Bird' of Them All": 64
"By the Light of the Silvery Moon": 278

Caddigan, Jack (songwriter): 155
Caire, Madeline (Gaby Deslys): 41
"Caissons Go Rolling Along, The": 206
"Calcio": 197
Camden, Harriet Parker (composer): 176
Camden and Atlantic Railroad: 301
Campanini, Cleofonte (conductor): 33
Cantor, Eddie (comedian): 281
"Captain Lindy, He Flew for the Red,
  White and Blue": 63
Carle, Richard (lyricist): 180, 388
Carmen: 36
Carnegie, Andrew (philanthropist): 97ff.
Carnegie Endowment for International
  Peace: 99
Carnegie Hero Fund: 99
Carnegie Institute (Pittsburgh): 99
Carnegie Steel Company: 98, 363
Carnes, Frederick G. (songwriter): 80
Carpender, Henry de la Bruyère (stock-
  broker): 226–27, 231
Carroll, Harry (songwriter): 73
"Carrollton March": 85, 86
"Cartoons in Tunes": 273
Caruso, Dorothy Benjamin (Mrs. Enrico
  Caruso): 41
Caruso, Enrico (tenor): 34
"Casey Jones": 93
Castle, Vernon (dancer): 21 ff.
"Castles by the Sea": 24
Castle School of the Dance: 23
"Castles in Europe": 25
"Castles in the Air": 24
"Castle Walk" (dance): 23
Catt, Mrs. Carrie Chapman (suffragette):
  141, 148

Cawthorn, Joseph (comedian): 372
"Central, Give Me New York Town":
  323
Century Magazine: 160
Chabas, Paul (artist): 162, 166
Chamberlin, Clarence (pilot): 63
Chambers, John Graham (sportsman):
  207
Chambers, Robert W. (author): 161
"Champagne Charley": 118, 119
Chaplin, Charlie (actor): 8
Chavez, Francisco (entertainer): 193
"Cherokee, The": 170
"Cherokee Outlet": 175
"Cheyenne": 184
"Chicago, Chicago, That Toddlin'
  Town": 101
Chicago and Alton Railroad: 121
Chicago Evening Post: 102
Chicago Exposition (1893): 261
Chicago Telegram: 101
Chicago Times: 102
"Chinese Honeymoon, The": 106
Christensen, Axel (songwriter): 70
"Christian Mission": 148
Christian Science Monitor: 26
Churchill, Winston: 143
"City of Bisbee March": 193
Clark, C. C. (composer): 101
Clark, Kenneth (songwriter): 203
Clarke, David (lyricist): 300
Clarke, Grant (lyricist): 154
Clayton, Stanley (composer): 363
Cleveland, President Grover: 318, 355,
  363
Clifford, Margaret (lyricist): 193
Clifton, Arthur (composer): 85
Cline, Maggie (comedienne): 278
"Coal Oil Johnny": 118
"Coal Oil Tommy": 118, 119
Cobb, J. (lyricist): 170
Cobb, Will D. (lyricist): 278
Coey, Charles (balloonist): 57, 58
"Coey Junior": 61
Cohan, George M. (stage performer): 137

Cole, Bob (songwriter): 202, 299, 388
"Cole 30 Flyer": 70
Collins, James (songwriter): 92
"Colonel McNeery": 102ff.
"Columbia": 64
"Coming Through the Rye": 317
Confare, Thomas B. (composer): 237
Conley, Larry (songwriter): 63
Conreid, Heinrich (director of Metropolitan Opera): 29, 36
Cooke, Alistair: (journalist): 5
Cooke, Jay (industrialist): 351
"Coquette": 13
Corbett, Gentleman Jim (boxer): 210
Coufal, Joseph F. (songwriter): 221
Covent Garden (London): 30
Cox, James M. (politician): 372
Cox, Palmer (writer): 289
Crandall, Charles D. (songwriter): 94
Croker, Richard (politician): 371
"Cross Is Not Greater Than His Grace, The": 151
Crystal Motion Picture Company: 16
Crystal Palace Exhibition (London): 83
Culebra, Panama: 344
Cullen, Robert D. (president of Reading Railroad): 86
Curtis, Virginia (songwriter): 230
Curtiss, Glenn H. (pilot): 62

Daggett, Parker H. (songwriter): 202
Dale, Alan (reporter): 43
"Dance of the Brownies, The": 289
"Dance of the Hogan Alley Hoboes": 284
Danks, H. P. (composer): 357
Davis, Gussie L. (songwriter): 94
"Dawn of Peace": 101
Dea, James O. (songwriter): 182
"Death Song of the Titanic": 246
"Deep in the Heart of Texas": 185
Dellafield, Henry (songwriter): 101
"Dennis McFlinn" (A. C. Weeks): 140
Depew, Chauncy (statesman): 389
Deslys, Gaby (dancer): 41 ff.

Deutzel, Gustav A. (carrousel builder): 255
DeVito, Joseph (songwriter): 237
Diamond Horseshoe (New York): 35
Dietz, Arthur (songwriter): 258
Dignowitz, James V. (songwriter): 202
Dillea, Herbert (orchestra leader): 241
Dillingham, Charles (producer): 23
Dixon, Mort (songwriter): 316
Dixon, Rose (songwriter): 316
Dockstader, Lew (singer): 260, 308
"Dr. Munyon": 376ff.
"Don't Forget That He's Your President": 136
"Don't Forget the Salvation Army": 156
"Don't Put the Poor Workingman Down": 360
Dooley, Martin (cartoon character): 102
"Dorando": 218, 219, 221
Dougherty, W. A., Jr. (songwriter): 205
Downs, William A. (songwriter): 8
Dreiser, Theodore (novelist): 171
Dresser, Louise (actress): 182
Dresser, Paul (songwriter): 171, 182
Drury Lane Theatre (London): 24
Dubin, Al (lyricist): 135
Dumont, Frank (lyricist): 91
Dunham, Billy (songwriter): 37
Dunlap, J. G. (songwriter): 357
Dunne, Finley Peter ("Mr. Dooley"): 101

Edison, Thomas A. (inventor): 81, 83
Edwards, Gus (composer): 33, 40, 67, 278, 376
Edwards, Ross (lyricist): 233
Elbel, Louis (songwriter): 199
"El Capitan": 113, 114
Elkins Act: 121
Emerson, Ida (songwriter): 322
"Enfin en Revue": 22
"Engineer's Love, An": 93
Eno, Paul (composer): 204
"Erie Railroad Polka": 86
Esquire: 157
Eugene, Paul (songwriter): 221

Europe, Jim (band leader): 24
Europe's Society Orchestra: 22
Evans, Zella (songwriter): 237
"Ev'ry Baby is a Sweet Bouquet": 286
"Everybody Works but Ma (She's an Advocate of Women's Rights)": 145, 146
"Eyes of Texas, The": 180

Fairbanks, Douglas (actor): 12
"Faithful Engineer, The": 93
Fall River Railroad Company: 49
Fall River Steamship Line: 51 ff.
Famous Players: 8
Farmer, Moses (electric-car manufacturer): 81
Farrar, Geraldine (soprano): 34, 40
"Fast Line Gallop": 86
"Fatal Wedding, The": 6
Federation of American Aero Clubs: 58
Federation of Organized Trade and Labor Unions: 362
Feeney, James L. (songwriter): 367
Feininger, Lyonel (painter): 288
Feist, Felix F. (songwriter): 263
Fernald, Albert H. (composer): 86
Fields, Kate (artist): 317
Fields, Lew (producer): 21
"Fight for Penn": 204
Fisk, Jim (financier): 51, 351
Fiske, Minnie Maddern (actress): 151
Fitzgibbons, Dave (composer): 352
Fitzsimmons, Bob (boxer): 210
"Flashes of Merriment": 362
Flatiron Building (New York): 324ff.
"Flatiron March and Two Step, The": 328
Fleming, Len (composer): 193
"Floradora Sextette": 231
"Flying Ballet": 241
Flying Horse Establishment: 255
"Foolish Questions": 267, 268
Foote, Irene (dancer): 21
Ford, Henry (automobile manufacturer): 331

"Ford March and Two Step, The": 68
"For Human Life (The Little Red Schoolhouse)": 5
Forrester, Dorothy (songwriter): 214
"For the Sake of Wife and Home": 233
Fortune, Michael (songwriter): 259
Foster, Stephen (composer): 176
"Four Years More in the White House": 134
"Foxy Grandpa": 269, 285, 287
Foy, Eddie (comedian): 240
"Free Lance, The": 114, 115
"Free Lunch Cadets, The": 111
Friday, Will H., Jr. (composer): 90
Frohman, Daniel (producer): 8
"From Earth to Mar": 69
Frost, Jack (songwriter): 290

"Gabrielle of the Lilies" ("Gaby Deslys"): 42
"Gaby Glide, The": 44ff.
Gadsden, James (minister to Mexico): 191
Gale, George W. (songwriter): 128
Gallagher, J. J. (songwriter): 143
Galli-Curci, Amelita (singer): 34
Galt, Mrs. Edith (Mrs. Woodrow Wilson): 134
"Galveston": 184
Garden, Mary (soprano): 29
Garfield, President James B.: 358
Gaskill, Clarence (songwriter): 273
"Gay Paree": 262
"George White's Scandals of 1921": 338
Gershwin, George (composer): 338
"Get on the Raft with Taft": 123, 124
Gibson, Charles Dana (writer): 157, 160, 231
Gibson, Sidney (composer): 246
"Gibson Bathing Girl, The": 158ff.
Gibson Girl: 157, 160
"Gibson Girl Review, The": 160
"Gibson Sailor Girl, The": 160
"Gibson Widow, The": 160
Gilbert and Sullivan operas: 112

Gilmore, Patrick Garfield (band leader):
  113
Gilson, J. W. (songwriter): 69
Gilson, Lottie (performer): 260, 278
"Girl with the Curls": 7, 13
"Git a Horse": 66
"Give Me a Spin in Your Mitchell, Bill":
  71, 72
"Gladiator, The": 110
Glogau, Jack (songwriter): 136
Goelet, Walter W. (Henry Hyatt): 274,
  277
Goethals, George W. (bridge builder):
  338, 341, 346
Goetz, E. Roy (songwriter): 381
Goldberg, Rube (cartoonist): 266ff.
Golden, Joseph A. (movie director): 16
"Goldilocks": 7
Goldstein, Gus (songwriter): 64
Gompers, Samuel (labor leader): 362,
  364, 367
"Goodbye, Little Girl, Goodbye": 278
"Good-bye Mister Caruso": 37
"Good Little Devil, A": 7, 9
Goodrich Girl: 160
Gordon, Mack (songwriter): 309
"Go Right Along Mister Wilson": 134,
  135
"Gospel of Wealth, The": 99
Gould, Jay (financier): 351, 361, 362
Graff, George, Jr. (songwriter): 136
Grafulla, C. S. (songwriter): 371
Grand Army of the Republic: 352ff.
"Grand Master Workman": 360
Grant, Bert (songwriter): 78
Grant, President Ulysses S.: 127, 351
Graumann's Hollywood Theatre: 8
"Great American Bears": 295
"Great Dog Show in M'Coogan Ave.,
  The": 284
"Great Harry K. Thaw Song, The": 236
"Green Goods Man, A": 171
Grey, Vivian (Mabel McKinley): 192
Griffith, David W. (movie producer): 6
"Grip, The": 361

"Grizzly Bear" (dance): 22
Grobe, Charles (songwriter): 382
Gruber, Edmund L. (songwriter): 206
Guild, T. H. (songwriter): 204
"Gus Edwards' Song Review": 278
Guyer, John R. (orchestra leader): 183
"Guys and Dolls": 156

Hagan, J. M. (songwriter): 127
Hagenbeck's Circus: 261
Hagenback's Wild Animal Show: 261
"Hail to the Boys of the U.S.A.": 221
"Hail to Yale": 202
"Hair": 114
Hall, A. Oakey (politician): 370
Hall, John P. (songwriter): 136
Hall, Mazie (Pearl White): 15
"Hallelujah Band, The": 148, 149
Hallelujah Females: 149
"Hall-Mills Case, The": 228, 229
Hammerstein, Oscar (producer): 26
Hammerstein, William (producer): 163
Hammerstein Roof Garden (New York):
  163, 268
Handy, Will (songwriter): 203
"Happy Hooligan": 285ff.
"Happy Land of Once upon a Time,
  The": 288
Hardman, Will J. (songwriter): 359
Harker, Norman L. (composer): 204
Harlem Opera House (New York): 27
Harrigan, Edward (satirist): 150, 361
Harrigan and Hart (songwriters): 328
Harris, Charles K. (songwriter): 319
Harris, Nathalie (author): 160
Hart, Tony (comedian): 150, 361
Hartley, Henry (bandmaster): 246
"Hats Off! To our Olympian Athletes":
  221
Hawk, S. M. (songwriter): 125
Hayes, Johnny (athlete): 217, 220
Hayes, President Rutherford B.: 357
Hea, Mrs. C. W. (lyricist): 246
Hearst, William Randolph (newspaper
  owner): 16, 227, 268, 284

Hein, Silvie (composer): 175
Heller, Grace (songwriter): 145
"Hello! All Right, Good-Bye": 323
"Hello Central, Give Me Heaven": 319ff.
"Hello, Central! Give Me No Man's
  Land": 324
"Hello Frisco": 323
"Hello, Hawaii, How Are You?": 323,
  324
"Hello Lindy": 63
"Hello! Mr. Moon Man, Hello!": 323
"Hello Ma Baby": 322
"Help! Help! Mr. Sennett, I'm Drowning
  in a Sea of Love": 7
"Henpecked, The": 22
Henry, O. (writer): 372
"Henry's Made a Lady Out of Lizzie": 68
Hepburn Act: 121
Herbert, Victor (composer): 288
"Here's to Good Old Whiskey, Drink it
  Down": 151
"Her First Biscuits": 6
"Hero of the European War, The": 135
"Hero of the Isthmus": 346
Herschell, Allan (carrousel builder): 256
Hersee, George W. (lyricist): 93
Hersey, June (songwriter): 185
Hewitt, J. F. (songwriter): 203
Hienrich, Anthony Philip (songwriter):
  180
Hill, F. L. (songwriter): 118
Hippodrome Theatre (New York): 24
Hirsch, Louis A. (composer): 45
Hirsh, A. M. (songwriter): 202
Hoffman, Max (songwriter): 299, 344
Hoier, Thomas (songwriter): 134
"Hold Fast": 75ff.
Holley, Mrs. M. A. (lyricist): 179
Holzman, Abe (songwriter): 122
Homer, Mrs. M. F. (composer): 194
Hough, Will M. (songwriter): 289
Howard, Eugene (comedian): 323
Howard, Joseph E. (songwriter): 289, 322
Howard, Willie (comedian): 132, 323
"How I Caught My Girl": 61

"Hurrah for Oklahoma! Patriotic Song
  and Chorus": 178
Hyatt, Henry (Jimmy Valentine): 274ff.

"I Didn't Raise My Boy to Be a Soldier":
  134
"I Dream Too Much": 258
"If I Was a Millionaire": 281
"If I Were a Bell": 156
"I Found a Million Dollar Baby in a Five
  and Ten Cent Store": 316
"Illinois Siren Song, The": 204
"I Love You in the Same Old Way": 389
"I Love Louisa": 258
"I'm Afraid to Come Home in the Dark":
  184
"I'm After Madame Tetrazzini's Job": 31
"I'm Climbing Up the Golden Stair to
  Glory": 151
"Imp" pictures: 7
Imrie, John (songwriter): 318
"I'm the Guy": 268, 270ff.
Independent Motion Picture Company: 7
Inglis, Richard (lyricist): 202
"In My Mercer Racing Car": 70
"In My Merry Oldsmobile": 278
"In My Rickenbacker Car": 74
"In Oklahoma": 176
"In Panama": 342, 343
"In Tammany Hall": 372
"In That City of Wealth and Fame": 237
"In the Baggage Car Ahead": 94, 95
"In the Shade of the Old Apple Tree":
  184
"Iola": 171, 192
I Puritani: 29
"Ironmaster, The": 100, 101
"Iroquois on Fire, The": 237ff.
Iroquois Theatre (Baltimore, Md.): 240
Irwin, Charles (lyricist): 179
"Isle of Bong-Bong, The": 289
"It's Your Country and My Country": 138
"I've Been Working on the Railroad":
  180
"I've Lost My Teddy Bear": 299

"I've Worked Eight Hours This Day":
362
"I Wants Dem Presents Back": 389

Jackson, Arthur (lyricist): 338
Jackson Automobile Company: 69
Janvier, Francis De Haes (writer): 170
Jeffries, James J. (boxer): 210
"Jeffries Crouch": 210
Jerome, William (lyricist): 52, 106, 182,
233, 352, 372
Jessel, George (comedian): 281
"Jim-a-da-Jeff": 211 ff.
"Jockey on the Carousel, The": 258
Johnson, Billy (songwriter): 202
Johnson, Howard (songwriter): 64
Johnson, J. W. (songwriter): 388
Johnson, Jack (boxer): 214
Johnson, Julius K. (songwriter): 62
Johnson, President Andrew: 79, 355
Johnson, Robert (songwriter): 151
Johnson, Rosamond (songwriter): 65,
299
Jolson, Al (actor): 43
Jones, Harold (composer): 246
Jost, J. W. (writer): 170
"Jumping Jupitor": 181
"June Bug": 62
"Just as the Ship Went Down": 244, 245
"Just Come Aroun' wid an Automobile":
66

Kalmar, Bert (lyricist): 323
Kamman, Effie F. (composer): 289
"Kansas Pacific Railway Grand March":
86
"Kareless Koon, an Ethiopian Two Step":
65
Keady, John Thomas (lyricist): 204
Kelly, "Honest John" (politician): 371
Kennedy, M. J. (songwriter): 178
Kerker, Gustave (musician): 27
Kerlin, Louise (Louise Dresser): 182
Kerr, Harry D. (songwriter): 122
Keystone Cops: 6

Kiellhoffer, B. A. (songwriter): 143
Kilrain, Jake (boxer): 209
"King of Kings, The": 278
"King of the Air": 62
"Kissing Papa Through the Telephone":
319
"Kiss Through the Telephone, The":
318, 319
Kern, Jerome (composer): 258
Klaw and Erlanger (producers): 288
Klein, Charles (lyricist): 114
Klicksman, F. Henri (songwriter): 133
Knight, A. P. (composer): 170
Knights of Labor: 360 ff.
Kohinoor, The: 28
Kohlman, Charles (songwriter): 107
Koster and Beal's Music Hall (New
York): 28
Kresge, Sebastian Spering (business-
man): 315
Kroger, Ida (songwriter): 263
Kunkel, Charles (composer): 358

La Bohème: 36
"Ladies World": 8
Laemmle, Carl (movie producer): 7, 69
La Hache, Theodore (musician): 86
La Juive: 41
"Lala Palooza": 268
Lampe, J. Bodewalt (composer): 346
Landis, Judge Kenesaw Mountain: 115,
118, 121
Lange, Arthur (songwriter): 138
Langhorne, Irene (Mrs. Gibson Lang-
horne): 161
La Traviata: 30
"La Woola Boola": 202
Lawrence, W. V. (songwriter): 357
Lee, Alfred (composer): 118
Leonard, Eddie (minstrel): 181, 182
Leopold, Fred (composer): 233
Lerman, J. W. (songwriter): 328
Leslie, Edgar (songwriter): 154, 323
Lessing, Edith Maida (lyricist): 246
"Levee Song": 180

Levey, Ethel (singer): 260
"Levine, Levine, the Jew with His Machine": 63, 64
Lewis, Sam M. (songwriter): 324
Leybourne (composer): 55
Life Magazine: 157, 160
"Lifting the Lid": 182
Lincoln, President Abraham: 355
Lindbergh, Charles A.: 63
"Line up for Bryan, the Battle Song of Democracy": 128
Linn, Grace Walls (songwriter): 67
"Listen to the Mocking Bird": 308
Little, George A. (composer): 35
"Little Abner": 269
"Little Bears and Tigers, The": 283
"Little Good-for Nothing's Good for Something, After All, The": 48
"Little Johnny Hayes": 221
"Little Mary": 7
"Little Nemo": 269, 285ff., 300
"Little Nemo and His Bear": 300
"Little Nemo in Slumberland": 285
Lloyd, Rosie (composer): 127
"Lo": 372
Loel, Harry G. (composer): 236
Loesser, Frank (composer): 156, 184
London Daily Mail: 56
London Prize Ring Code: 207
"Look at Me, Bing! Bang! I'm the Guy": 273
"Look Out for Jimmy Valentine": 279, 280
"Lottery of Life, The": 118
Louisiana Purchase Exposition: 258ff.
Louisville and Nashville Railroad: 86
"Love Story of the Packard and the Ford, The": 73
Lubin Company: 16
Lucia di Lammermoor: 34
Luks, George (artist): 288
Lyceum Theatre (London): 118

McCarres, Charles (lyricist): 17
McConnell, George B. (songwriter): 135

McCormack, John (tenor): 30, 34, 262
McCoy, Winsor (cartoonist): 285
McCree, Junie (songwriter): 61
McDonald, C. P. (songwriter): 69
Mack, Keller (songwriter): 301
McKenna, John J. (politician): 102
McKinley, Mabel (Vivien Grey): 192
McKinley, President William: 246, 318
"Mackintosh" law: 306
McLaughlin, James A. (songwriter): 177
McManus, George (cartoonist): 285
McPherson, Aimee Semple (evangelist): 148
"McSorleys, The": 150
Macy's Department Store (New York): 248
Madame Butterfly: 388
Madden, Ed (lyricist): 40, 278, 344
Maddux, W. P. (songwriter): 205
Madison Square Garden (New York): 232
"Madison Square March and Two Step, The": 328
"Maggie Murphy's Home": 284
Magruder, James E. (musician): 55
"Maid and the Mummy, The": 180
"Manhattan Beach March, The": 113
Manhattan Opera Company (New York): 27, 30
Manhattan Opera House (New York): 26, 29, 34
"Man of the Hour, The": 130
"Man Who Broke the Bank at Monte Carlo, The": 352
"Man Who Broke the Brokers Down in Wall Street, The": 352
"March King, U.S.A., The": 113
"March of the 1/8 Brigade": 347, 348
Marda, L. (songwriter): 67
Marine Corps Band: 359
Marsh, S. H. (songwriter): 56
Martin, John Ames (editor of *Life Magazine*): 157
Maryland Journal and Baltimore Advertiser: 54

"Mary Pickford, the Darling of Them All": 9
"Mary Pickford Studios": 9
Mason, Jack (lyricist): 155
Maxwell, Perriton (writer): 162
"Mayor of Tokio, The": 180, 388
Mead, Frederick (songwriter): 221
Meck, John S. (songwriter): 70
"Meet Me in St. Louis, Louis": 260
"Meet Me on the Boardwalk, Dearie": 302, 303
Meineke, Charles (composer): 85, 86
Melba, Nellie (soprano): 29
Merchants Exchange Building (New York): 350
Merrill, Blanche (songwriter): 132
"Merry Go Round, The": 389
"Message of the Dying Engineer, The": 93
Metropolitan Opera Company (New York): 26, 29, 34ff.
Metropolitan Railroad: 80
"Mexican Rope Artist, The": 263
Micary, Vincent L. (songwriter): 63
"Midnight Sons, The": 21
"Mike and Ike": 268
Miles, A. H. (lyricist): 207
Mills, Kerry (songwriter): 260
"Miss Mazie" (Peal White): 15
"Monte Cristo": 15
"Mr. Bluebeard": 240, 242
"Mr. Dooley": 101ff.
"Mr. Dooley March": 106
"Mr. Ford's Little Jitney Bus": 68
Mitchell, S. N. (lyricist): 357
"Monte Cristo": 15
Mooney, William (politician): 367, 368
Moore, Gladys Mary Smith (Mary Pickford): 12
Moore, Owen (actor): 8, 12
Moret, Neil (lyricist): 182
Morgan, Irving J. (songwriter): 384
Morgan, J. P. (financier): 98
Morgan, Jimmie (songwriter): 134
Morse, Theodore F. (composer): 154, 189
Mott, Lucretia (suffragette): 139

Muir, Duncan J. (songwriter): 352
Mullaly, W. S. (composer): 91
Murphy, Charles Francis (politician): 371
"My Alamo Love": 181
"My Boy Bill": 389
"My Cousin Caruso": 38ff.
"My Creole Belle": 65
"My Dad's the Engineer": 93
"My Doughnut Girl": 156
Myers, Gene (composer): 284
"My Faith Loooks Up to Thee, My Faith So Small, So Slow": 151
"My Heart Belongs to Daddy": 202
"My LuLu San": 388
"My Pretty Little Kickapoo": 172ff.
Myrow, Joseph (songwriter): 309
"My Salvation Army Girl": 155

Nathan, Casper (songwriter): 133
National American Woman Suffrage Association: 141, 144
National Police Gazette: 209
"Navajo": 175, 184
"N.C.R., The": 335
"Nearer My God to Thee": 246, 247
Nemo, Captain (Verne character): 287
Nesbit, Evelyn (actress): 231
Newcomb, Bobby (composer): 360
New Haven Railroad: 54
"Newlyweds and Their Baby, The": 269, 285, 286, 389
"New Orleans and Great Western Railroad Polka": 86
New York, New Haven and Hartford Railroad: 86
"New York, O What a Charming City!": 183
New York Evening Journal: 232
New York Life Insurance Company: 28
New York Society for the Suspension of Vice: 162
New York Stock Exchange: 352
New York World: 62
"Noise by Bert Grant": 269

North Chicago City Railway: 80
Northern Pacific Railroad: 351
Norton, George A. (songwriter): 184
Norworth, Jack (composer): 182, 298
"No Wealth Without Labor": 361

"Oh Boundless Salvation": 156
"Oh, You September Morn": 166
"Oh! You Suffragette": 142ff.
"Oklahoma": 176ff.
"Oklahoma—Land of the Fair God": 177
"Oklahoma, the New State": 177, 178
Old Colony Railroad: 52
Old Colony Steamboat Company: 52
"Old Fall River Line": 49, 54
Oldfield, Barney (racing driver): 66
"Old Fox, The": 211
"Old Oaken Bucket, The": 183
Olympia Theatre (New York): 28
Olympic games: 215, 220
"Once More He Is Our President": 137
"On the Banks of the Wabash": 171, 182
"On the Boardwalk in Atlantic City": 309
"On the Merry-Go-Round": 254
"On the Old Fall River Line": 49, 50,
    52ff.
"On Wisconsin!": 205
Opper, Frederick Burr (cartoonist): 285,
    287
"Orchid, The": 21
Orlob, Harold (songwriter): 251
Orth, Frank (songwriter): 301
Osborn, A. H. (songwriter): 203
Oslin, Rev. S. J. (songwriter): 178
"Our Good and Honest Taft": 128, 129
"Our Soldiers Again Are Marching":
    353, 354
Outcault, Richard (cartoonist): 284
Outlook (magazine): 337
"Overland Success Grand March, The":
    74
"Over There": 137

Parkhurst, Mrs. Emmeline (suffragette):
    141, 143

Pathé Frères (moviemakers): 16
Pagliacci: 40
Paguet, P. (manufacturer): 255
Palace of Peace (The Hague): 99
"Panama Canal March, The": 346
Panama Railroad Company: 339–40
"Parisian Model, The": 298
Parker, W. C. (songwriter): 358
Patterson, Michael J. (songwriter): 221
Paul, Alice (suffragette): 141 ff., 147, 148
Paxton, C. D. (songwriter): 69
"Peace Conference, The": 384
"Peacemaker, The": 384
Peace Society of New York: 99
Peachblow, Penelope (Gibson Girl): 160
Pearson, William J. (Salvation Army
    leader): 151
"Peg of My Heart Girl": 278
"Pelican": 266
Pennsylvania Railroad: 86, 98
"Perils of Pauline": 17
Perkins, Ray (songwriter): 7
Permenter, Stephen C. (songwriter): 180
Perry, Commodore Oliver H.: 382
Peters, William Frederick (composer):
    388
Petty, George (artist): 157
Petty Girls: 157
Philadelphia and Reading Railroad: 86
Piantadosi, Al (songwriter): 37, 134, 155
Pickford, Mary (actress): 5ff.
Pietri, Dorando (athlete): 217
"Pig Woman": 226, 230
"Pike, The": 261
Pilcer, Harry (composer): 45, 48
Pinafore: 112
Playboy Magazine: 157
Pond, George W. (songwriter): 203
Pons, Lily (soprano): 258
"Poor Pauline": 13
Porter, Cole (composer): 179, 202
"Porters on a Pullman Train": 94
Powers Film Company: 16
Poznanski, Joseph (songwriter): 352
Price, Georgie (actor): 281

"Princeton Cannon Song, The": 203
  "Princeton Jungle March": 203
  Professor Bear (orchestra leader): 55
  Pryor, Arthur (band leader): 113
  Puck, Eva (actor): 174
  Puck, Harry (actor): 174
  Pullman Palace Car Company: 363
  "Pullman Porters on Parade": 94
  Purdy, W. T. (songwriter): 205
  Puschett, Joseph (songwriter): 251

Queen of the Sound (*Commonwealth*, ship): 52

Radford, Dave (songwriter): 9
"Railroad Conductors, The": 91, 92
"Railroad March for the Fourth of July": 86
Railton, George S. (Salvation Army leader): 150
"Ramble Song": 203
Rainier (automobile): 68
"Ravings by Rube Goldberg": 269
"Reading Railroad and Its President, The": 86
"Red Wing": 171, 192
Reed, Dave, Jr. (songwriter): 66, 309
Reed, Nellie (dancer): 241
Rehm, William C. (composer): 86
"Reilly and the 400": 284
Remick, Jerome H., Company (music publisher): 166
Repaid, Billy (songwriter): 137
Reszke, Jean de (tenor): 35
"Retrieved Reformation, A": 274, 278
Richards, Lucenia W. (suffragette): 145
Rickenbacker, Captain Eddie (pilot): 74
"Riding on the Dummy": 80
"Rights of Ladies": 140
Ring, Blanche (comedienne): 254
"Ring the Bell, Watchman": 151
Ritchie Brothers: 306
"Roads of Destiny": 274, 278
Robbins, C. A. (songwriter): 206
Robinson, Mrs. I. C. (songwriter): 177

Rock Island Railroad: 86
Rockefeller, John D. (financier): 115ff.
Rogers, Charles ("Buddy," actor): 13
Rogers, Gus (comedian): 344
Rogers, Max (comedian): 344
Rogers, Will (performer): 107, 263
"Rogers Brothers in Ireland, The": 344
"Rogers Brothers in Panama, The": 344
"Rogers Brothers in Paris, The": 344
"Roosevelt Bears": 295
"Roosevelt, the Peace Victor": 384
Roosevelt, President Franklin D.: 129
Roosevelt, President Theodore: 120, 138, 259, 293, 294, 300, 340, 341, 384
Root, Elihu (secretary of war): 126
Rosenfeld, Monroe (songwriter): 127
"Rose of No Man's Land, The": 155
Rough Riders of the World: 262
"Ruined Through the Strike": 363, 364
Runyon, Damon (writer): 156
Ryan, Paddy (boxer): 208

St. Clair, Floyd J. (songwriter): 290
St. Louis Globe-Democrat: 262
Saltus, Edgar (writer): 326
"Salt Water Taffy": 307
Salvation Army: 148ff.
"Salvation Army, Oh!": 150
Salvation Army Singers: 282
"Salvation Lassie of Mine": 155
"Salvation Nell": 151ff.
"San Antonio": 184ff.
San Francisco News Letter: 55
"Sans Souci" (New York restaurant): 24
"Santa Maria, My Joy, My Pride": 28
"Satan Don't Bother Me": 149
"Saved from Death": 93, 94
Scheu, A. F. (songwriter): 118
Schindle, Baron (Jimmy Valentine), 282
Schoenbein, Maximilian (Jimmy Valentine): 282
Scannel, Tom (boxer): 208
"School Days": 33, 278
Schroder, George (songwriter): 309
Schultze, Charles E. (cartoonist): 285

Schwab, Charles M.: (financier): 98
Schwartz, Howard (songwriter): 258
Schwartz, Jean (composer): 106, 182,
    323, 372
Scotti, Antonio (opera singer): 34
Sears, Paul H. (lyricist): 202
"See That You're Born in Texas": 179
Sefton, H. F. (songwriter): 318
Sekoson, Leon (songwriter): 221
Selman, Alfred (composer): 160
Sembrich, Marcella (soprano): 34
"Seminole": 175
"Semper Fidelis": 113
Sennett, Mack (movie producer): 6
"September Morn": 166
"September Morn (I'd Like to Meet
    Her): 164ff.
"September Morning": 162, 163
Seymour, Horatio (politician): 371
Shackford, Charles (songwriter): 87
Shapiro Bernstein & Company (music
    publishers): 230, 236
Sheafe, Mark W. (songwriter): 206
"She Couldn't Keep Away from the Ten
    Cent Store": 309ff.
Sheffield, W. Kyle (composer): 202
Sheldon, Edward (songwriter): 151
Sherman, Stanley S. (songwriter): 176
Sherman Anti-Trust Act: 120
Sherwood, Josephine (songwriter): 66
"Shew Fly, Don't Bother Me": 149
Shinburn, Max (Jimmy Valentine): 282
"Shine On, Harvest Moon": 182
Shirley family (theater troupe): 149
Shisler, Charles (songwriter): 273
Shubert, Lee and Jack (theatrical team):
    43
"Signal Man": 90, 91
"Sillysonnets": 273
Silver, Morris S. (lyricist): 237
"Silver Heels": 192
"Silver King, The": 5
Silverman, Dave (songwriter): 63
Sinclair, John Lang (lyricist): 180
Sloane, A. Baldwin (composer): 372

Small, Solomon (songwriter): 250
Smalley, Victor H. (songwriter): 58
"Smick, Smack, Smuck": 111, 112
Smith, Al (politician): 372
Smith, Gladys (Mary Pickford): 5ff.
Smith, Harry B. (lyricist): 114, 288
Smith, William H. (songwriter): 202
Snider, C. Ellsworth (lyricist): 189
Society of St. Tammany: 368
Soldiers' and Sailors' National Union
    League: 355
"Solid Men to the Front": 371
"Sombrero": 182, 183
"Song Book of the Salvation Army, the
    Bandsman and Songster": 151
"Song of the Aeroplane, The" ("The
    Flying Machine"): 56
"Song of the N.C.R., The": 330ff., 336
"Song of the Rail": 92, 93
"Song of the Red Man, The": 170
"Songs of Peace and War": 151
Sousa, John Philip: 67, 110ff.
"Sousa's Band Is on Parade Today":
    107ff.
"Southern Railway March": 86
"South Sea Bubble": 349
"South Sea Company": 349
Spencer, Herbert (composer): 309
Speroy, Robert (songwriter): 290
Sprague, Frank Julian: 82, 83
"Spring Chicken, The": 180
"Standard Oil": 115ff.
Stanley, Jack (composer): 35
Stanton, Elizabeth Cady (suffragette):
    139
"Stars and Stripes Forever, The": 113,
    115
"Step into Line for Taft": 127, 128
Sterling, Andrew B. (lyricist): 52, 138,
    174, 260
Stevens, George Alexander (poet): 254
"Stick to the Union Jack": 365, 366
Stillman, Byron X. (songwriter): 285, 287
Stock Exchange Building (New York):
    347, 351

Stone, Lucy (suffragette): 139
Stonington Steamship Line: 51
Storace, Stephen (composer): 170
"Storm the Forts of Darkness": 151
Story, Chick (songwriter): 155
"Streets of Cairo": 261
"Streets of Paris": 262
"Strolling 'Long the Pike": 263
"Studebaker Grand March, The": 67
Stultz, R. M. (songwriter): 352
"Suffrage March": 145
Suffragist movement: 141
Sullivan, Daisy (songwriter): 9
Sullivan, John Lawrence (boxer): 208, **210**
"Sullivan's Grand March": 209
Sulzer, Governor William (New York): 372
"Summer Widowers, The": 22
Sunday, Billy (evangelist): 148
"Sunny Jim": 289, 290
"Sunshine of Paradise Alley, The": 389
Sutherland, Victor (actor): 16
Swander, Don (songwriter): 185
Sweeney, Peter B. (politician): 370
"Swing, The": 206
Swinnerton, James (cartoonist): 283, 284
"Syncopated Walk, The": 23
"Syracuse Rail Road Quick Step": 86

Taft, President William Howard: 130, 341
"Take Back Your Gold": 127
"Take Me Out to the Ball Game": 298
"Take Me Up with You Dearie": 61
Taming of the Shrew, The: 13
"Tammany": 278, 373ff.
"Tammany, a Pale Face Pow-Wow": 372
Tammany Hall: 368ff.
"Tammany on Parade": 372
Tammany Society: 368
Tanguay, Eva (actress): 132
Taylor, Laurette (actress): 278
"Tech Triumph": 205
"Teddy and the Bear": 295

"Teddy Bear": 294
"Tenderfoot, The": 181
"Tenting on the Old Camp Ground": 147
"Tess of the Storm Country": 8
Tetrazzini, Luisa (soprano): 29ff.
Texas: 185
"Texas, Pride of the South": 185
"Texas Dan": 181
"Texas and Oregon Grand March": 180
"Texas Star, The": 183
"Texian Hymn": 180
"Texian Hymn of Liberty": 179
"Texian Song of Liberty, The": 179
"Texian War Song, The": 179
"That Charlie Chaplin Walk": 9
Thaw, Harry Kendall (murderer): 231, 233
Theatre Arts Magazine: 43
"Theodore": 121, 122
Theodore Bear and Company (toy manufacturer): 295
Thomas, R. R., Motor Car Company: 57
Thomas Flyer (automobile): 57, 58
Thornton, Bonnie (singer): 260
"There's Something Else Goes with It": 68
"They Wanted a Song Bird in Heaven, So God Took Caruso Away": 35
"Those Wedding Bells Shall Not Ring Out": 127
"Three Old Sports from Oklahoma": 171
"Three Times Three for Harvard": 202
Tiemann, Daniel F. (politician): 369
Tilden, Samuel J. (politician): 371
Tinney, Frank (entertainer): 43, 308
Titanic (ship): 243, 248
"Titanics Disaster, The": 248
"Tommy Polka": 382
"Touchdown": 202, 203
Tourison, C. E. (songwriter): 203
"Treaty of Peace, The": 384
"Trolley Car Swing, The": 78
Tuskegee Institute (Alabama): 106
Tweed, William Marcy (politician): 369ff.

"Twenty Thousand Leagues Under the Sea": 287
"Typical Tune of Zanzibar, A": 114

"Uncle Sam Won't Go to War": 133
"Uncle Tom's Cabin": 13
"Union Pacific Galop": 86
Universal Pictures: 69
University of Michigan: 199
University of Texas: 180
"Up in a Balloon": 55
U.S. Marine Band: 110, 359
U.S. Naval Academy Band: 206

Valentine, Jimmy (Henry Hyatt): 274ff.
Vance, Add (songwriter): 107
Varga, Alberto (artist): 157
Varga Girl: 157
"Venerable Sage": 360
"Vera Violetta": 43, 45
Verne, Jules (writer): 287
Verner, H. C. (songwriter): 364
"Veteran's Vote, The": 358
Victoria (New York theatre): 28
"Victors, The": 199ff.
Victor Talking Machine Company: 41
"Violin Maker of Cremona, The": 6
Vogel, Victor (songwriter): 285, 287
Von Alstyne, Egbert (composer): 175, 184
Von Tilzer, Albert: 298
Von Tilzer, Harry (composer): 49, 52, 61, 174

Wabash Railroad: 86
Wagler, F. A. (composer): 179
"Wake Up, America!": 136, 137
Walkemus, L. F. (composer): 246
Walker, Raymond (composer): 17
Wallack Theatre (New York): 278
Wallerstein, Anton (composer): 54
Ward, Artemis (writer): 107
Warner, H. B.: 278
Warren, Betty (Mary Pickford): 6
Warrens of Virginia: 6

Washington, Booker T. (Negro educator): 106
"Washington and Lee Swing, The": 206
"Washington Post March, The": 113, 115
Watch Your Step: 23, 24
Watson, Thomas A.: 316
"Way Down in Colon Town": 344
Webster, Mrs. Priscilla V. B. (songwriter): 176
"We March to Victory": 203
West, Mae (actress): 43
West, Paul (songwriter): 166, 286, 389
"We Stand for Peace While Others War": 133
Westendorf, Thomas (songwriter): 316, 319
"We Take Our Hats Off to You, Mr. Wilson": 130ff.
"What Drink Did": 6
"What Price Crime": 282
"When America Is Captured by the Japs": 383, 385ff., 389ff.
"When East Meets West": 338
"When Johnny Comes Marching Home": 113
"When the Lusitania Went Down": 134
White, Pearl (Mazie White, actress): 13ff.
White, Stanford (financier): 231, 232
"White House Bears": 295
White Star Company: 250
Whitford, Annabelle (actress): 160
Whiting, Richard A. (songwriter): 9
"Who Paid the Rent for Mrs. Rip Van Winkle when Rip Van Winkle was Away?": 45
"Who Stole the Hat?": 154
"Why Don't They Set Him Free?": 234, 235
Whyte, Francis P. (Jimmy Valentine): 274
Whyte, William Pinckney (Jimmy Valentine): 274
"Widowers": 22

Williams, Harry (songwriter): 184
Williams, W. R. (songwriter): 133
"Will You Be My Teddy Bear?": 299
Wilson, President Woodrow: 133, 138, 144, 147
Winchell, Walter (journalist): 281
Wind, I. P. (composer): 86
Winne, J. M. (songwriter): 309
Winner, Septimus (songwriter): 308
Winstein, Frank (composer): 193
Winter Garden (New York): 43
"With Mary Ann on the Merry-Go-Round": 251 ff.
Wizard of Oz, The: 300
"Wondrous Telephone, The": 319
"Won't You Come Over to My House?": 184
"Won't You Come Up and Spoon in Coey's Balloon, 'Chicago' ": 58ff.
Wood, Leo (songwriter): 74
Wood, Will (songwriter): 346
Woolworth, Frank Winfield (businessman): 313, 315

Work, Henry Clay (songwriter): 151
Wright, Frank Lloyd (architect): 326
Wright, Orville and Wilbur (inventors): 56
Wuerthner, Julius (composer): 201
Wurlitzer Company: 113

Yale Football Association: 197
"Yankee Doodle": 86
"Yellow Kid": 284
"Yellow Rose of Texas, The": 180
"You Do Something to Me": 202
Young, Joe (lyricist): 78, 324
Young's Million Dollar Pier (Atlantic City, N.J.): 256, 307
"You're the Top": 202

Zickel, Harry H. (songwriter): 68
Ziegfeld, Florenz (producer): 263, 298
Ziegfeld Follies: 160, 161, 323
Zimmerman, Charles A. (composer): 206
Zukor, Adolph (producer): 8

The paper on which this book was printed bears the watermark of the University of Oklahoma Press and has an effective life of at least three hundred years.

UNIVERSITY OF OKLAHOMA PRESS

NORMAN